THE ADULT LEARNER'S GUIDE TO ALTERNATIVE AND EXTERNAL DEGREE PROGRAMS

THE ADULT LEARNER'S GUIDE TO ALTERNATIVE AND EXTERNAL DEGREE PROGRAMS

Eugene Sullivan

AMERICAN COUNCIL ON EDUCATION
Series on Higher Education
ORYX PRESS
1993

The rare Arabian Oryx is believed to have inspired the myth of the unicorn. This desert antelope became virtually extinct in the early 1960s. At that time several groups of international conservationists arranged to have 9 animals sent to the Phoenix Zoo to be the nucleus of a captive breeding herd. Today the Oryx population is nearly 800, and over 400 have been returned to reserves in the Middle East.

Copyright © 1993 by The Oryx Press
4041 North Central at Indian School Road
Phoenix, Arizona 85012-3397

Published simultaneously in Canada

Printed and Bound in the United States of America

∞ The paper used in this publication meets the minimum requirements of American National Standard for Information Science—Permanence of Paper for Printed Library Materials, ANSI Z39.48, 1984.

Library of Congress Cataloging-in-Publication Data
Sullivan, Eugene J.
    The adult learner's guide to alternative and external degree programs / by Eugene Sullivan.
        p. cm. — (American Council on Education/Oryx series on higher education)
    Includes bibliographical references (p.) and indexes.
    ISBN 0-89774-815-8 (alk. paper)
    1. Universities and colleges—United States—Directories.
2. Adult education—United States—Directories. 3. University extension—United States—Directories. 4. Continuing education—United States—Directories. 5. Degrees, Academic—United States—Directories. I. Title. II. Series.
L901.S84 1993   93-32154
378.73—dc20   CIP

Contents

Acknowledgments

I am indebted to many colleagues for their counsel, advice, and support, especially Tim Peterson and Rita Alford. Tim's assistance was immensely helpful, particularly in the design of the survey instruments used to collect data. Rita's dedication, conscientiousness, and unfailing good humor were very much in evidence in her preparation of the manuscript. I am grateful to Gwen Dozier for her assistance with the drafts of the introductory and supplemental sections and for her helpful replies to numerous inquiries about the book. My thanks to Kent Warren and Catherine Marineau for their especially valuable comments and suggestions. I appreciate all the institutions that agreed to be included in the book and that took the time to respond to the survey questions. Throughout, I have been inspired by all those adult learners who are so eager to find degree programs that are responsive to their needs, circumstances, and aspirations.

Introduction

The Adult Learner's Guide to Alternative and External Degree Programs includes a wide range of information that allows users to:

- identify a variety of alternative and external degree programs
- determine the extent to which quality processes are present in these programs
- design a program of study that may include courses from more than one degree program
- obtain credit for prior institutional and extrainstitutional learning

The *Guide* is designed to provide adults with the information necessary to make sound degree program decisions. It also will assist those who counsel adults in both school and work settings: librarians providing information to patrons who inquire about degree programs for adults; college and university administrators who plan degree programs for the decision-makers in accrediting bodies and state degree program approval agencies; and others interested in the field of alternative and external education.

The programs listed in the *Guide* are the result of an extensive and thorough survey of all accredited colleges and universities in the United States. The survey was conducted by the American Council on Education (ACE). The purpose of the survey was to identify two types of degree programs that best serve adult learners: alternative and external degree programs. Alternative programs include evening, weekend, or other academic programs specifically designed to accommodate the needs of adults. They are primarily campus based (i.e., 25 percent or more of the degree requirements must be completed on campus). External programs are those in which fewer than 25 percent of the degree requirements are campus based and generally provide distance learning options.

The *Guide* is divided into two parts: The first includes alternative degree programs and the second includes external degree programs. This information is followed by seven appendices that provide information about the elements that make up a quality degree program. Finally an Alphabetical Index of Institutions is included as well as an Index to Fields of Study for both the alternative and external degree programs. The latter index includes a symbol indicating level of degree for each program offered. A List of Abbreviations and Acronyms used in this *Guide* is provided on pages xi–xii.

By including different types of degree programs, the *Guide* provides you with access to a variety of relevant educational opportunities. It may be possible for you to design a program of study that combines courses from both alternative and external degree programs.

All of the institutions included in the *Guide* are accredited by an agency recognized by the Council on Postsecondary Accreditation (COPA). COPA is a national umbrella organization that works to support, coordinate, and improve all nongovernmental accrediting activities conducted at the postsecondary level in the United States. Although institutional accreditation indicates that the basic foundation for quality education programs is present, it is only a partial indicator. For just as quality cannot be "inspected" in a manufacturing process, neither can it be "accredited" in an education program. Rather, quality must be built into the detailed processes of teaching, learning, and program administration; indeed, it resides in the details. The *Guide* is intended to assist you in exploring those details.

There are 192 alternative degree programs and 91 external degree programs included in the *Guide*. Each program entry contains the following information: degree(s) offered; program mission statement or program description; accreditation; admission and credit hour requirements; credit awards for prior learning and limits to them; credit awards for standardized examinations; average degree completion time; student support services; distance learning options; available informational materials; program age, enrollment, and number of degrees conferred; percentage of bachelor's degree holders admitted to graduate school; geographic admission restrictions; tuition and fees; and for entries in the External Degree section of the *Guide,* minimum campus time.

Appendix A contains the *Principles of Good Practice for Alternative and External Degree Programs for Adults*. The *Principles*, developed by ACE and The Alliance: An Association for Alternative Degree Programs for Adults, supplements institutional accreditation by providing a more specific measure of quality. The *Principles* provides the prospective student with the means to determine, in advance of enrollment, whether the processes for providing and maintaining a quality education program are, indeed, in place. For more on using the *Principles*, please see Appendix A.

Library resources and services are of particular importance to students enrolled in alternative and external degree programs. The Association of College and Research Libraries (ACRL) recognized this need when it decided to revise its *Guidelines for Extended Campus Library Services* in 1990. In making this decision, ACRL also recognized the growing presence of diverse educational opportunities in higher education. You are encouraged to read the *Guidelines* in Appendix B and determine whether the programs that you are considering cite them.

Frequently, adult learners achieve college-level learning in settings outside of the traditional classroom (see Appendix C). Extrainstitutional learning occurs in military service, through courses sponsored by an employer, or by independent study. Various types of extrainstitutional learning have been evaluated for academic credit purposes by ACE. Descriptions of this learning along with ACE credit recommendations may be found in the following ACE publications: *Guide to the Evaluation of Educational Experiences in the Armed Services; National Guide to Educational Credit for Training Programs;* and *Guide to Educational Credit by Examination.* For further information on these and other publications, see "ACE Publications" in Appendix D, "Supplemental References."

Another way to demonstrate extrainstitutional learning is with portfolio assessment instruments and guides developed by the Council on Adult and Experiential Learning. For more information on these instruments and guides, see "CAEL Publications" in Appendix D, "Supplemental References."

Most of the institutions included in the *Guide* award academic credit for extrainstitutional learning when that learning is:

- assessed by qualified faculty members
- judged comparable to learning outcomes expected in the program
- found relevant to the learner's program of study

To make credit determinations for extrainstitutional learning, institutions should have policies and procedures in place. ACE developed a model policy to assist institutions with this process (see Appendix E). You may wish to find out if these elements are in place at the institution under consideration.

With regard to transfer credit, the college where credit has been earned is referred to as the "sending institution." The college accepting this prior credit is referred to as the "receiving institution." If you have already earned college credit, you will need to determine the procedures and practices of the receiving institution that guide the acceptance and application of traditional transfer credit. ACE, COPA, and the American Association of Collegiate Registrars and Admissions Officers developed a joint statement on this subject to assist institutions with decisions affecting both traditional and nontraditional transfer credit. This statement is found in Appendix F.

Because both alternative and external degree programs are included in the *Guide,* you may, as suggested earlier, be able to design a program of study with more than one institution. This would have to be worked out carefully in advance with institutional academic advisers and faculty members. It would entail prior agreement between you and the respective institutions about your degree plan. This kind of arrangement, which may be described as an individualized program articulation, would facilitate the flow of transfer credit and increase access to a broader range of educational opportunities.

The National Universities Degree Consortium (NUDC) offers another way of accessing the resources of multiple institutions. NUDC consists of nine land grant universities that offer bachelor's degree programs with the assistance of the cablecast facilities of Mind Extension University (ME/U). Please see Appendix G for more information.

The *Guide* is intended as a starting point for investigating alternative and external degree programs. Users should contact, visit, and compare institutions and programs before making decisions. In particular, be sure to check such transitory information as tuition and possible additional program offerings.

Users of the *Guide* should bear in mind that all information has been supplied either by the institutions or through public sources. The editors have assumed all information supplied by the institutions to be factual and accurate. Listings are not meant to be comparative in nature nor is a listing in this directory meant to be an endorsement of any institution by The Oryx Press or by the American Council on Education.

List of Abbreviations and Acronyms

AA	Associate of Arts	COPA	Council on Postsecondary Accreditation
AALS	Associate of Arts in Liberal Studies	Ctr.	Center
AAS	Associate in Applied Science	DANTES	Defense Activity for Non-Traditional Education Support
ACE	American Council on Education		
ACRL	Association of College and Research Libraries	Dept.	Department
		Dr.	Drive
ACT	American College Testing	E.	East
Admin.	Administration	Ed.	Education
ADN	Associate Degree in Nursing	Elem.	Elementary
AGS	Associate of General Studies	EMBA	Executive Master of Business Administration
AP	Advanced Placement		
Approx.	Approximately	Engr.	Engineering
AS	Associate of Science	Est.	Established
A/V	Audiovisual	Exec.	Executive
Ave.	Avenue	Expy.	Expressway
BA	Bachelor of Arts	GED	Test of General Educational Development
BALS	Bachelor of Arts in Liberal Studies	Gen.	General
BBA	Bachelor of Business Administration	GMAT	Graduate Management Admission Test
BCS	Bachelor of Continuing Studies	GRE	Graduate Record Examination
BFA	Bachelor of Fine Arts	HCF	Health Care Facility
BGS	Bachelor of General Studies	HS	High School
BIS	Bachelor of Independent Studies	Hwy.	Highway
Bldg.	Building	Indiv.	Individualized
BLS	Bachelor of Liberal Studies	Info.	Information
BM	Bachelor of Music	Inst.	Institute
BPA	Bachelor of Public Administration	Inter.	Interdisciplinary
BS	Bachelor of Science	Ln.	Lane
BSCS	Bachelor of Science in Computer Science	MA	Master of Arts
BSET	Bachelor of Science in Engineering Technology	MAEd	Master of Arts in Education
		MALS	Master of Arts in Liberal Studies
BSIT	Bachelor of Science in Industrial Technology	MAT	Master of Arts in Teaching
		Max.	Maximum
BSN	Bachelor of Science in Nursing	MBA	Master of Business Administration
BSPS	Bachelor of Science in Professional Studies	ME	Master of Engineering
		MEd	Master of Education
BSW	Bachelor of Social Work	MFA	Master of Fine Arts
Bus.	Business	Mgmt.	Management
BUS	Bachelor of University Studies	MHR	Management of Human Relations
CAI	Computer-Assisted Instruction	Min.	Minimum
CCAF	Community College of the Air Force	MLA	Master of Liberal Arts
CIS	Computer Information Systems	MM	Master of Management
CJ	Criminal Justice	MN	Master of Nursing
CLAST	College Level Academic Skills Test	MOS	Military Occupational Specialties
CLEP	College Level Examination Program	MPA	Master of Public Administration
Comm.	Communication	MPH	Master of Public Health

MPS	Master of Pastoral Studies	**Pkwy.**	Parkway
MRE	Master of Religious Education	**Rm.**	Room
MS	Master of Science	**S.**	South
MSEd	Master of Science in Education	**Sci.**	Science
MSHA	Master of Science in Health Administration	**SLIS**	Specialist in Library and Information Science
MSW	Master of Social Work	**Soc.**	Sociology
N.	North	**SOC**	Servicemembers Opportunity College
N/A	Not applicable	**Sq.**	Square
NLN	National League for Nursing	**St.**	Street
NTE	National Teacher Examination	**Ste.**	Suite
NY	New York	**Svcs.**	Services
Org.	Organizational	**TECEP**	Thomas Edison College Examination Program
OT	Occupational Therapy		
PACE	Program for Adult College Education	**Telc.**	Telecommunications
PhD	Doctor of Philosophy	**TOEFL**	Test of English as a Foreign Language
Pl.	Place	**TV**	Television
P.O.	Post Office	**Univ.**	University
PONSI	Program on Noncollegiate Sponsored Instruction	**US**	United States
		USAFI	United States Armed Forces Institute
Psych.	Psychology	**W.**	West
PTSD	Part-Time Studies Division		

PART I
Alternative Degree Programs

Alabama

1. Birmingham-Southern College

Adult Studies Program
Box A-52
Arkadelphia Rd.
Birmingham, AL 35254

Degrees Offered: Bachelor of Arts and Bachelor of Science (Majors: Accounting; Business Administration; Economics; Early Childhood or Elementary Education; Educational Services; Human Resources Management; or individualized interdisciplinary majors based on a student's individual needs); Master of Arts in Public and Private Management.

Program Mission Statement/Description: Birmingham-Southern College's purpose is to offer a liberal arts education of traditional breadth and distinctive quality. The Adult Studies Program serves adults whose working schedule and educational needs are most suited to learning outside the traditional college framework. Adult students attend courses taught evenings and weekends by regular college faculty and by successful practitioners in the Birmingham area. These students receive the traditional Birmingham-Southern College degree but proceed toward graduation at their own pace. The Master of Arts in Public and Private Management is designed for persons who hold or aspire to hold midlevel management or executive positions. It is an innovative graduate program organized around three levels of study, including general management, required courses in basic disciplines of management, and electives. Specific areas of concentration include public or private sector management, health care management, or educational leadership.

Accreditation: Southern Association of Colleges and Schools; American Assembly of Collegiate Schools of Business; National Association of Schools of Music; and National Council for Accreditation of Teacher Education.

Admission Requirements:

Undergraduate	Graduate
HS/GED Diploma	Undergraduate Degree
Essay/Written Work	Interview
Full-Time Employment	Essay/Written Work
Prefer Employment	Recommendations
Experience	GRE, GMAT, or MAT

Credit Awards for Prior Learning: Portfolio Assessment; Transfer Credit.

Limits to Credit Awards for Prior Learning: We will accept up to 18 units (courses) of credit (72 semester hours).

Credit Awards for Examinations: CLEP General Exams; CLEP Subject Exams; College Board AP Exams; Departmental Exams.

Estimated Average Completion Time: Bachelors' Degrees: 6 years (part-time), 4 years (full-time); Graduate Degrees: MA 3 years (part-time), 2 years (full-time).

Credit Hour Requirements:

Degree	Total Hours	Academic Residency*
Bachelor's**	36 units	18 units
Graduate**	16 units	14 units

*Hours that must be earned at the institution exclusive of credit-by-exam, portfolio assessment, etc.

**Bachelor's degree 1 unit = 4 semester hours; Master's 1 unit = 3 semester hours (48 hours).

Distance Learning Options: Cooperative Education (Bachelor only); Independent Study; Supervised Fieldwork.

Student Support Services Available: Academic Advising; Career Counseling; Counseling/Testing; Financial Aid; Job Placement Assistance; Orientation.

Other Student Services: Back-to-college workshops are noncredit seminars offered free to the public twice a year. People considering beginning or continuing their college educations learn study techniques, language skills, and receive a review of basic mathematics. A course called "Life Experience and Learning" is a seminar designed to help returning students make the transition into college. Required for all new college students and those who have been out of school for over 10 years, this college credit course builds on basic academic skills: reading, writing, and critical thinking.

Informational Materials Available: Exam Preparation Guides; Institutional Catalog; Prior Learning Guides; Program Brochure.

Program Age, Enrollment, and Degrees Conferred:

Degree	Year Est.	Current Enrollment	Degrees Conferred
BA/BS	1975	424	618
MA in Public Mgmt.	1982	105	100

Percentage of Bachelor's Degree Holders Admitted to Graduate School: Information not available.

Geographic Admission Restrictions: Although we have no geographic restrictions, since we offer mostly evening classes, it would be difficult for long-distance commuters to attend class conveniently.

Tuition and Fees:

	Undergraduate	Graduate
In-State Tuition	$105.00/credit	$310.00/credit
Out-of-State Tuition	$105.00/credit	$310.00/credit
Application Fee	$25.00	$25.00
Graduation Fee	$50.00	
Credit-by-Exam Fee	$50.00	

Other Fees: Lab fees for certain courses vary $25.00-$45.00 per course.

Other Pertinent Information: "Birmingham-Southern has developed a Model Liberal Arts Program for Adults,"—The Kellogg Foundation; "Birmingham-Southern College was named the best liberal arts college in the Southern Region"—*U.S. News and World Report*, Oct. 26, 1987; "Birmingham-Southern is one of the (50 best bargains in colleges)"—*Good Housekeeping*," 1989; The Money College Guide 1990, compiled by the editors of *Money Magazine*, listed Birmingham-Southern College in the Top 100 Private Schools among "America's Best College Buys."

2. Jacksonville State University

227 Stone Center
Jacksonville, AL 36265

Degrees Offered: Bachelor of General Studies.

Program Mission Statement/Description: The General Studies degree program meets the academic needs not ordinarily available in other degree programs of the university. This degree is designed to allow students greater freedom in selecting a course of study.

Accreditation: Southern Association of Colleges and Schools.

Admission Requirements: HS/GED Diploma; ACT or SAT Tests.

Credit Awards for Prior Learning: ACE Military Recommendations; Transfer Credit.

Limits to Credit Awards for Prior Learning: All work from each college will be reflected on the JSU record and will become part of the student's cumulative record. Credits on which a "C" grade or better have been earned will be accepted as an equivalent course or, if there is not an equivalent course, as an elective. Grades of "D" are acceptable if the student has an overall "C" average in the work presented for transfer. Grades of "D" are not acceptable in English 101. Grades of "D" will not be allowed to count toward fulfilling required courses in the major, minor, and teaching field. Students may transfer from a junior college at any time. It is recommended, however, that they not earn credit beyond 64 semester hours (96 quarter hours). Although an unlimited number of hours is acceptable from a four-year college or university. Students under academic probation at other accredited colleges/ universities are admissible to JSU on probation. Students under academic suspension at the last college/university attended may not be admitted to JSU. They may, however, petition the Admissions Committee for consideration of their individual situation.

Credit Awards for Examinations: ACT Proficiency Exams; CLEP General Exams; CLEP Subject Exams; DANTES Subject Tests; College Board AP Exams.

Estimated Average Completion Time: 7.5-8 years (part-time), 5 years (full-time).

Credit Hour Requirements: 128 hours total; 32 hours academic residency (hours that must be earned at the institution exclusive of credit-by-exam, portfolio assessment, etc.).

Distance Learning Options: Television Courses.

Student Support Services Available: Academic Advising; Career Counseling; Counseling/Testing; Financial Aid; Job Placement Assistance; Orientation; Tutoring.

Informational Materials Available: Institutional Catalog.

Program Age, Enrollment, and Degrees Conferred:

Degree	Year Est.	Current Enrollment	Degrees Conferred
BGS	1988	0	0

Percentage of Bachelor's Degree Holders Admitted to Graduate School: Information not available.

Geographic Admission Restrictions: None.

Tuition and Fees:

	Undergraduate
In-State Tuition per credit	$55.00
Out-of-State Tuition per credit	$82.50
Application Fee	$15.00
Graduation Fee	$11.00
Credit-by-Exam Fee	$38.00

3. Troy State University at Dothan

P.O. Drawer 8368
Dothan, AL 36304-0368

Degrees Offered: Associate of Science in General Education; Associate of Applied Science; Bachelor of Science; Bachelor of Applied Science; Master of Science; Master of Business Administration; Master of Education Specialist.

Program Mission Statement/Description: Troy State University is a commuter university of predominantly nontraditional, adult students with approximately 95 percent of its student body residing within a 50-mile radius of Dothan. Within this radius, it is the only comprehensive university. Troy State University at Dothan is dedicated to the preprofessional and professional preparation of students in a variety of fields in the arts and sciences, business, education, and applied sciences.

Accreditation: Southern Association of Colleges and Schools.

Admission Requirements:

Undergraduate	Graduate
HS/GED Diploma	Undergraduate Degree GRE, MAT, or NTE Exams

Credit Awards for Prior Learning: ACE Military Recommendations; Transfer Credit.

Credit Awards for Examinations: CLEP General Exams; CLEP Subject Exams; DANTES Subject Tests.

Estimated Average Completion Time: Associates' Degrees: 3 years (part-time), 2 years (full-time); Bachelors' Degrees: 5-6 years (part-time), 4 years (full-time); Graduate Degrees: 2-3 years (part-time), 1 year (full-time).

Credit Hour Requirements:

Degree	Total Hours	Academic Residency*
Associate's quarter hour	90	22
Bachelor's quarter hour	180	45
Graduate (MS)	50	40
Graduate (MBA)	60	50

*Hours that must be earned at the institution exclusive of credit-by-exam, portfolio assessment, etc.

Distance Learning Options: Independent Study—Bachelor, Graduate, and Associate; Supervised Fieldwork—Bachelor and Graduate only; Television Courses—Associate and Bachelor only.

Student Support Services Available: Academic Advising; Career Counseling; Counseling/Testing; Financial Aid; Job Placement Assistance; Orientation; Tutoring

Informational Materials Available: Institutional Catalog; Program Brochure.

Program Age, Enrollment, and Degrees Conferred:

Degree	Year Est.	Current Enrollment	Degrees Conferred
Associate's	1970	1933	21
BS	1970	269	unknown
MS	1970	162	unknown
EDS	1981	4	unknown

Percentage of Bachelor's Degree Holders Admitted to Graduate School: Information not available.

Geographic Admission Restrictions: None.

Tuition and Fees:

	Undergraduate	Graduate
In-State Tuition per quarter	$490.00	$49.00
Out-of-State Tuition per quarter	$784.00	$78.00
Application Fee	$15.00	$15.00
Graduation Fee	$12.00	$12.00

4. University of Alabama at Birmingham

Master of Science in Health Administration Executive
  Program
Webb Bldg., Rm. 560
UAB Station
Birmingham, AL 35294-3361

Degrees Offered: Master of Science in Health Administration.

Program Mission Statement/Description: The Master of Science in Health Administration (MSHA) Executive Program is designed for experienced health services professionals who want to seek an advanced degree without career interruption, during an intensive 24-month period.

Instructional design and methodology include reading assignments, video presentations, computer-aided instruction, and electronic mail. The program consists of on-campus sessions, weekend cluster groups (regional), and off-campus study.

Accreditation: Southern Association of Colleges and Schools.

Admission Requirements: Employment/Experience: 3 years at midlevel; Essay/Written Work; GRE or GMAT; Interview; Recommendations; Undergraduate Degree.

Credit Awards for Prior Learning: None.

Credit Awards for Examinations: None.

Estimated Average Completion Time: Graduate Degrees: 2 years (full-time).

Credit Hour Requirements: 60 credit hours.

Distance Learning Options: Correspondence Courses; Electronic Mail; Independent Study; Study Guides.

Student Support Services Available: Academic Advising; Orientation.

Informational Materials Available: Program Brochure.

Program Age, Enrollment, and Degrees Conferred:

Degree	Year Est.	Current Enrollment	Degrees Conferred
MSHA Executive Program	1991	17	0

Geographic Admission Restrictions: None.

Tuition and Fees: For Two-Year Program; Nonlocal In-State and Out-of-State Tuition $18,600.00, Application fee $25.00. Local In-State and Out-of-State Tuition $15,300.00. $9,300.00 per calendar year includes tuition, lodging, fees, books, and materials.

5. University of South Alabama

Department of Adult Personalized Study
Alpha East 214
Mobile, AL 36688

Degrees Offered: Bachelor of Arts; Bachelor of Science.

Program Mission Statement/Description: The Department of Adult Personalized Study provides opportunity for adult students through three alternative educational programs: The Personalized Study Program for Adults (PSPA); The Weekend College; Media-Assisted Courses.

Accreditation: Southern Association of Colleges and Schools.

Admission Requirements: HS/GED Diploma; Interview.

Credit Awards for Prior Learning: ACE Military Recommendations; ACE/PONSI Recommendations; Transfer Credit.

Limits to Credit Awards for Prior Learning: Maximum of 48 quarter hours accepted from ACE.

Credit Awards for Examinations: CLEP General Exams; CLEP Subject Exams; College Board AP Exams; Departmental Exams.

Estimated Average Completion Time: 24 quarter hours (part-time), 16 quarter hours (full-time).

Caveats Regarding Time Estimates: Part-time estimate is based on 8 hours per quarter. Both estimates exclude transfer, CLEP, or other alternative credit.

Credit Hour Requirements: 192 hours total; 48 hours academic residency (hours that must be earned at the institution exclusive of credit-by-exam, portfolio assessment, etc.).

Distance Learning Options: A/V Cassettes; Cooperative Education; Independent Study; Study Guides.

Student Support Services Available: Academic Advising; Career Counseling; Counseling/Testing; Financial Aid; Job Placement Assistance; Orientation; Tutoring; Health Services.

Informational Materials Available: Institutional Catalog; Program Brochure.

Program Age, Enrollment, and Degrees Conferred:

Degree	Year Est.	Current Enrollment	Degrees Conferred
Bachelor's	1980	500	196

Percentage of Bachelor's Degree Holders Admitted to Graduate School: Information not available.

Geographic Admission Restrictions: None.

Tuition and Fees: $36.00 per credit; Application Fee $15.00; Graduation Fee $20.00.

Credit-by-Exam Fee Varies.

Other Fees: Out-of-State Fees; Less than 6-hour course load $67.00, 6-11 hour course load $134.00, and 12 hours or greater course load $200.00.

Other Pertinent Information: This is not a distance-learning program. It is a personalized program that offers adult students support, advising, flexibility, and the maximum opportunity at our university to use prior learning experience.

Alaska

6. Alaska Pacific University

Degree Completion Program
Adult and Continuing Education
4101 University Dr.
Anchorage, AK 99508

Degrees Offered: Bachelor of Arts in Organizational Administration.

Program Mission Statement/Description: Degree Completion Program is a unique alternative to the traditional method of pursuing a degree. It is designed especially for adults who want to earn a degree while on the job, in classes close to home and coordinated with their schedules.

Accreditation: Northwest Association of Schools and Colleges.

Admission Requirements: Employment/Experience; Essay/Written Work; HS/GED Diploma; Interview; Prior Credits: 60-64; GPA of 2.0; Recommendation.

Credit Awards for Prior Learning: ACE Military Recommendations; Portfolio Assessment; Transfer Credit.

Limits to Credit Awards for Prior Learning: Portfolio—32 credits.

Credit Awards for Examinations: CLEP General Exams; CLEP Subject Exams; College Board AP Exams; DANTES Subject Tests.

Estimated Average Completion Time: 16 months (full-time).

Caveats Regarding Time Estimates: Bachelor's degree student must transfer in 60-64 credit hours. Sixteen months is full-time continuous, and one night a week, and must be taken as a whole unit. If transferred hours do not meet Alaska Pacific University's GURs, students must take additional classes to do so. We offer intensive weekend sessions of some classes to enable degree completion students (and others who might be interested) to complete their GURs. These sessions run Friday evenings and all day Saturdays for the same number of contact hours as traditional format classes.

Credit Hour Requirements: 128 hours total; 32 hours academic residency (hours that must be earned at the institution exclusive of credit-by-exam, portfolio assessment, etc.).

Distance Learning Options: Supervised Fieldwork.

Student Support Services Available: Academic Advising; Career Counseling; Counseling/Testing; Financial Aid; Orientation; Tutoring.

Informational Materials Available: Institutional Catalog; Program Brochure.

Program Age, Enrollment, and Degrees Conferred:

Degree	Year Est.	Current Enrollment	Degrees Conferred
Organizational Administration	1988	252	107

Percentage of Bachelor's Degree Holders Admitted to Graduate School: 27 percent.

Geographic Admission Restrictions: Students have to attend class in Wasilla or Anchorage.

Tuition and Fees: In-State Tuition: $258.00 per credit; Out-of-State Tuition: $258.00 per credit; Graduation Fee $50.00; Credit-by-Exam Fee CLEP $37.00; Challenged Classes $50.00 per credit.

Other Fees: $6200.00 tuition for 16-month program of 39 credits.

Arizona

7. University of Phoenix

Branch Campus Alternative Degree Program
4615 East Elwood St.
P.O. Box 52069
Phoenix, AZ 85072-2069

Degrees Offered: Associate of Arts in Business; Bachelor of Arts in Management; Bachelor of Science in Business Administration; Bachelor of Science in Nursing; Master of Business Administration; Master of Arts in Organizational Management; Master in Nursing; Master of Arts in Education; Master of Counseling; Master of Science in Computer Information Systems.

Program Mission Statement/Description: The University of Phoenix is a private, postsecondary institution that provides education and professional renewal services designed specifically for working adults. The university identifies and develops programs which respond to the professional and career goals of its target population and the education and training needs of the organizations in which they are employed.

Accreditation: North Central Association of Colleges and Schools; National League for Nursing.

Admission Requirements:

Undergraduate	Graduate
HS/GED Diploma	Undergraduate Degree
Recommendations	Recommendations
Two years prior employment	Three years prior employment
Prior Credits: 24	GRE

Other Admission Requirements: Institutional exam; Current employment; TOEFL if primary language is not English. For BSN, program-equivalent of an associate's degree in nursing (56 specific credits).

Credit Awards for Prior Learning: ACE Military Recommendations; ACE/PONSI Recommendations; Portfolio Assessment; Transfer Credit.

Limits to Credit Awards for Prior Learning: Maximum lower division credits 60; University of Phoenix major course of study must be completed.

Credit Awards for Examinations: ACT Proficiency Exams; CLEP General Exams; CLEP Subject Exams; DANTES Subject Tests.

Estimated Average Completion Time: Associates' Degrees: 2 years (full-time); Bachelors' Degrees: 3 years (full-time); Graduate Degrees: MBA, MN 2 years (full-time); MAEd one year (full-time); MAOM 1.5 years (full-time); MC 1.5 years (full-time).

Caveats Regarding Time Estimates: Time to complete associate's or bachelor's degree varies depending on number of credits students transfer or earn for prior learning.

Credit Hour Requirements:

Degree	Total Hours	Academic Residency*
Associate's	60	39
Bachelor's (BSBS)	120	38
Bachelor's (BAM)	120	32
Bachelor's (BSN)	126	40
Graduate (MBA, MA)	37	31
Graduate (MAEd)	17	11
Graduate (MAEd with specialization)	35-38	29-32
Graduate (MC)	52	52
Graduate (MAOM)	40	31
Graduate (MSCIS)	39	30

*Hours that must be earned at the institution exclusive of credit-by-exam, portfolio assessment, etc.

Distance Learning Options: Electronic Mail (Bachelor and Graduate only); Directed/Independent Study.

Student Support Services Available: Academic Advising; Counseling/Testing; Financial Aid; Orientation.

Informational Materials Available: Exam Preparation Guides; Institutional Catalog; Prior Learning Guides; Program Brochure.

Program Age, Enrollment, and Degrees Conferred:

Degree	Year Est.	Current Enrollment	Degrees Conferred
BSBA/BAM	1978	6376	11,272
BAM	1978	1112	1200
BSN	1982	894	1900
MAOM	1988	826	613
MBA	1979	1967	5905
MN	1987	149	63
MSCIS	1991	63	N/A
AA	1990	107	68
MAEd	1991	310	1288
MC	1990	106	57

Percentage of Bachelor's Degree Holders Admitted to Graduate School: Information not available.

Geographic Admission Restrictions: Our access and on-line programs have no geographic restrictions. We have campus-based offerings in Salt Lake City, Utah; Denver, Colorado; Albuquerque, New Mexico; Phoenix, and Tucson, Arizona; San Jose, San Diego, and Orange County, California; Puerto Rico; and Hawaii. Attendance at these campuses is restricted to proximity to a campus.

Tuition and Fees:

	Undergraduate	Graduate
In-State Tuition per credit	$166.00	$180.00
Application Fee	$48.00	$48.00
Graduation Fee	$50.00	$50.00

Arkansas

8. Southern Arkansas University

SAU Box 1240
Magnolia, AR 71753

Degrees Offered: Bachelor of Science in Industrial Technology; Bachelor of Business Administration.

Program Mission Statement/Description: Bachelor of Science in Industrial Technology (BSIT)–This program is designed to accommodate the continuing education needs of employees who have a terminal associate's degree to enhance their career advancement in areas combining skilled crafts and highly scientific professions. Core curriculum offered on weekends. Bachelor of Business Administration (BBA)–Students seeking this degree may major in accounting, administrative services, computer information systems, economics, finance, general business, management, or marketing. A combination major is available in industrial management. Core curriculum offered on weekends.

Accreditation: North Central Association of Colleges and Schools; National Council for the Accreditation of Teacher Education; National League for Nursing.

Admission Requirements: HS/GED Diploma; Associate's Degree; ACT Test Scores.

Credit Awards for Prior Learning: ACE Military Recommendations; Portfolio Assessment; Transfer Credit amount 68 hours maximum depending upon degree requirements, etc.

Limits to Credit Awards for Prior Learning: Up to nine hours of credit in the BSIT program can be transferred in via prior higher education achievement, military training, work experience, or technical electives.

Credit Awards for Examinations: CLEP Subject Exams; DANTES Subject Tests.

Limits to Credit Awards for Examinations: Exams do not meet residency requirements.

Estimated Average Completion Time: 4 years (full-time).

Caveats Regarding Time Estimates: No student can expect to take more than six years to graduate under the SAU catalog issue in effect at the time of entrance at SAU-Magnolia. Requests to waive this policy should be submitted to the Vice President for Academic Affairs for review.

Credit Hour Requirements: Information not available.

Distance Learning Options: Supervised Fieldwork/Internships/practicums; Television Courses–Limited PBS telecourses.

Student Support Services Available: Academic Advising; Career Counseling; Counseling/Testing; Financial Aid; Tutoring.

Informational Materials Available: Exam Preparation Guides; Institutional Catalog; Program Brochure.

Program Age, Enrollment, and Graduates:

Degree	Year Est.	Current Enrollment	Degrees Conferred
BSIT	1989	30	0
BBA	1989	15	0

Percentage of Bachelor's Degree Holders Admitted to Graduate School: Information not available.

Geographic Admission Restrictions: None.

Tuition and Fees: In-State Tuition $56.00 per credit; Out-of-State Tuition $86.00 per credit; Credit-by-Exam Fee Pending; Off-Campus Course Tuition $95.00 per credit for the BSIT program; Athletic Fee per hour (off-campus courses exempt) $4.00.

California

9. Chabot College

Program for Adult College Education
25555 Hesperian Blvd.
Hayward, CA 94545

Degrees Offered: Associate of Arts.

Program Mission Statement/Description: Program for Adult College Education (PACE) is a program for working adults. Students attend class one evening per week plus all day every other Saturday. Additionally, PACE students enroll in a telecourse. In five terms, students are able to earn an AA degree and fulfill lower division requirements of the California State University system.

Accreditation: Western Association of Schools and Colleges.

Admission Requirements: HS/GED Diploma; students must be eligible for English 1A (College Level English).

Credit Awards for Prior Learning: ACE Military Recommendations; Transfer Credit.

Limits to Credit Awards for Prior Learning: ACE Military recommendations: maximum of 10 units accepted.

Credit Awards for Examinations: CLEP General Exams.

Limits to Credit Awards for Examinations: College Board AP Exams 10 units.

Estimated Average Completion Time: 3-4 years (part-time), 2 years (full-time).

Credit Hour Requirements: 90 hours total; 18 hours academic residency (hours that must be earned at the institution exclusive of credit-by-exam, portfolio assessment, etc.).

Distance Learning Options: A/V Cassettes; Independent Study; Television Courses.

Student Support Services Available: Academic Advising; Career Counseling; Counseling/Testing; Financial Aid; Job Placement Assistance; Orientation; Tutoring.

Informational Materials Available: Institutional Catalog; Program Brochure.

Program Age, Enrollment, and Degrees Conferred:

Degree	Year Est.	Current Enrollment	Degrees Conferred
Associate of Arts	1989	319	0

Geographic Admission Restrictions: None.

Tuition and Fees: In-State Tuition: $35.00 per credit; Out-of-State Tuition: $70.00 per credit; Credit-by-Exam Fee: Same as tuition.

Other Pertinent Information: PACE is a district program available at both of our colleges, Las Positas and Chabot. PACE is "housed" at Chabot.

---

10. Cuyamaca College

Weekend College
2950 Jamacha Rd.
El Cajon, CA 92019

Degrees Offered: Associate of Arts and Associate of Science in Business Administration, General Studies, Liberal Studies, Real Estate, Business Microcomputers, and Paralegal Studies.

Program Mission Statement/Description: The mission of the Grossmont-Cuyamaca Community College District as approved by the governing board is to be a responsive leader in developing effective and efficient quality educational programs, classes and services to meet the needs of students for transfer to baccalaureate institutions, job entry and job reentry skills, and for lifelong and cultural enrichment necessary to a productive and socially responsible life. The Cuyamaca Weekend College is an innovative concept designed for busy people who want to attend college but cannot attend during the week when most courses are offered. This program enables students to attend Cuyamaca College on weekends only and earn an associate's degree in two years. New courses are offered each month and usually meet Friday evenings and all day on Saturday. A full complement of general education courses are offered in the Weekend College program. Course fees are the same as other Cuyamaca College courses.

Accreditation: Western Association of Schools and Colleges.

Admission Requirements: HS/GED Diploma or students who are 18 years of age and have the ability to benefit from the instruction offered may attend Cuyamaca.

Credit Awards for Prior Learning: Transfer Credit.

Other Options: Cuyamaca will give credit for physical education for military.

Credit Awards for Examinations: ACT Proficiency Exams; College Board AP Exams; Departmental Exams.

Estimated Average Completion Time: 4 years (part-time), 2 years (full-time).

Credit Hour Requirements: 60 hours total; 12 hours academic residency (hours that must be earned at the institution exclusive of credit-by-exam, portfolio assessment, etc.).

Distance Learning Options: Independent Study; Television Courses.

Student Support Services Available: Academic Advising; Career Counseling; Counseling/Testing; Financial Aid; Job Placement Assistance; Orientation; Tutoring.

Informational Materials Available: Institutional Catalog; Program Brochure.

Program Age, Enrollment, and Degrees Conferred: Information not available.

Geographic Admission Restrictions: Students are eligible to attend Cuyamaca College as California residents if they have been physically present and have established intent for one year prior to the residence determination date. A student classified as a nonresident is required to pay nonresident tuition in addition to other fees required by the institution.

Tuition and Fees: In-State Tuition: $50.00 per credit; Out-of-State Tuition: $96.00 per credit

11. Fresno Pacific College

Management of Human Relations Program
1717 S. Chestnut Ave.
Fresno, CA 93702

Degrees Offered: Bachelor of Arts in Management of Human Relations.

Program Mission Statement/Description: This is a compressed time program for working adults who have at least 7 years of postsecondary experience and are presently employed. This program includes a high regard for the individual student, concern for the maximum development of his/her potential, and a commitment to high ethical standards.

Accreditation: Western Association of Schools and Colleges.

Admission Requirements: HS/GED Diploma; Interview; Essay/Written Work; Recommendations; Prior Employment/Experience: 7 years; Prior Credits: 60.

Credit Awards for Prior Learning: ACE/Recommendations; Portfolio Assessment; Transfer Credit.

Limits to Credit Awards for Prior Learning: 70 semester units from an accredited two-year institution; 30 semester units from portfolio assessment.

Credit Awards for Examinations: CLEP General Exams; CLEP Subject Exams; College Board AP Exams.

Limits to Credit Awards for Examinations: 30 units of test credits.

Estimated Average Completion Time: 13 months or 56 weeks.

Caveats Regarding Time Estimates: This MHR program takes 56 weeks to complete if the student has already completed 60 units of college work and all general education requirements.

Credit Hour Requirements: 124 hours total; 30 hours academic residency (hours that must be earned at the institution exclusive of credit-by-exam, portfolio assessment, etc.).

Distance Learning Options: Correspondence Courses; Independent Study.

Student Support Services Available: Academic Advising; Counseling/Testing; Financial Aid; Orientation; Tutoring.

Informational Materials Available: Institutional Catalog; Prior Learning Guides; Program Brochure.

Program Age, Enrollment, and Degrees Conferred:

Degree	Year Est.	Current Enrollment	Degrees Conferred
MHR	1991	32	0

Percentage of Bachelor's Degree Holders Admitted to Graduate School: Information not available.

Geographic Admission Restrictions: None.

Tuition and Fees: In-State Tuition $7500.00; Out-of-State Tuition $7500.00; Application Fee $30.00; Graduation Fee $30.00.

Other Fees: Books/Materials/Research fee $350.00 (total both semesters). Student Associate fee $40.00 (total both semesters). Assessment fee for life-learning papers $20.00 per unit.

12. Mount Saint Mary's College

10 Chester Pl.
Los Angeles, CA 90007

Degrees Offered: Bachelor of Science in Business, Bachelor of Arts in Psychology, Associate of Arts in Occupational Therapy Assistant.

Program Mission Statement/Description: Educational programs leading to associates' and baccalaureates' degrees, offered on time schedules convenient for women and men who work or are otherwise unable to attend class during traditional daytime class hours. The degrees are essentially the same as those offered daytime students at Mount St. Mary's College students. Teaching/learning methodologies and schedules selected for students are those shown to be appropriate and effective for adult learners.

Accreditation: Western Association of Schools and Colleges.

Admission Requirements: HS/GED Diploma; Recommendations.

Credit Awards for Prior Learning: ACE Military Recommendations; Portfolio Assessment; Transfer Credit.

Limits to Credit Awards for Prior Learning: Maximum 36 semesters, 54 quarter transfer credits accepted for AA degree. Maximum 66 semester transfer credits for bachelor's degree.

Credit Awards for Examinations: CLEP General Exams; CLEP Subject Exams; College Board AP Exams; Departmental Exams.

Estimated Average Completion Time: Associates' Degrees: 3 years (part-time), 2 years (full-time); Bachelors' Degrees: 5 years (part-time), 4 years (full-time).

Credit Hour Requirements:

Degree	Total Hours
Associate's	60 credit hours
Bachelor's	129 credit hours

Distance Learning Options: Independent Study; Supervised Fieldwork.

Student Support Services Available: Academic Advising; Career Counseling; Counseling/Testing; Financial Aid; Job Placement Assistance; Orientation; Tutoring.

Informational Materials Available: Institutional Catalog; Program Brochure.

Program Age, Enrollment, and Degrees Conferred:

Degree	Year Est.	Current Enrollment	Degrees Conferred
AA	1990	30	0
BSC Business	1990	50	0
BA Psychology	1990	10	0

Percentage of Bachelor's Degree Holders Admitted to Graduate School: Information not available.

Geographic Admission Restrictions: None.

Tuition and Fees: In-State Tuition $200.00 per credit; Out-of-State Tuition $200.00 per credit; Application Fee $25.00; Graduation Fee $100.00.

Other Fees: Portfolio Application/Counseling: $100.00; Portfolio Evaluation/Decision and Credit for Extrainstitutional Learning Evaluation: $300.00 for 3 units or less; for each additional course: $100.00; Credential Evaluation: $75.00.

---

13. Saint Mary's College of California

School of Extended Education
P.O. Box 4700
Moraga, CA 94575

Degrees Offered: Bachelor of Arts in Management; Bachelor of Arts in Health Services Administration; Master of Science in Health Services Administration; Master of Science in Procurement and Contract Management.

Program Mission Statement/Description: The goals of the school are: to provide the competence and knowledge adults need in the world of work; to provide for the underlying intellectual processes which allow learning to become a lifelong experience; to develop an appreciation of the life of the mind so that learning does become a central goal in life; to enhance students critical thinking skills; and to encourage high ethical standards and a concern for human values.

Accreditation: Western Association of Schools and Colleges.

Admission Requirements:

Undergraduate	Graduate
HS/GED Diploma	Undergraduate Degree
Essay/Written Work	Interview
Recommendations	Essay/Written Work
Employment/Experience	Recommendations
Prior Credits: 60	Employment/Experience

Credit Awards for Prior Learning: ACE Military Recommendations; ACE/PONSI Recommendations; Portfolio Assessment; Transfer Credit.

Limits to Credit Awards for Prior Learning: On portfolio, 30. On transfer credits, 64 lower division. (No limit as such on upper division but at most 26 can be counted towards degree.)

Credit Awards for Examinations: CLEP Subject Exams; DANTES Subject Tests.

Estimated Average Completion Time: Bachelors' Degrees: 15 months to complete program of 30 credits (part-time); Graduate Degrees: 21 months (part-time).

Caveats Regarding Time Estimates: Students engage in continuous intensive program but typically also are working. No "semester" units.

Credit Hour Requirements:

Degree	Total Hours	Academic Residency*
Bachelor's	120	30
Graduate (MS)	14 quarter courses	

*Hours that must be earned at the institution exclusive of credit-by-exam, portfolio assessment, etc.

Distance Learning Options: None.

Student Support Services Available: Academic Advising; Career Counseling; Financial Aid; Job Placement Assistance; Orientation.

Informational Materials Available: Institutional Catalog; Prior Learning Guides; Program Brochure.

Program Age, Enrollment, and Degrees Conferred:

Degree	Year Est.	Current Enrollment	Degrees Conferred
BA: Mgmt and HSA	1977	600	3500
MS HSA	1983	80	300
MS PCM	1985	40	300

Percentage of Bachelor's Degree Holders Admitted to Graduate School: Information not available.

Geographic Admission Restrictions: Students must be in area to attend weekly classes.

Tuition and Fees: Undergraduate $8,664.00 for 18-month program; Graduate Master of Science in Health Services Administration $8,568.00 for 21-month program; Master of Science in Procurement and Contract Management $9,891.00 for 21-month program; Application Fee $35.00.

Other Fees: Graduate Tuition fee for Health Services $8,360.00; Mgmt/Procurement $9,282.00.

14. Sonoma State University

External Master of Arts in Psychology Programs
Dept. of Psychology
1801 E. Cotati Ave.
Rohnert Park, CA 94928

Degrees Offered: Master of Arts in Psychology.

Program Mission Statement/Description: Designed for self-directed individuals who may already be in the professional workplace and are unable to attend a residential MA program, the external MA in Psychology provides an alternative approach to professional preparation in psychology. It provides the opportunity to develop a 30-semester-unit curriculum, primarily tutorial in nature, working closely with an advisor from the faculty.

Accreditation: Western Association of Schools and Colleges.

Admission Requirements: Undergraduate Degree; Employment/Experience: 1 year post-bachelor of arts; Essay/Written Work; GRE or MAT, plus local writing exam; Interview; Recommendations.

Other Admission Requirements: Some prior work at Sonoma State. A course in the history of psychology.

Credit Awards for Prior Learning: Portfolio Assessment.

Limits to Credit Awards for Prior Learning: 15 units.

Credit Awards for Examinations: None.

Estimated Average Completion Time: 1.5 years (full-time), 2.5 years (part-time).

Credit Hour Requirements: 30 semester hours.

Distance Learning Options: Independent Study.

Student Support Services Available: Academic Advising; Career Counseling; Financial Aid; Orientation.

Informational Materials Available: Institutional Catalog; Program Brochure.

Program Age, Enrollment, and Graduates:

Degree	Year Est.	Current Enrollment	Degrees Conferred
MA Psychology	1972	20	Info. not available

Geographic Admission Restrictions: Students are expected to reside in the greater San Francisco Bay Area or Northern California coastal region.

Tuition and Fees: In-State Tuition $85.00 per credit; Out-of-State Tuition $85.00 per credit; Application Fee $35.00; Graduation Fee $13.00.

15. University of San Francisco

College of Professional Studies
Ignatian Heights
San Francisco, CA 94117

Degrees Offered: Bachelor of Science in Organizational Behavior; Bachelor of Science in Information Systems Management; Bachelor of Science in Applied Economics; Bachelor of Public Administration; Master of Human Resources and Organization Development; Master of Public Administration; Master of Nonprofit Administration; Master of Public Administration/Health Services Administration; Master of Education.

Program Mission Statement/Description: The College of Professional Studies at the University of San Francisco offers to midcareer professionals in the private, public, and nonprofit sectors interdisciplinary programs that emphasize the integration of theory and practice in developing the knowledge and skills for effective organizational leadership as they relate to human, technical, and financial resources.

Accreditation: Western Association of Schools and Colleges.

Admission Requirements:

Undergraduate	Graduate
HS/GED Diploma	Undergraduate Degree
Interview	Interview
Recommendations	Essay/Written Work
Employment/Experience	Recommendations
	Employment/Experience: 2 years or more

Credit Awards for Prior Learning: ACE Military Recommendations; ACE/PONSI Recommendations; Transfer Credit; Portfolio Assessment; CLEP.

Limits to Credit Awards for Prior Learning: Transfer—no limit although some credit may be "add on" given requirements for graduation; ACE (PONSI or Military)—no limit, although credit may be "add on"; Portfolio—30 unit limit.

Credit Awards for Examinations: CLEP General Exams; CLEP Subject Exams.

Estimated Average Completion Time: Bachelors' Degrees: 24 months (full-time); Graduate Degrees: 30 months (full-time).

Caveats Regarding Time Estimates: All students are full-time.

Credit Hour Requirements:

Degree	Total Hours	Academic Residency*
Bachelor's	36	30
Graduate	36	30

*Hours that must be earned at the institution exclusive of credit-by-exam, portfolio assessment, etc.

Distance Learning Options: None.

Student Support Services Available: Academic Advising; Counseling/Testing; Financial Aid; Job Placement Assistance Career Counseling; Orientation; Tutoring.

Informational Materials Available: Institutional Catalog; Program Brochure.

Other Information Available: Program fact sheets.

Program Age, Enrollment, and Degrees Conferred:

Degree	Year Est.	Current Enrollment	Degrees Conferred
BS-OB/BPA	1977	585	5550
BS-ISM/BS-AE	1980	330	1000
MHROD	1980	175	800
MPA	1977	30	260
MPA/HSA	1986	125	550
MNA	1983	25	120

Percentage of Bachelor's Degree Holders Admitted to Graduate School: 25 percent.

Geographic Admission Restrictions: None.

Tuition and Fees:

	Undergraduate	Graduate
In-State Tuition per credit	$305.00	$322.00
Out-of-State Tuition per credit	$305.00	$322.00
Application Fee	$35.00	$35.00

Colorado

16. Adams State College

Dept. of Teacher Education
Alamosa, CO 81102

Degrees Offered: Master of Arts in Elementary Education, Field-Based; Master of Arts in Secondary Education, Field-Based.

Program Mission Statement/Description: The Department of Teacher Education offers graduate programs leading to the Master of Arts in Elementary Education, Secondary Education and Special Education-Teacher I Moderate Needs. Graduate programs assume that the teacher holds the initial level of certification in an academic area or grade level and that the teacher has had successful experience in the classroom. The program of study for the Master of Arts degree builds upon the concept developed at the undergraduate level that the teacher is a decision maker. Thus, the courses offered in the three graduate programs emphasize the development of increasing skill in teacher decision making and a more in depth conceptual understanding of both the decision process and the basic areas in and underlying teacher decisions. The program leading to the Master of Arts in Elementary Education and in Secondary Education has a core of professional education courses as well as requirements for each individual to take advanced level preparation in a specified teaching field. The program also provides for individual interests by including a series of approved electives from which each individual can make choices.

Accreditation: North Central Association of Colleges and Schools; National Council for Accreditation of Teacher Education.

Admission Requirements: GRE; Undergraduate Degree; Current standard teaching certificate in subject matter area.

Credit Awards for Prior Learning: Transfer Credit.

Limits to Credit Awards for Prior Learning: Transfer credits—6 semester hours of graduate credit appropriate to the degree program.

Credit Awards for Examinations: None.

Estimated Average Completion Time: Graduate Degrees: 14 months (full-time).

Caveats Regarding Time Estimates: 14 month cycle is completed from June of the first summer through July of the second summer.

Credit Hour Requirements:

Degree	Total Hours	Academic Residency*
Graduate	30 (MA)	16

*Hours that must be earned at the institution exclusive of credit-by-exam, portfolio assessment, etc.

Distance Learning Options: A/V Cassettes; Correspondence Courses; Electronic Mail; Independent Study; Phone/Mail Instruction; Study Guides; Supervised Fieldwork; Television Courses.

Student Support Services Available: Academic Advising; Career Counseling; Counseling/Testing; Financial Aid; Job Placement Assistance; Orientation; Tutoring.

Informational Materials Available: Exam Preparation Guides; Institutional Catalog; Program Brochure.

Program Age, Enrollment, and Degrees Conferred:

Degree	Year Est.	Current Enrollment	Degrees Conferred
MA Elem. Education	1977	27	0
MA Secondary Education	1977	20	0

Geographic Admission Restrictions: None.

Tuition and Fees: In-State Tuition $62.00 per credit; Out-of-State Tuition $171.00 per credit; Application Fee $10.00.

Other Pertinent Information: All graduate students pay in-state tuition fees during summer sessions, regardless of residency classification.

---

17. Metropolitan State College

Adult Learning Services
Campus Box 50
P.O. Box 173362
Denver, CO 80217

Degrees Offered: Individualized Major and Minor Degrees offered through contract option.

Program Mission Statement/Description: As a large, urban undergraduate institution of higher education, Metropolitan State College of Denver has a commitment to respond to the learning needs of a socially, culturally, and educationally diverse population. One growing segment of this population consists of adults, nontraditional learners whose needs are sometimes not met by the existing catalog major and/or minor offerings. The Contract Major/Minor option provides an opportunity for this special population to be involved with a faculty advisory committee in the individualization of a degree program that may combine a selection of courses drawn from departments within and/or across the three schools of the college.

Accreditation: North Central Association of Colleges and Schools.

Admission Requirements: HS/GED Diploma.

Other Admission Requirements: Admission requirements differ according to age. There are two categories, those less than 20 and those 20 years of age and older. Based on the college's modified open admissions system, each category has its own admission requirements and procedures.

Credit Awards for Prior Learning: ACE Military Recommendations; ACE/PONSI Recommendations; Portfolio Assessment; Transfer Credit.

Limits to Credit Awards for Prior Learning: 60 semester hours total.

Credit Awards for Examinations: CLEP General Exams; CLEP Subject Exams; College Board AP Exams; Departmental Exams.

Estimated Average Completion Time: 6-10 years (part-time), 4 years (full-time).

Credit Hour Requirements: 120 hours total; 30 hours academic residency (hours that must be earned at the institution exclusive of credit-by-exam, portfolio assessment, etc.).

Distance Learning Options: Cooperative Education; Correspondence Courses; Independent Study; Supervised Fieldwork; Television Courses.

Student Support Services Available: Academic Advising; Career Counseling; Counseling/Testing; Financial Aid; Job Placement Assistance; Orientation; Tutoring; Disabled Student Services; Off-Campus Housing Services; Office of International Programs; Child Care Center.

Informational Materials Available: Institutional Catalog; Prior Learning Guides; Program Brochure.

Other Information Available: Appropriate flyers.

Program Age, Enrollment, and Degrees Conferred:

Degree	Year Est.	Current Enrollment	Degrees Conferred
Contract Major	1974	250	Unknown

Percentage of Bachelor's Degree Holders Admitted to Graduate School: 10-15 percent.

Geographic Admission Restrictions: None.

Tuition and Fees: In-State Tuition: $62.00 per credit; Out-of-State Tuition: $232.00 per credit; Application Fee $10.00; Credit-by-Exam Fee $10.00 per credit hour.

Other Fees: Student Activity Fee $17.00. Athletic Fee $16.00. Telephone Registration $4.00 Facility $13.50. AHEC Bond $22.00. Information Technology Fee $12.50. Extended Studies $10.00 per credit hour added to basic tuition. Graduation Fee $20.00; Health Insurance $165.00.

---

18. National Technological University (NTU)

700 Centre Ave.
Fort Collins, CO 80526

Degrees Offered: Master of Science in Computer Engineering; Master of Science in Computer Science; Master of Science in Electrical Engineering; Master of Science in Engineering Management; Master of Science in Management of Technology; Master of Science in Manufacturing Systems Engineering; and Master of Science in Materials Science and Engineering.

Program Mission Statement/Description: In summary, National Technological University has a mission to (a) serve the advanced educational needs of graduate engineers, technical professionals and managers; (b) award degrees and certificates at the master's level to qualified candidates; (c) explore, develop, and use advanced educational and telecommunications technologies in delivering instructional programs to graduate engineers and technical professionals at their employment locations; and (d) provide a satellite network infrastructure linking technical professionals and managers nationally, and potentially internationally, in research seminars, technology transfer activities and related technical exchanges.

Accreditation: North Central Association of Colleges and Schools.

Admission Requirements: Undergraduate Degree.

Credit Awards for Prior Learning: None.

Credit Awards for Examinations: None.

Estimated Average Completion Time: Graduate Degrees: MS 3 years (part-time).

Caveats Regarding Time Estimates: All students are part-time.

Credit Hour Requirements: 30 credit hours.

Distance Learning Options: A/V Cassettes; Television Courses.

Student Support Services Available: Academic Advising.

Informational Materials Available: Institutional Catalog; Program Brochure.

Program Age, Enrollment, and Degrees Conferred:

Degree	Year Est.	Current Enrollment	Degrees Conferred
Comp. Engr./Sci.	Unknown	437	67
Electrical Engr.	Unknown	243	26
Engr. Management	Unknown	215	20
Material Sci./Engr.	Unknown	7	0
Manuf. System Engr.	Unknown	62	8
Mgmt. of Technology	Unknown	58	0

Geographic Admission Restrictions: None.

Tuition and Fees: Out-of-State Tuition $475.00 per credit; Application Fee $50.00 per credit.

19. Pikes Peak Community College

5675 S. Academy Blvd., Box 33
Colorado Springs, CO 80906

Degrees Offered: Associate of General Studies.

Program Mission Statement/Description: The Associate of General Studies degree provides an educational plan which allows students to create a personalized program by blending a variety of occupational and technical courses with liberal arts and science courses.

Accreditation: North Central Association of Colleges and Schools.

Admission Requirements: As an "open door" institution, Pikes Peak Community College has no admission requirements. Students do take a placement test to determine the course level in which they may enroll.

Credit Awards for Prior Learning: ACE Military Recommendations; ACE/PONSI Recommendations; Portfolio Assessment; Transfer Credit.

Limits to Credit Awards for Prior Learning: Up to 50 percent of the degree can be completed with awarded credits (portfolio, standardized tests, published guide recommendations). No more than 25 percent of the degree requirements can be met with portfolio awarded credits. For military students in Servicemember Opportunity Col-lege, up to 75 percent of a degree could be awarded through these methods and would be cited in a formal agreement with the student. This is to comply with SOC guidelines.

Credit Awards for Examinations: ACT Proficiency Exams; CLEP General Exams; CLEP Subject Exams; College Board AP Exams; DANTES Subject Tests.

Limits to Credit Awards for Examinations: Same as for prior learning options.

Estimated Average Completion Time: Associates' Degrees: 3-5 years (part-time), 2-4 years (full-time).

Credit Hour Requirements:

Degree	Total Hours	Academic Residency*
Associate's	60	15

*Hours that must be earned at the institution exclusive of credit-by-exam, portfolio assessment, etc.

Distance Learning Options: A/V Cassettes; Independent Study; Study Guides; Supervised Fieldwork; Television Courses.

Student Support Services Available: Academic Advising; Career Counseling; Counseling/Testing; Financial Aid; Job Placement Assistance; Orientation; Tutoring.

Informational Materials Available: Institutional Catalog; Prior Learning Guides; Program Brochure.

Program Age, Enrollment, and Degrees Conferred:

Degree	Year Est.	Current Enrollment	Degrees Conferred
AA	1967	973	8603
AS	1967	495	369
AGS	1967	849	4302

Geographic Admission Restrictions: None.

Tuition and Fees: In-State Tuition $39.25 per credit; Out-of-State Tuition $157.00 per credit; Application Fee $11.00; Graduation Fee $15.00.

Other Fees: Administrative fee for evaluation of prior learning $50-$75. Tuition for off-campus, independent study courses $50/semester hour.

Other Pertinent Information: 25 percent of degree may be fulfilled through successful completion of campus-based independent studies.

20. Regis University

School for Professional Studies
West 50th Ave. and Lowell Blvd.
Denver, CO 80221

Degrees Offered: Bachelor of Arts; Bachelor of Science; Master of Arts in Adult Christian Community Development; Master of Science in Management; Master of Business Administration; Master of Non-Profit Management; Master of Science in Computer Information Science; Master of Community Service and Administration, Master of Arts in Liberal Studies.

Program Mission Statement/Description: The School for Professional Studies of Regis University offers a spectrum of undergraduate and graduate educational programs designed to meet the needs of experienced, reflective adults. The heart of this educational approach rests on belief in the capacity of adult learners to engage in creative, analytic and critical reasoning. This allows students to experience the substantive academic, professional, and personal growth which flows from a collaborative and integrative model of learning. Our programs are flexible and serve the process of learning wherever it occurs—in the formal classroom, the workplace, the marketplace, or the home. Learning sites are spread across geographically distributed campuses and utilize a variety of learning and delivery models as well as a wide range of teaching and professional expertise. This diversity of place and form is bound together by a paramount concern for the interests and needs of the learners in a context of academic quality, fiscal integrity, and management excellence.

Accreditation: North Central Association of Colleges and Schools.

Admission Requirements:

Undergraduate	Graduate
HS/GED Diploma	Undergraduate Degree
Essay/Written Work	Interview
Employment/Experience: 3 years	Essay/Written
	Recommendations
	Employment/Experience: 3 years
	GMAT

Other Admission Requirements: Undergraduate age requirement of 23 years. Requirements may differ from program to program.

Credit Awards for Prior Learning: ACE Military Recommendations; ACE/PONSI Recommendations; Portfolio Assessment; Transfer Credit.

Limits to Credit Awards for Prior Learning: 36 hours undergraduate credit limit for portfolio earned credits. No limit to ACE PONSI and Transfer Credit.

Credit Awards for Examinations: CLEP General Exams; CLEP Subject Exams; DANTES Subject Tests; Departmental Exams.

Estimated Average Completion Time: Bachelors' Degrees: 2-3 years (part-time); Graduate Degrees: MS and MBA 2-3 years (part-time).

Caveats Regarding Time Estimates: Above estimates assume approximately 50-60 transfer credits.

Credit Hour Requirements:

Degree	Total Hours	Academic Residency*
Bachelor's	128	30
MS	34	34
MBA	30	26
MA	36	18

*Hours that must be earned at the institution exclusive of credit-by-exam, portfolio assessment, etc.

Distance Learning Options: Independent Study; Study Guides; Supervised Fieldwork (Bachelor and Graduate).

Student Support Services Available: Academic Advising; Career Counseling; Counseling/Testing; Financial Aid; Job Placement Assistance; Orientation; Academic Computing; Wellness Center; Campus Ministry.

Informational Materials Available: Institutional Catalog; Program Brochure.

Program Age, Enrollment, and Degrees Conferred:

Degree	Year Est.	Current Enrollment	Degrees Conferred
BA	1978	0	154
BS	1978	3500	4528
MBA	1978	700	795
MS Management	1989	224	15
MS CIS	1991	45	0
MA ACCD	1982	216	215
Masters of Nonprofit Mgmt.	1990	49	0
MA Liberal Studies	1991	23	0

Percentage of Bachelor's Degree Holders Admitted to Graduate School: Information not available.

Geographic Admission Restrictions: None.

Tuition and Fees:

	Undergraduate	Graduate
In-State Tuition per credit	$168.00	$210.00
Out-of-State Tuition per credit	$168.00	$210.00
Application Fee	$60.00	$75.00
Graduation Fee	$80.00	$80.00
Credit-by-Exam Fee	$45.00	

Note: Tuition and fees may differ from program to program.

21. University of Colorado

Center for Advanced Training in Engineering and Computer
   Science
Campus Box 435
Boulder, CO 80309

Degrees Offered: Master of Engineering in Aerospace Engineering; Master of Engineering in Mechanical Engineering; Master of Civil Engineering; Master of Engineering in Engineering Management; Master of Engineering in Telecommunication; Master of Engineering in Computer Science; Master of Engineering in Electrical/Computer Engineering; Master of Engineering in Software Engineering.

Program Mission Statement/Description: The Center for Advanced Training in Engineering and Computer Science (CATECS) provides quality graduate education in engineering, computer science and selected areas of business and administration to working professionals via distance learning modalities.

Accreditation: North Central Association of Colleges and Schools; Accreditation Board for Engineering and Technology.

Admission Requirements: Recommendations; Undergraduate Degree. Admission requirements vary with individual degree programs.

Credit Awards for Prior Learning: Transfer Credit.

Limits to Credit Awards for Prior Learning: Varies per department. In general, transfer credits are limited up to 9 (12 upon petition).

Credit Awards for Examinations: None.

Estimated Average Completion Time: 3.5 years (part-time).

Caveats Regarding Time Estimates: Based upon completion of one graduate course per semester (including summer).

Credit Hour Requirements: Total Hours: 30 credits hours.

Distance Learning Options: A/V Cassettes; Independent Study; Television Courses.

Student Support Services Available: Academic Advising.

Informational Materials Available: Institutional Catalog; Program Brochure.

Program Age, Enrollment, and Degrees Conferred: Information not available.

Percentage of Bachelor's Degree Holders Admitted to Graduate School: Information not available.

Geographic Admission Restrictions: None.

Tuition and Fees: In-State Tuition $283-$332.00 per credit; Out-of-State Tuition $283-$332.00 per credit.

Other Pertinent Information: CATES students may take courses by (1) Live TV with 2-way interactive audio or (2) Videotape cassettes.

Connecticut

22. Albertus Magnus College

Accelerated Degree Program
700 Prospect St.
New Haven, CT 06511

Degrees Offered: Associate of Arts Degree in Liberal Studies; Bachelor of Arts; Bachelor of Fine Arts.

Program Mission Statement/Description: Within the college's primary mission of educating men and women for leadership, the Continuing Education program has the special responsibility of providing educational programs to the adult population of the local community. The chief vehicle for meeting this responsibility is the Accelerated Degree Program (ADP) which is designed and scheduled to allow the nontraditional learner to complete his or her education in the most efficient and economical manner. The curriculum of the ADP, though grounded in the liberal arts, recognizes that most students enrolled in the program are already engaged in careers and have specific life goals in mind. In addition to the ADP, Continuing Education has the flexibility to provide other educational experiences designed to respond quickly to the needs of the community.

Accreditation: New England Association of Schools and Colleges, Inc.

Admission Requirements:

Undergraduate	Graduate
HS/GED Diploma	Undergraduate Degree
Interview	Interview
Recommendations	Essay/Written Work
	Recommendations

Credit Awards for Prior Learning: Portfolio Assessment; Transfer Credit.

Other Options: The State of Connecticut allows colleges to grant credit for noncollegiate courses after the state has given approval to each school's policy for granting credit. Albertus Magnus currently grants credit for 7 American Institute of Banking credits.

Limits to Credit Awards for Prior Learning: A limit of 21 credits.

Credit Awards for Examinations: ACT Proficiency Exams; CLEP General Exams; CLEP Subject Exams; College Board AP Exams.

Estimated Average Completion Time: Associates' Degrees: 4 years (part-time), 2 years (full-time); Bachelors' Degrees: 8 years (part-time), 4 years (full-time); Graduate Degrees: certificates 2 years (part-time), 1 year (full-time).

Credit Hour Requirements:

Degree	Total Hours	Academic Residency*
Associate's	60	21
Bachelor's	120	30

*Hours that must be earned at the institution exclusive of credit-by-exam, portfolio assessment, etc.

Distance Learning Options: Cooperative Education; Independent Study; Supervised Fieldwork.

Student Support Services Available: Academic Advising; Career Counseling; Counseling/Testing; Financial Aid; Job Placement Assistance; Orientation; Tutoring.

Informational Materials Available: Institutional Catalog; Program Brochure.

Program Age, Enrollment, and Degrees Conferred:

Degree	Year Est.	Current Enrollment	Degrees Conferred
AA	1977	150	100
BA	1975	200	100
BFA	1989	10	6

Percentage of Bachelor's Degree Holders Admitted to Graduate School: 40-50 percent (includes law schools).

Geographic Admission Restrictions: None.

Tuition and Fees: In-State Tuition $585.00 per credit; Out-of-State Tuition $585.00 per credit; Graduation Fee $70.00; Registration fee 5 times per year, $10 each time; Matriculation Fee $25.00.

23. Bridgeport Engineering Institute

785 Unquowa Rd.
Fairfield, CT 06430

Degrees Offered: Bachelor of Science in Electrical Engineering; Bachelor of Science in Mechanical Engineering; Bachelor of Science in Information Systems Engineering; Bachelor of Science in Manufacturing Engineering; Associate in Engineering.

Program Mission Statement/Description: The Bridgeport Engineering Institute is an independent, nonprofit, evening college of engineering offering the residents of Southwest Connecticut and nearby New York a quality education at the associate and baccalaureate level in engineering and related fields attainable through part-time evening study. In support of this mission and to meet the needs of its students, their employers, and the community at large, the College is committed to providing student support services needed by fully employed individuals; providing special courses in engineering and related fields, particularly in

emerging technologies to graduate engineers, managers, and others who wish to advance their professional development; maintaining a close working relationship with industry to better understand their needs and identify new opportunities to serve them.

Accreditation: New England Association of Schools and Colleges, Inc.

Admission Requirements: HS/GED Diploma; Interview.

Credit Awards for Prior Learning: Portfolio Assessment; Transfer Credit.

Credit Awards for Examinations: CLEP General Exams; CLEP Subject Exams; College Board AP Exams; Departmental Exams.

Estimated Average Completion Time: Associates' Degrees: 4 years (part-time); Bachelors' Degrees: 6 years (part-time).

Caveats Regarding Time Estimates: It is difficult and unusual for a student to carry 12 credits (4 courses) in an evening college. The above estimates assume no previous college work, and the student follows recommended program of 24 credits/year average.

Credit Hour Requirements:

Degree	Total Hours	Academic Residency*
Associate's	70	24
Bachelor's	139	36

*Hours that must be earned at the institution exclusive of credit-by-exam, portfolio asessment, etc.

Distance Learning Options: None.

Student Support Services Available: Academic Advising; Career Counseling; Financial Aid; Orientation; Tutoring.

Informational Materials Available: Institutional Catalog; Program Brochure.

Program Age, Enrollment, and Degrees Conferred:

Degree	Year Est.	Current Enrollment	Degrees Conferred
BS	1963	462	1000
AS	1958	22	150

Percentage of Bachelor's Degree Holders Admitted to Graduate School: 19 percent.

Geographic Admission Restrictions: None.

Tuition and Fees: In-State Tuition $210.00 per credit; Out-of-State Tuition $210.00 per credit; Application Fee $50.00; Graduation Fee $50.00; Credit-by-Exam Fee $40.00.

24. Fairfield University

General Studies Bachelor's Degree Program
Fairfield, CT 06430

Degrees Offered: Bachelor of Arts; Bachelor of Science.

Program Mission Statement/Description: The General Studies curriculum leading to a Bachelor of Arts or Bachelor of Science degree is intended for mature students with considerable life-work experience and with personal and career goals which cannot be fulfilled by traditional majors. The General Studies Bachelor's Degree Program recognizes the maturity and high level of motivation of these students, as well as the time pressures under which they work.

Accreditation: New England Association of Schools and Colleges, Inc.

Admission Requirements: HS/GED Diploma; Interview; open to person 25 years of age or older with 3 years interruption in formal education.

Credit Awards for Prior Learning: ACE Military Recommendations; ACE/PONSI Recommendations; Portfolio Assessment; Transfer Credit.

Limits to Credit Awards for Prior Learning: A maximum of 75 total credits may be earned for prior non-collegiate sponsored or unsponsored learning.

Credit Awards for Examinations: ACT Proficiency Exams; CLEP General Exams; CLEP Subject Exams; College Board AP Exams; DANTES Subject Tests; Departmental Exams.

Estimated Average Completion Time: The timing is dependent on number of transfer and prior learning credits and student's time availability. A full-time student could complete in 2 years (or less) if he or she had the maximum in advanced standing.

Credit Hour Requirements: 120 hours total; 60 hours academic residency (hours that must be earned at the institution exclusive of credit-by-exam, portfolio assessment, etc.).

Distance Learning Options: A/V Cassettes; Independent Study; Television Courses.

Student Support Services Available: Academic Advising; Career Counseling; Counseling/Testing; Financial Aid; Orientation; Tutoring.

Informational Materials Available: Institutional Catalog; Program Brochure.

Program Age, Enrollment, and Degrees Conferred:

Degree	Year Est.	Current Enrollment	Degrees Conferred
Bachelor's	1982	9	12

Percentage of Bachelor's Degree Holders Admitted to Graduate School: Information not available.

Geographic Admission Restrictions: None.

Tuition and Fees: In-State Tuition $200.00 per credit; Out-of-State Tuition $200.00 per credit; Application Fee $35.00; Graduation Fee $60.00; Credit-by-Exam Fee $38.00 (CLEP); Portfolio Analysis Fee $150.00.

25. Saint Joseph College

Weekend College
1678 Asylum Ave.
West Hartford, CT 06117

Degrees Offered: Bachelor of Arts in American Studies; Bachelor of Science in Business Administration; Bachelor of Science in Nursing; Bachelor of Science in Social Work.

Program Mission Statement/Description: Weekend College is geared to mature, self-motivated individual whose education has largely taken place outside of the classroom. Applicants to the Weekend College are generally adults (23 years or older) who work full-time while studying part-time. The weekend format offers an opportunity to earn a degree by enrolling in specially designed classes that meet on the weekends. The design offers many students an alternative means of completing their education. Students who do not plan to work toward a degree are also welcome to enroll in weekend credit courses.

Accreditation: New England Association of Schools and Colleges, Inc.; Council on Social Work Education; American Dietetic Association; National League for Nursing.

Admission Requirements: HS/GED Diploma; Interview.

Credit Awards for Prior Learning: ACE Military Recommendations; ACE/PONSI Recommendations; Portfolio Assessment; Transfer Credit.

Credit Awards for Examinations: CLEP General Exams; CLEP Subject Exams; College Board AP Exams; Departmental Exams.

Estimated Average Completion Time: 6-8 years (part-time), 4 years (full-time).

Caveats Regarding Time Estimates: Weekend College schedules and format make full-time enrollment (12 credits/semester) difficult.

Credit Hour Requirements: 120 hours total; 60 hours

academic residency (hours that must be earned at the institution exclusive of credit-by-exam, portfolio assessment, etc.).

Distance Learning Options: Independent Study.

Student Support Services Available: Academic Advising; Career Counseling; Counseling/Testing; Financial Aid; Job Placement Assistance; Orientation; Tutoring.

Informational Materials Available: Institutional Catalog; Program Brochure.

Program Age, Enrollment, and Degrees Conferred:

Degree	Year Est.	Current Enrollment	Degrees Conferred
Weekend College Degree Programs	1985	450	32

Percentage of Bachelor's Degree Holders Admitted to Graduate School: Information not available.

Geographic Admission Restrictions: None.

Tuition and Fees: In-State Tuition $225.00 per credit; Application Fee $25.00; Graduation Fee $50.00; Credit-by-Exam Fee one-third of per-credit-hour tuition; Portfolio development per credit fee $65.00 (undergraduate). Registration fee $25.00.

26. University of Hartford

Office of University College
200 Bloomfield Ave.
West Hartford, CT 06117

Degrees Offered: All of the undergraduate and most of the graduate programs at the university are open to part-time study. Sixteen of the undergraduate and many of the graduate degrees may be obtained by enrolling in evening courses only. The nontraditional programs at the university apply to undergraduate study only and may not be used to earn graduate credit.

Program Mission Statement/Description: The primary purpose of the nontraditional programs at the university is to supplement the traditional undergraduate degree programs. They offer qualified students alternative methods to earn college credits that may be applied toward a traditional degree. All undergraduate degree recipients must earn at least 30 credits at the university.

Accreditation: New England Association of Schools and Colleges, Inc.; National Accrediting Agency for Clinical Laboratory Sciences, Committee on Allied Health Education and Accreditation of the American Medical Association; National League for Nursing; National Council for Accreditation of Teacher Education; National Association of Schools of Art and Design; National Association of Schools of Music; Engineering Accreditation Board for Engineering and Technology, Inc.

Admission Requirements:

Undergraduate	Graduate
HS/GED Diploma	Undergraduate Degree
Recommendations	Essay/Written Work
	Recommendations
	GRE, GMAT, MAT

Other Admission Requirements: Auditions are required in the Music School and portfolios are required in the Art School.

Credit Awards for Prior Learning: ACE Military Recommendations; Portfolio Assessment; Transfer Credit.

Credit Awards for Examinations: ACT Proficiency Exams; CLEP General Exams; CLEP Subject Exams; College Board AP Exams; DANTES Subject Tests; Departmental Exams.

Estimated Average Completion Time: Associates' Degrees: 4 years (part-time); Bachelors' Degrees: 9 years (part-time).

Credit Hour Requirements:

Degree	Total Hours	Academic Residency*
Associate's	60	30
Bachelor's	120	30
Graduate	Varies by program	

*Hours that must be earned at the institution exclusive of credit-by-exam, portfolio assessment, etc.

Distance Learning Options: Cooperative Education; Supervised Fieldwork.

Student Support Services Available: Academic Advising; Career Counseling; Counseling/Testing; Financial Aid; Job Placement Assistance; Orientation; Tutoring.

Informational Materials Available: Institutional Catalog; Prior Learning Guides; Program Brochure.

Program Age, Enrollment, and Degrees Conferred: Information not available.

Percentage of Bachelor's Degree Holders Admitted to Graduate School: Information not available.

Geographic Admission Restrictions: Residency requirements tend to limit students to commuter distance.

Tuition and Fees: In-State Tuition $210.00 per credit; Application Fee $35.00; Graduation Fee $65.00; Credit-by-Exam Fee $30.00; Portfolio Analysis Fee $100.00 + $40.00 per credit.

District of Columbia

27. The American University

Bachelor of Arts in Liberal Studies Degree Program
4400 Massachussets Ave., NW
Washington, DC 20016

Degrees Offered: Bachelor of Liberal Studies.

Program Mission Statement/Description: The Bachelor of Arts in Liberal Studies degree program features a multidisciplinary major that permits adults to choose courses that relate directly to personal and professional goals. Adult students will find this degree program to have considerable value as they look to link their career goals to academic objectives that are not bounded by a single discipline. This linkage will occur as students develop their major by studying broadly in the humanities, the social sciences, or the natural sciences and then completing an 18-24 credit specialization.

Accreditation: Middle States Association of Colleges and Schools.

Admission Requirements: HS/GED Diploma; Prior Credits.

Other Admission Requirements: Students who do not wish to have their high school records considered for admission must show completion of 15 semester hours from American University, or any accredited college, with a 3.0 average. They may then transfer into the program.

Credit Awards for Prior Learning: ACE Military Recommendations; ACE/PONSI Recommendations; Portfolio Assessment; Transfer Credit.

Other Options: Military credit is awarded on a case-by-case basis. Credit is awarded in those areas judged academically appropriate by the admissions office.

Limits to Credit Awards for Prior Learning: A total of 75 credits may be transferred from 4-year institutions; 30 credits may be transferred from 2-year institutions. A maximum of 30 credits from portfolio assessment may be applied to a student's program. Such credit is used for elective credit only.

Credit Awards for Examinations: CLEP Subject Exams; College Board AP Exams.

Estimated Average Completion Time: 2-6 years (part-time), 2-4 years (full-time).

Credit Hour Requirements:

Degree	Total Hours	Academic Residency*
Bachelor's	120	45

*Hours that must be earned at the institution exclusive of credit-by-exam, portfolio assessment, etc.

Distance Learning Options: Cooperative Education.

Student Support Services Available: Academic Advising; Career Counseling; Counseling/Testing; Financial Aid; Job Placement Assistance; Orientation; Tutoring.

Informational Materials Available: Institutional Catalog; Prior Learning Guides (Portfolio Assessment only); Program Brochure.

Program Age, Enrollment, and Degrees Conferred: BA in Liberal Studies. Other information not available.

Percentage of Bachelor's Degree Holders Admitted to Graduate School: Information not available.

Geographic Admission Restrictions: None.

Tuition and Fees: In-State Tuition $1353.00/3 credits; Portfolio Assessment Fee $250.00; Application for Portfolio Program $25.00.

28. Mount Vernon College

Evening and Weekend College
Office of Continuing Education
2100 Foxhall Rd., NW
Washington, DC 20007

Degrees Offered: Bachelor of Arts; Associate in Arts.

Program Mission Statement/Description: The Evening and Weekend College is a degree program developed to meet the needs of adults in the Washington area. All courses necessary for a degree will be offered during weekend and evening hours, making it possible to pursue an education while actively engaged in family and career. The flexible class scheduling which characterizes this program will require that students be energetic and self-directed. Students are expected to attend all scheduled classes and to work independently to achieve course goals.

Accreditation: Middle States Association of Colleges and Schools; Foundation for Interior Design Education Research.

Admission Requirements: HS/GED Diploma; Interview.

Credit Awards for Prior Learning: Portfolio Assessment; Transfer Credit.

Limits to Credit Awards for Prior Learning: 90 transfer credits. 12 portfolio type assessment credits. Students must complete at least 30 of the last 36 credit hours toward the BA or AA degrees at Mount Vernon College.

Credit Awards for Examinations: CLEP Subject Exams; College Board AP Exams.

Estimated Average Completion Time: Associates' Degrees: 3-4 years (part-time), 2 years (full-time); Bachelors' Degrees: 5-6 years (part-time), 4 years (full-time).

Credit Hour Requirements:

Degree	Total Hours	Academic Residency*
Associate's	60	30
Bachelor's	120	30

*Hours that must be earned at the institution exclusive of credit-by-exam, portfolio asessment, etc.

Distance Learning Options: Independent Study; Supervised Fieldwork.

Student Support Services Available: Academic Advising; Career Counseling; Financial Aid Counseling/Testing; Job Placement Assistance; Orientation; Tutoring.

Informational Materials Available: Institutional Catalog; Program Brochure.

Program Age, Enrollment, and Degrees Conferred: Information not available.

Percentage of Bachelor's Degree Holders Admitted to Graduate School: 15 percent.

Geographic Admission Restrictions: None.

Tuition and Fees: In-State Tuition $294.00 per credit; Application Fee $20.00; Matriculation Fee $100.00; Work/Life Experience Fee $225.00.

---

29. Trinity College

Weekend College
125 Michigan Ave., NE
Washington, DC 20017

Degrees Offered: Bachelor of Arts in Business Administration; Bachelor of Arts in Communications; Bachelor of Arts in Economics; Bachelor of Arts in Education; Bachelor of Arts in Human Relations; Bachelor of Arts in International Studies; Bachelor of Arts in Public Affairs; Bachelor of Arts in Sociology.

Program Mission Statement/Description: Trinity's Weekend College offers women the opportunity to earn an undergraduate degree by attending classes entirely on weekends. Classes are scheduled on Friday night, Saturday morning, and Saturday afternoon for women of all ages who are seeking a quality education but are unable to attend classes during the week.

Accreditation: Middle States Association of Colleges and Schools.

Admission Requirements: Essay/Written Work; HS/GED Diploma; Interview; Recommendations.

Credit Awards for Prior Learning: Portfolio Assessment; Transfer Credit.

Limits to Credit Awards for Prior Learning: No more than 96 credits transferred in apply to degree. No more than 64 credits will apply from a 2-year college. Portfolio assessment: maximum 30 credits.

Credit Awards for Examinations: CLEP Subject Exams; DANTES Subject Tests.

Estimated Average Completion Time: 5-6 years (part-time).

Caveats Regarding Time Estimates: All weekend students are part-time.

Credit Hour Requirements: 128 hours total; 32 hours academic residency (hours that must be earned at the institution exclusive of credit-by-exam, portfolio assessment, etc.).

Distance Learning Options: None.

Student Support Services Available: Academic Advising; Career Counseling; Financial Aid; Job Placement Assistance; Orientation; Tutoring.

Informational Materials Available: Institutional Catalog; Program Brochure.

Program Age, Enrollment, and Degrees Conferred:

Degree	Year Est.	Current Enrollment	Degrees Conferred
BA	1984	500	85

Percentage of Bachelor's Degree Holders Admitted to Graduate School: Information not available.

Geographic Admission Restrictions: None.

Tuition and Fees: In-State Tuition $226.00 per credit; Application Fee $30.00; Graduation Fee $100.00; Credit-by-Exam Fee $40.00.

Florida

30. Barry University

Frank J. Rooney School
of Adult and Continuing Education
11300 NE 2nd Ave.
Miami Shores, FL 33161

Degrees Offered: Bachelor of Professional Studies; Bachelor of Liberal Studies; Bachelor of Science in Technology; Bachelor of Science in Accounting; Bachelor of Science in Management; Bachelor of Science in Management Information Systems.

University Mission Statement/Description: The purpose of the Frank J. Rooney School of Adult and Continuing Education is to provide adult students with undergraduate credit and noncredit programs which recognize educational needs of the adult learner and promote lifelong learning. These degree and certificate programs are designed for adult men and women who, because of family and work responsibilities, are unable to attend class in a traditional manner or at traditional times.

Accreditation: Southern Association of Colleges and Schools.

Admission Requirements: Employment/Experience; HS/GED Diploma; Interview; Application and two official transcripts of credits taken at all colleges attended and, if applicable, CLEP, DANTES transcripts, or, if no college credit or fewer than 12 credits have been earned, two official transcripts indicating graduation from high school or GED.

Credit Awards for Prior Learning: ACE/PONSI Recommendations; Portfolio Assessment; Transfer Credit.

Limits to Credit Awards for Prior Learning: Portfolio limit: 45 credits. Transfer limit: 64 credits from community/junior college, 90 credits maximum.

Credit Awards for Examinations: CLEP General Exams; CLEP Subject Exams; DANTES Subject Tests.

Limits to Credit Awards for Examinations: CLEP—30 credits.

Estimated Average Completion Time: For students with an associate's degree: 2 years (part-time); for students with no college credit: 4 years (part-time).

Credit Hour Requirements: 120 hours total (minimum); 30 hours academic residency (hours that must be earned at the institution exclusive of credit-by-exam, portfolio assessment, etc.).

Distance Learning Options: None.

Student Support Services Available: Academic Advising; Career Counseling; Counseling/Testing; Financial Aid; Job Placement Assistance; Orientation; Personal Counseling; English and Mathematics Skills Clinics.

Informational Materials Available: Institutional Catalog; Prior Learning Guides; Program Brochure; Student Bulletin.

Program Age, Enrollment, and Degrees Conferred: Information not available.

Percentage of Bachelor's Degree Holders Admitted to Graduate School: 15 percent.

Geographic Admission Restrictions: None.

Tuition and Fees: In-State Tuition $145.00 per credit; Application Fee $25.00; Graduation Fee $40.00; Credit-by-Exam Fee $20.00 per credit; Portfolio Administrative Fee $400.00.

31. Bethune-Cookman College

Continuing Education Program
640 2nd Ave.
Daytona Beach, FL 32114

Degrees Offered: Bachelor of Arts; Bachelor of Sciences.

Program Mission Statement/Description: The Continuing Education Program at Bethune-Cookman College seeks to serve the total college by providing educational services to the nontraditional matriculating student. The program provides the means by which the college enriches, expands, and extends its primary mission of teaching, research, and community service. The purpose of the program is to extend the resources of the college to a wide range of individuals, special interest groups, and targeted audiences not otherwise served by on-going programs. It is designed to satisfy the noncredit, credit, and degree needs of individuals through its offerings of undergraduate courses and programs. These programs are directed specifically toward those individuals whose interests are in occupational and professional development, personal enrichment, community problems, and critical issues.

Accreditation: Southern Association of Colleges and Schools.

Admission Requirements: HS/GED Diploma; Recommendations; Admissions application and physical.

Credit Awards for Prior Learning: Transfer Credit.

Credit Awards for Examinations: ACT Proficiency Exams; CLEP General Exams; CLEP Subject Exams; College Board AP Exams.

Estimated Average Completion Time: Bachelors' Degrees: 7 years (part-time), 5 years (full-time).

Credit Hour Requirements:

	Total Hours	Academic Residency*
Bachelors' Degrees	124	30

*Hours that must be earned at the institution exclusive of credit-by-exam, portfolio assessment, etc.

Distance Learning Options: Supervised Fieldwork.

Student Support Services Available: Academic Advising; Career Counseling; Counseling/Testing; Financial Aid; Job Placement Assistance; Orientation; Tutoring.

Informational Materials Available: Institutional Catalog; Program Brochure; Continuing Education Brochure.

Program Age, Enrollment, and Degrees Conferred:

Degree	Year Est.	Current Enrollment	Degrees Conferred
BA and BS	1979	211	67

Percentage of Bachelor's Degree Holders Admitted to Graduate School: 22 percent.

Geographic Admission Restrictions: None.

Tuition and Fees: In-State Tuition $167.00 per credit; Out-of-State Tuition $167.00 per credit; Application Fee: $25.00; Graduation Fee: $65.00.

32. Jacksonville University

College of Weekend Studies
2800 University Blvd., N.
Jacksonville, FL 32211

Degrees Offered: Bachelor of General Studies; Bachelor of Science; Executive Master of Business Administration; Master of Arts in Teaching; and Bachelor of Science in Nursing.

Program Mission Statement/Description: The College of Weekend Studies is designed to provide opportunities in higher education to adult students who have job or family responsibilities during the week. The college offers a complete undergraduate program in 6 different academic areas and is committed to (1) making private higher education available at a reduced cost to adult students, whose financial obligations might otherwise limit their academic choices only to institutions in the public sector; (2) developing a learning philosophy and environment congenial to the strengths of the adult learner; (3) scheduling classes in a time frame which allows room for the nontraditional student's work and family responsibilities; (4) developing mechanisms to recognize and evaluate college-level learning which adult students may have acquired outside the traditional classroom; (5) building an academic advising system which responds to the needs of the adult learner; and (6) encouraging the university to provide support services in an appropriate time frame for the nontraditional student.

Accreditation: Southern Association of Colleges and Schools; National League for Nursing.

Admission Requirements:

Undergraduate	Graduate
HS/GED Diploma	Undergraduate Degree
Interview	Interview
Employment/Experience:	Recommendations
5 years	Employment/Experience:
Essay/Written Work	5 years
Prior Credits: 30	
Executive MBA	

Credit Awards for Prior Learning: ACE Military Recommendations; ACE/PONSI Recommendations; Portfolio Assessment; Transfer Credit.

Limits to Credit Awards for Prior Learning: Transfer—64 credit limit from lower division institution; a Portfolio—30 credit limit; CLEP—30 credit limit.

Credit Awards for Examinations: CLEP General Exams; CLEP Subject Exams; DANTES Subject Tests; Departmental Exams.

Estimated Average Completion Time: Bachelors' Degrees: 5 years (part-time), 2 years (full-time); Graduate Degrees: EMBA 16 months, MAT 18 months, both (part-time).

Caveats Regarding Time Estimates: Less than 10 percent of students in nontraditional programs are full-time.

Credit Hour Requirements:

Degree	Total Hours	Academic Residency*
Bachelor's	128	32
Exec MBA	43	43
MAT Ed Leadership	36	43

*Hours that must be earned at the institution exclusive of credit-by-exam, portfolio assessment, etc.

Distance Learning Options: Independent Study.

Student Support Services Available: Academic Advising; Career Counseling; Counseling/Testing; Financial Aid; Job Placement Assistance; Orientation; Tutoring.

Informational Materials Available: Exam Preparation Guides; Institutional Catalog; Prior Learning Guides; Program Brochure; Audio Informational Tape.

Program Age, Enrollment, and Degrees Conferred:

Degree	Year Est.	Current Enrollment	Degrees Conferred
BS/BGS	1986	193	52
EMBA	1984	43	175
MAT Ed Leadership	1989	32	0
BSN	1991	0	0

Percentage of Bachelor's Degree Holders Admitted to Graduate School: 25 percent.

Geographic Admission Restrictions: None.

Tuition and Fees: In-State Tuition $126.00 per credit; Out-of-State Tuition $126.00 per credit; Application Fee $25.00; Credit-by-Exam Fee $12.00 per credit; $25.00 registration.

33. Nova University

3301 College Ave.
Fort Lauderdale, FL 33314

Degrees Offered: Bachelor of Science; Bachelor of Arts; Master of Science; Master of Arts; Doctor of Education; Doctor of Computer Science; Doctor of Business; Doctor of Philosophy; Juris Doctor.

Program Mission Statement/Description: Nova University is committed to the idea that education should not be time bound or place bound and uses a variety of educational technologies. Through its educational offerings, research projects, and programs of public service, the university encourages the free exchange of ideas and the search for knowledge that is the cornerstone of the academic tradition.

Accreditation: Southern Association of Colleges and Schools; American Bar Association/Association of American Law Schools; American Psychological Association; American Speech-Language-Hearing Association.

Admission Requirements:

Undergraduate	Graduate
HS/GED Diploma	Undergraduate Degree
Interview	Interview
Recommendations	Essay/Written Work
Employment/Experience	Recommendations
	Employment/Experience
	GRE, LSAT

Other Admission Requirements: SAT/ACT Test. Test required in Hospitality Education. TOEFL exam required for all international students.

Credit Awards for Prior Learning: ACE Military Recommendations; ACE/PONSI Recommendations; Portfolio Assessment; Transfer Credit.

Other Options: Standard grants for previously evaluated experiences, training, and licenses are used by James Farquhar Center; life experience is used against specific course requirements by Hospitality Education.

Limits to Credit Awards for Prior Learning: There is a limit of 90 credits that can be awarded for the above options. In the Shepard Broad Law Center, 1.5 years (i.e., 3 semesters), generally no more than one year of transfer credit (i.e., 2 semesters), is accepted. Transfer credit must come from another law school accredited by the American Bar Association (or foreign law school for a foreign attorney). In the School of Psychology and the School of Business and Entrepreneurship, a maximum of 6 graduate-level semester hours can be awarded.

Credit Awards for Examinations: ACT Proficiency Exams; CLEP General Exams; CLEP Subject Exams; College Board AP Exams; DANTES Subject Tests; Departmental Exams.

Limits to Credit Awards for Examinations: There is a 90-credit limit on credit that can be awarded for the above examinations through the James Farquhar Center.

Estimated Average Completion Time: Bachelors' Degrees: 6 years (part-time), 4 years (full-time) in James Farquhar Center, Hospitality Education, Computer and Information Sciences; Graduate Degrees: Oceanographic Center 2-4 years (part-time), 1.75 years (full-time); JD (Shepard Broad Law Center) 4 years part-time, 3 years full-time; School of Psychology MS 4 years part-time, 2.50 years full-time; Computer and Information Sciences 3 years part-time, 1.5 years MS, and 4 years EdD and DSc full-time; School of Business and Entrepreneurship 2 years part-time.

Credit Hour Requirements:

Degree	Total Hours	Academic Residency*
Bachelor's	120-136	30

*Hours that must be earned at the institution exclusive of credit-by-exam, portfolio assessment, etc.

Distance Learning Options: Cooperative Education (bachelor's only); Electronic Mail; Independent Study; Supervised Fieldwork; Weekend Courses (School of Psychology).

Student Support Services Available: Academic Advising; Career Counseling; Counseling/Testing; Financial Aid; Job Placement Assistance; Orientation; Tutoring.

Informational Materials Available: Exam Preparation Guides; Institutional Catalog; Prior Learning Guides; Program Brochure.

Program Age, Enrollment, and Degrees Conferred:

Degree	Year Est.	Current Enrollment	Degrees Conferred
James Farquhar Center			
Education	1976	500	742
Psychology	1976		
Bus. Admin.	1976	350	723
Studies, Prof. Mgmt. Admin.	1981	1000	583
Master Bus. Admin.	1973	320	2155
General Studies	1989	20	
Applied Prof. Studies	1990		
Hospitality Education			
Hospitality Management	1988	200	3
Oceanographic Center			
MS	1981	40	20
Shepard Broad Law Center			
JD	1974	739	2635
School of Psychology			
MS Mental Health Counseling	1989	300	
MS School Guidance and Counseling	1991		
The School of Business and Entrepreneurship			
MBA	1973	320	2155
Ex MBA-Banking	1985	20	28
MPA	1982	20	59
Ex MBA-Real Estate	1989	50	0
MIBA	1985	20	33
MS/Gerontology	1988	15	3
MS/HSA	1986	30	56
MS/HRM	1980	12	164
MS/HS	1980	12	144
MAC	1983	100	59
ScD	1986	22	1
MS	1974	65	256
BS	1975	120	600

Percentage of Bachelor's Degree Holders Admitted to Graduate School: 33 percent Hospitality Education; 40 percent Computer and Information Science.

Geographic Admission Restrictions: None.

Tuition and Fees:

	Undergraduate	Graduate
In-State Tuition	$115-210.00/credit	$225.00/credit
Out-of-State Tuition	$210-345.00/credit	$225-250.00/credit
Application Fee	$30.00	$25-30.00
Graduation Fee	$30.00	$30.00
Credit-by-Exam Fee	$40.00	
James Farquhar Center	$125.00	

Computer and Information Sciences (Undergraduate and Graduate).

Other Pertinent Information: Hospitality Education—All students are industry professionals; average age of students is 35; courses are held in local hotels. Oceanographic Center—Courses are offered in the evenings; sessions are 3 hours long, one night per week, over a 12-week term; each specialty typically has 2 courses offered per term.

34. Palm Beach Atlantic College

Bachelor's Degree in Human Resource Management Program
901 S. Flager
West Palm Beach, FL 33401

Degrees Offered: Bachelor of Human Resource Management.

Program Mission Statement/Description: Traditionally, college education has been available only to those with time and money to spend several years away from work and usually away from home. People who either choose or need to work find few practical ways of continuing their education. To meet the needs of the working adult, Palm Beach Atlantic College offers the Bachelor's Degree in Human Resource Management, (HRM) with features for adults with other responsibilities. HRM Classroom Course—30 credits. Portfolio—up to 30 credits (includes career credentials and training, life learning papers). Thesis Project—6 credits (an applied research project based on a complete literature search project focuses on a problem related to student's community or employment).

Accreditation: Southern Association of Colleges and Schools.

Admission Requirements: Essay/Written Work; HS/GED Diploma; Interview; Prior Credits: minimum 40; English Composition I and II.

Credit Awards for Prior Learning: ACE Military Recommendations; ACE/PONSI Recommendations; Portfolio Assessment; Transfer Credit.

Other Options: Life learning papers—paper written in a particular discipline and graded by a professor in that discipline for one, 2, or 3 credits. Maximum of 30 credits total for any form of life learning credit.

Limits to Credit Awards for Prior Learning: Maximum of 30 credits.

Credit Awards for Examinations: None.

Estimated Average Completion Time: One year (if admitted with 60 credits).

Caveats Regarding Time Estimates: Program is designed to be full-time, one night each week, for 54 weeks.

Credit Hour Requirements: 128 credit hours.

Distance Learning Options: None.

Student Support Services Available: Academic Advising; Career Counseling; Counseling/Testing; Financial Aid; Job Placement Assistance; Orientation; Tutoring.

Informational Materials Available: Institutional Catalog; Program Brochure.

Program Age, Enrollment, and Degrees Conferred:

Degree	Year Est.	Current Enrollment	Degrees Conferred
Bachelor of HRM	1988	175	50

Percentage of Bachelor's Degree Holders Admitted to Graduate School: 5 percent.

Geographic Admission Restrictions: None.

Tuition and Fees: In-State Tuition $165.00 per credit; Out-of-State Tuition $165.00 per credit; Application Fee $25.00; Graduation Fee $55.00; Credit-by-Exam Fee $30.00.

35. Saint Leo College

Center for Continuing Education
Box 2248
St. Leo, FL 33574

Degrees Offered: Bachelor of Arts in Business Administration; Bachelor of Arts in Psychology; Bachelor of Arts in Criminology; Bachelor of Arts in Religious Studies; Bachelor of Arts in Elementary Education; Bachelor of Science in Health Care Administration; Associate of Arts in Liberal Arts.

Program Mission Statement/Description: The primary mission of the Center for Continuing Education is to make the academic programs of the college accessible to adult students and distant learners.

Accreditation: Southern Association of Colleges and Schools.

Admission Requirements: HS/GED Diploma.

Other Admission Requirements: Health Care Administration requires RN as prerequisite. Elementary Education requires ACT or SAT scores and Florida CLAST test. As entrance requirement, passing score varies by year completed.

Credit Awards for Prior Learning: ACE Military Recommendations; ACE/PONSI Recommendations; Transfer Credit; RN license with school diploma; Police Academy certificates.

Limits to Credit Awards for Prior Learning: All credit will transfer if "C" or better, but not all credit counts to reduce degree requirements. Each degree program has its own rules.

Credit Awards for Examinations: ACT Proficiency Exams; CLEP General Exams; CLEP Subject Exams; College Board AP Exams; DANTES Subject Tests; Departmental Exams.

Limits to Credit Awards for Examinations: Maximum CLEP credit 30.

Estimated Average Completion Time: Associates' Degrees: 3 years (part-time), 2 years (full-time).; Bachelors' Degrees: 4 years (part-time), 2 years (full-time).

Credit Hour Requirements:

Degree	Total Hours	Academic Residency*
Associate's	60	15
Bachelor's	120	30

*Hours that must be earned at the institution exclusive of credit-by-exam, portfolio assessment, etc.

Distance Learning Options: A/V Cassettes (Associate and Bachelor); Independent Study; Phone/Mail Instruction; Supervised Fieldwork.

Student Support Services Available: Academic Advising; Career Counseling; Counseling/Testing; Financial Aid; Orientation; Tutoring.

Informational Materials Available: Institutional Catalog; Program Brochure.

Program Age, Enrollment, and Degrees Conferred:

Degree	Year Est.	Current Enrollment	Degrees Conferred
Health Care Admin.	1989	700	500
Business Admin.	1989	300	800
Criminology	1989	200	1000
Psychology	1989	300	500
Religious Studies	1989	12	150
Elementary Ed.	1991	162	0

Percentage of Bachelor's Degree Holders Admitted to Graduate School: Of those who apply 80 percent are accepted into their first choice Graduate School.

Geographic Admission Restrictions: Since residence is required, student needs to be on campus for a 6-9 semester hours at some time in junior or senior year. 100 percent of students from Florida.

Tuition and Fees: In-State Tuition $84.00 per credit; Application Fee $25.00; Graduation Fee $70.00.

Other Fees: Directed Study Fee $84.00 per semester hour.

36. Southeastern University of the Health Science

College of Pharmacy
1750 NE 168th St.
North Miami Beach, FL 33162

Degrees Offered: Postbaccalaureate Pharmacy Doctorate.

Program Mission Statement/Description: The program is to help meet the needs of the BS and MS degree pharmacists aspiring to earn a PharmD Degree. Pharmacists are able to pursue their education on a part-time basis. It is a campus-based program. While the program is uncompromising in quality, it is highly flexible and geared to meeting the needs of the working pharmacist in south Florida. Courses are offered in the evenings, and students can vary their course load according to their work schedule.

Accreditation: The American Council on Pharmaceutical Education.

Admission Requirements: Recommendations; Undergraduate Degree; GPA 2.0 or above on a 4.0 scale and BS in Pharmacy from an ACPE accredited college of pharmacy.

Credit Awards for Prior Learning: Portfolio Assessment.

Limits to Credit Awards for Prior Learning: Some credit for prior learning is available for those who meet certain life experience and exam requirements. Write to the institution for a complete description of the requirements.

Credit Awards for Examinations: Departmental Exams.

Estimated Average Completion Time: 6 years (part-time).

Credit Hour Requirements: Graduate degrees (Total Hours) Postgraduate 52.

Distance Learning Options: Supervised Fieldwork.

Student Support Services Available: Academic Advising; Financial Aid.

Informational Materials Available: Institutional Catalog; Program Brochure.

Program Age, Enrollment, and Degrees Conferred:

Degree	Year Est.	Current Enrollment	Degrees Conferred
Postgrad. Pharmacy	1988	77	10

Geographic Admission Restrictions: None.

Tuition and Fees: Graduate In-State Tuition $224.00 per credit; Graduate Out-of-State Tuition $224.00 per credit;

Application Fee $100.00.

37. University of Miami

Bachelor of Continuing Studies Program
P.O. Box 248005
Coral Gables, FL 33124

Degrees Offered: Bachelor of Continuing Studies.

Program Mission Statement/Description: The Bachelor of Continuing Studies (BCS) Program was established to provide an opportunity for mature persons to receive a bachelor's degree through the University of Miami in a course of study designed to augment their present career or to prepare them for new employment opportunities. The far-reaching goal of the program is life enrichment through personal development and academic participation.

Accreditation: Southern Association of Colleges and Schools.

Admission Requirements: Essay/Written Work; HS/GED Diploma; Interview; Recommendations if student's previous GPA is below 2.00 and application must be sent to faculty review committee.

Credit Awards for Prior Learning: ACE Military Recommendations; Transfer Credit.

Limits to Credit Awards for Prior Learning: Transfer credits: junior/community college—within first 64 credits of college work; upper-division course requirements may not be satisfied with junior college/community college credits; university does not accept C- or below; credits not accepted from institutions not accredited by appropriate regional accrediting association; last 45 credits must be taken in residency. ACE Military recommendation: usually credit given in elective area; may not take place of subjects required for graduation.

Credit Awards for Examinations: ACT Proficiency Exams; CLEP General Exams; CLEP Subject Exams; College Board AP Exams.

Limits to Credit Awarded for Examination: 60 credits.

Estimated Average Completion Time: 5.5 years (part-time).

Caveats Regarding Time Estimates: True only for students starting with 0 credits; assumes student takes 6 credits fall/spring semester and 3 credits each summer session (2).

Credit Hour Requirements: 120 hours total; 45 hours academic residency (hours that must be earned at the institution exclusive of credit-by-exam, portfolio assessment, etc.).

Distance Learning Options: Supervised Fieldwork.

Student Support Services Available: Academic Advising; Career Counseling; Counseling/Testing; Financial Aid; Job Placement Assistance; Orientation; Tutoring.

Informational Materials Available: Exam Preparation Guides; Institutional Catalog; Program Brochure.

Program Age, Enrollment, and Degrees Conferred:

Degree	Year Est.	Current Enrollment	Degrees Conferred
Bachelor of Continuing Studies	1989	150	0

Percentage of Bachelor's Degree Holders Admitted to Graduate School: Information not available.

Geographic Admission Restrictions: None.

Tuition and Fees: In-State Tuition $200.00 per credit; Application Fee $35.00; Credit-by-Exam Fee $35.00.

38. The University of Tampa

School of Continuing Studies
401 W. Kennedy Blvd.
Tampa, FL 33606

Degrees Offered: Bachelor of Liberal Studies; Bachelor of Science in Computer Information Systems; Bachelor of Management and Marketing.

Program Mission Statement/Description: The primary mission of the School of Continuing Studies is to extend the instructional resources of the university to nontraditional learners through the following academic programs: Evening College, Summer Sessions, Training and Professional Development, International Education, and Community Services.

Accreditation: Southern Association of Colleges and Schools.

Admission Requirements: HS/GED Diploma; Students must demonstrate maturity and motivation, must submit transcripts of any previous college work and high school transcript or GED scores, if less than 24 hours of college credit have been earned.

Credit Awards for Prior Learning: ACE Military Recommendations; ACE/PONSI Recommendations; Portfolio Assessment; Transfer Credit.

Limits to Credit Awards for Prior Learning: Transfer credits: 93 hours total; maximum of 64 from community college. ACE/PONSI: 60 hours. ACE/Military: 30 hours. Portfolio Assessment: 10 hours.

Credit Awards for Examinations: ACT Proficiency Exams; CLEP General Exams; CLEP Subject Exams; College Board AP Exams; DANTES Subject Tests.

Estimated Average Completion Time: 3-6 years (part-time), 4 years (full-time).

Credit Hour Requirements: 124 hours total; 31 hours academic residency (hours that must be earned at the institution exclusive of credit-by-exam, portfolio assessment, etc.).

Distance Learning Options: Correspondence Courses; Independent Study; Supervised Fieldwork.

Student Support Services Available: Academic Advising; Career Counseling; Counseling/Testing; Financial Aid; Job Placement Assistance; Orientation; Tutoring; Preenrollment by mail.

Informational Materials Available: Exam Preparation Guides; Institutional Catalog; Prior Learning Guides; Program Brochure.

Program Age, Enrollment, and Degrees Conferred:

Degree	Year Est.	Current Enrollment	Degrees Conferred
Bachelor of Liberal Studies	1986	73	30

Percentage of Bachelor's Degree Holders Admitted to Graduate School: 20 percent.

Geographic Admission Restrictions: None.

Tuition and Fees: In-State Tuition $145.00 per credit; Out-of-State Tuition $205.00 per credit; Application Fee $25.00; Graduation Fee $35.00.

Other Fees: $125.00 for portfolio development advising; $50.00 per course for assessment fee.

39. University of West Florida

11000 University Pkwy.
Pensacola, FL 32514

Degrees Offered: Bachelor of Science in Business Administration; Master in Business Administration; Master of Arts; Master of Science; Master of Education.

Program Mission Statement/Description: The primary mission of the university is to educate men and women to think, communicate effectively, cultivate an appreciation for life, and act with reason and effectiveness. To achieve this mission, the university gives the highest priority to teaching and the active involvement of students in learning process. Further, the university believes that students should interact with faculty who possess intellectual vitality, who extend their knowledge through research and creative activities, and who enhance their understanding of contemporary society through service.

Accreditation: Southern Association of Colleges and Schools.

Admission Requirements: GRE; GMAT; Undergraduate Degree.

Credit Awards for Prior Learning: ACE Military Recommendations; ACE/PONSI Recommendations; Transfer Credit.

Limits to Credit Awards for Prior Learning: Transfer—60 semester hours from Community/Junior College; ACE—30 semester hours; Military—30 semester hours.

Credit Awards for Examinations: CLEP General Exams; CLEP Subject Exams; College Board AP Exams; DANTES Subject Tests; Departmental Exams.

Estimated Average Completion Time: Associates' Degrees: 2-3 years (part-time), 2 years (full-time); Bachelors' Degrees: 5-6 years (part-time), 4 years (full-time); Graduate Degrees: 1-1.5 years (part-time), 1.5-2 years (full-time).

Credit Hour Requirements:

Degree	Total Hours	Academic Residency*
Associate's	60	36
Bachelor's	120	30
Graduate	30-42	
		30

*Hours that must be earned at the institution exclusive of credit-by-exam, portfolio assessment, etc.

Distance Learning Options: Cooperative Education (Bachelor only); Independent Study; Supervised Fieldwork.

Student Support Services Available: Academic Advising; Career Counseling; Counseling/Testing; Financial Aid; Job Placement Assistance; Orientation; Tutoring.

Informational Materials Available: Institutional Catalog; Program Brochure.

Program Age, Enrollment, and Degrees Conferred: Information not available.

Percentage of Bachelor's Degree Holders Admitted to Graduate School: Information not available.

Geographic Admission Restrictions: None.

Tuition and Fees:

	Undergraduate	Graduate
In-State Tuition	$44.02/credit	$76.73/credit
Out-of-State Tuition	$154.39/credit	$238.66/credit
Application Fee	$15.00	$15.00

Georgia

40. Brenau College

Brenau Professional College
1 Centennial Circle
Gainesville, GA 30501

Degrees Offered: Bachelor of Arts and Bachelor of Science in Business Administration, Human Resource Management, Public Administration, Education in Middle Grades and Elementary; Bachelor of Science in Nursing; Bachelor of Fine Arts in Interior Design; Master of Business Administration; Master of Education in Middle Grades and Elementary.

Program Mission Statement/Description: The Professional College offers to both men and women baccalaureate programs, master's programs, and opportunities for non-credit professional development on the main campus and at off-campus locations. The baccalaureate programs provide foundations for individual and professional growth and competence. The master's programs encourage students to develop the proficiency and professionalism necessary to meet the challenges inherent in their fields of study.

Accreditation: Southern Association of Colleges and Schools.

Admission Requirements:

Undergraduate	Graduate
HS/GED Diploma	Undergraduate Degree
Prior Credits	Interview (education only)
	Recommendations
	GRE, GMAT, or MAT

Credit Awards for Prior Learning: ACE/PONSI Recommendations; ACE Military Recommendations; Portfolio Assessment; Transfer Credit.

Limits to Credit Awards for Prior Learning: In no case will lower-division transfer credit exceed 120 quarter hours. As a Servicemembers Opportunity College (SOC), Brenau College transfers all ACE-approved military credit.

Credit Awards for Examinations: ACT Proficiency Exams; CLEP General Exams; CLEP Subject Exams; College Board AP Exams; DANTES Subject Tests; Departmental Exams.

Limits to Credit Awards for Examinations: CLEP General maximum limit of 45 quarter hours; CLEP Subject maximum limit of 35 quarter hours.

Estimated Average Completion Time: Bachelors' Degrees: 3.5 years (part-time), 2.5 years (full-time); Graduate Degrees: 2.5 year (part-time), 1.5 year (full-time).

Caveats Regarding Time Estimates: Most students enter with transfer credit from other institutions. Graduation time is quite variable. Graduate students are limited to 10 hours of transfer credit.

Credit Hour Requirements:

Degree	Total Hours	Academic Residency*
Bachelor's	196	45
Graduate (MBA)	50	40
Graduate (MED)	55	45

*Hours that must be earned at the institution exclusive of credit-by-exam, portfolio assessment, etc.

Distance Learning Options: A/V Cassettes; Independent Study; Newspaper Courses; Supervised Fieldwork; Selected on-line computer classes are available via modem.

Student Support Services Available: Academic Advising; Career Counseling; Counseling/Testing; Financial Aid; Job Placement Assistance; Orientation.

Informational Materials Available: Institutional Catalog; Prior Learning Guides; Program Brochure.

Program Age, Enrollment, and Degrees Conferred:

Degree	Year Est.	Current Enrollment	Degrees Conferred
Business Admin.	1975	331	Unknown
Human Resource Mgmt.	1980	55	Unknown
Public Admin.	1978	121	Unknown
Interior Design	1986	43	Unknown
Education	1960	162	Unknown
Nursing	1986	100	Unknown
Master of Bus. Admin.	1983	253	Unknown
Master of Ed.	1974	126	Unknown

Percentage of Bachelor's Degree Holders Admitted to Graduate School: 20-30 percent.

Geographic Admission Restrictions: None.

Tuition and Fees:

	Undergraduate	Graduate
In-State Tuition	$95.00/credit	$77.00/credit
Application Fee	$30.00	$30.00
Graduation Fee	$75.00	$75.00
Credit-by-Exam Fee	$50.00	

41. Georgia Southern University

Landrum Box 8092
Statesboro, GA 30460

Degrees Offered: Bachelor of General Studies; Executive Master of Business Administration.

Program Mission Statement/Description: The Bachelor of General Studies program provides opportunities for nontraditional college students who are interested in combining a liberal arts background with some degree of specialization. It offers a solid core curriculum program along with the freedom to choose from a wide range of concentrations. Executive MBA—requirements in the Executive Master of Business Administration (MBA) include the satisfactory completion of the 21-month lockstep schedule of 75 quarter hours. This includes successful completion of the Independent Project (MBA 858).

Accreditation: Southern Association of Colleges and Schools; American Assembly of Collegiate Schools of Business.

Admission Requirements:

Undergraduate	Graduate
HS/GED Diploma	Undergraduate Degree
Recommendations	GMAT, SAT scores for
Employment/Experience:	first-year students; college
5 years	transcripts for transfers.

Credit Awards for Prior Learning: ACE Military Recommendations; Transfer Credit.

Limits to Credit Awards for Prior Learning: No graduate transfer credit — Executive MBA is a lockstep program.

Credit Awards for Examinations: CLEP Subject Exams; College Board AP Exams; DANTES Subject Tests; Departmental Exams.

Estimated Average Completion Time: Bachelors' Degrees: 4 years (full-time); Graduate Degrees: Executive MBA 21 months (full-time).

Credit Hour Requirements:

Degree	Total Hours	Academic Residency*
Bachelor's	190	45
Graduate	75	75

*Hours that must be earned at the institution exclusive of credit-by-exam, portfolio assessment, etc.

Distance Learning Options: None.

Student Support Services Available: Academic Advising; Career Counseling; Counseling/Testing; Financial Aid; Job Placement Assistance; Orientation; Tutoring.

Informational Materials Available: Exam Preparation Guides; Institutional Catalog; MBA Program Brochure.

Program Age, Enrollment, and Degrees Conferred:

Degree	Year Est.	Current Enrollment	Degrees Conferred
BGS	1986	5	0
Executive MBA	1986	13	27

Percentage of Bachelor's Degree Holders Admitted to Graduate School: Information not available.

Geographic Admission Restrictions: None.

Tuition and Fees: In-State Tuition $34.00 per credit; Out-of-State Tuition $102.00 per credit; Application Fee $10.00; Graduation Fee $16.00; Credit-by-Exam Fee: $15.00.

Other Fees: College fee (if enrolled in more than 5 quarter hours) $108.00. All fees, including books for Executive MBA $200.00 per quarter hour. Motor vehicle registration $10.00.

Other Pertinent Information: Although the general studies degree allows for study in several areas, it is organized to provide an academically sound program with carefully planned concentrations. The student who earns this degree will have achieved a broad education that meets high standards of learning.

42. Oglethorpe University

Evening-Weekend Program
4484 Peachtree Rd.
Atlanta, GA 30319

Degrees Offered: Bachelor of Arts; Bachelor of Business Administration.

Program Mission Statement/Description: The Evening-Weekend Program serves 2 groups: those who wish to take a limited number of courses for special purposes and those who desire to earn baccalaureate degrees. Degree programs are offered in Accounting, Business Administration and Behavioral Sciences, and the Individually Planned Major.

Accreditation: Southern Association of Colleges and Schools.

Admission Requirements:

Undergraduate	Graduate
HS/GED Diploma	Undergraduate Degree Recommendations GRE, NTE, MAT

Credit Awards for Prior Learning: ACE/PONSI Recommendations; Transfer Credit.

Limits to Credit Awards for Prior Learning: 60 semester hours for RN hospital program. 30 for PONSI.

Credit Awards for Examinations: CLEP General Exams; College Board AP Exams.

Limits to Credit Awards for Examinations: CLEP—30 hours.

Estimated Average Completion Time: Bachelors' Degrees: 6-8 years (part-time), 4 years (full-time).

Credit Hour Requirements: 120 hours total; 45 hours academic residency (hours that must be earned at the institution exclusive of credit-by-exam, portfolio assessment, etc.).

Distance Learning Options: None.

Student Support Services Available: Academic Advising; Career Counseling; Counseling/Testing; Financial Aid; Job Placement Assistance; Orientation; Tutoring.

Informational Materials Available: Institutional Catalog; Program Brochure.

Program Age, Enrollment, and Degrees Conferred: Information not available.

Percentage of Bachelor's Degree Holders Admitted to Graduate School: About 20 percent from the Evening/Weekend Adult Program.

Geographic Admission Restrictions: None.

Tuition and Fees:

	Undergraduate
Tuition	$210.00/credit
Application Fee	$25.00
Graduation Fee	$65.00

Hawaii

43. Hawaii Loa College

Bachelor in Organizational Managerial Degree Program
45-045 Kamehameha Hwy.
Kaneohe, HI 96744

Degrees Offered: Bachelor in Organizational Management.

Program Mission Statement/Description: To provide an accelerated and practical program leading to a degree for working adults.

Accreditation: Western Association of Schools and Colleges.

Admission Requirements: HS/GED Diploma; Interview; Prior Credits: 60; Recommendations.

Credit Awards for Prior Learning: ACE Military Recommendations; ACE/PONSI Recommendations; Portfolio Assessment; Transfer Credit.

Limits to Credit Awards for Prior Learning: 30 credits.

Credit Awards for Examinations: ACT Proficiency Exams; CLEP General Exams; CLEP Subject Exams; College Board AP Exams; DANTES Subject Tests; Departmental Exams.

Limits to Credit Awards for Examinations: 30 credits.

Estimated Average Completion Time: Information not available.

Credit Hour Requirements: 124 hours total; 30 hours academic residency (hours that must be earned at the institution exclusive of credit-by-exam, portfolio assessment, etc.).

Distance Learning Options: Supervised Fieldwork.

Student Support Services Available: Academic Advising; Financial Aid; Orientation; Tutoring.

Informational Materials Available: Institutional Catalog; Program Brochure.

Program Age, Enrollment, and Graduates:

Degree	Year Est.	Current Enrollment	Degrees Conferred
January	1989	36	8

Percentage of Bachelor's Degree Holders Admitted to Graduate School: Information not available.

Geographic Admission Restrictions: None.

Tuition and Fees: In-State Tuition $7,500.00*; Application Fee $35.00; Credit-by-Exam Fee $215.00.

*Total tuition for 40 credits.

Other Fees: Prior learning $30 per essay; $30 per hour portfolio evaluation.

Other Pertinent Information: The program lasts 18 months with classes meeting one night per week and every other Saturday for 4 hours.

Illinois

44. DePaul University

School for New Learning
25 East Jackson Blvd.
Chicago, IL 60604

Degrees Offered: Bachelor of Arts; Master of Arts.

Program Mission Statement/Description: The School for New Learning (SNL) expresses DePaul University's mission to provide quality education, service, and research. It fosters collaboration between the adult student and the urban community for the enhancement of learning. Through the individualized character of its education and its cooperative learning environment, SNL implements DePaul's philosophy of personalism. The School for New Learning teaches adults exclusively and certifies their competence in the acquisition of knowledge and skills, however gained. By focusing on the outcomes of learning, SNL guides students in an educational process that values their experience and helps them transform it into new learning. The faculty, selected from both professional and academic ranks, have expertise in content and in the ability to teach in a learner-centered, trans-disciplinary manner. SNL conducts research in the theories and practice of adult and competence-based education.

Accreditation: North Central Association of Colleges and Schools.

Admission Requirements:

Undergraduate	Graduate
Interview	Undergraduate Degree
Essay/Written Work	Interview
	Essay/Written Work
	Recommendations
	Employment/Experience: 3 years area of profession

Other Admission Requirements: For the BA program, students must successfully complete a "Discovery Workshop," prior to applying for admission. Graduate applicants are required to complete the "Professional Assessment Workshop" prior to being admitted to the program.

Credit Awards for Prior Learning: Portfolio assessment.

Limits to Credit Awards for Prior Learning: Both programs are competence- rather than credit-hour based. Prior learning in any form is assessed in terms of the competence requirements of the programs.

Credit Awards for Examinations: ACT Proficiency Exams; CLEP General Exams; CLEP Subject Exams; College

Board AP Exams; DANTES Subject Tests; Departmental Exams.

Estimated Average Completion Time: Bachelors' Degrees: 2.5-3 years (part-time); Graduate Degrees: 18-24 months (part-time).

Caveats Regarding Time Estimates: Because of the great variance of prior learning students bring to the program, as well as variance in their pacing through the program, the time to completion varies considerably among students.

Distance Learning Options: Independent Study; Supervised Fieldwork.

Student Support Services Available: Academic Advising; Career Counseling; Counseling/Testing; Financial Aid; Job Placement Assistance; Orientation; Tutoring.

Informational Materials Available: Institutional Catalog; Program Brochure.

Program Age, Enrollment, and Degrees Conferred:

Degree	Year Est.	Current Enrollment	Degrees Conferred
Bachelor of Arts	1972	1300	1300
Master of Arts	1985	100	40

Percentage of Bachelor's Degree Holders Admitted to Graduate School: 45 percent.

Geographic Admission Restrictions: None.

Tuition and Fees:

	Undergraduate	Graduate
In-State Tuition	$183.00/sem.	$203.00/sem.
Application Fee	$50.00	

Other Pertinent Information: The School for New Learning has been recognized nationally as a premier institution for adult degree programs.

45. Southern Illinois University at Edwardsville

Office of Continuing Education
Box 1084
Edwardsville, IL 62026

Degrees Offered: Bachelor of Science in Nursing; Master of Business Administration; Master of Science in Education; Master of Public Administration; Master of Marketing Research.

Program Mission Statement/Description: Consistent with its particular commitment to southwestern Illinois and with its pursuit of academic excellence, the Southern Illinois University at Edwardsville (SIUE) strives to enhance regional access to the educational opportunities it offers. It recognizes an obligation to provide developmental opportunities for the educationally dispossessed; it pursues a commitment to meet the special needs of nontraditional students; and it makes every effort to maintain admissions standards, fees, schedules, and calendars which will encourage access and support the progress of all its students.

Accreditation: North Central Association of Colleges and Schools; American Assembly of Collegiate Schools of Business; National Council for the Accreditation of Teacher Education; National League for Nursing.

Admission Requirements: Undergraduate—HS/GED Diploma; Graduate—Undergraduate Degree, Prior Credits: up to 50 hours, GMAT (MBA), MAT (MSEd), GRE, (MAEd), and programs have specific admissions requirements. Students should consult the university catalog and graduate catalog for details.

Credit Awards for Prior Learning: ACE Military Recommendations; Transfer Credit.

Limits to Credit Awards for Prior Learning: Undergraduate—transfer limits are set by each school or program; ACE Military recommendations are limited to 3 quarter hours of PE and 3 hours of health. Graduate—transfer credits must be at least a grade of B or above; cannot exceed one-third of the total hours required for the master's degree; and must be earned within 6 years prior to the completion of the SIUE degree.

Credit Awards for Examinations: CLEP General Exams; CLEP Subject Exams; College Board AP Exams; Departmental Exams.

Limits to Credit Awards for Examinations: CLEP Subject—maximum of 48 hours which must be approved by the departments that offer the comparable courses. CLEP General—scores must be above the 50th percentile. College Board AP—maximum of 16 hours. Dept./Institution Exams—maximum of 48 hours with a grade of C or above.

Estimated Average Completion Time: Bachelors' Degrees: 2.5 years (part-time); Graduate Degrees: MBA/MSEd 3 years (part-time) 1.5 years (full-time)

Credit Hour Requirements:

Degree	Total Hours	Academic Residency*
Bachelor's	192 quarter hours	48
Graduate (MBA)	52	35
Graduate (MSEd)	48	32

*Hours that must be earned at the institution exclusive of credit-by-exam, portfolio assessment, etc.

Distance Learning Options: Independent Study (Graduate only); Supervised Fieldwork.

Student Support Services Available: Academic Advising; Career Counseling; Counseling/Testing; Financial Aid; Job Placement Assistance; Orientation; Tutoring.

Informational Materials Available: Exam Preparation Guides; Institutional Catalog; Program Brochure; Financial Aid Brochure; Graduate Catalog; Undergraduate Catalog.

Program Age, Enrollment, and Graduates:

Degree	Year Est.	Current Enrollment	Degrees Conferred
BSN Completion	1980	197	*
MBA Off-Campus	1973	350	*
MSEd Off-Campus	1982	230	*

*Not available—data are included with on-campus totals.

Percentage of Bachelor's Degree Holders Admitted to Graduate School: Information not available.

Geographic Admission Restrictions: None.

Tuition and Fees:

	Undergraduate	Graduate
In-State Tuition	$40.50/credit	$43.50/credit
Out-of-State Tuition	$121.50/credit	$130.20/credit
Application Fee	$10.00 (MBA)	
Graduation Fee	$10.00	$10.00

Off-Campus fee $29.40 per course.

Indiana

46. Indiana University Northwest

3400 Broadway
Gary, IN 46408

Degrees Offered: Associate of General Studies; Bachelor of General Studies.

Program Mission Statement/Description: To serve the needs of students who cannot take advantage of the traditional formal programs; to enrich further their personal development for social or cultural reasons; to develop and maintain a vocational or professional competence.

Accreditation: North Central Association of Colleges and Schools.

Admission Requirements: HS/GED Diploma. Provisional acceptance, if individual does not have high school diploma or GED. Twelve hours of college "C" work.

Credit Awards for Prior Learning: ACE Military Recommendations; ACE/PONSI Recommendations; Portfolio Assessment; Transfer Credit.

Limits to Credit Awards for Prior Learning: Portfolio—15 hours for associate's degree; 30 hours for bachelor's degree. Transfer—90 hours maximum for bachelor; 45 hours maximum for associate.

Credit Awards for Examinations: CLEP General Exams; CLEP Subject Exams; DANTES Subject Tests; Departmental Exams.

Estimated Average Completion Time: Associates' Degrees: 4 years (part-time), 2.5 years (full-time); Bachelors' Degrees: 7 years (part-time), 5 years (full-time).

Credit Hour Requirements:

Degree	Total Hours	Academic Residency*
Associate's	60	15
Bachelor's	120	30

*Hours that must be earned at the institution exclusive of credit-by-exam, portfolio assessment, etc.

Distance Learning Options: Correspondence Courses; Supervised Fieldwork.

Student Support Services Available: Academic Advising; Career Counseling; Counseling/Testing; Financial Aid; Job Placement Assistance; Orientation; Tutoring.

Informational Materials Available: Program Brochure; Institutional Catalog.

Program Age, Enrollment, and Degrees Conferred:

Degree	Year Est.	Current Enrollment	Degrees Conferred
AGS	1977	80	80
BGS	1977	158	198

Percentage of Bachelor's Degree Holders Admitted to Graduate School: 10 percent.

Geographic Admission Restrictions: None.

Tuition and Fees: In-State Tuition $59.65 per credit; Out-of-State Tuition $150.40 per credit; Application Fee $20.00; Credit-by-Exam Fee $30.35; Student Activity Fee $1.50 per credit hour; Parking Permit $1.15 per credit hour.

47. Indiana Wesleyan University

Leadership Education for Adult Professionals Program
4406 S. Harmon St.
Marion, IN 46953

Degrees Offered: Associate of Science in Business; Bachelor of Science in Business Administration; Bachelor of Science in Management; Master of Science in Business Administration; Master of Science in Management.

Program Mission Statement/Description: Indiana Wesleyan University proposes to "search for truth by study in liberal arts and in professional education within the framework of Christian faith and philosophy so that the person is developed for service to God and man in the church and in society." A committed faculty leads in maintaining a climate where students are challenged to develop in academic knowledge, wholesome personal growth, professional competence, responsible citizenship, social relationships, and spiritual life. Out of the desire to serve the adult population and in the spirit of open inquiry, the Leadership Education for Adult Professionals (LEAP) program was developed. Indiana Wesleyan University understands the special requirements of adults who are interested in receiving an associate's, bachelor's, or master's degree but who must also continue meeting their professional and personal commitments. The LEAP program, designed for those working adults, combines theory with practical experience.

Accreditation: North Central Association of Colleges and Schools.

Admission Requirements:

Undergraduate	Graduate
HS/GED Diploma	Undergraduate Degree
Recommendations	Recommendations
Employment/Experience: 2 years	Employment/Experience: 3 years

Other Admission Requirements: AS requires 24 credits transferable semester hours including 6 hours in General Education. BS requires 60 credits transferable semester hours.

Credit Awards for Prior Learning: ACE Military Recommendations; ACE/PONSI Recommendations; Portfolio Assessment; Transfer Credit.

Other Options: Educational Credential Evaluations for Foreign Students.

Limits to Credit Awards for Prior Learning: Portfolio assessment—18 hours credit for associate's degree, 40 hours credit for undergraduate degree. Maximum of 62 semester hours transferable from evaluated coursework completed at colleges or universities not approved by COPA.

Credit Awards for Examinations: CLEP General Exams; CLEP Subject Exams; DANTES Subject Tests.

Estimated Average Completion Time: Associates' Degrees: 16 months (full-time); Bachelors' Degrees: 16 months (full-time); Graduate Degrees: MSM—16 months (full-time). MBA—22 months (full-time).

Caveats Regarding Time Estimates: Lockstep program; intense coursework. Students meet in class one night per week for 4 hours and out of class one night per week for 4 hours. No course waivers are permitted. Prerequisites may be required for MBA students.

Credit Hour Requirements:

Degree	Total Hours	Academic Residency*
Associate's	64	40
Bachelor's	124	40
Graduate (MBA)	37	37
Graduate (MSM)	30	30

*Hours that must be earned at the institution exclusive of credit-by-exam, portfolio assessment, etc.

Distance Learning Options: None.

Student Support Services Available: Academic Advising; Financial Aid; Orientation.

Informational Materials Available: Program Brochure; Institutional Catalog; Prior Learning Guides.

Program Age, Enrollment, and Degrees Conferred:

Degree	Year Est.	Current Enrollment	Degrees Conferred
BSBA	1985	408	532
BSM	1985	154	350
MBA	1985	535	533
MSM	1985	200	373
ASB	1990	170	0

Percentage of Bachelor's Degree Holders Admitted to Graduate School: Information not available.

Geographic Admission Restrictions: None.

Tuition and Fees:

	Undergraduate	Graduate
In-State Tuition	$145.00/credit	$203.00/credit
Application Fee	$10.00	$10.00
Graduation Fee	$54.00	$54.00
Credit-by-Exam Fee	$25.00/credit	

Other Fees: Associate's Degree tuition for In-State $125.00. Books—$796.00 (MSM), $756.00 (UG), $740.00 (Associate). Portfolio Submission $150.00, Edition. Resource Fee $200.00, Credit-by-Assessment $25/hour certified learning. $35/hour life experience essays.

Other Pertinent Information: Stand alone elective courses are offered to corporations on a contractual basis. Unclassified student status is available for those not pursuing a degree from Indiana Wesleyan University for a maximum of 18 credit hours.

48. Martin Center College

2171 Avondale Pl.
P.O. Box 18567
Indianapolis, IN 46218

Degrees Offered: Bachelor of Arts; Bachelor of Science.

Program Mission Statement/Description: Martin Center College (MCC) offers the baccalaureate degree specifically designed to assist low-income, minority, and adult-aged persons. The philosophy of MCC is that a college education should be made available to all who can benefit. MCC recognizes that students vary in their personal circumstances, career goals, prior learning experiences, and educational needs and these factors are taken into consideration.

Accreditation: North Central Association of Colleges and Schools.

Admission Requirements: HS/GED Diploma.

Credit Awards for Prior Learning: ACE Military Recommendations; ACE/PONSI Recommendations; Portfolio Assessment; Transfer Credit.

Limits to Credit Awards for Prior Learning: ACE military recommendations are not "duplicated" or increased because of length of service.

Credit Awards for Examinations: CLEP Subject Exams; DANTES Subject Tests; Departmental Exams.

Estimated Average Completion Time: 3-4 years (part-time), 2-3 years (full-time).

Credit Hour Requirements: 128 hours total; 32 hours academic residency (hours that must be earned at the institution exclusive of credit-by-exam, portfolio assessment, etc.).

Distance Learning Options: None.

Student Support Services Available: Academic Advising; Career Counseling; Counseling/Testing; Financial Aid; Job Placement Assistance; Orientation; Tutoring; Health Care Support; Death and Dying Support Group (year round); Arrangements for childcare at a preschool.

Informational Materials Available: Institutional Catalog; Prior Learning Guides; Program Brochure.

Program Age, Enrollment, and Degrees Conferred:

Degree	Year Est.	Current Enrollment	Degrees Conferred
Baccalaureate Degree	1980	850	301

Percentage of Bachelor's Degree Holders Admitted to Graduate School: 30 percent.

Geographic Admission Restrictions: None.

Tuition and Fees:

	Undergraduate
In-State Tuition	$150.00/credit
Out-of-State Tuition	$150.00/credit
Application Fee	$10.00
Graduation Fee	$60.00

Other Pertinent Information: There is no restriction to age-span, and learning times are accommodated to adult lifestyle. All students must complete a final project exhibiting their learning, and community projects are encouraged. Typical student is African American, low-income, and around 40 years of age.

49. University of Evansville

External Studies Program
1800 Linda Ave.
Evansville, IN 47722

Degrees Offered: Bachelor of Arts; Bachelor of Science.

Program Mission Statement/Description: Through the External Studies Program, qualified adults may participate in the design of an individualized degree program. This program allows for special use of resources and learning opportunities outside the classroom setting.

Accreditation: North Central Association of Colleges and Schools.

Admission Requirements: HS/GED Diploma; Interview.

Credit Awards for Prior Learning: ACE Military Recommendations; ACE/PONSI Recommendations; Portfolio Assessment; Transfer Credit.

Credit Awards for Examinations: CLEP General Exams; CLEP Subject Exams; DANTES Subject Tests; Departmental Exams.

Estimated Average Completion Time: 2-10 years (part-time).

Credit Hour Requirements: 124 hours total; 24 hours academic residency (hours that must be earned at the institution exclusive of credit-by-exam, portfolio assessment, etc.).

Distance Learning Options: None.

Student Support Services Available: Academic Advising; Orientation.

Informational Materials Available: Institutional Catalog; Program Brochure.

Program Age, Enrollment, and Graduates: Information not available.

Percentage of Bachelor's Degree Holders Admitted to Graduate School: Information not available.

Geographic Admission Restrictions: None.

Tuition and Fees: In-State Tuition $160.00; Out-of-State Tuition $160.00; Application Fee $20.00; Graduation Fee $20.00; Credit-by-Exam Fee $25.00/semester hour.

Other Fees: Intensive Advising $70.00.

50. Valparaiso University

Valparaiso, IN 46383

Degrees Offered: Bachelor of Arts; Master of Arts in Liberal Studies; Master of Science in Nursing; Master of Arts in Applied Behavioral Science; Master of Education; Master of Music.

Program Mission Statement/Description: Valparaiso University seeks to meet the needs of nontraditional students, particularly in the region of Northwest Indiana. The university offers programs that enable the undergraduate student to achieve a bachelor's degree, and it offers graduate programs that permit persons with the baccalaureate to attain higher levels of knowledge and specialization that enhance professional abilities.

Accreditation: North Central Association of Colleges and Schools; National Association for Accreditation of Teacher Education; National Association of Schools of Music; National League for Nursing.

Admission Requirements:

Undergraduate	Graduate
HS/GED Diploma	Undergraduate Degree
Essay/Written Work	
Recommendations	

Other Admission Requirements: Interview may be required when the credentials suggest this to be appropriate.

Credit Awards for Prior Learning: Transfer Credit.

Credit Awards for Examinations: ACT Proficiency Exams; CLEP General Exams; CLEP Subject Exams; College Board AP Exams; DANTES Subject Tests; Departmental Exams.

Estimated Average Completion Time: Bachelors' Degrees: 8 years (part-time); Graduate Degrees: 5 years, JD (part-time). Master's 1.5 years (full-time), JD 3 years (full-time).

Credit Hour Requirements:

Degree	Total Hours	Academic Residency*
Bachelor's	124	30
Graduate (JD)	90	47
Graduate (MAABS)	42	37
Graduate (MSN)	36	27
Graduate (MED)	33	24
Graduate (MALS)	33	30
Graduate (MM)	30	27

*Hours that must be earned at the institution exclusive of credit-by-exam, portfolio assessment, etc.

Distance Learning Options: Cooperative Education; Independent Study; Supervised Fieldwork.

Student Support Services Available: Academic Advising; Career Counseling; Counseling/Testing; Financial Aid; Job Placement Assistance; Orientation; Tutoring.

Informational Materials Available: Institutional Catalog.

Program Age, Enrollment, and Degrees Conferred:

Degree	Year Est.	Current Enrollment	Degrees Conferred
J.D.	1879	499	3299
MALS	1963	53	1207
MAABS	1986	36	23
MED	1972	23	433
MSN	1989	14	0
MMusic	1981	4	25

Percentage of Bachelor's Degree Holders Admitted to Graduate School: 10 percent.

Geographic Admission Restrictions: None.

Tuition and Fees:

	Undergraduate	Graduate
In-State Tuition	$115.00/credit	$135.00/credit
Out-of-State Tuition	$115.00/credit	$135.00/credit
Application Fee	$30.00	$30.00
Graduation Fee	$20.00	$20.00

Iowa

51. Iowa Wesleyan College

Office of Continuing Education
601 N. Main St.
Mount Pleasant, IA 52641

Degrees Offered: Bachelor of Arts in Accounting; Bachelor of Arts in Business Administration; Bachelor of Arts in Elementary Education; Bachelor of Arts in Psychology; Bachelor of Arts in Sociology; Bachelor of Arts in Criminal Justice; Bachelor of Science in Nursing; Bachelor of General Studies.

Program Mission Statement/Description: The primary function of the Office of Continuing Education is to provide credit and noncredit courses, workshops, seminars, and conferences for adults in southeastern Iowa who are interested in a degree, personal enrichment, self-development, or a program looking toward career advancement. The Continuing Education Office cooperates with the divisions of the college to offer several degree programs at various locations to persons unable to attend traditional day classes.

Accreditation: North Central Association of Colleges and Schools.

Admission Requirements: HS/GED Diploma; 2.00 GPA on previous college transcripts.

Credit Awards for Prior Learning: ACE Military Recommendations; ACE/PONSI Recommendations; Portfolio Assessment; Transfer Credit.

Limits to Credit Awards for Prior Learning: Up to 30 semester hours on credit for extrainstitutional prior learning; up to 64 hours for community college transfer courses; up to 94 hours for four-year college transfer courses.

Credit Awards for Examinations: CLEP Subject Exams; Departmental Exams.

Limits to Credit Awards for Examinations: Up to 30 semester hours.

Estimated Average Completion Time: 2-7 years (part-time); 4 years (full-time).

Caveats Regarding Time Estimates: Completion through part-time study depends upon the number of transfer credits, program of study, etc.

Credit Hour Requirements: 124 hours total; 30 hours academic residency (hours that must be earned at the institution exclusive of credit-by-exam, portfolio assessment, etc.).

Distance Learning Options: Independent Study; Supervised Fieldwork; Television Courses.

Student Support Services Available: Academic Advising; Career Counseling; Financial Aid; Job Placement Assistance; Tutoring.

Informational Materials Available: Exam Preparation Guides; Institutional Catalog; Prior Learning Guides; Program Brochure; Course Requirement Worksheets; Financial Aid Information; Course Schedule Brochures.

Program Age, Enrollment, and Graduates:

	Year Est.	Current Enrollment	Degrees Conferred
BA - Business Admin.	1985	130	37
BA - Elem. Education	1987	27	12
BA - C.J., Soc, Psych	1987	12	1
BSN	1986	46	27
BGS	1985	7	15

Note: All figures are based on 1985-90 data; most programs were actually started prior to 1985.

Percentage of Bachelor's Degree Holders Admitted to Graduate School: Information not available.

Geographic Admission Restrictions: See Program Mission Statement/Description.

Tuition and Fees: In-State Tuition $115.00 per credit; Out-of-State Tuition $115.00 per credit; Graduation Fee $35.00; Credit-by-Exam Fee $15-30.00 per credit hour.

52. Kirkwood Community College

Integrated Career Studies Program
6301 Kirkwood Blvd.
P.O. Box 2068
Cedar Rapids, IA 52406

Degrees Offered: Associate of Applied Science in Integrated Career Studies.

Program Mission Statement/Description: This program is primarily directed toward the adult learner with previous work experience. It is designed to allow students to develop and pursue an individualized program of study that meets their own personal and career goals.

Accreditation: North Central Association of Colleges and Schools.

Admission Requirements: Essay/Written Work; HS/GED Diploma; Interview; Asset Evaluation Test.

Credit Awards for Prior Learning: ACE Military Recommendations; Portfolio Assessment; Transfer Credit; Occupational Work assessment.

Limits to Credit Awards for Prior Learning: 10 credit hours for previous work experience. Up to one-third of total program hours (maximum 21 credit hours) may be waived. This would include the 10 credit hours for work experience. The last 16 hours of coursework must be completed at Kirkwood.

Credit Awards for Examinations: ACT Proficiency Exams; CLEP General Exams; CLEP Subject Exams; DANTES Subject Tests; Departmental Exams.

Estimated Average Completion Time: 3-5 years (part-time), 2 years (full-time).

Credit Hour Requirements: 64 hours total; 16 hours academic residency (hours that must be earned at the institution exclusive of credit-by-exam, portfolio assessment, etc.).

Distance Learning Options: Cooperative Education; Independent Study; Study Guides; Supervised Fieldwork; Television Courses.

Student Support Services Available: Academic Advising; Career Counseling; Counseling/Testing; Financial Aid; Job Placement Assistance; Orientation; Tutoring.

Informational Materials Available: Exam Preparation Guides; Institutional Catalog; Program Brochure; self-help pamphlets from the counseling office.

Program Age, Enrollment, and Degrees Conferred:

Degree	Year Est.	Current Enrollment	Degrees Conferred
AAS	1989	20	1

Geographic Admission Restrictions: None.

Tuition and Fees: In-State Tuition $37.00 per credit; Out-of-State Tuition $79.00 per credit; Credit-by-Exam Fee $50.00

53. Loras College

Tri College Degree Program
1450 Alta Vista
Dubuque, IA 52004

Degrees Offered: Associate of Arts; Bachelor of Arts; Master of Arts.

Program Mission Statement/Description: The Tri College degree program of Loras College, Clarke College, and the University of Dubuque is designed to serve the academic needs of persons 24 years old and older through part-time study and assessment of prior learning. Master of Arts Programs are designed for part-time study in Education, English, History, Physical Education, and Psychology.

Accreditation: North Central Association of Colleges and Schools.

Admission Requirements:

Undergraduate	Graduate
HS/GED Diploma	GRE, GMAT
Interview	

Credit Awards for Prior Learning: ACE Military Recommendations; ACE/PONSI Recommendations; Portfolio Assessment; Transfer Credit.

Limits to Credit Awards for Prior Learning: Maximum of 30 in any area. Must earn minimum of 30 credits of coursework for the degree.

Credit Awards for Examinations: ACT Proficiency Exams; CLEP General Exams; CLEP Subject Exams; College Board AP Exams; DANTES Subject Tests; Departmental Exams.

Estimated Average Completion Time: Associates' Degrees: 4 years (part-time), 2 years (full-time); Bachelors' Degrees: 6-8 years (part-time), 4 years (full-time); Graduate Degrees: 3-4 years (part-time), 2 years (full-time).

Caveats Regarding Time Estimates: Most MA students are part-time. Only full-time study in psychology is possible, and few students opt for the full-time mode.

Credit Hour Requirements:

Degree	Total Hours	Academic Residency*
Associate's	60	15
Bachelor's	120	30
Graduate	30-38	24-29

*Hours that must be earned at the institution exclusive of credit-by-exam, portfolio assessment, etc.

Distance Learning Options: Independent Study; Supervised Fieldwork; Internships (Associate and Bachelor only).

Student Support Services Available: Academic Advising; Career Counseling; Counseling/Testing; Financial Aid; Job Placement Assistance; Orientation; Tutoring.

Informational Materials Available: Institutional Catalog; Prior Learning Guides; Program Brochure; Financial Aid and Counseling Center Information.

Program Age, Enrollment, and Degrees Conferred: Information not available.

Percentage of Bachelor's Degree Holders Admitted to Graduate School: Information not available.

Geographic Admission Restrictions: None.

Tuition and Fees: In-State Tuition $235.00 per credit; Out-of-State Tuition $235.00 per credit; Application Fee $15.00; Graduation Fee $15.00/$30.00; Credit-by-Exam Fee 20% of tuition-per-credit fee.

54. North Iowa Area Community College

Evening Dean
500 College Dr.
Mason City, IA 50401

Degrees Offered: Associate of Arts Degree; Associate of General Studies Degree; Associate of Science in Business.

Program Mission Statement/Description: To provide courses and services to maximize recruitment and retention of older students.

Accreditation: North Central Association of Colleges and Schools.

Admission Requirements: HS/GED Diploma.

Credit Awards for Prior Learning: ACE Military Recommendations; Portfolio Assessment; Transfer Credit.

Credit Awards for Examinations: CLEP General Exams; CLEP Subject Exams; College Board AP Exams; Departmental Exams.

Limits to Credit Awards for Examinations: 12 hours.

Estimated Average Completion Time: Information not available.

Credit Hour Requirements: Associates' Degrees 60 credit hours.

Distance Learning Options: Independent Study; Television Courses.

Student Support Services Available: Academic Advising; Career Counseling; Counseling/Testing; Financial Aid; Job Placement Assistance; Orientation; Tutoring.

Informational Materials Available: Institutional Catalog; Prior Learning Guides; Program Brochure.

Program Age, Enrollment, and Graduates: Information not available.

Geographic Admission Restrictions: None.

Tuition and Fees: In-State Tuition $41.00 per credit; Out-of-State Tuition $46.50 per credit; Graduation Fee $20.00; Credit-by-Exam Fee $50.00.

55. Simpson College

Adult and Continuing Education
701 N. C St.
Indianola, IA 50125

Degrees Offered: Bachelor of Arts in Accounting; Bachelor of Arts in Computer Science; Bachelor of Arts in Communication Studies; Bachelor of Arts in English; Bachelor of Arts in Management.

Program Mission Statement/Description: Simpson College provides courses and degree programs for students who wish to attend part-time. Courses are offered in day, evening, Saturday, and accelerated formats. Adult students meet the same graduation requirements as do traditional students (competencies, general, and major requirements). Classes are held on campus and in West Des Moines, 25 miles away from the main campus.

Accreditation: North Central Association of Colleges and Schools.

Admission Requirements: HS/GED Diploma.

Other Admission Requirements: Acceptance for enrollment is based on review by vice president if student wishes to seek degree.

Credit Awards for Prior Learning: ACE Military Recommendations; ACE/PONSI Recommendations; Portfolio Assessment; Transfer Credit; Professional Certification Courses.

Limits to Credit Awards for Prior Learning: Students who transfer from a 4-year institution must complete at least 32.00 hours at Simpson for a BA degree. Students who transfer from a 2-year institution must complete at least 64.00 hours at Simpson for a BA degree.

Credit Awards for Examinations: CLEP General Exams; CLEP Subject Exams; DANTES Subject Tests; Departmental Exams.

Limits to Credit Awards for Examinations: CLEP 24 semester hours, DANTES 16 hours, Professional Certification 16 hours, Departmental Exams 16 hours.

Estimated Average Completion Time: 5.5 years (part-time), 4 years (full-time).

Credit Hour Requirements: 128 hours total; 64 hours academic residency (hours that must be earned at the institution exclusive of credit-by-exam, portfolio assessment, etc.).

Distance Learning Options: Cooperative Education; Supervised Fieldwork; Independent Study.

Student Support Services Available: Academic Advising; Career Counseling; Counseling/Testing; Financial Aid; Job Placement Assistance; Orientation; Tutoring.

Informational Materials Available: Exam Preparation Guides; Institutional Catalog; Prior Learning Guides; Program Brochure.

Program Age, Enrollment, and Degrees Conferred: Information not available.

Percentage of Bachelor's Degree Holders Admitted to Graduate School: Information not available.

Geographic Admission Restrictions: None.

Tuition and Fees: In-State Tuition $140.00 per credit; Out-of-State Tuition $140.00 per credit; Application Fee $25.00; Graduation Fee $30.00; Credit-by-Exam Fee $50.00; Portfolio Assessment Fee $50.00.

---

56. Teikyo Marycrest University

1607 W. 12th St.
Davenport, IA 52804

Degrees Offered: Bachelor of Arts; Bachelor of Science; Master of Arts; Master of Science.

Program Mission Statement/Description: Teikyo Marycrest University, a private, coeducational university, prepares students of all faiths through liberal and professional studies on the undergraduate and graduate levels for service that contributes to the good of society.

Accreditation: North Central Association of Colleges and Schools.

Admission Requirements:

Undergraduate	Graduate
HS/GED Diploma	Undergraduate Degree
Interview	
Recommendations	

Other Admission Requirements: Graduate application. If English is not the primary language, TOEFL score of 550 is required. Official transcripts. Undergraduate GPA of 2.8 on 4.0 system. MA in Education: Current elementary teaching certificate.

Credit Awards for Prior Learning: ACE Military Recommendations; ACE/PONSI Recommendations; Portfolio Assessment; Transfer Credit.

Limits to Credit Awards for Prior Learning: Baccalaureate: maximum of 66 semester hours from junior college; maximum of 90 semester hours from 4-year college.

Credit Awards for Examinations: CLEP General Exams; CLEP Subject Exams; DANTES Subject Tests; Departmental Exams.

Estimated Average Completion Time: Associates' Degrees: 2.5-3 years (part-time), 2 years (full-time). Bachelors' Degrees: 4.5-5 years (part-time), 4 years (full-time). Graduate Degrees: MA/MS 3 years (part-time); MS Program only, 16 months-2 years (full-time).

Caveats Regarding Time Estimates: MA degree programs are offered only on a part-time basis. MS degree programs are offered on part-time or full-time basis.

Credit Hour Requirements:

Degree	Total Hours	Academic Residency*
Associate's	60	30
Bachelor's	120	30
Graduate (MA/MS)	30-36	30

*Hours that must be earned at the institution exclusive of credit-by-exam, portfolio assessment, etc.

Distance Learning Options: Cooperative Education (Bachelor only); Independent Study; Supervised Fieldwork (Bachelor only); Television Courses.

Student Support Services Available: Academic Advising; Career Counseling; Counseling/Testing; Financial Aid; Job Placement Assistance; Orientation.

Informational Materials Available: Institutional Catalog; Program Brochure.

Program Age, Enrollment, and Degrees Conferred:

Degree	Year Est.	Current Enrollment	Degrees Conferred
BA/BS Weekend College	1981	300	40
MA Ed.	1972	240	25
MS Computer Science	1982	45	10

Percentage of Bachelor's Degree Holders Admitted to Graduate School: 27 percent of the 62 who responded to a recent questionnaire (population 216) were attending graduate school.

Geographic Admission Restrictions: None.

Tuition and Fees:

	Undergraduate	Graduate
In-State Tuition	$295.00/credit	$295.00/credit
Out-of-State Tuition	$295.00/credit	$295.00/credit
Application Fee	$25.00	$25.00
Graduation Fee	$35.00	$35.00
Credit-by-Exam Fee	$25.00	
Student Activity Fee	$3.00/sem. hour	

Other Pertinent Information: An Associate of Arts (AA) degree from an accredited institution satisfies the general education requirements for the baccalaureate degree. Courses in general education and those in selected majors are offered at off-campus sites.

57. Waldorf College

Adult Degree Program
106 S. 6th St.
Forest City, IA 50436

Degrees Offered: Associate of Arts.

Program Mission Statement/Description: Waldorf College Adult Degree Program is designed to serve the working adult. Classes are offered in an accelerated format so students can complete an associate's degree in 2-3 years while attending class in the evening.

Accreditation: North Central Association of Schools and Colleges.

Admission Requirements: HS/GED Diploma.

Credit Awards for Prior Learning: ACE Military Recommendations; ACE/PONSI Recommendations; Portfolio Assessment; Transfer Credit.

Limits to Credit Awards for Prior Learning: Total of 32 hours.

Credit Awards for Examinations: CLEP General Exams; CLEP Subject Exams.

Estimated Average Completion Time: 4 years (part-time), 2 years (full-time).

Credit Hour Requirements: 64 hours total; 32 hours academic residency (hours that must be earned at the institution exclusive of credit-by-exam, portfolio assessment, etc.).

Distance Learning Options: Independent Study; Television Courses.

Student Support Services Available: Academic Advising; Career Counseling; Counseling/Testing; Financial Aid; Orientation; Tutoring.

Informational Materials Available: Institutional Catalog; Program Brochure.

Program Age, Enrollment, and Degrees Conferred:

Degree	Year Est.	Current Enrollment	Degrees Conferred
AA	1989	107	3

Geographic Admission Restrictions: None.

Tuition and Fees: In-State Tuition $95.00 per credit; Out-of-State Tuition $95.00 per credit; Graduation Fee $15.00.

Other Pertinent Information: The program offers courses in 4 10-week semesters each year. Courses offered are in general education, business, computer science, preengineering, rehabilitation, and training.

Kansas

58. Baker University

School for Professional & Graduate Studies
6800 College Blvd., Ste. 500
Overland Park, KS 66211

Degrees Offered: Bachelor of Business Administration; Master of Science in Management; Master in Business Administration; and Master of Liberal Arts.

Program Mission Statement/Description: The School of Professional and Graduate Studies, operating within framework of the Baker University institutional mission, provides opportunities for adult students to pursue undergraduate and graduate degrees in a nontraditional setting. In recognition that the need for formal learning continues throughout life, Baker seeks to serve the needs of these students by offering educational programs in liberal arts and professional studies.

Accreditation: North Central Association of Colleges and Schools.

Admission Requirements:

Undergraduate	Graduate
HS/GED Diploma	Undergraduate Degree
Recommendations	Recommendations
Employment/Experience:	Employment/Experience
3 years	
Prior Credits: 60	

Other Admission Requirements: TOEFL score of 600 for international students (all programs). Normally applicants should be at least 23 years of age for undergraduate programs and 25 years of age for graduate programs.

Credit Awards for Prior Learning: ACE Military Recommendations; ACE/PONSI Recommendations; Transfer Credit; Portfolio Assessment.

Limits to Credit Awards for Prior Learning: Credit only granted for undergraduate programs.

Credit Awards for Examinations: CLEP General Exams; CLEP Subject Exams; DANTES Subject Tests; ACT/PEP; Certified Professional Secretary Exam.

Estimated Average Completion Time: Bachelors' Degrees: BBA—18 months (full-time); Graduate Degrees: MLA 2-3 years (part-time), MLA 1-2 years; MSM 17 months; MBA 23 months (full-time).

Caveats Regarding Time Estimates: The BBA, MSM, MBA are lockstep, accelerated programs with specified curriculum and learning groups.

Credit Hour Requirements:

Degree	Total Hours	Academic Residency*
Bachelor's	124	44
Graduate (MLA)	36	30
Graduate (MSM)	34	34
Graduate (MBA)	46	46

*Hours that must be earned at the institution exclusive of credit-by-exam, portfolio assessment, etc.

Distance Learning Options: Correspondence Courses; Independent Study; Television Courses.

Student Support Services Available: Academic Advising; Career Counseling; Financial Aid; Job Placement Assistance; Orientation.

Informational Materials Available: Institutional Catalog; Prior Learning Guides; Program Brochure.

Program Age, Enrollment, and Degrees Conferred:

Degree	Year Est.	Current Enrollment	Degrees Conferred
BBA	1988	165	33
MSM	1988	148	42
MBA	1990	73	0
MLA	1975	69	315

Percentage of Bachelor's Degree Holders Admitted to Graduate School: Information not available.

Geographic Admission Restrictions: None.

Tuition and Fees:

	Undergraduate	Graduate
In-State Tuition	$145.00/credit	$145.00/credit
Application Fee	$20.00/credit	$20.00/credit
Graduation Fee	$40.00	$40.00

Other Fees: MSM and MBA tuition $195.00 including computer. Registration fee BBA—$10.00, MSM—$10.00, and MBA—$10.00. Educational resource fee BBA—$900.00, MSM—$980.00, and MBA—$1200.00. MLA varies with each course.

59. Bethel College

Contract Degree Program
300 E. 27th St.
North Newton, KS 67117

Degrees Offered: Bachelor of Science in Business Administration; Bachelor of Science in Nursing; Bachelor of Science in Teacher Education; Bachelor of Social Work; Bachelor of Arts in Teacher Education; and Bachelor of Arts in Liberal Arts.

Program Mission Statement/Description: Program mission is to try to make baccalaureate-level college education as accessible as possible to adult learners in terms of programs, degrees, and course formats; courses offered, times of course offerings, and formats of course offerings; sites and locations of course offerings; and support systems to aid adult students in course and degree programs.

Accreditation: North Central Association of Schools and Colleges.

Admission Requirements: Employment/Experience: depends on degree profession; Essay/Written Work; HS/GED Diploma; Interview; Prior Credits: 60; Recommendations some programs may have an age or out-of-school time requirement.

Credit Awards for Prior Learning: ACE Military Recommendations; ACE/PONSI Recommendations; Portfolio Assessment; Transfer Credit.

Credit Awards for Examinations: ACT Proficiency Exams; CLEP General Exams; CLEP Subject Exams; College Board AP Exams; Departmental Exams.

Estimated Average Completion Time: 4 years (full-time).

Credit Hour Requirements: Bachelors' Degrees 124 total hours.

Limits to Credit Awards for Prior Learning: A candidate for a baccalaureate degree shall have earned at Bethel a minimum of 30 hours of credit. At least 24 of the last 30 hours or 50 of the last 60 hours must be completed in residence. All credit by exam, ACCK interterm courses, and courses taken in approved cooperative programs such as mathematics, computer science, and special education shall count as resident credit. Work taken in Bethel study abroad programs at Wuppertal is also credited as resident credit. An associated degree candidate must earn not less than 30 of the required 62 hours, inclusive of the last 10, at Bethel College. Transfer students must present at least 9 hours of residence work in their major field.

Distance Learning Options: A/V Cassettes; Cooperative Education; Independent Study; Phone/Mail Instruction; Study Guides; Supervised Fieldwork.

Student Support Services Available: Academic Advising; Career Counseling; Counseling/Testing; Financial Aid; Job Placement Assistance; Orientation; Tutoring.

Informational Materials Available: Institutional Catalog; Prior Learning Guides; Program Brochure.

Program Age, Enrollment, and Degrees Conferred:

Degree	Year Est.	Current Enrollment	Degrees Conferred
Contract Degree	1974	10	59

Percentage of Bachelor's Degree Holders Admitted to Graduate School: Estimate of 20 percent of adult learners seek admission to graduate school.

Geographic Admission Restrictions: Determined by student's ability to meet individual course requirements.

Tuition and Fees: Full-time tuition (12-16.5 hours—$3399.00. Fees charged to all full-time students—$96.00. Fees for students who are studying off campus (Urban Life, CUTE, Study Abroad, etc.)—$22.00. Part-time 6-11 hours—$244.00. Part-time 1-5 hours—$122.00. CLEP per credit hour $10.00. Credit-by-Exam Fee—$10.00.

60. Kansas City Kansas Community College

Program for Adult College Education (PACE)
7250 State Ave.–CEB
Kansas City, KS 66112

Degrees Offered: Associate of Arts with Liberal Arts Emphasis; Associate of Applied Science in Carpentry; Associate of General Studies; Associate of Science.

Program Mission Statement/Description: To deliver high-quality, low-cost, and accessible college education to working adults who have been underserved in the past, using a delivery system that enables completion of the AA degree in a reasonable time—2.5 years (5 semesters) or less. Development of individual reading, writing, and analytical skills for maximum democratic and cultural participation by working people in society is the ultimate goal.

Accreditation: North Central Association of College and Schools; National League for Nursing; American Board of Funeral Service Education Inc.

Admission Requirements: HS/GED Diploma; Interview; minimum age 23.

Credit Awards for Prior Learning: ACE Military Recommendations; ACE/PONSI Recommendations; Portfolio Assessment; Transfer Credit.

Other Options: UBC carpentry apprenticeship, or other union apprenticeships; transfer agreement with local Vo-Tech school; Fire Academy; Police Academy; Dale Carnegie Speech course; and Bethany Hospital (Radiology and Respiratory Therapy).

Limits to Credit Awards for Prior Learning: 30 hours cumulative. 15 hours in any one category on testing. 15-hour residency required. Last 10 hours must be completed at Kansas City Kansas Community College.

Credit Awards for Examinations: CLEP General Exams; CLEP Subject Exams; College Board AP Exams; DANTES Subject Tests; Departmental Exams; CPS exam; International Baccalaureate Program.

Limits to Credit Awards for Examinations: CLEP Subject—15, College Board—0, Dept.—15, CLEP General—30, DANTES—15, CPS—15, IBP—30.

Estimated Average Completion Time: 5-10 years (part-time), 5 semesters (2.5 years) or less (full-time).

Caveats Regarding Time Estimates: PACE students typically reduce degree completion time through transfer credits. Experiential or awarded credit tends not to transfer to 4-year institutions. Part-time study is possible but lengthens degree completion time. PACE is geared to full-time students who want to graduate in 5 semesters.

Credit Hour Requirements: 60 hours total; 15 hours academic residency (hours that must be earned at the institution exclusive of credit-by-exam, portfolio assessment, etc.).

Distance Learning Options: A/V Cassettes; Independent Study; Phone/Mail Instruction; Television Courses; Weekend Seminar.

Student Support Services Available: Academic Advising; Career Counseling; Counseling/Testing; Financial Aid; Job Placement Assistance; Orientation; Tutoring; Adult Transfer Option Information for Bachelor Completion.

Informational Materials Available: Institutional Catalog; Program Brochure; Student Handbook; Financial Aid Information.

Program Age, Enrollment, and Degrees Conferred:

Degree	Year Est.	Current Enrollment	Degrees Conferred
PACE AA	1982	350	400

Geographic Admission Restrictions: None.

Tuition and Fees: In-State Tuition $25.00 per credit; Out-of-State Tuition $68.00 per credit; Graduation Fee $20.00; Credit-by-Exam Fee $25.00 per hour; Late enrollment $5.00, Drop/Add $1.00 per class.

Other Pertinent Information: Off-campus classes are available in different inner-city locations, suburban communities, or at the worksite. Retention rate is much higher than average. Percentage of Honor Roll students is much higher than average.

61. Ottawa University

1001 S. Cedar
Ottawa, KS 66067

Degrees Offered: Bachelor of Arts in Business Administration; Bachelor of Arts in Health Care and Administration; Bachelor of Arts in Human Resources; Bachelor of Arts in Human Services-Psychology; Bachelor of Arts in Education; Master of Arts in Human Resources. Individual major and other selected social science and humanities focus areas. Master of Arts in Human Resources.

Program Mission Statement/Description: The purpose of Ottawa University is to provide the highest possible quality education for the development of individual students in the context of its Christian heritage, its liberal arts emphasis, and its coeducational community of concern and scholarship. Among its stated purposes, the University seeks to admit and retain students interested in completing a college degree through two nonresidential centers in Kansas City, Kansas, and Phoenix, Arizona.

Accreditation: North Central Association of Colleges and Schools.

Admission Requirements:

Undergraduate	Graduate
HS/GED Diploma	Undergraduate Degree
Interview	Interview
Essay/Written Work	Essay/Written Work
Recommendations	

Other Admission Requirements: The BA program requires an initial general education course—the Pro Seminar. The MA program requires evidence of a knowledge of introductory statistics. A foundation of 4 core courses is prior to courses in an area of concentration.

Credit Awards for Prior Learning (undergraduate program only): ACE Military Recommendations; ACE/PONSI Recommendations; Portfolio Assessment; Transfer Credit.

Other Options: Certain health care programs (e.g., nursing and respiratory therapy) have been evaluated for awarding credit.

Limits to Credit Awards for Prior Learning: Assessment of courses completed and transcripted by unaccredited institutions may be made, and acceptable credits will be transferred and recorded after a student has successfully completed 20 semester hours of credit with the university. In the MA program, a maximum of 9 credit hours of graduate study completed at an accredited institution with a grade of B or higher may be accepted into the degree program.

Credit Awards for Examinations (undergraduate program only): ACT Proficiency Exams; CLEP General Exams; CLEP Subject Exams; College Board AP Exams; DANTES Subject Tests; Departmental Exams.

Limits to Credit Awards for Examinations: CLEP and other lower division credits limited to a maximum of 72 semester hours of credit toward the BA degree.

Estimated Average Completion Time: Bachelors' Degrees: 2.5 years (part-time); Graduate Degrees: 2 years (part-time).

Caveats Regarding Time Estimates: The typical student entering the BA degree completion program has 2 years of study (60-72 semester hours) prior to entry into the program. Many students also qualify for some credit through portfolio assessment.

Credit Hour Requirements:

Degree	Total Hours	Academic Residency*
Bachelor's	128	24
Graduate (MA)	36	27

*Hours that must be earned at the institution exclusive of credit-by-exam, portfolio assessment, etc.

Distance Learning Options: Electronic Mail (Graduate only); Independent Study (Bachelor only); Supervised Fieldwork; Directed study under the guidance of a faculty member.

Student Support Services Available: Academic Advising; Career Counseling; Financial Aid; Orientation; Tutoring; Life/Work Planning Workshops and Job Search Workshops.

Informational Materials Available: Institutional Catalog; Program Brochure; Interview with faculty in Kansas City or Phoenix strongly recommended.

Program Age, Enrollment, and Graduates:

Degree	Year Est.	Current Enrollment	Degrees Conferred
BA—Kansas City	1974	231	1833
BA—Phoenix	1977	226	479
MA in Human Resources	1988	47	27

Percentage of Bachelor's Degree Holders Admitted to Graduate School: Information not available.

Geographic Admission Restrictions: Students must reside in metropolitan Kansas City or Phoenix or be able to come to these centers for advising/instruction or live in areas where groups of students study together with faculty sent from either Kansas City or Phoenix. This last option has included Wilmington (DE), New Orleans (LA), and Milwaukee (WI).

Tuition and Fees:

	Undergraduate	Graduate
In-State Tuition	$122.00/credit	$175.00/credit
Out-of-State Tuition	$122.00/credit	$175.00/credit
Application Fee	$25.00	$40.00
Graduation Fee	$40.00	$50.00
Credit-by-Exam Fee	$75.00	

Other Fees: Portfolio assessment fee $300; fee per semester hour of credit awarded through portfolio assessment $40.

Other Pertinent Information: Other locations: Ottawa University Kansas City, 10865 Grandview, Overland Park, KS 66210. Ottawa University Phoenix, 2340 W. Mission Lane, Phoenix, AZ 85021.

Kentucky

62. Campbellsville College

Organizational Administration Major
200 W. College St.
Campbellsville, KY 42718

Degrees Offered: Bachelor of Science in Organizational Administration.

Program Mission Statement/Description: The Organizational Administration major is intended to serve nontraditional (adult) learners, preparing them for administrative leadership positions, with coursework presented from a Christian perspective.

Accreditation: Southern Association of Colleges and Schools.

Admission Requirements: HS/GED Diploma; Prior Credits: 60 semester hours.

Other Admission Requirements: Cumulative GPA 2.25 or above. Completion of 6 hours Freshman English with C or better grades. Completion of College Algebra course or equivalent. Age 23 (conditional acceptance for minor exceptions by Admissions Committee approval).

Credit Awards for Prior Learning: ACE Military Recommendations; Portfolio Assessment; Transfer Credit.

Limits to Credit Awards for Prior Learning: Portfolio assessment—32 semester hours maximum.

Credit Awards for Examinations: CLEP General Exams; CLEP Subject Exams.

Estimated Average Completion Time: Bachelors' Degrees: 4-6 years (part-time), 4 years (full-time).

Caveats Regarding Time Estimates: Excludes students who enroll in single courses.

Credit Hour Requirements: 128 hours total; 30 hours academic residency (hours that must be earned at the institution exclusive of credit-by-exam, portfolio assessment, etc.).

Distance Learning Options: Cooperative Education; Correspondence Courses; Independent Study; Supervised Fieldwork.

Student Support Services Available: Academic Advising; Financial Aid; Job Placement Assistance; Orientation; Tutoring.

Informational Materials Available: Institutional Catalog; Program Brochure.

Program Age, Enrollment, and Degrees Conferred:

Degree	Year Est.	Current Enrollment	Degrees Conferred
BS (Org. Admin.)	1990	13	0

Percentage of Bachelor's Degree Holders Admitted to Graduate School: Information not available.

Geographic Admission Restrictions: None.

Tuition and Fees: In-State Tuition $145.00 per credit; Graduation Fee $10.00; Credit-by-Exam Fee CLEP Standard Charge; GRE Exams.

Other Pertinent Information: A degree-completion major for students with 60 semester hours completed is offered in the evening program and at off-campus sites; program is intended for nontraditional students who work days. Experiential learning credit based on work experience or other experience may be coordinated with the major in Organizational Administration to complete a degree.

63. Midway College

512 E. Stephens St.
Midway, KY 40347

Degrees Offered: Associate of Arts in Business Administration; Associate of Arts in Computer Information Systems; Associate's Degree in Nursing; Bachelor of Arts in Business Administration.

Program Mission Statement/Description: To provide a quality education for working adults utilizing a 9-week modular scheduling system so that nontraditional students have the opportunity to complete a college degree in the evenings. The mission also requires that students provide service to the community.

Accreditation: Southern Association of Colleges and Schools; National League for Nursing.

Admission Requirements: HS/GED Diploma; Interview.

Credit Awards for Prior Learning: ACE/PONSI Recommendations; Transfer Credit.

Limits to Credit Awards for Prior Learning: 32 transfer hours for associate's degree; 90 hours for baccalaureate degree.

Credit Awards for Examinations: CLEP General Exams; CLEP Subject Exams; College Board AP Exams.

Estimated Average Completion Time: Associates' Degrees: 4 years (part-time), 2.5 years (full-time); Bachelors' Degrees: 6-6.5 years (part-time), 4.5-5 years (full-time).

Credit Hour Requirements: Information not available.

Distance Learning Options: Independent Study; Supervised Fieldwork.

Student Support Services Available: Academic Advising; Career Counseling; Counseling/Testing; Financial Aid; Job Placement Assistance; Orientation; Tutoring.

Informational Materials Available: Institutional Catalog; Program Brochure.

Program Age, Enrollment, and Degrees Conferred:

Degree	Year Est.	Current Enrollment	Degrees Conferred
AA in Bus. Admin.	1988	0	0
BA in Bus. Admin.	1990	6	0
AA in Nursing	1990	40	0

Percentage of Bachelor's Degree Holders Admitted to Graduate School: Information not available.

Geographic Admission Restrictions: None.

Tuition and Fees: In-State Tuition $110.00 per credit; Application Fee $15.00; Nursing is $110 per contact hour.

---

64. Spalding University

Weekend College
851 S. Fourth St.
Louisville, KY 40203

Degrees Offered: Bachelor of Arts or Bachelor of Science degree with majors in Business Administration, Communication, Liberal Studies, and Nursing. Associate of Arts in Business Administration.

Program Mission Statement/Description: Spalding University is an urban, independent, coeducational university whose mission is to offer undergraduate education of high quality in the liberal arts and sciences and in selected professional areas of study. A Weekend College was established in 1980, which offers adult learners an opportunity to earn a degree by enrolling in specially designed classes. These classes meet only 5 times within a 11-12 week term, and the main order of business is learning. The Weekend College student pursues an education while actively involved with family and career responsibilities, integrates study and work in a unique way, meets new people, explores new ideas, reexamines the past, and searches for a new future.

Accreditation: Southern Association of Colleges and Schools; National League for Nursing; National Council for the Accreditation of Teacher Education; Council on Social Work Education.

Admission Requirements: The Weekend College maintains a flexible admission policy. For the adult learner, recent achievements and motivation to learn are more reliable indicators of success in a college degree program than are the records of high school or college classes taken a number of years previously. For this reason, admission to Spalding University Weekend College is based on an interview with the Weekend College director. The initial interview is designed to assist adults in assessing whether college, in general, or this program, in particular, will be a beneficial learning experience for them. The joint decision concerning admission to Weekend College is made as a result of the interview process.

Credit Awards for Prior Learning: ACE Military Recommendations; ACE/PONSI Recommendations; Portfolio Assessment; Transfer Credit.

Limits to Credit Awards for Prior Learning: Candidates for a Spalding University degree must complete 32 of the last 42 semester hours of coursework at the university. Extrainstitutional or experiential learning may not be applied to the last 32 semester hours. Credit is considered only for those students who are matriculating for a degree at Spalding University and is awarded at the time of approval and payment of fees. Any extrainstitutional or experiential learning credit must fit the student's degree requirements, at least as electives. Not more than 60 credit hours required for graduation are awarded for experiential learning. No more than 30 of these credits may be awarded on the basis of portfolio evaluation, and those may not be applied to the last 32 hours.

Credit Awards for Examinations: ACT Proficiency Exams; CLEP General Exams; CLEP Subject Exams; DANTES Subject Tests; Departmental Exams.

Estimated Average Completion Time: Associates' Degrees: 2-3 years (part-time), 2 years (full-time); Bachelors' Degrees: 4 years.

Caveats Regarding Time Estimates: Weekend College has 4 terms per academic year where a student may take a maximum of 9 semester hours per term. This allows a student to complete 36 hours per year. Because most students transfer in credits from other accredited universities and use the experiential learning process, the majority receive a bachelor's degree in less than 4 years.

Credit Hour Requirements:

Degree	Total Hours	Academic Residency*
Associate's	63	32
Bachelor's	128-129	32

*Hours that must be earned at the institution exclusive of credit-by-exam, portfolio assessment, etc.

Distance Learning Options: Cooperative Education; Independent Study; Supervised Fieldwork.

Student Support Services Available: Academic Advising; Career Counseling; Counseling/Testing; Financial Aid; Job Placement Assistance; Orientation; Tutoring.

Informational Materials Available: Exam Preparation Guides; Institutional Catalog; Prior Learning Guides; Program Brochure.

Program Age, Enrollment, and Degrees Conferred: Information not available.

Percentage of Bachelor's Degree Holders Admitted to Graduate School: Information not available.

Geographic Admission Restrictions: None.

Tuition and Fees: In-State Tuition: $200.00 per credit; Out-of-State Tuition: $200.00 per credit; Application Fee: $20.00; Graduation Fee: $50.00; Credit-by-Exam Fee: 1/3 tuition. All undergraduate tuition is $200.00 per credit for less than 12 hours and $3300.00 per semester for 12-18 credit hours or $7,100.00 per year for 36 credit hours from first semester through summer sessions.

Louisiana

65. Loyola University

Loyola Institute for Ministry Extension Program
Box 67
6363 Saint Charles Ave.
New Orleans, LA 70118

Degrees Offered: Master of Religious Education; Master of Pastoral Studies.

Program Mission Statement/Description: Loyola's Institute for Ministry Extension (LIMEX) program mission is to provide a professionally oriented program of graduate education which seeks to increase the competencies of practitioners in the areas of religious education and pastoral ministries. LIMEX responds to the expressed educational needs of dioceses with little or no access to residential programs by offering on-site programs. LIMEX addresses adult practitioners within the actual context of their ministry. The educational process is carried out in learning groups, each led by a LIMEX certified facilitator. Sessions for each course employ a learning design in which lectures in printed form and other required and suggested readings are correlated with the participant's experience by means of reflective processes assisted by video tapes.

Accreditation: Southern Association of Colleges and Schools.

Admission Requirements: Essay/Written Work; Recommendations; Undergraduate Degree; 2.5 GPA.

Credit Awards for Prior Learning: None.

Credit Awards for Examinations: None.

Estimated Average Completion Time: 3.5 years (part-time).

Caveats Regarding Time Estimates: Students complete the degree in an agreed upon time frame based on a consensus decision of their learning group.

Credit Hour Requirements: 30 credit hours.

Distance Learning Options: None.

Student Support Services Available: Academic Advising; Orientation.

Informational Materials Available: Institutional Catalog; Program Brochure; Program Prospectus.

Program Age, Enrollment, and Graduates:

Degree	Year Est.	Current Enrollment	Degrees Conferred
MRE, MPS	1983	435	481

Geographic Admission Restrictions: None.

Tuition and Fees: In-State Tuition $123.00 per credit; Application Fee $20.00; Outside Reading Fee $20.00.

66. Tulane University

University College
125 Gibson Hall
New Orleans, LA 70118

Degrees Offered: Bachelor of Arts in Paralegal Studies; Bachelor of Arts in Social Studies; Bachelor of Science in Computer Information Systems; Bachelor of General Studies; Associate of Arts in Paralegal Studies; Associate of Science in Computer Information Systems.

Program Mission Statement/Description: From its inception, Tulane has accepted a basic responsibility for the continuing education of adults. University College shares in the traditions of Tulane, extending the commitments and resources of the university beyond customary academic boundaries. By serving the educational needs and interests of diverse populations, University College provides access to Tulane's academic environment for adults returning for part-time study, for international students, for the employed seeking to improve their skills, and for other special students. In addition, those of precollege age and senior citizens enjoy the resource of Tulane through University College programs.

Accreditation: Southern Association of Colleges and Schools.

Admission Requirements: HS/GED Diploma; Interview.

Credit Awards for Prior Learning: Transfer Credit.

Credit Awards for Examinations: CLEP Subject Exams.

Estimated Average Completion Time: Associates' Degrees: 3 years (part-time), 2 years (full-time); Bachelors' Degrees: 6 years (part-time), 4 years (full-time); Graduate Degrees: MLA: 2-3 years (part-time), 12-15 months (full-time).

Credit Hour Requirements:

Degree	Total Hours	Academic Residency*
Associate's	64	32
Bachelor's	128	32

*Hours that must be earned at the institution exclusive of credit-by-exam, portfolio assessment, etc.

Distance Learning Options: Independent Study; Supervised Fieldwork.

Student Support Services Available: Academic Advising; Career Counseling; Counseling/Testing; Financial Aid; Job Placement Assistance; Orientation; Tutoring.

Informational Materials Available: Institutional Catalog; Program Brochure.

Program Age, Enrollment, and Degrees Conferred:

Degree	Year Est.	Current Enrollment	Degrees Conferred
BA	1940	800	799
BS	1940	400	698
BGS	1980	180	101
AA	1988	90	47
AS	1988	40	5

Percentage of Bachelor's Degree Holders Admitted to Graduate School: Information not available.

Geographic Admission Restrictions: None.

Tuition and Fees: In-State Tuition $129.00 per credit; Out-of-State Tuition $129.00 per credit; Application Fee $15.00.

Maine

67. University of Maine

Bachelor of University Studies Degree Program
122 Chadbourne Hall
Orono, ME 04469

Degrees Offered: Bachelor of University Studies.

Program Mission Statement/Description: The Bachelor of University Studies Degree Program presents to the highly motivated, adult, part-time student the opportunity to coordinate the offerings of the Continuing Education Division and summer session into an individually planned degree program. This program is designed specifically and solely for adult part-time students. Each student, in consultation with an academic advisor, designs a program leading to specific educational goals but not necessarily within any one department, division, school, or college.

Accreditation: New England Association of Schools and Colleges, Inc.

Admission Requirements: Essay/Written Work; HS/GED Diploma; Interview; Prior Credits: 18 credit hours; Recommendations; Minimum GPA 2.0.

Credit Awards for Prior Learning: ACE Military Recommendations; Transfer Credit.

Limits to Credit Awards for Prior Learning: Credits transferred from regionally accredited institutions only.

Credit Awards for Examinations: ACT Proficiency Exams; CLEP General Exams; CLEP Subject Exams; College Board AP Exams; Departmental Exams.

Estimated Average Completion Time: 8 semester hours (part-time), 4 semester hours (full-time).

Caveats Regarding Time Estimates: Many students, particularly classified employees of the university, will take one course per semester including summer session.

Credit Hour Requirements: 120 hours total; 30 hours academic residency (hours that must be earned at the institution exclusive of credit-by-exam, portfolio assessment, etc.).

Distance Learning Options: Cooperative Education; Independent Study; Supervised Fieldwork; Television Courses.

Student Support Services Available: Academic Advising; Career Counseling; Counseling/Testing; Financial Aid; Job Placement Assistance; Orientation; Tutoring.

Informational Materials Available: Institutional Catalog; Program Brochure.

Program Age, Enrollment, and Graduates:

Degree	Year Est.	Current Enrollment	Degrees Conferred
BUS	1976	219	81

Percentage of Bachelor's Degree Holders Admitted to Graduate School: Records indicate 4 graduates have earned master degrees; some have earned PhDs.

Geographic Admission Restrictions: None.

Tuition and Fees:

	Undergraduate	Graduate
In-State Tuition	$69.00/credit	$90.00/credit
Out-of-State Tuition	$195.00/credit	$254.00/credit
Application Fee	$20.00	$25.00
Graduation Fee	$20.00	$20.00

Maryland

68. Anne Arundel Community College

Continuing Education and Credit Program
101 College Pkwy.
Arnold, MD 21012

Degrees Offered: Associate of Arts.

Program Mission Statement/Description: Weekend College and Telecourse offerings are designed for students who want to begin or continue their college education but cannot fit regular class attendance into their busy schedules. Credit classes are available in nontraditional formats to meet students' needs.

Accreditation: Middle States Association of Colleges and Schools.

Admission Requirements: HS/GED Diploma.

Credit Awards for Prior Learning: ACE Military Recommendations; Transfer Credit.

Limits to Credit Awards for Prior Learning: No limit; however, students must satisfy 30 credit residency requirement; 50 percent of credit counting toward degree completion must be earned in the classroom.

Credit Awards for Examinations: ACT Proficiency Exams; CLEP General Exams; CLEP Subject Exams; College Board AP Exams; DANTES Subject Tests; Departmental Exams.

Estimated Average Completion Time: 4 years (part-time), 2 years (full-time).

Credit Hour Requirements: 60 hours total; 30 hours of academic residency (hours that must be earned at the institution exclusive of credit-by-exam, portfolio assessment, etc.).

Distance Learning Options: Cooperative Education; Independent Study; Television Courses.

Student Support Services Available: Career Counseling; Counseling/Testing; Financial Aid; Job Placement Assistance; Orientation Academic Advising; Tutoring.

Informational Materials Available: Institutional Catalog; Program Brochure.

Program Age, Enrollment, and Degrees Conferred: Information not available.

Geographic Admission Restrictions: None.

Tuition and Fees: In-State Tuition $88.00 per credit; Out-of-State Tuition $176.00 per credit; In-County Fee $40.00; Graduation Fee $20.00; Credit-by-Exam Fee $15.00; Registration fee $20.00.

69. College of Notre Dame of Maryland

Weekend College
4701 N. Charles St.
Baltimore, MD 21210

Degrees Offered: Bachelor of Arts in Business; Bachelor of Arts in Communication Arts; Bachelor of Arts in Computer Information Systems; Bachelor of Arts in Elementary Education; Bachelor of Arts in Human Services; Bachelor of Arts in Liberal Arts; Bachelor of Arts in Religious Studies; Bachelor of Science in Nursing.

Program Mission Statement/Description: In 1975, the College of Notre Dame of Maryland responded to the need of employed adults to earn a bachelor's degree by establishing the Weekend College. The Weekend College is designed to help women and men meet new educational demands—career related or personal—by offering degree programs on weekends. The Weekend College at the College of Notre Dame of Maryland is founded on the principles of adult learning and on the belief that adults learn best in an environment which considers their needs and life responsibilities. The program enables students to successfully integrate their education with their individual life-styles. Learning takes place within the framework of a unique and stimulating educational structure. Teacher and student form a partnership of participation and interaction. At the same time, students are encouraged to realize their full potential through increased awareness of themselves and their environment. The day-to-day pursuits of living are looked upon, not as a barrier to higher education, but as a stimulus for increased learning.

Accreditation: Middle States Association of Colleges and Schools; National League for Nursing.

Admission Requirements: Essay/Written Work; HS/GED Diploma; Interview.

Credit Awards for Prior Learning: ACE Military Recommendations; ACE/PONSI Recommendations; Portfolio Assessment; Transfer Credit.

Limits to Credit Awards for Prior Learning: Total credits cannot exceed 30 credits.

Credit Awards for Examinations: ACT Proficiency Exams; CLEP Subject Exams.

Estimated Average Completion Time: 5-7 years (part-time).

Credit Hour Requirements: 120 hours total; 45 hours academic residency (hours that must be earned at the institution exclusive of credit-by-exam, portfolio asessment, etc.).

Distance Learning Options: Independent Study; Supervised Fieldwork.

Student Support Services Available: Academic Advising; Career Counseling; Counseling/Testing; Financial Aid; Job Placement Assistance; Orientation.

Informational Materials Available: Program Brochure.

Program Age, Enrollment, and Degrees Conferred:

Degree	Year Est.	Current Enrollment	Degrees Conferred
BA	1975	1150	600
BSN	1978	250	500

Percentage of Bachelor's Degree Holders Admitted to Graduate School: Information not available.

Geographic Admission Restrictions: None.

Tuition and Fees:

	Undergraduate	Graduate
In-State Tuition	$136.00/credit	$169.00/credit
Out-of-State Tuition	$136.00/credit	$169.00/credit
Application Fee	$25.00	$25.00
Graduation Fee	$50.00	$50.00

Other Fees: Registration fee $15.00.

70. Columbia Union College

Adult Evening Program
7600 Flower Ave.
Takoma Park, MD 20912

Degrees Offered: Bachelor of Science in Business Administration; Bachelor of Science in Health Care Administration; Bachelor of Science in Organization Management.

Program Mission Statement/Description: The Columbia Union College Adult Evening Program offers working professionals who have earned at least 60 semester hours of credit an opportunity to complete a baccalaureate degree in as little as 18 months by attending class one night per week.

Accreditation: Middle States Association of Colleges and Schools.

Admission Requirements: Employment/Experience; Essay/Written Work; HS/GED Diploma; Interview; Prior Credits: 60; Cumulative GPA 2.0 minimum.

Credit Awards for Prior Learning: ACE Military Recommendations; ACE/PONSI Recommendations; Portfolio Assessment; Transfer Credit.

Limits to Credit Awards for Prior Learning: 24 semester hours portfolio credit; 70 semester hours transfer from 2-year college.

Credit Awards for Examinations: ACT Proficiency Exams; CLEP General Exams; CLEP Subject Exams; College Board AP Exams; DANTES Subject Tests; Departmental Exams.

Limits to Credit Awards for Examinations: 24 hours credit by examination.

Estimated Average Completion Time: 18 months (full-time).

Credit Hour Requirements: 120 hours total; 36 hours academic residency (hours that must be earned at the institution exclusive of credit-by-exam, portfolio assessment, etc.).

Distance Learning Options: None.

Student Support Services Available: Academic Advising; Counseling/Testing; Financial Aid; Orientation.

Informational Materials Available: Institutional Catalog; Prior Learning Guides; Program Brochure.

Program Age, Enrollment, and Degrees Conferred:

Degree	Year Est.	Current Enrollment	Degrees Conferred
BS	1984	350	550

Percentage of Bachelor's Degree Holders Admitted to Graduate School: 25 percent.

Geographic Admission Restrictions: None.

Tuition and Fees: In-State Tuition $175.00 per credit; Out-of-State Tuition $175.00 per credit; Application Fee $25.00; Graduation Fee $195.00; Credit-by-Exam Fee $35.00.

Other Pertinent Information: Classes in each major run sequentially; each class is from 6:00-10:10 pm for 6 weeks.

71. Montgomery Community College

Weekend College Program
20200 Observation Dr.
Germantown, MD 20876

Degrees Offered: Associate of Arts in Computer Applications; Associate of Arts in General Studies; Associate of Arts with electives in Business Transfer; Desktop Publishing and Management; Humanities; Social Science; Technical Writing.

Program Mission Statement/Description: The Weekend College program offered by the Germantown campus of Montgomery College is designed to provide a solid general education and technical skills in selected fields of study via an intense but convenient class schedule.

Accreditation: Middle States Association of Colleges and Schools.

Admission Requirements: HS/GED Diploma; assessment testing in English, mathematics, and reading.

Credit Awards for Prior Learning: ACE Military Recommendations; ACE/PONSI Recommendations; Transfer Credit.

Limits to Credit Awards for Prior Learning: 45 transfer; 24 military (USAFI) and service-training.

Credit Awards for Examinations: CLEP Subject Exams; College Board AP Exams.

Estimated Average Completion Time: 3 years (part-time).

Caveats Regarding Time Estimates: The maximum a student can take is 3 courses at a time which, if taken, will complete the degree in 3 years. Most students take only one course at a time.

Credit Hour Requirements: 62 hours total; 17 hours academic residency (hours that must be earned at the institution exclusive of credit-by-exam, portfolio assessment, etc.).

Distance Learning Options: Although not offered by the Weekend College program, students may complete some courses through the Montgomery College of the Air Telecourse and electronic mail programs.

Student Support Services Available: Academic Advising; Career Counseling; Counseling/Testing; Financial Aid; Job Placement Assistance; Orientation.

Informational Materials Available: Institutional Catalog; Program Brochure.

Program Age, Enrollment, and Degrees Conferred:

Degree	Year Est.	Current Enrollment	Degrees Conferred
Associate's	1990	550	0

Geographic Admission Restrictions: None.

Tuition and Fees: In-State Tuition $47.00 per credit; Out-of-County $89.00 per credit; Out-of-State Tuition $123.00 per credit. A Consolidated Fee of 10 percent of tuition.

72. Mount Saint Mary's College

Bachelor of General Studies Program
Emmitsburg, MD 21727

Degrees Offered: Bachelor of General Studies.

Program Mission Statement/Description: Mount Saint Mary's College offers a Bachelor of Arts and Bachelor of Science in General Studies to meet the educational needs of adults whose formal education has been interrupted for any reason. Men and women who can add work/life experience to earlier college training may complete their requirements for a bachelor's degree.

Accreditation: Middle States Association of Colleges and Schools.

Admission Requirements: HS/GED Diploma; Interview; Prior Credits: 85.

Credit Awards for Prior Learning: ACE Military Recommendations; ACE/PONSI Recommendations; Portfolio Assessment; Transfer Credit.

Limits to Credit Awards for Prior Learning: USAFI—30 hours; Military Service Schools—9 hours; diploma nursing programs; civil service training programs; courses and institutes sponsored by industry and business —30 hours;

proficiency in communication arts; foreign language, music, art and significant community service—30 hours; lifework experience that is considered truly educational—30 hours.

Credit Awards for Examinations: ACT Proficiency Exams; CLEP General Exams; CLEP Subject Exams; College Board AP Exams; DANTES Subject Tests.

Limits to Credit Awards for Examinations: CLEP—30 hours.

Estimated Average Completion Time: 3-4 years (part-time), 3 semesters (full-time).

Credit Hour Requirements: 120 hours total; 30 hours academic residency (hours that must be earned at the institution exclusive of credit-by-exam, portfolio assessment, etc.).

Distance Learning Options: Independent Study; Supervised Fieldwork.

Student Support Services Available: Academic Advising; Career Counseling; Counseling/Testing; Financial Aid; Job Placement Assistance; Orientation; Tutoring.

Informational Materials Available: Exam Preparation Guides; Institutional Catalog; Program Brochure.

Program Age, Enrollment, and Degrees Conferred:

Degree	Year Est.	Current Enrollment	Degrees Conferred
BA/BS General Studies	1971	15	550

Percentage of Bachelor's Degree Holders Admitted to Graduate School: 20 percent.

Geographic Admission Restrictions: None.

Tuition and Fees: In-State Tuition $59.00 per credit; Out-of-State Tuition $168.00 per credit; Application Fee $25.00; Graduation Fee $20.00.

73. University of Maryland University College

University Blvd. at Adelphi Rd.
College Park, MD 20742

Degrees Offered: Bachelor of Arts; Bachelor of Science; Associate in Arts (available only to active-duty military personnel); Masters of General Administration; Master of Science in Computer Systems Management; Master of Science in Engineering Management; Master of International Management; Master of Science in Technology Management; Master of Science in Telecommunications Management.

Program Mission Statement/Description: The mission of the University of Maryland University College is to provide access to public higher education for adult learners. University of Maryland University College is foremost a teaching institution, although applied research and public service are also integral to its mission. University College offers a primary concentration leading to either a Bachelor of Arts or a Bachelor of Science in 32 areas including management, fire science, computer science, and the social sciences. The Graduate School of the University of Maryland University College is dedicated to providing high-quality programs for midcareer individuals who want to further develop their professional management and technical abilities. Our 6 graduate degree programs are designed specifically to combine management theories and concepts with their practical application in various specialized areas and technical disciplines. Our faculty has extensive experience, many in a technical environment, and is selected on the basis of managerial expertise, teaching ability, and advanced education.

Accreditation: Middle States Association of Colleges and Schools.

Admission Requirements:

Undergraduate	Graduate
HS/GED Diploma	Undergraduate Degree
Employment/Experience: Varies	

Other Admission Requirements: MS in Engineering Management requires acceptable scores on the GRE or GMAT. Minimum GPA requirements vary for each degree program. All executive degree programs require a personal interview.

Credit Awards for Prior Learning: ACE Military Recommendations; ACE/PONSI Recommendations; Portfolio Assessment; Transfer Credit.

Limits to Credit Awards for Prior Learning: Not applicable for graduate studies.

Credit Awards for Examinations: ACT Proficiency Exams; CLEP General Exams; CLEP Subject Exams; College Board AP Exams; DANTES Subject Tests; Departmental Exams.

Estimated Average Completion Time: Varies for all degrees.

Caveats Regarding Time Estimates: 7-year time limit for all graduate programs.

Credit Hour Requirements:

Degree	Total Hours	Academic Residency*
Associate's	60	15
Bachelor's	120	30
Graduate	36	30

*Hours that must be earned at the institution exclusive of credit-by-exam, portfolio assessment, etc.

Distance Learning Options: A/V Cassettes; Cooperative Education; Correspondence Courses; Electronic Mail; Independent Study; Phone/Mail Instruction; Study Guides; Supervised Fieldwork; Television Courses.

Student Support Services Available: Academic Advising; Career Counseling; Counseling/Testing; Financial Aid; Orientation; Tutoring.

Informational Materials Available: Institutional Catalog; Prior Learning Guides; Program Brochure.

Program Age, Enrollment, and Degrees Conferred:

Degree	Year Est.	Current Enrollment	Degrees Conferred
Bachelor's	1948	11715	Unknown
Master's	1978	3679	724

Percentage of Bachelor's Degree Holders Admitted to Graduate School: Information not available.

Geographic Admission Restrictions: Bachelor of Science in Fire Science is offered in the District of Columbia and in the following states: Delaware, Maryland, New Jersey, North Carolina, West Virginia, Virginia.

Tuition and Fees:

	Undergraduate	Graduate
In-State Tuition	$127.00/credit	$190.00/credit
Out-of-State Tuition	$132.00/credit	$260.00/credit
Application Fee	$25.00	$25.00
Graduation Fee	$25.00	$25.00
Course Registration Fee	$3.00	$5.00
Credit-by-Exam Fee: Current tuition rate		

Massachusetts

74. Bentley College

175 Forest St.
Morison Hall, Rm. 200
Waltham, MA 02154

Degrees Offered: Bachelor of Science in Professional Studies.

Program Mission Statement/Description: Offering students increased options in academic concentrations, the Bachelor of Science in Professional Studies was developed to expand the educational and career path opportunities available to Bentley graduates. The degree program combines the fundamentals of liberal arts with a strong foundation in introductory and advanced business courses in addition to a specialization in one of the following disciplines: government, applied ethics, behavioral science, communication, or legal studies. The liberal arts electives can be fulfilled by a variety of alternative academic formats. A directed study or seminar can be arranged under the guidance of a faculty member. This individualized project gives students the chance to research a specialized topic. Additionally, internships provide students with work experience in their area of secondary specialization and can be arranged through the appropriate department.

Accreditation: New England Association of Schools and Colleges Inc.; American Assembly of Collegiate Schools of Business.

Admission Requirements: HS/GED Diploma.

Other Admission Requirements: Students must complete 5 courses, including a first-year English course and a college math course with a 2.0 cumulative average to matriculate into the degree program.

Credit Awards for Prior Learning: ACE/PONSI Recommendations*; Portfolio Assessment; Transfer Credit.

Limits to Credit Awards for Prior Learning: No more than 75 credits (out of a total of 120 credits) may be awarded through transfer credit. However, students must complete a residency requirement of 45 Bentley credits to graduate.

Credit Awards for Examinations: ACT Proficiency Exams*; CLEP General Exams; CLEP Subject Exams; College Board AP Exams; Departmental Exams.

*In process of reviewing for applicability.

Limits to Credit Awards for Examinations: No more than 30 credits in proficiency and CLEP credit may be awarded.

Estimated Average Completion Time: 7-8 years (part-time).

Caveats Regarding Time Estimates: Estimate completion time assumes that students start the program without bringing in any transfer credit. Eighty percent of degree-seeking students transfer in an average of 11 courses out of a 40-course BS program, so they may complete in a 5-6 year time frame. Some students enroll full-time periodically to shorten their time spent pursuing the degree.

Credit Hour Requirements: 120 hours total; 45 hours academic residency (hours that must be earned at the institution exclusive of credit-by-exam, portfolio assessment, etc.).

Distance Learning Options: Independent Study; Supervised Fieldwork.

Student Support Services Available: Academic Advising; Career Counseling; Counseling/Testing; Financial Aid; Job Placement Assistance; Orientation; Tutoring. A variety of student services and academic support workshops as well as the library and athletic facilities are available to students.

Informational Materials Available: Exam Preparation Guides; Institutional Catalog; Prior Learning Guides; Program Brochure.

Program Age, Enrollment, and Degrees Conferred:

Degree	Year Est.	Current Enrollment	Degrees Conferred
BS Prof. Studies	1986	40	3

Percentage of Bachelor's Degree Holders Admitted to Graduate School: Information not available.

Geographic Admission Restrictions: None.

Tuition and Fees: In-State Tuition $625.00 per credit; Application Fee $45.00; Graduation Fee $35.00; Credit-by-Exam Fee $25.00.

Other Pertinent Information: Required and elective courses are available on weeknights and Saturdays during 2 7-week summer sessions each year and during intensive one-week sessions in the winter session and in the summer.

75. Boston Architectural Center

320 Newbury St.
Boston, MA 02115

Degrees Offered: Bachelor of Architecture.

Program Mission Statement/Description: The mission of the Boston Architectural Center (BAC) is to prepare students for the practice of architecture, interior design, and the allied professions. Now in its 103rd year, the BAC continues to pursue its original purposes by administering the only architecture degree-granting, concurrent work curriculum program in the United States. It also continues to offer a stimulating and informal gathering place for practitioners in the profession.

Accreditation: New England Association of Schools and Colleges Inc.; National Architectural Accrediting Board.

Admission Requirements: HS/GED Diploma.

Credit Awards for Prior Learning: Portfolio Assessment; Transfer Credit.

Credit Awards for Examinations: None.

Estimated Average Completion Time: 6 plus years.

Caveats Regarding Time Estimates: Full-time is a relative term. The BAC is not a college-type program, but rather alternative in the full sense of the term. For example, a full-time BAC student takes 6-9 credits in the evenings, while earning approximately 8 credits in an architectural or related work setting during the days. The combination day-and-night schedule results in an average of 15-16 credits per semester.

Credit Hour Requirements: 177 total credits (123 credits for academic course work and 54 credits for work-related experience).

Distance Learning Options: None.

Student Support Services Available: Academic Advising; Career Advisement; Counseling; Financial Aid; Job Placement Assistance; Orientation; Tutoring.

Informational Materials Available: Program Brochure; Institutional Catalog; Work Curriculum Notes.

Program Age, Enrollment, and Degrees Conferred:

Degree	Year Est.	Current Enrollment	Degrees Conferred
Bachelor of Architecture	1978	550	500

Percentage of Bachelor's Degree Holders Admitted to Graduate School: 10 percent; most qualify for the Architect Registration Exam one year after graduation.

Geographic Admission Restrictions: None.

Tuition and Fees: In- and Out-of-State Tuition: $1,550.00 per semester; Application Fee, $50.00; Registration Fee, $150.00.

Other Pertinent Information: The center has evolved from its founding in 1883 as the Architectural Association at Boston. In 1890, it was reincorporated as the Boston Architectural Center to "provide instruction in architecture and related fields . . . for those interested in the practice of architecture or the allied arts, especially those whose (related) employment might interfere with such education in day schools and universities."

76. College of Our Lady of the Elms

Continuing Education and Graduate Programs
291 Springfield St.
Chicopee, MA 01013

Degrees Offered: Bachelor of Arts; Bachelor of Science; Master of Arts in Teaching; Master of Arts in Theology.

Program Mission Statement/Description: The college believes that the opportunity to learn should extend over the student's lifetime; include both personal enrichment and professional growth; accommodate the student's life and work schedules; and provide quality educational experiences.

Accreditation: New England Association of Schools and Colleges Inc.; Council on Social Work Education; National League for Nursing.

Admission Requirements:

Undergraduate	Graduate
HS/GED Diploma	Undergraduate Degree
Interview	Interview
Essay/Written Work	Essay/Written Work
Recommendations	Recommendations

Credit Awards for Prior Learning: ACE Military Recommendations; ACE/PONSI Recommendations; Portfolio Assessment; Transfer Credit.

Limits to Credit Awards for Prior Learning: 30 credits.

Credit Awards for Examinations: ACT Proficiency Exams; CLEP General Exams; CLEP Subject Exams; College Board AP Exams; DANTES Subject Tests; Departmental Exams; National League for Nursing Mobility Exams.

Estimated Average Completion Time: 3.5 years (part-time), 2 years (full-time); Bachelors' Degrees: 6 years (part-time), 4 years (full-time); Graduate Degrees: 3.5 years (part-time), 2 years (full-time).

Credit Hour Requirements:

Degree	Total Hours	Academic Residency*
Bachelor's	120	30
Graduate	33	21

*Hours that must be earned at the institution exclusive of credit-by-exam, portfolio assessment, etc.

Distance Learning Options: Independent Study.

Student Support Services Available: Academic Advising; Career Counseling; Financial Aid; Job Placement Assistance; Orientation; Tutoring.

Informational Materials Available: Exam Preparation Guides; Institutional Catalog; Prior Learning Guides; Program Brochure.

Program Age, Enrollment, and Degrees Conferred:

Degree	Year Est.	Current Enrollment	Degrees Conferred
BA/BS Evening	1978	400	Unknown
BA Weekend College		200	Unknown

Percentage of Bachelor's Degree Holders Admitted to Graduate School: Information not available.

Geographic Admission Restrictions: None.

Tuition and Fees:

	Undergraduate	Graduate
In-State Tuition	$222.00/credit	$236.00/credit
Out-of-State Tuition	$222.00/credit	$236.00/credit
Application Fee	$25.00	$30.00
Graduation Fee	$60.00	
Registration Fee	$20.00	$20.00

77. Emmanuel College

Adult Learner Degree Program
400 The Fenway
Boston, MA 02115

Degrees Offered: Bachelor in Liberal Arts; Bachelor of Science in Health Administration; Bachelor of Science in Business Administration; Bachelor of Science in Nursing; Master of Arts in Human Resource Management; Master of Arts in Education; Master of Arts in Educational Pastoral Ministry; Master of Arts in Clinical Pastor Counseling; Master of Arts in Public Policy Making; Master in School Administration; Master in School Special Education Technology.

Program Mission Statement/Description: Emmanuel College believes that learning is a lifelong opportunity to define personal meaning and value and implements this philosophy by enabling women and men 23 years of age or older to meet their educational needs on a timely basis. Students may study part-time or full-time. Courses may be scheduled in late afternoons, evenings, and weekends and may also be taken during the summer intersessions as well as during the fall and spring semesters. Accelerated courses are also offered at off-campus sites.

Accreditation: New England Association of Schools and Colleges, Inc.; National League for Nursing.

Admission Requirements:

Undergraduate	Graduate
HS/GED Diploma	Undergraduate Degree
Interview	Interview
Recommendations	Essay/Written Work
Prior Credits: 80 credits max.	Recommendations
Essay/Written Work	Employment/Experience
Employment/Experience	GRE, MAT

Credit Awards for Prior Learning: ACE Military Recommendations; ACE/PONSI Recommendations; Portfolio Assessment; Transfer Credit.

Limits to Credit Awards for Prior Learning: Portfolio is called Life-Work-Experience Credits and is limited to maximum of 16 credits.

Credit Awards for Examinations: ACT Proficiency Exams; CLEP General Exams; CLEP Subject Exams; DANTES Subject Tests; Departmental Exams.

Estimated Average Completion Time: Bachelors' Degrees: 3-4 years (part-time), 2-3 years (full-time). Graduate Degrees: Masters' Degrees: 2.5 years (part-time), 1.5 (full-time).

Credit Hour Requirements:

Degree	Total Hours	Academic Residency*
Bachelor's	128	48
Graduate	36	30

*Hours that must be earned at the institution exclusive of credit-by-exam, portfolio asssessment, etc.

Distance Learning Options: None.

Student Support Services Available: Academic Advising; Career Counseling; Counseling/Testing; Financial Aid; Job Placement Assistance; Orientation; Tutoring.

Informational Materials Available: Institutional Catalog; Prior Learning Guides; Program Brochure.

Program Age, Enrollment, and Degrees Conferred: Information not available.

Percentage of Bachelor's Degree Holders Admitted to Graduate School: Information not available.

Geographic Admission Restrictions: None.

Tuition and Fees:

	Undergraduate	Graduate
In-State Tuition	$162.00/credit	$315.00/credit
Out-of-State Tuition	$162.00/credit	$315.00/credit
Application Fee	$30.00	$40.00
Graduation Fee	$100.00	$100.00

78. Framingham State College

University Studies Program
100 State St.
Framingham, MA 01701

Degrees Offered: Bachelor of Arts in Liberal Studies.

Program Mission Statement/Description: The Liberal Studies Program grants college credit for a number of nontraditional learning experiences (employment, independent study, community service, travel, military service, etc.). It provides access to higher education for students with a background of knowledge that has been acquired by such nontraditional learning.

Accreditation: New England Association of Schools and Colleges, Inc.

Admission Requirements: Employment/Experience: Varies; HS/GED Diploma; Interview; Recommendations.

Credit Awards for Prior Learning: ACE Military Recommendations; ACE/PONSI Recommendations; Portfolio Assessment; Transfer Credit.

Credit Awards for Examinations: CLEP General Exams; CLEP Subject Exams; College Board AP Exams; DANTES Subject Tests; U.S. Armed Forces Institute Examinations (USAFI).

Estimated Average Completion Time: Information not available.

Credit Hour Requirements: 128 hours total; 32 hours academic residency (hours that must be earned at the institution exclusive of credit-by-exam, portfolio assessment, etc.).

Distance Learning Options: A/V Cassettes; Cooperative Education; Correspondence Courses; Independent Study; Newspaper Courses; Study Guides; Television Courses.

Student Support Services Available: Academic Advising; Career Counseling; Counseling/Testing; Financial Aid; Job Placement Assistance; Orientation; Tutoring; Special Program for Adults Returning to College.

Informational Materials Available: Institutional Catalog; Prior Learning Guides; Program Brochure; Liberal Studies Program Catalog.

Program Age, Enrollment, and Degrees Conferred:

Degree	Year Est.	Current Enrollment	Degrees Conferred
BA	1973	150	300

Percentage of Bachelor's Degree Holders Admitted to Graduate School: Approximately one third of the program graduates have been accepted by graduate schools.

Geographic Admission Restrictions: Students must complete a minimum of 32 semester hours at Framingham State College.

Tuition and Fees: In-State Tuition $62.50 per credit; Out-of-State Tuition $82.50 per credit; Application Fee $25.00; Graduation Fee $25.00; Assessment Fee (evaluation of student's life experience credits) $550.00. Miscellaneous registration fees $65.50.

Other Pertinent Information: Once accepted into the program, the student attends information meetings that assist him/her in the preparation of a portfolio (resume) documenting credit-worthy life experiences. The portfolio is then evaluated by a committee, and college credit is awarded. The committee serves as the student's advisors, providing academic guidance while the student completes the program requirements.

79. Harvard University Extension School

20 Garden St.
Cambridge, MA 02138

Degrees Offered: Bachelor of Liberal Arts; Master of Liberal Arts; Associate in Arts.

Program Mission Statement/Description: These programs are designed to meet the needs of adults who could not otherwise afford a Harvard University education, in terms of time or money. Students may proceed at their own pace, enrolling in one to 4 evening courses per term at reasonable rates.

Accreditation: New England Association of Colleges and Schools, Inc.

Admission Requirements: Students complete essay on application form, but it does not play role in admission decision. The main criteria for admission to Bachelor of Liberal Arts (ALB) or Master of Liberal Arts (ALM) is the successful completion of three extension school courses (12 credits) with B or higher grades.

Credit Awards for Prior Learning: Transfer Credit.

Limits to Credit Awards for Prior Learning: ALB: Maximum transfer credit: 64 units.

Credit Awards for Examinations: CLEP General Exams; CLEP Subject Exams.

Limits to Credit Awards for Examinations: CLEP: maximum of 3, toward ALB only.

Estimated Average Completion Time: Bachelors' Degrees: 4.5-5 years; Graduate Degrees: ALM 4 years (part-time), 2 years (full-time).

Caveats Regarding Time Estimates: In 1989/90, on average, ALB students enrolled in slightly over 4 courses per year and brought in 48 transfer credits. Amount of time it takes to earn an ALB degree depends on amount of transfer credits, number of courses per term. ALM students must

complete degree requirements, including the thesis, within 5 years of admission to the program.

Credit Hour Requirements:

Degree	Total Hours	Academic Residency*
Associate's	64	64
Bachelor's	128	64
Graduate (ALM)	40	40

*Hours that must be earned at the institution exclusive of credit-by-exam, portfolio assessment, etc.

Distance Learning Options: None.

Student Support Services Available: Academic Advising; Financial Aid; Orientation

Informational Materials Available: Institutional Catalog.

Program Age, Enrollment, and Degrees Conferred:

Degree	Year Est.	Current Enrollment	Degrees Conferred
ALB	1913	511	1124
ALM	1980	332	384

Percentage of Bachelor's Degree Holders Admitted to Graduate School: 25-30 percent.

Geographic Admission Restrictions: None.

Tuition and Fees:

	Undergraduate	Graduate
In-State Tuition	$71.25/credit	$190.00/credit
Out-of-State Tuition	$71.25/credit	$190.00/credit
Application Fee	$50.00	$75.00

80. Quincy College

Accelerated Business Degree Program
34 Coddington St.
Quincy, MA 02169

Degrees Offered: Associate in Science in Business.

Program Mission Statement/Description: Our mission in the Accelerated Business Degree program and other special programs is to overcome obstacles that prevent people from completing their educations. This program addresses obstacles of cost, duration of program, and travel by providing a low-cost degree alternative in an accelerated schedule at a variety of satellite campuses.

Accreditation: New England Association of Schools and Colleges, Inc.

Admission Requirements: HS/GED Diploma.

Credit Awards for Prior Learning: ACE Military Recommendations; Transfer Credit; Limited Acceptance of Work Experience.

Limits to Credit Awards for Prior Learning: Total of 30 credits from outside sources is maximum, including transfer credit, military, CLEP, etc.

Credit Awards for Examinations: CLEP Subject Exams; DANTES Subject Tests.

Limits to Credits Awarded for Examinations: Same as prior learning options.

Estimated Average Completion Time: 4 years (part-time); 2 years (full-time).

Credit Hour Requirements: 60 hours total; 30 hours academic residency (hours that must be earned at the institution exclusive of credit-by-exam, portfolio assessment, etc.).

Distance Learning Options: None.

Student Support Services Available: Academic Advising; Career Counseling; Financial Aid; Tutoring.

Informational Materials Available: Institutional Catalog; Program Brochure.

Program Age, Enrollment, and Degrees Conferred:

Degree	Year Est.	Current Enrollment	Degrees Conferred
AS	1982	200	150

Geographic Admission Restrictions: None.

Tuition and Fees: In-State Tuition $64.00 per credit; Out-of-State Tuition $64.00 per credit; Application Fee $15.00; Graduation Fee $20.00; Credit-by-Exam Fee $190.00 per course; Registration fee $10.00 per course.

Other Pertinent Information: The program is currently in transition to new sites that will accommodate more students. The program has been expanded and updated this year. Enrollment is expected to increase as new sites are readied.

81. Regis College

Division of Nursing
235 Wellesley St.
Weston, MA 02193

Degrees Offered: Bachelor of Science in Nursing.

Program Mission Statement/Description: The purpose of the nursing program at Regis College is to provide a Bachelor of Science Degree in Nursing. The program is designed to serve the registered nurse population to prepare them for professional nursing practice. One of the further aims of the program is to provide a foundation for future graduate education in nursing. The nursing program subscribes to and functions within the stated mission and goals of Regis College, a liberal arts institution. The program is based upon the belief that the liberal arts and nursing education provide essential preparation for a variety of roles within the nursing profession.

Accreditation: New England Association of Schools and Colleges, Inc.; National League for Nursing.

Admission Requirements: Interview; must be a registered nurse in Massachusetts.

Credit Awards for Prior Learning: Transfer Credit.

Credit Awards for Examinations: ACT Proficiency Exams; CLEP Subject Exams.

Estimated Average Completion Time: 3 years (part-time).

Caveats Regarding Time Estimates: Program is a part-time schedule.

Credit Hour Requirements: 38 hours total; 18 hours academic residency (hours that must be earned at the institution exclusive of credit-by-exam, portfolio assessment, etc.).

Distance Learning Options: Independent Study.

Student Support Services Available: Academic Advising; Career Counseling; Counseling/Testing; Financial Aid; Job Placement Assistance; Orientation; Tutoring.

Informational Materials Available: Institutional Catalog; Program Brochure.

Program Age, Enrollment, and Degrees Conferred:

Degree	Year Est.	Current Enrollment	Degrees Conferred
BS	1983	100	76

Percentage of Bachelor's Degree Holders Admitted to Graduate School: 10 percent accepted to accredited graduate programs.

Geographic Admission Restrictions: None.

Tuition and Fees: Application Fee: $30.00; Graduation Fee: $100.00; Credit-by-Exam Fee: $200.00 per 28 credits.

82. Simmons College

Continuing Education
300 The Fenway
Boston, MA 02115

Degrees Offered: Bachelor of Science; Bachelor of Arts.

Program Mission Statement/Description: Simmons offers its courses to women beyond the age of traditional college students (aged 23 or older) who work on a flexible basis. There are many reasons why women enter the program: to complete an undergraduate degree; to obtain prerequisites for graduate school; to expand competence as a professional; to gain enrichment; or for younger women, to take courses as a guest student from another college.

Accreditation: New England Association of Schools and Colleges, Inc.

Admission Requirements: HS/GED Diploma; Interview; Recommendations; Transcripts of any postsecondary coursework. Qualifications for acceptance are flexible, although readiness and ability to handle coursework at Simmons are important factors.

Credit Awards for Prior Learning: Portfolio Assessment; Transfer Credit.

Limits to Credit Awards for Prior Learning: Total credits that may be transferred from all sources—80.

Credit Awards for Examinations: ACT Proficiency Exams; CLEP General Exams; CLEP Subject Exams; College Board AP Exams; NLN Level II Mobility Exams.

Limits to Credit Awards for Examinations: ACT—32 credits, CLEP—32 credits, NLN—18.

Estimated Average Completion Time: 4 years (part-time).

Credit Hour Requirements: 128 hours total; 48 hours academic residency (hours that must be earned at the institution exclusive of credit-by-exam, portfolio assessment, etc.).

Distance Learning Options: None.

Student Support Services Available: Academic Advising; Career Counseling; Counseling/Testing; Financial Aid; Job Placement Assistance; Orientation; Tutoring.

Informational Materials Available: Exam Preparation Guides; Institutional Catalog; Prior Learning Guides; Program Brochure.

Program Age, Enrollment, and Degrees Conferred:

Degree	Year Est.	Current Enrollment	Degrees Conferred
Bachelor's	1964	110	475

Percentage of Bachelor's Degree Holders Admitted to Graduate School: Information not available.

Geographic Admission Restrictions: None.

Tuition and Fees: In-State Tuition $402.00 per course; Out-of-State Tuition $402.00 per course; Application Fee $35.00. Credit for prior learning seminar $1,000.00. Registration Fee $60.00. Nursing courses 4 credits $820.00, 5 credits $1025.00. Nonnursing courses 4 credits $550.00.

Other Pertinent Information: RNs may select the evening or the weekend option for the nursing courses.

---

83. Springfield College

School of Human Services
Locklin Hall, Alden St.
Springfield, MA 01109

Degrees Offered: Bachelor of Science in Human Services (including an International Human Resource Development Program); Master of Science in Human Services (Tracks: Administration, Gerontology or Community Psychology, Community-Based Development); Master of Science in Social Work.

Program Mission Statement/Description: The School of Human Services was created both as an educational center and as a resource center to focus on the urgent need for changes in the way we address human needs in our time.

In considering the development of our programs, the School of Human Services is concerned about inequality and inequities, about cruelty and injustice, about racism, sexism, ageism. These concerns dictate that the programs have to focus on support to help people cope with pressures, problems, and oppression and on development of empowerment and social change toward a more humane society and a more humane world. The educational model is designed for experienced adults who can teach and learn from each other. The college offers intense, accelerated programs which usually combine day-long classes with independent and group study as well as with community-based projects. Most of our programs are offered from three central sites and, where possible, work is extended to the communities in which students live and work.

Accreditation: New England Association of Schools and Colleges, Inc.

Admission Requirements:

Undergraduate	Graduate
HS/GED Diploma	Undergraduate Degree
Interview	Interview
Essay/Written Work	Essay/Written Work
Recommendations	Recommendations
Employment/Experience: (5 years in human service experience)	Employment/Experience: (5 years in human service experience)

Other Admission Requirements: Completed application form. English language proficiency for international students and English-as-a-second language (ESL) students.

Credit Awards for Prior Learning: ACE Military Recommendations; ACE/PONSI Recommendations; Portfolio Assessment; Transfer Credit.

Limits to Credit Awards for Prior Learning: Masters program no more than 10 transfer credits. Undergraduate no more than 72 credits can be transferred.

Credit Awards for Examinations: CLEP General Exams; CLEP Subject Exams; DANTES Subject Tests.

Limits to Credit Awards for Examinations: No more than 72 credits.

Estimated Average Completion Time: Bachelors' Degrees: varies—3 years (part-time), 20-24 months (full-time); Graduate Degrees: MSHS—20-24 months (part-time), 16 months (full-time); MSSW—2 years (part-time), 16 months (full-time).

Caveats Regarding Time Estimates: The 20-24 month estimate is based on the assumption that students transfer or claim 72 credits and need only to complete their residency requirements. It can take as little as 16 months (4 academic terms) to complete the residency requirements.

Credit Hour Requirements:

Degree	Total Hours	Academic Residency*
Bachelor's	120	48
Graduate (MSHS)	36	24
Graduate (MSSW)	61	30

*Hours that must be earned at the institution exclusive of credit-by-exam, portfolio assessment, etc.

Distance Learning Options: Independent Study; Supervised Fieldwork.

Student Support Services Available: Academic Advising; Career Counseling; Counseling/Testing; Financial Aid; Job Placement Assistance; Orientation; Tutoring; Advocacy, Support Workshops; Referral.

Informational Materials Available: Institutional Catalog; Prior Learning Guides; Program Brochure; Financial Aid Information.

Program Age, Enrollment, and Degrees Conferred:

Degree	Year Est.	Current Enrollment	Degrees Conferred
BSHS	1976	448	1340
MSHS	1979	142	650
MSSW	1986	71	30

Percentage of Bachelor's Degree Holders Admitted to Graduate School: 48 percent apply to graduate school; 98 percent are accepted.

Geographic Admission Restrictions: None.

Tuition and Fees:

	Undergraduate	Graduate
In-State Tuition	$1752.00/sem.	$1752.00/sem.
Out-of-State Tuition	$1752.00/sem.	$1752.00/sem.
Application Fee	$10.00	$10.00
Graduation Fee	$20.00	$20.00
Portfolio Fee	$200.00	$200.00

Other Pertinent Information: (1) MSHS program is currently being offered in Gothenberg, Sweden. (2) The School of Human Services participates in an International Center for the Study of Social Reality and Social Development along with the University of Gothenberg, Sweden, and the University of Puerto Rico. These 3 institutions formed the center to work collaboratively on research and educational exchange. 3). SHS is also the home base for Jane Sapp's Center for Cultural and Community Development—a resource, organizing, and educational center for cultural/community workers.

84. Tufts University

Resumed Education for Adult Learners
Office of Undergraduate Education
Ballou Hall
Medford, MA 02155

Degrees Offered: Bachelor of Arts; Bachelor of Science.

Program Mission Statement/Description: Resumed Education for Adult Learners (REAL) offers an alternative admissions process for applicants 25 years or older. Option to take part-time program. Support seminar, all majors, student services, and financial aid available.

Accreditation: New England Association of Schools and Colleges, Inc.

Admission Requirements: Employment/Experience; Essay/Written Work; Interview; Prior Credits: 2 courses; Recommendations.

Credit Awards for Prior Learning: Transfer Credit.

Limits to Credit Awards for Prior Learning: Up to one half the total number of courses (17 out of 34) may be transferred.

Credit Awards for Examinations: College Board AP Exams.

Estimated Average Completion Time: Ordinarily, Tufts students cannot be part-time; REAL students may be part-time. Typically, students transfer with 1-2 years credit. Theoretically, they could complete the 4-year requirement in 2 years. Most, however, take 2.5-3 years.

Credit Hour Requirements: 34 hours total; 17 hours academic residency (hours that must be earned at the institution exclusive of credit-by-exam, portfolio assessment, etc.).

Distance Learning Options: None.

Student Support Services Available: Academic Advising; Career Counseling; Counseling/Testing; Financial Aid; Job Placement Assistance; Orientation; Tutoring.

Informational Materials Available: Institutional Catalog; Program Brochure.

Program Age, Enrollment, and Degrees Conferred: Information not available.

Percentage of Bachelor's Degree Holders Admitted to Graduate School: 50 percent (approximately).

Geographic Admission Restrictions: None.

Tuition and Fees: In-State Tuition $1938.00 per semester; Application Fee $45.00.

85. University of Massachusetts/Boston

Harbor Campus
College of Public and Community Service
Boston, MA 02125

Degrees Offered: Bachelor of Arts; Bachelor of Science in Criminal Justice; Masters in Human Services.

Program Mission Statement/Description: The college was established in 1973 to serve adults working in or preparing for careers in public and community service. One thousand students are currently enrolled, representing a diverse population: 30 percent persons of color, 70 percent women, average age 39 years. The curriculum of the college is competence based, requiring students to meet the criteria and standard of each of 50 competencies for the BA degree. The college provides a variety of learning options: courses, independent study, and internships. Career concentrations are offered in human services, law, gerontology, community planning, criminal justice (12 competencies are required) supported by general education competencies (20) and the required applied language and math competencies (14). The remaining 4 competencies are designated as independent interest competencies. Prior learning and transfer credits can be accommodated in the curriculum.

Accreditation: New England Association of Schools and Colleges, Inc.

Admission Requirements:

Undergraduate	Graduate
HS/GED Diploma	Undergraduate Degree
Essay/Written Work	Interview
Recommendations	Essay/Written Work
Employment/Experience	Employment/Experience: Several years
	Recommendations

Other Admission Requirements: The BA program requires attendance at a formal admissions seminar which is offered every Tuesday at 9:00 a.m. and 6:00 p.m. at the college.

Credit Awards for Prior Learning: Transfer Credit.

Other Options: Credit for prior learning is assessed in the self-assessment course which is required of all entering students. Students must provide evidence to meet the criteria and standards of specific competencies for academic credit.

Limits to Credit Awards for Prior Learning: Within certain centers (departments), limits have been set on the amount of transfer credit (4 competencies within a career center), but prior learning credit is not limited. No transfer credit can be applied to the reading/writing/math competencies; and a college, diagnostic test is required for the ALM competencies.

Credit Awards for Examinations: Departmental Exams.

Estimated Average Completion Time: Bachelors' Degrees: 6 semesters (full-time); Graduate Degrees: 4 semesters (full-time).

Credit Hour Requirements: See Program Mission Statement/Description.

Distance Learning Options: Independent Study; Study Guides (Bachelor only); Supervised Fieldwork.

Student Support Services Available: Academic Advising; Career Counseling; Counseling/Testing; Financial Aid; Orientation; Tutoring; Critical Skills Program; Learning Disability Counseling; English as a Second Language; Personal Counseling.

Informational Materials Available: Program Brochure; Admission Seminar/Information Session.

Program Age, Enrollment, and Degrees Conferred:

Degree	Year Est.	Current Enrollment	Degrees Conferred
BA	1973	1000	1696
MS	1985	98	59

Percentage of Bachelor's Degree Holders Admitted to Graduate School: 43 percent of graduates have been accepted to accredited graduate schools.

Geographic Admission Restrictions: None.

Tuition and Fees:

	Undergraduate	Graduate
In-State Tuition	$80.50/credit	$100.00/credit
Out-of-State Tuition	$283.00/credit	$295.50/credit

86. Wellesley College

Elizabeth Kaiser Davis Degree Program
Office of the Dean of Continuing Education
Wellesley, MA 02181

Degrees Offered: Bachelor of Arts.

Program Mission Statement/Description: The Elizabeth Kaiser Davis Degree Program offers educational opportunity for women beyond traditional college age. The program is designed for women who wish to work toward the Bachelor of Arts degree at Wellesley College. Davis Scholars enroll in the same courses as the traditionally aged Wellesley undergraduates and meet the same degree requirements. They may enroll on a part-time or full-time basis. Prospective candidates for the BA degree are women, usually over the age of 24, whose education has been interrupted for at least 2 years.

Accreditation: New England Association of Schools and Colleges, Inc.

Admission Requirements: Essay/Written Work; HS/GED Diploma; Interview; Recommendations. Transcripts from secondary school and all colleges and universities previously attended by the applicant are also required.

Credit Awards for Prior Learning: Transfer Credit.

Limits to Credit Awards for Prior Learning: At least 16 of the 32 units required for the BA degree must be completed at Wellesley. There is no time limitation for completion of the degree. The college will accept for credit only those courses that are comparable to courses offered in the liberal arts curriculum at Wellesley. One Wellesley unit is equal to 4 semester hours or 6 quarter hours. The registrar will evaluate credit earned at accredited colleges with the official transcript, catalog, and degree requirements from those colleges.

Credit Awards for Examinations: College Board AP Exams.

Limits to Credit Awards for Examinations: No more than 8 AP examinations.

Estimated Average Completion Time: 3-5 years (part-time), 2-4 years (full-time).

Caveats Regarding Time Estimates: Time to complete the degree varies because each student proceeds at her own pace, taking as few as one course per term to a full academic load of 4 courses per term. At least 16 of the 32 courses required for the BA degree must be completed at Wellesley.

Credit Hour Requirements: 128 hours total; 64 hours academic residency (hours that must be earned at the institution exclusive of credit-by-exam, portfolio assessment, etc.).

Distance Learning Options: None.

Student Support Services Available: Academic Advising; Career Counseling; Counseling/Testing; Financial Aid; Job Placement Assistance; Orientation; Tutoring. Special support services for the adult learner provided by the dean, the coordinator and peer advisors.

Informational Materials Available: Institutional Catalog; Program Brochure; Financial Aid Brochure.

Program Age, Enrollment, and Degrees Conferred:

Degree	Year Est.	Current Enrollment	Degrees Conferred
BA	1969	170	420

Percentage of Bachelor's Degree Holders Admitted to Graduate School: Each year approximately 37 percent of the total college graduates continue on to graduate and professional schools.

Geographic Admission Restrictions: Foreign student applicants who reside outside the United States may apply for fall admission only and must submit all application materials by December 1 of the previous year.

Tuition and Fees: In-State Tuition $1996.00 per semester; Out-of-State Tuition $1996.00 per semester; Application Fee $40.00; Student Activity Fee $14.00 per course; Facility Fee $25.00 per course.

Other Pertinent Information: Liberal arts curriculum: students may choose from 900 courses and 45 majors. Financial aid available. Application deadlines: March 1 for fall semester, December 1 for spring semester.

87. Western New England College

Division of Continuing Education
1215 Wilbraham Rd.
Springfield, MA 01119

Degrees Offered: Associate of Arts in Liberal Studies; Bachelor of Arts in Liberal Studies.

Program Mission Statement/Description: The Associate of Arts in Liberal Studies is particularly appropriate for nontraditional students who are entering or reentering college after a long pause in their formal education. The 2-year degree may be designed by the student, with the assistance of an academic advisor, to serve as a career development tool as well as preparing for upper-level study in a 4-year degree program. The Bachelor of Arts in Liberal Studies may be structured to satisfy the broad interest of older students who wish to further their formal education without reference to specific career preparation or as preparation for graduate study. Advisors can give more information and guidance on this flexible degree option.

Accreditation: New England Association of Schools and Colleges, Inc.

Admission Requirements: HS/GED Diploma; Interview.

Credit Awards for Prior Learning: ACE Military Recommendations; ACE/PONSI Recommendations; Transfer Credit.

Limits to Credit Awards for Prior Learning: Maximum of 90 transfer credits (maximum of 70 from community colleges and/or exams).

Credit Awards for Examinations: ACT Proficiency Exams; CLEP General Exams; CLEP Subject Exams; College Board AP Exams; DANTES Subject Tests; Departmental Exams.

Limits to Credit Awards for Examinations: 70 semester hours.

Estimated Average Completion Time: Associates' Degrees: 3 years (part-time); Bachelors' Degrees: 6 years (part-time).

Credit Hour Requirements:

Degree	Total Hours	Academic Residency*
Associate's	60	30
Bachelor's	120	30

*Hours that must be earned at the institution exclusive of credit-by-exam, portfolio assessment, etc.

Distance Learning Options: Independent Study; Supervised Fieldwork.

Student Support Services Available: Academic Advising; Career Counseling; Counseling/Testing; Financial Aid; Job Placement Assistance; Orientation; Tutoring.

Informational Materials Available: Institutional Catalog; Program Brochure. Information available through telephone advisory toll-free 1-800-325-1122.

Program Age, Enrollment, and Degrees Conferred:

Degree	Year Est.	Current Enrollment	Degrees Conferred
AALS	1990-91	24	7
BALS	1990-91	68	21

Percentage of Bachelor's Degree Holders Admitted to Graduate School: Approximately 75 percent of bachelor's degree holders.

Geographic Admission Restrictions: None, but part-time nature of these degrees dictates that most students come from western Massachusetts and northwestern Connecticut.

Tuition and Fees: In-State Tuition $222.00 per credit; Out-of-State Tuition $222.00 per credit; Application Fee $30.00; Graduation Fee $50.00; Credit-by-Exam Fee; Registration Fee $10.00; General Services Fees $7.00.

Michigan

88. Aquinas College

Continuing Education Program
1607 Robinson Rd., SE
Grand Rapids, MI 49506

Degrees Offered: Associate of Arts; Associate of Arts in Gerontology; Associate in Ministry; Associate of Science; Bachelor of Arts; Bachelor of Arts in General Education; Bachelor of Science in Business Administration; Master in the Art of Teaching; Master of Management.

Program Mission Statement/Description: The mission of Aquinas College is to provide a liberal arts education with a career orientation in a Catholic Christian context to all students capable of profiting from such an education regardless of their sex, age, religion, ethnicity, or racial background. Continuing education programs at Aquinas are designed and intended for persons beyond conventional college age who are established in their adult lives and careers and whose education has been interrupted.

Accreditation: North Central Association of Colleges and Schools.

Admission Requirements:

Undergraduate	Graduate
HS/GED Diploma	Undergraduate Degree
Interview	
Employment/Experience	

Other Admission Requirements: Teacher certification for admission to Master in the Art of Teaching Program (MAT). GMAT score of 40th percentile for admission to Master of Management (MM), undergraduate GPA of 2.75 for MM and 3.0 for MAT.

Credit Awards for Prior Learning: Transfer Credit; Life Experience Credit.

Life Experience Credit Limits to Credit Awards for Prior Learning: Life experience credit is not considered residency credit.

Credit Awards for Examinations: CLEP General Exams; College Board AP Exams.

Other Exam Options: Credit-by-Exam.

Limits to Credit Awards for Examinations: Minimum score for AP is 3. Minimum score CLEP is 45th percentile.

Estimated Average Completion Time: Associates' Degrees: 3.5 years (part-time), 2 years (full-time); Bachelors' Degrees: 6.5 years (part-time), 4 years (full-time); Graduate Degrees: MM—4 years (part-time), 1.5 years (full-time); MAT—3 years (part-time).

Credit Hour Requirements:

Degree	Total Hours	Academic Residency*
Associate's	64	30
Bachelor's	124	30
Graduate Management	39	30
Master of Art in Teaching	36	30

*Hours that must be earned at the institution exclusive of credit-by-exam, portfolio assessment, etc.

Distance Learning Options: Independent Study; Supervised Fieldwork (associate and bachelor only).

Student Support Services Available: Academic Advising; Career Counseling; Counseling/Testing; Financial Aid; Job Placement Assistance; Orientation; Tutoring; Day Care; and Health Care. Special advisor available for veterans.

Informational Materials Available: Institutional Catalog; Program Brochure.

Program Age, Enrollment, and Degrees Conferred:

Degree	Year Est.	Current Enrollment	Degrees Conferred
Continuing Education	1969	1412	3224
MM	1978	650	63
MA	1987	60	1

Percentage of Bachelor's Degree Holders Admitted to Graduate School: Estimated placement rate is 90 percent—includes employment and graduate school.

Geographic Admission Restrictions: None.

Tuition and Fees:

	Undergraduate	Graduate
In-State Tuition	$196.00/credit	$219.00/credit
Out-of-State Tuition	$196.00/credit	$219.00/credit
Application Fee	$20.00	$20.00
Credit-by-Exam Fee	$10.00	

89. Central Michigan University

Extended Degree Program
130 Rowe Hall
Mount Pleasant, MI 48324

Degrees Offered: Master of Science in Administration with concentrations in General Administration, Health Services Administration, Public Administration, Software

Engineering Administration, and Human Resources Administration; Master of Arts in Education with a concentration in Community College Education; Bachelor of Science in Community Development; and Bachelor of Science in Administration with concentrations in Guest Services Administration, Industrial Administration, Organizational Administration, and Service Sector Administration.

Program Mission Statement/Description: Central Michigan University (CMU) believes that adults with full-time work and family responsibilities should still have access to higher education. CMU established the Extended Degree Program to offer working adults the opportunity to earn a degree on a part-time basis. Classes are offered on a compressed format at night through local CMU centers in 23 states and several Canadian provinces.

Accreditation: North Central Association of Colleges and Schools.

Admission Requirements:

Undergraduate	Graduate
HS/GED Diploma	Undergraduate Degree
	Undergraduate GPA of 2.5

Credit Awards for Prior Learning: ACE Military Recommendations; Portfolio Assessment; Transfer Credit.

Limits to Credit Awards for Prior Learning: Undergraduate students may not apply more than 60 semester hours of prior learning credit.

Credit Awards for Examinations: CLEP General Exams; CLEP Subject Exams.

Limits to Credit Awards for Examinations: There are limits on credit awards; students need to consult an academic advisor.

Estimated Average Completion Time: Bachelors' Degrees: 3 years (part-time); Graduate Degrees: 2 years (part-time).

Credit Hour Requirements: Bachelors' Degrees: 124 credit hours; MS in Administration: 36 credit hours; MA in Education: 30 credit hours.

Distance Learning Options: Correspondence Courses; Independent Study; Study Guides; Television Courses.

Student Support Services Available: Academic Advising; Financial Aid; Orientation.

Informational Materials Available: Institutional Catalog; Prior Learning Guides; Program Brochure.

Program Age, Enrollment, and Degrees Conferred:

Degree	Year Est.	Current Enrollment	Degrees Conferred
MS in Administration	1983	6000	4500
MA in Education	1977	150	300
BS w/ Major in Admin.	1985	3000	400
BS in Comm. Dev.	1975	300	100

Percentage of Bachelor's Degree Holders Admitted to Graduate School: Information not available.

Geographic Admission Restrictions: None.

Tuition and Fees:

	Undergraduate	Graduate
In-State Tuition	$115.00/credit	$155.00/credit
Out-of-State Tuition	$115.00/credit	$155.00/credit
Application Fee	$40.00	$40.00
Graduation Fee	$35.00	$35.00
Prior Learning Processing Fee	$65.00	$65.00
Prior Learning Recording Fee	$25.00/credit	$25.00/credit

90. Kellogg Community College

Guaranteed Evening Program
Open Entry, Open Exit Program
450 North Ave.
Battle Creek, MI 49017

Degrees Offered: Associate in Arts; Associate in Applied Science with Concentration in Liberal Arts, Elementary Education, Business Management, Computer Information Systems, and Industrial Skills Training.

Program Mission Statement/Description: Provide an opportunity for students to obtain associates' degrees in specified programs by attending evenings only. A 4-year schedule of classes is provided with a guarantee that the classes will run as scheduled even if enrollment is low. Provides a delivery system for the industrial skills areas that individualizes instruction, is competency based, and features flexible scheduling. Persons may enroll at any time during the year and may be given credit for previously learned skills.

Accreditation: North Central Association of Colleges and Schools.

Admission Requirements: HS/GED Diploma. Assessment testing required for certain courses.

Credit Awards for Prior Learning: ACE Military Recommendations; Portfolio Assessment; Transfer Credit; Interviews.

Credit Awards for Examinations: CLEP Subject Exams; College Board AP Exams; Departmental Exams.

Estimated Average Completion Time: 4-5 years (part-time), 2 years (full-time).

Credit Hour Requirements: 62 hours total; 24 hours academic residency (hours that must be earned at the institution exclusive of credit-by-exam, portfolio assessment, etc.).

Distance Learning Options: Cooperative Education; Independent Study; Supervised Fieldwork; Television Courses.

Student Support Services Available: Academic Advising; Career Counseling; Counseling/Testing; Financial Aid; Job Placement Assistance; Orientation; Tutoring.

Informational Materials Available: Institutional Catalog; Program Brochure.

Program Age, Enrollment, and Degrees Conferred: Information not available.

Percentage of Bachelor's Degree Holders Admitted to Graduate School: Information not available.

Geographic Admission Restrictions: None.

Tuition and Fees: In-State Tuition $29.50 per credit; Graduation Fee $10.00; Credit-by-Exam Fee $5.00; per clock hour fee $2.93.

91. Marygrove College

8425 W. McNichols
Detroit, MI 48221

Degrees Offered: Bachelor of Arts; Bachelor of Science; Bachelor of Music; Bachelor of Fine Arts; Bachelor of Social Work; Bachelor of Business Administration; Associate of Arts; Associate of Science; Master of Arts; Master of Education.

Program Mission Statement/Description: Cognizant that job and family responsibilities often preclude full-time study during the day, Marygrove College offers all academic programs on a part-time basis and several programs that can be completed in the evening. Recognizing further that learning derived from life experience and from individual study is of significant academic value and can often be equated with college-level studies, Marygrove provides a number of options for validating and measuring such learning.

Accreditation: North Central Association of Colleges and Schools.

Admission Requirements:

Undergraduate	Graduate
HS/GED Diploma	Undergraduate Degree
Interview	Interview
Recommendations	Essay/Written Work
	GRE MAT

Credit Awards for Prior Learning: ACE/PONSI Recommendations; Portfolio Assessment.

Limits to Credit Awards for Prior Learning: Bachelors' Degrees: Maximum of 32 semester hours for all prior learning methods, including credit by examination. Associates' Degrees: Maximum of 16 semester hours for all prior learning methods. Master's Degree program: Maximum of 6 semester hours for all prior learning methods.

Credit Awards for Examinations: CLEP General Exams; CLEP Subject Exams; College Board AP Exams; Departmental Exams.

Limits to Credit Awards for Exams: Same as prior learning limits.

Estimated Average Completion Time: Associates' Degrees: 4 years (part-time), 2 years (full-time); Bachelors' Degrees: 6-7 years (part-time), 4 years (full-time); Graduate Degrees: 3 years (part-time), 1.5 years (full-time).

Credit Hour Requirements:

Degree	Total Hours	Academic Residency*
Associate's	64	48
Bachelor's	128	96
Graduate (MA)	36	30
Graduate (MEd)	30	30

*Hours that must be earned at the institution exclusive of credit-by-exam, portfolio assessment, etc.

Distance Learning Options: Cooperative Education (associate, bachelor, and graduate); Independent Study (bachelor and graduate); Television Courses (bachelor only).

Student Support Services Available: Academic Advising; Career Counseling; Counseling/Testing; Financial Aid; Job Placement Assistance; Orientation; Tutoring.

Informational Materials Available: Exam Preparation Guides; Institutional Catalog; Program Brochure.

Program Age, Enrollment, and Degrees Conferred: Information not available.

Percentage of Bachelor's Degree Holders Admitted to Graduate School: 20 percent.

Geographic Admission Restrictions: None.

Tuition and Fees:

	Undergraduate	Graduate
In-State Tuition	$231.00/credit	$243.00/credit
Out-of-State Tuition	$231.00/credit	$243.00/credit
Application Fee	$15.00	$15.00
Graduation Fee	$50.00	$50.00
Credit-by-Exam Fee varies by exam		
Portfolio Assessment Fee	$60.00/course	$60.00/course
Individualized Faculty Assistance Fee	$100.00	$100.00

92. Western Michigan University

Division of Continuing Education
A 103 Ellsworth
Kalamazoo, MI 49008

Degrees Offered: Bachelor of Science in General University Studies, Bachelor of Science in Production Technology, Master in Educational Leadership, Master in Elementary Education and Reading, Master in Business Administration, Master in Public Administration, Master of Engineering Management, Master of Individual Engineering.

Program Mission Statement/Description: To provide complete degree programs to qualified adult/part-time students at accessible locations off campus.

Accreditation: North Central Association of Colleges and Schools, Council on Social Work Education; National Council for the Accreditation of Teacher Education; Accreditation Board for Engineering and Technology, Inc.; American Assembly of Collegiate Schools of Business.

Admission Requirements:

Undergraduate	Graduate
HS/GED Diploma	Undergraduate Degree
Employment/Experience: 5 years	GRE
Prior Credits: 62	

Credit Awards for Prior Learning: ACE Military Recommendations; ACE/PONSI Recommendations; Portfolio Assessment; Transfer Credit.

Limits to Credit Awards for Prior Learning: Maximum 60 credits; average 15-20 credits.

Credit Awards for Examinations: CLEP General Exams; CLEP Subject Exams; College Board AP Exams; DANTES Subject Tests; Departmental Exams.

Estimated Average Completion Time: Bachelors' Degrees: 7-8 years (part-time), 4-5 year (full-time); Graduate Degrees: 3 years (part-time), 2 years (full-time).

Credit Hour Requirements: Bachelors' Degrees: 122 credit hours; Graduate Degrees: 30-60 credit hours.

Distance Learning Options: A/V Cassettes; Cooperative Education (Graduate); Correspondence Courses; Electronic Mail (Graduate); Independent Study (Bachelor and Graduate); Newspaper Courses; Phone/Mail Instruction (Bachelor and Graduate); Study Guides; Supervised Fieldwork (Bachelor and Graduate); Television Courses.

Student Support Services Available: Academic Advising; Career Counseling; Counseling/Testing; Financial Aid; Job Placement Assistance.

Informational Materials Available: Institutional Catalog; Program Brochure.

Program Age, Enrollment, and Degrees Conferred:

Degree	Year Est.	Current Enrollment	Degrees Conferred
General Univ. Studies	1985	500	141
General Univ. Studies	1986	500	103
General Univ. Studies	1987	600	159
General Univ. Studies	1988	600	128
General Univ. Studies	1989	700	119
General Univ. Studies	1990	750	114
General Univ. Studies	1991	750	121

Percentage of Bachelor's Degree Holders Admitted to Graduate School: Information not available.

Geographic Admission Restrictions: None.

Tuition and Fees:

	Undergraduate	Graduate
In-State Tuition	$87.50/credit	$107.50/credit
Application Fee	$25.00	$15.00
Graduation Fee	$30.00	$30.00
Credit-by-Exam Fee	$25.00	

Minnesota

93. College of St. Scholastica

Encore! Program
1200 Kenwood Ave.
Duluth, MN 55811

Degrees Offered: Bachelor of Arts; Master of Arts.

Program Mission Statement/Description: To make a college degree feasible to all able adults. To provide additional college-level learning to meet the demands of the region.

Accreditation: North Central Association of Colleges and Schools; American Physical Therapy Association, Council on Social Work Education; National Accrediting Agency for Clinical Laboratory Sciences; National League for Nursing; American Dietetic Association; Committee on Health Education and Accreditation, American Medical Association.

Admission Requirements:

Undergraduate	Graduate
HS/GED Diploma	Undergraduate Degree
Interview	Interview
Essay/Written Work	Essay/Written Work
Employment/Experience: one year	GRE

Credit Awards for Prior Learning: ACE Military Recommendations; ACE/PONSI Recommendations; Portfolio Assessment; Transfer Credit.

Limits to Credit Awards for Prior Learning: 144 quarter credits may be earned. The remaining 48 must be earned under College of St. Scholastica jurisdiction.

Credit Awards for Examinations: ACT Proficiency Exams; CLEP General Exams; CLEP Subject Exams; College Board AP Exams; DANTES Subject Tests; Departmental Exams.

Estimated Average Completion Time: Bachelors' Degrees: 4 years (full-time); Graduate Degrees: 3 years (full-time).

Caveats Regarding Time Estimates: The physical therapy program is a 5-year course of study and is in transition to a 6-year master's only program.

Credit Hour Requirements:

Degree	Total Hours	Academic Residency*
Bachelor's	192	48
Graduate	50-55	50-55

*Hours that must be earned at the institution exclusive of credit-by-exam, portfolio assessment, etc.

Distance Learning Options: A/V Cassettes; Cooperative Education; Independent Study; Study Guides; Supervised Fieldwork.

Student Support Services Available: Academic Advising; Career Counseling; Counseling/Testing; Financial Aid; Job Placement Assistance; Orientation; Tutoring; Peer Advising for New Students; Support Programs for Disadvantaged, Low Income Minority and Single-Parent Students Services.

Informational Materials Available: Institutional Catalog; Prior Learning Guides; Program Brochure; Workshop Series Covering Study Skills, Transitions, Financial Aid, and Career Guidance; College Readiness Advising.

Program Age, Enrollment, and Degrees Conferred:

Degree	Year Est.	Current Enrollment	Degrees Conferred
BA	1982	600	800

Percentage of Bachelor's Degree Holders Admitted to Graduate School: Information not available.

Geographic Admission Restrictions: None.

Tuition and Fees:

	Undergraduate	Graduate
In-State Tuition	$190.00/quarter	$200.00/quarter
Out-of-State Tuition	$190.00/quarter	$200.00/quarter
Application Fee	$15.00	$50.00
Credit-by-Exam Fee	$15.00/credit	

Other Pertinent Information: The program at the College of St. Scholastica is called Encore! and is designed for individuals aged 23 and older who want to earn an undergraduate degree. Special emphasis is placed on individual counseling and on identifying those individuals who will make successful college students. Support services are tailored to the needs of returning adults and are available as soon as the individual applies to the college. Workshops to identify self-imposed obstacles are conducted for applicants to reduce first quarter stress. Student services have been tailored to meet the needs of adult students and are available at all hours of the day. Master's programs are designed for practitioners.

---

94. Concordia College

School of Adult Learning
275 N. Syndicate
St. Paul, MN 55104

Degrees Offered: Bachelor of Arts in Organizational Management and Communications.

Program Mission Statement/Description: The Concordia School of Adult Learning, an integral part of the Concordia College community, was created particularly for the adult student. Supportive of the mission of the entire college, the Concordia School of Adult Learning uses responsive and innovative methods of outreach to enable students to achieve educational and professional goals. The Concordia School of Adult Learning will benefit all by providing quality educational programs, increased enrollments, and a positive witness to Christ's Church for life-long learning.

Accreditation: North Central Association of Colleges and Schools.

Admission Requirements: Employment/Experience: If under age 25; Essay/Written Work; Prior Credits: 90; Recommendations; (2.0 GPA).

Credit Awards for Prior Learning: ACE Military Recommendations; ACE/PONSI Recommendations; Portfolio Assessment; Transfer Credit.

Limits to Credit Awards for Prior Learning: 48 credits maximum for nontraditional. 45 credits maximum life experience essays (portfolio).

Credit Awards for Examinations: CLEP General Exams; CLEP Subject Exams; DANTES Subject Tests; Departmental Exams.

Estimated Average Completion Time: Bachelors' Degrees: 15 months (full-time).

Caveats Regarding Time Estimates: Only full-time permitted.

Credit Hour Requirements: 192 hours total; 61 hours academic residency (hours that must be earned at the institution exclusive of credit-by-exam, portfolio assessment, etc.).

Distance Learning Options: Study Guides.

Student Support Services Available: Academic Advising; Counseling/Testing; Financial Aid; Job Placement Assistance; Orientation; Tutoring.

Informational Materials Available: Exam Preparation Guides; Institutional Catalog; Program Brochure.

Program Age, Enrollment, and Degrees Conferred:

Degree	Year Est.	Current Enrollment	Degrees Conferred
BA	1985	260	391

Percentage of Bachelor's Degree Holders Admitted to Graduate School: Information not available.

Geographic Admission Restrictions: None.

Tuition and Fees: In-State Tuition $158.00 per credit; Application Fee $10.00; Graduation Fee $60.00.

95. Mankato State University

Alternative Degree Program
Mankato, MN 56001

Degrees Offered: Associate of Arts in Liberal Studies; Bachelor of Science in Open Studies; Associate of Arts in Open Studies; Master of Science in Continuing Studies.

Program Mission Statement/Description: Alternative degree programs are designed for the student whose personal, educational, or career goals require a program not confined to the demands of a specific discipline.

Accreditation: North Central Association of Colleges and Schools.

Admission Requirements:

Undergraduate	Graduate
HS/GED Diploma	Undergraduate Degree
Essay/Written Work	GRE
ACT or SAT	

Credit Awards for Prior Learning: ACE Military Recommendations; Transfer Credit.

Credit Awards for Examinations: CLEP General Exams; CLEP Subject Exams; College Board AP Exams; DANTES Subject Tests; Departmental Exams; International Baccalaureate.

Limits to Credit Awards for Examinations: CLEP—16 credits per subject. CLEP General—9 credits per exam (none allowed for English).

Estimated Average Completion Time: Associates' Degrees: 2-3 years; Bachelors' Degrees: 5-6 years; Graduate Degrees: 2-7 years.

Caveats Regarding Time Estimates: Students often mix full- and part-time quarters of attendance.

Credit Hour Requirements:

Degree	Total Hours	Academic Residency*
Associate's	96	30
Bachelor's	192	45
Graduate	45-51	30

*Hours that must be earned at the institution exclusive of credit-by-exam, portfolio assessment, etc.

Distance Learning Options: Independent Study; Supervised Fieldwork (bachelor and graduate only); Television Courses (associate and bachelor only).

Student Support Services Available: Academic Advising; Career Counseling; Counseling/Testing; Financial Aid; Job Placement Assistance; Orientation; Tutoring.

Informational Materials Available: Institutional Catalog; Program Brochure.

Program Age, Enrollment, and Degrees Conferred:

Degree	Year Est.	Current Enrollment	Degrees Conferred
Open Studies BS	1970	153	572
Open Studies AS	1974	9	531
Liberal Studies AA	1972	16	236
Cont. Studies MS	1969	71	292

Percentage of Bachelor's Degree Holders Admitted to Graduate School: Information not available.

Geographic Admission Restrictions: None.

Tuition and Fees:

	Undergraduate	Graduate
In-State Tuition	$36.30/credit	$52.00/credit
Out-of-State Tuition	$62.30/credit	$75.00/credit
Application Fee	$15.00	$15.00
Credit-by-Exam Fee	$5.00/credit	
Activity Fee $6.05/credit for first 12 credits		

96. Minneapolis Community College

College for Working Adults
1501 Hennepin Ave.
Minneapolis, MN 55403

Degrees Offered: Associate of Arts; Associate of Science in General Business, Management, Marketing, and Accounting.

Program Mission Statement/Description: The purpose of the College for Working Adults (WA) is to allow a working adult to earn a degree nearly as quickly as a full-time day student by minimizing the amount of time spent on campus. The College for Working Adults program is centered around 3 unique characteristics: (1) A coherent, interdisciplinary, theme-based curriculum to which adults can relate life experience. (2) A delivery system that uses telecourses, weekend conference seminars, and weekly, evening workshop courses. (3) A student-centered organization structure. Each quarter the student concentrates on a CWA block of courses in one of 4 disciplines—social sciences; humanities, communications and the arts; science and technology; or business. All coursework and assignments during the quarter are interrelated.

Accreditation: North Central Association of Colleges and Schools.

Admission Requirements: HS/GED Diploma.

Credit Awards for Prior Learning: Transfer Credit.

Limits to Credit Awards for Prior Learning: The college has a residence requirement of 30 credits. Therefore, a student could enter with 60-65 credits depending on the degree plan.

Credit Awards for Examinations: CLEP General Exams; CLEP Subject Exams; Departmental Exams.

Estimated Average Completion Time: Associates' Degrees: depends on number of credits taken per quarter (part-time), 2-3 years (full-time).

Credit Hour Requirements:

Degree	Total Hours	Academic Residency*
Associate's (quarter)	90-96	30

*Hours that must be earned at the institution exclusive of credit-by-exam, portfolio assessment, etc.

Distance Learning Options: A/V Cassettes; Independent Study.

Student Support Services Available: Academic Advising; Career Counseling; Counseling/Testing; Financial Aid; Orientation; Tutoring.

Informational Materials Available: Institutional Catalog; Program Brochure; Audiocasette Tape.

Program Age, Enrollment, and Degrees Conferred: AA—Information not available; AS—Information not available.

Geographic Admission Restrictions: None.

Tuition and Fees: In-State Tuition $32.75 per credit; Out-of-State Tuition $49.25 per credit; Application Fee $15.00; Graduation Fee, Credit-by-Exam Fee half of the cost of the course; Telecourse Fee $15.00.

---

97. Northwestern College

Adult Degree Completion Program
3003 N. Snelling Ave.
St. Paul, MN 55113

Degrees Offered: Bachelor of Science in Organizational Administration.

Program Mission Statement/Description: The Bachelor of Science in Organizational Administration prepares students to skillfully carry out the job responsibilities of employees in an organization. The organization can be a business, nonprofit, school, or government workplace. Emphasis is placed on oral and written communication skills, developing problem-solving techniques, and respecting other people for their own ideas, differences, and uniqueness. Particular emphasis is placed on integrating Christian values, ethics, and faith in the curriculum.

Accreditation: North Central Association of Colleges and Schools.

Admission Requirements: HS/GED Diploma; Prior Credits 86; Minimum Age 25 years.

Credit Awards for Prior Learning: ACE Military Recommendations; ACE/PONSI Recommendations; Portfolio Assessment; Transfer Credit; Professional technical credit for licenses such as real estate and financial counselor.

Limits to Credit Awards for Prior Learning: Professional technical—60 quarter credits.

Credit Awards for Examinations: CLEP General Exams; CLEP Subject Exams; DANTES Subject Tests.

Estimated Average Completion Time: Bachelors' Degrees: 15 months (full-time).

Caveats Regarding Time Estimates: We began this Adult Degree Completion Program September 1990.

Credit Hour Requirements:

Degree	Total Hours	Academic Residency*
Bachelor's	188	45

*Hours that must be earned at the institution exclusive of credit-by-exam, portfolio assessment, etc.

Distance Learning Options: None.

Student Support Services Available: Academic Advising; Financial Aid; Job Placement Assistance; Orientation.

Informational Materials Available: Institutional Catalog; Prior Learning Guides; Program Brochure.

Program Age, Enrollment, and Degrees Conferred:

Degree	Year Est.	Current Enrollment	Degrees Conferred
BS	1990	0	0

Percentage of Bachelor's Degree Holders Admitted to Graduate School: Information not available.

Geographic Admission Restrictions: None.

Tuition and Fees: In-State Tuition $160.00 per credit; Application Fee $15.00; Graduation Fee $30.00; Textbooks/Supplies Fee $500.00; Entire Program Portfolio Fee varies ($500.00 suggested).

---

98. University of Minnesota

107 Armory
15 Church St. SE
Minneapolis, MN 55455

Degrees Offered: Bachelor of Arts and Bachelor of Science in individually designed fields of study.

Program Mission Statement/Description: The mission of the Program for Individualized Learning (PIL) is to serve students who seek innovative opportunities for individualized undergraduate education. The program does this by offering a distinctive BA or BS degree for intellectually independent students; teaching individual curriculum development, independent study design, and reflective analysis; analyzing and assessing learning gained outside of the classroom; fostering active learning through inquiry; and encouraging the integration of social involvement and ethical awareness with intellectual pursuits.

Accreditation: North Central Association of Colleges and Schools.

Admission Requirements: To qualify for admission to PIL, students must demonstrate an understanding of why they want a bachelor's degree and how PIL will help them to achieve that goal; the ability to describe their proposed field of study and identify ways of acquiring learning in the liberal arts; the skills needed to design independent learning projects; a command of written English.

Credit Awards for Prior Learning: Transfer Credit.

Other Options: The above option has been used in individual cases but not "generically." We review each student's prior learning as it relates to her or his goals and to the university's educational standards.

Limits to Credit Awards for Prior Learning: We are not a credit-based program. Theoretically, it is possible for all of the learning in a degree program to be prior learning. Realistically, however, this is not the case.

Credit Awards for Examinations: CLEP General Exams; CLEP Subject Exams; College Board AP Exams; Departmental Exams.

Estimated Average Completion Time: Bachelors' Degrees: 5 years (part-time), 3 years (full-time).

Caveats Regarding Time Estimates: Most students enter with some prior college, so graduate in less than the above time spans. Variations are quite wide.

Credit Hour Requirements: Academic residency (hours that must be earned at the institution exclusive of credit-by-exam, portfolio assessment, etc.)—45 hours, but must satisfy graduation criteria rather than meet specific credit hour requirement.

Minimum Campus Time Required: Quarterly visits to campus are expected of students.

Distance Learning Options: A/V Cassettes; Correspondence Courses; Independent Study; Phone/Mail Instruction; Television Courses.

Student Support Services Available: Academic Advising; Career Counseling; Counseling/Testing; Financial Aid; Job Placement Assistance; Orientation; Tutoring. Full-time students can use any/all services available to any University of Minnesota students. There are some limitations for part-time students.

Informational Materials Available: Institutional Catalog; Program Brochure; Student Handbook (for enrolled students only).

Program Age, Enrollment, and Graduates:

Degree	Year Est.	Current Enrollment	Degrees Conferred
BA/BS	1971	180	522

Percentage of Bachelor's Degree Holders Admitted to Graduate School: 50-60 percent.

Geographic Admission Restrictions: PIL serves students who live in Minnesota, Iowa, North Dakota, South Dakota, Wisconsin, and Manitoba. PIL will also attempt to serve former University of Minnesota students who live outside the region. Students living outside the Twin Cities metropolitan area must have at least 60 quarter credits of prior college work. They must also have access to appropriate educational resources.

Tuition and Fees: In-State Tuition (1992-93) $71.00; Application Fee $25.00; Credit-by-Exam Fee $40.00; "Continuing registration" for quarters when students are not otherwise registered for programmatic registrations—$50.00 per quarter.

Mississippi

99. Millsaps College

Adult Degree Program
P.O. Box 150035
Jackson, MS 39210

Degrees Offered: Bachelor of Liberal Studies.

Program Mission Statement/Description: The Adult Degree Program (ADP) enables nontraditional students to pursue an undergraduate degree while continuing their other professional, family, and community responsibilities.

Accreditation: Southern Association of Colleges and Schools.

Admission Requirements: Essay/Written Work; HS/GED Diploma; Interview; Recommendations. Transcripts from earlier college work.

Credit Awards for Prior Learning: ACE Military Recommendations; ACE/PONSI Recommendations; Portfolio Assessment; Transfer Credit.

Limits to Credit Awards for Prior Learning: No more than 12 hours per academic department; no more than 30 hours from all sources; must be among first 90 semester hours toward the 120 semester hour degree.

Credit Awards for Examinations: ACT Proficiency Exams; CLEP Subject Exams; College Board AP Exams; Departmental Exams.

Estimated Average Completion Time: 6-7 years (part-time), 4 years (full-time).

Caveats Regarding Time Estimates: Most of our ADP students have one, 2, or 3 years of previous college work. A few have been without any education beyond high school. One of those, at age 54, graduated in 7 years, Phi

Beta Kappa and worked the entire time in a full-time job plus being a wife, mother, daughter, and active in the community. ADP students are regularly inducted into the academic honor fraternities.

Credit Hour Requirements: 120 hours total; 30 hours academic residency (hours that must be earned at the institution exclusive of credit-by-exam, portfolio assessment, etc.).

Distance Learning Options: Independent Study; Supervised Fieldwork.

Student Support Services Available: Academic Advising; Career Counseling; Counseling/Testing; Financial Aid; Job Placement Assistance; Orientation; Tutoring.

Other Student Services: Adult Student Association provides a social dimension for students with two parties per year; Millsaps College has a student lounge for ADP students; the required reentry seminar provides excellent support; the office of Adult Learning has a mid-week campuswide celebration during National Adult and Continuing Education Week.

Informational Materials Available: Exam Preparation Guides; Institutional Catalog; Prior Learning Guides; Program Brochure; Handbooks in ADP Guidelines and Procedures and Independent Studies.

Program Age, Enrollment, and Degrees Conferred:

Degree	Year Est.	Current Enrollment	Degrees Conferred
Bachelor of Liberal Studies	1982	93	39

Percentage of Bachelor's Degree Holders Admitted to Graduate School: 20 percent.

Geographic Admission Restrictions: The nature of our ADP requires campus presence. Students commute from as far as 100 miles away. There are no out-of-state students thus far.

Tuition and Fees: In-State Tuition $300.00 per credit; Out-of-State Tuition $300.00 per credit; Application Fee $20.00; Graduation Fee $50.00; Credit-by-Exam Fee $45.00.

Other Fees: Student Activities Fee ($50.00 full-time, $2.00/ semester hour, part-time. Provides access to programs, student newspaper subscription, etc. Parking permit; computer and science lab fees for certain courses.

Other Pertinent Information: A 3-semester hour re-entry seminar required of all students entering the interdisciplinary Adult Degree Program. Independent Directed Studies via Learning Contracts. Nonacademic credit for prior experiential learning. The option of designing an interdisciplinary major.

100. Mississippi State University

Office of Continuing Education
P.O. Drawer 5247
Mississippi State, MS 39762

Degrees Offered: Master of Arts in Political Science; Master of Arts in Public Policy Administration; Master of Business Administration; Bachelor of General Studies.

Program Mission Statement/Description: Continuing Education at Mississippi State University is dedicated to extending educational opportunities, through a variety of learning options to individuals not being served through traditional programs. The primary purpose is to provide programs tailored to the need of lifelong learners.

Accreditation: Southern Association of Colleges and Schools.

Admission Requirements: GRE; Recommendations; Undergraduate Degree.

Credit Awards for Prior Learning: Transfer Credit.

Credit Awards for Examinations: CLEP Subject Exams; College Board AP Exams.

Limits to Credit Awards for Examinations: Undergraduate credit only.

Estimated Average Completion Time: Bachelors' Degrees: MA—2.5 years, MBA—2.5 years (part-time).

Credit Hour Requirements:

Degree	Total Hours	Academic Residency*
Graduate (MA/MBA)	30	21

*Hours that must be earned at the institution exclusive of credit-by-exam, portfolio assessment, etc.

Distance Learning Options: Intensive semester; weekend classes.

Student Support Services Available: Academic Advising; Career Counseling; Orientation.

Informational Materials Available: Institutional Catalog; Program Brochure.

Program Age, Enrollment, and Degrees Conferred:

Degree	Year Est.	Current Enrollment	Degrees Conferred
MBA	1970	40	69
MA PPA	1981	24	22
MA PS	1984	14	14

Percentage of Bachelor's Degree Holders Admitted to Graduate School: Information not available.

Geographic Admission Restrictions: None.

Tuition and Fees: In-State Tuition $90.00 per credit; Out-of-State Tuition $164.00 per credit.

Missouri

101. Avila College

Weekend College
11901 Wornall Rd.
Kansas City, MO 64145

Degrees Offered: Associate of General Studies; Bachelor of General Studies.

Program Mission Statement/Description: Avila's Weekend College is designed for students who find the weekend a convenient and attractive time for learning and studying. It is designed to service students who, because of job and family responsibilities, find Saturday and Sunday classes compatible with their life-styles and goals. The Weekend College is for people of all ages. It is for people interested in a degree. It is for people pursuing a career. It is for personal growth. In other words, Avila's Weekend College is for anyone who wishes to enrich weekends by attending college classes.

Accreditation: North Central Association of Colleges and Schools.

Admission Requirements: HS/GED Diploma; Recommendations; ACT or SAT score levels.

Credit Awards for Prior Learning: Portfolio Assessment; Transfer Credit.

Limits to Credit Awards for Prior Learning: Transfer from 2-year colleges has a 64-credit limit. Transfer from a 4-year college has a 98-credit limit. Portfolio limit is 25% of total requirements.

Credit Awards for Examinations: CLEP General Exams; CLEP Subject Exams; Departmental Exams.

Limits to Credit Awards for Examinations: CLEP limit is 25% of total requirements.

Estimated Average Completion Time: Associates' Degrees: 4 years (part-time), 2 years (full-time); Bachelors' Degrees: 8 years (part-time), 4 years (full-time).

Credit Hour Requirements:

Degree	Total Hours	Academic Residency*
Associate's	64	18
Bachelor's	128	30

*Hours that must be earned at the institution exclusive of credit-by-exam, portfolio assessment, etc.

Distance Learning Options: None.

Student Support Services Available: Academic Advising; Career Counseling; Counseling/Testing; Financial Aid; Job Placement Assistance; Orientation; Tutoring.

Informational Materials Available: Institutional Catalog; Prior Learning Guides; Program Brochure.

Program Age, Enrollment, and Degrees Conferred:

Degree	Year Est.	Current Enrollment	Degrees Conferred
AGS	1984	2	3
BGS	1984	25	60

Percentage of Bachelor's Degree Holders Admitted to Graduate School: Information not available.

Geographic Admission Restrictions: None.

Tuition and Fees: In-State Tuition $151.00 per credit; Application Fee $20.00; Graduation Fee $70.00; Credit-by-Exam Fee $20.00.

102. Fontbonne College

6800 Wydown Boulevard
Options Program
St. Louis, MO 63105

Degrees Offered: Bachelor of Business Administration; Master of Business Administration.

Program Mission Statement/Description: The Options Program, operating within the framework of the Fontbonne College institutional mission, provides opportunities for adult students to pursue undergraduate and graduate degrees in a nontraditional setting. It recognizes the needs of these students by offering educational programs in liberal arts and professional studies. The specific goals of the Fontbonne College Options Program are to extend opportunities for higher education to individuals whose occupations, family responsibilities, or personal preference impede their ability to enroll in traditional campus-based programs; to provide programs for degree completion that require mastery of stated learning outcomes; to equip students with skills that enhance personal and professional development, including written and oral communication, problem solving, group interaction, and decision making; to provide curricula that draws upon theories, knowledge, and resources from all relevant disciplines; to furnish educational opportunities for a variety of professional careers and to extend the range of career choices for students; to foster academic excellence in professional and graduate endeavors; to provide learning experiences that encourage critical thinking, analytical reading and quantitative reasoning; to provide an educational curriculum to encourage commitment to ethical values, social issues, and environmental concerns; to expose students to learning experiences that further awareness of the international community; to offer opportunities to explore and understand the application of Christian principles in a professional environment.

Accreditation: North Central Association of Colleges and Schools.

Admission Requirements:

Undergraduate	Graduate
HS/GED Diploma	Undergraduate Degree
Recommendations	Employment/Experience:
Employment/Experience:	(3 years)
(2 years)	
Prior Credits: 60 semester hours	

Other Admission Requirements: Bachelor of Business Administration: 2.0 GPA/Minimum age of 25 years/ TOEFL (if applicable). Master of Business Administration: 2.5 GPA/TOEFL (if applicable).

Credit Awards for Prior Learning: ACE Military Recommendations; ACE/PONSI Recommendations; Transfer Credit; CLEAR—Credit for Life Experience that is Academically Related to Fontbonne College course(s).

Limits to Credit Awards for Prior Learning: BBA: Maximum of 72 credits from a community college. CLEAR maximum of 32 credits. All nontraditional credit (CLEAR, CLEP, PEP, ACE, etc.) max of 48 credits. MBA: transfer maximum of 6 credits, depending on age and content.

Credit Awards for Examinations: CLEP Subject Exams; DANTES Subject Tests; Departmental Exams.

Estimated Average Completion Time: Bachelors' Degrees: 22 months (full-time); Graduate Degrees: 24 months (full-time).

Caveats Regarding Time Estimates: BBA must complete a total minimum of 128 credits for the degree. The core is 45 credits and students enter with a minimum of 60. All General Education Requirements (GER) must be satisfied. Part-time study is not allowed.

Credit Hour Requirements: Bachelors' Degrees: 45 credit hours; Graduate Degrees: 43 credit hours; Distance Learning Options: None.

Student Support Services Available: Academic Advising; Financial Aid; Orientation.

Informational Materials Available: Institutional Catalog; Program Brochure.

Program Age, Enrollment, and Degrees Conferred:

Degree	Year Est.	Current Enrollment	Degrees Conferred
BBA	1991	32	0
MBA	1991	32	0

Percentage of Bachelor's Degree Holders Admitted to Graduate School: No BBA graduates until 1993.

Geographic Admission Restrictions: None.

Tuition and Fees:

	Undergraduate	Graduate
In-State Tuition	$173.00/credit	$242.00/credit
Application Fee	$20.00	$20.00
Registration Fee	$30.00	$30.00
Parking Permit	$30.00	$30.00
(Fontbonne campus only)		

Other Pertinent Information: The Options Program was created in 1991 to serve the unique educational needs of the working adult. Offerings include the Bachelor of Business Administration (BBA) and the Master of Business Administration (MBA) programs. Options is dedicated to coursework and experiences that are directly applicable to employment; cases and assignments are "real life" and practical, not simply theoretical or "textbook." Options uses a classroom style and course content that are very interactive, goal oriented, outcome driven, practical and stimulating to the student; there are no dry lectures or esoteric trivia. Options faculty are highly skilled individuals who know their fields intimately and in-depth because they work them every day; there are no impractical teachings that no longer fit in today's modern business world.

Options gives you flexibility and choice of degrees: BBA or MBA. Meeting times and days: courses meet one night a week (your choice) from 6 to 10 p.m. Location: courses are offered in a location convenient for you. Starting date: new groups can start in any month of the year and are not tied to standard semester or quarter system calendars. Options students learn together in small groups (generally 16 students) which are enhanced by a study group approach and collaboration on projects. The Options MBA degree is designed to utilize computer data bases, word processing, and spreadsheets for classroom work and assignments. A lap-top computer is provided to each MBA student; it remains the student's property upon completion of all program requirements. Fontbonne's Options Program provides a unique, flexible, and practical approach to educational advancement for the working adult.

103. Longview Community College

Program for Adult College Education
500 Longview Rd.
Lee's Summit, MO 64081

Degrees Offered: Associate in Arts Degree.

Program Mission Statement/Description: The Program for Adult College Education (PACE) is designed for working adults who want to attend college and complete a degree. PACE differs from traditional programs by offering both interdisciplinary and traditional courses in a unique delivery system which involves scheduling classes so that they are more convenient for working adults. Students are encouraged to enroll for a block of three courses in a single discipline area each semester. The first class meets one evening a week at a variety of convenient locations around the metropolitan area. Instruction for the second course is provided partly by VHS videotapes that the students check out of the library for home viewing. The third class meets 4 weekends per semester on the college campus. Since most courses carry 4 hours of credit, students are able to earn up to 12 hours each semester and should be able to complete the 62 hours required for the Associate in Arts degree in approximately 5 semesters. Students in traditional night classes need as many as 5 or 6 years to complete the same degree. The mission of the program is to provide a convenient and rapid way for the working adult to earn a traditional degree that will transfer to a 4-year institution.

Accreditation: North Central Association of Colleges and Schools.

Admission Requirements: This is an open admission public institution, so actually anyone is able to enroll even if they have no high school diploma or GED.

Credit Awards for Prior Learning: Transfer Credit.

Limits to Credit Awards for Prior Learning: No limit on credits but must earn at least 15 credits here to have a degree granted from this college.

Credit Awards for Examinations: CLEP Subject Exams.

Estimated Average Completion Time: Associates' Degrees: 3 years (part-time), 2 years (full-time).

Credit Hour Requirements:

Degree	Total Hours	Academic Residency*
Associate	62	15

*Hours that must be earned at the institution exclusive of credit-by-exam, portfolio assessment, etc.

Distance Learning Options: A/V Cassettes; Independent Study; Television Courses.

Student Support Services Available: Academic Advising; Career Counseling; Counseling/Testing; Financial Aid; Job Placement Assistance; Tutoring; Telephone Advising; Enrollment with Payment by Mail or Credit Card.

Informational Materials Available: Institutional Catalog; Program Brochure; Current Schedule of Classes.

Program Age, Enrollment, and Degrees Conferred:

Degree	Year Est.	Current Enrollment	Degrees Conferred
AA	1979	1200	1100

Geographic Admission Restrictions: No restrictions, but fees are higher for geographic differences.

Tuition and Fees:

	Undergraduate
In-State Tuition	$56.00 per credit
Out-of-State Tuition	$84.00 per credit
Graduation Fee	$30.00
Credit-by-Exam Fee	$25.00

104. Research College of Nursing

Accelerated Bachelor of Science in Nursing Degree Option
2316 East Meyer Blvd.
Kansas City, MO 64132

Degrees Offered: Bachelor of Science in Nursing.

Program Mission Statement/Description: Research College of Nursing is a private institution of higher learning committed primarily to excellence in nursing education. The academic community provides an atmosphere that is scholarly, conducive to learning and directed toward the development of the individual. Through the individual the college provides service to society. Research College of Nursing encourages scholarship and development of new knowledge as a goal in itself and as a means of maintaining teaching excellence and providing service to society.

Accreditation: North Central Association of Colleges and Schools; National League for Nursing.

Admission Requirements: HS/GED Diploma; Interview; 2.8/4.00 GPA (first degree).

Credit Awards for Prior Learning: Transfer Credit.

Credit Awards for Examinations: ACT Proficiency Exams (RN/BSN); CLEP Subject Exams.

Limits to Credit Awards for Examinations: CLEP and ACT-PEP for a total not to exceed 32 credit hours.

Estimated Average Completion Time: Bachelors' Degrees: 4-5 years (part-time), 2-2.5 years (full-time).

Caveats Regarding Time Estimates: Accelerated Option—three 16 week blocks; 40 hours/week 59 credit hours. 15 hours residency requirement at Rockhurst College. Prerequisites, as needed.

Credit Hour Requirements: 128 hours total; 36 hours academic residency (hours that must be earned at the institution exclusive of credit-by-exam, portfolio assessment, etc.).

Distance Learning Options: None.

Student Support Services Available: Academic Advising; Career Counseling; Counseling/Testing; Financial Aid; Job Placement Assistance; Orientation; Tutoring; Housing.

Informational Materials Available: Exam Preparation Guides; Institutional Catalog; Program Brochure; Financial Aid Packets; Scholarships.

Program Age, Enrollment, and Degrees Conferred:

Degree	Year Est.	Current Enrollment	Degrees Conferred
Accelerated Option	1991	10	0

Percentage of Bachelor's Degree Holders Admitted to Graduate School: No graduates as yet.

Geographic Admission Restrictions: None.

Tuition and Fees: In-State Tuition $14,385.00 per year; Graduation Fee $50.00; Credit-by-Exam Fee same as standard CLEP fees.

Other Pertinent Information: Research College of Nursing is in partnership with Rockhurst College (Jesuit). Graduates receive a joint degree from these two institutions.

Nebraska

105. Bishop Clarkson College

333 S. 44th St.
Omaha, NE 68131-3799

Degrees Offered: Bachelor of Science in Nursing; Master of Science in Nursing; Master of Science in Health Services Management; Associate of Science in Radiology; Bachelor of Science in Radiology Technology.

Program Mission Statement/Description: It is the mission of Bishop Clarkson College to offer academic programs of high quality which consider the uniqueness of each student. The college programs promote the integration of the liberal arts with the competency associated with professional education. Coordination of academic and experiential learning is emphasized. The college provides the student with a foundation of learning necessary for the development of logical thinking, critical analysis, literacy, values, historical awareness and the comprehensive knowledge related to the major area of study. The college views excellence in education as its primary commitment. Community service is also seen as an important component of the college mission. Although research is not a primary aspect of the mission of the college, the college is committed to the support and utilization of research investigation and findings.

Accreditation: North Central Association of Colleges and Schools; National League for Nursing.

Admission Requirements:

Undergraduate	Graduate
HS/GED Diploma	Undergraduate Degree
Interview	Essay/Written Work
Recommendations	Recommendations
	GRE, GMAT

Other Admission Requirements: Upper half of high school class. ACT composite 19. Undergraduate GPA 3.0. Nursing license for MSN; 500 or better in TOEFL for foreign students.

Credit Awards for Prior Learning: Transfer Credit.

Credit Awards for Examinations: ACT Proficiency Exams; CLEP Subject Exams; DANTES Subject Tests; Departmental Exams.

Estimated Average Completion Time: Associates' Degrees: 2 years; Bachelors' Degrees: 6 years (part-time), 4 years (full-time); Graduate Degrees: 4 years (part-time), 2 years (full-time).

Caveats Regarding Time Estimates: Time to complete assumes continuous enrollment; however, nontraditional students may "stop out" a semester which delays completion.

Credit Hour Requirements:

Degree	Total Hours	Academic Residency*
Associate	67	15
Bachelor's	128	15
Graduate (MSN)	36	18
Graduate (MS)	36	18

*Hours that must be earned at the institution exclusive of credit-by-exam, portfolio assessment, etc.

Distance Learning Options: A/V Cassettes; Electronic Mail; Independent Study (Associate and Bachelor only); Phone/Mail Instruction; Study Guides; Supervised Fieldwork (Associate and Bachelor only); Computer-Assisted Instruction (CAI) and Externships.

Student Support Services Available: Academic Advising; Career Counseling; Counseling/Testing; Financial Aid; Job Placement Assistance; Orientation; Tutoring; Library, Education Resource Center, Computer Labs, and Short Term Housing.

Informational Materials Available: Exam Preparation Guides; Institutional Catalog; Program Brochure; Handbooks describing services and guides to preparation of formal papers.

Program Age, Enrollment, and Degrees Conferred:

Degree	Year Est.	Current Enrollment	Degrees Conferred
BSN	1981	460	361
MSN	1990	0	50
MS	1990	10	0
AS	1991	7	0
BS	1991	0	0

Percentage of Bachelor's Degree Holders Admitted to Graduate School: 25 percent.

Geographic Admission Restrictions: Foreign students must score at 500 or better on TOEFL.

Tuition and Fees:

	Undergraduate	Graduate
In-State Tuition	$190.00/credit	$209.00/credit
Application Fee	$15.00	$15.00
Graduation Fee	$150.00	$150.00
Credit-by-Exam Fee	Varies	

Other Fees: Enrollment Fee—$20.00; Late Registration $25.00; Associate of Science in Radiology Technology is a flat fee of $1500.00 per year.

Other Pertinent Information: Graduate courses meet on campus only 3 weekends per 12 week trimester. Geographically distant RN students in the baccalaureate program (advanced placed) meet 3-4 times with faculty each semester. On-campus evaluations are required for students residing outside Nebraska.

106. Creighton University

University College of Creighton
California St. at 24th
Omaha, NE 68178

Degrees Offered: Bachelor of Science in Atmospheric Sciences; Bachelor of Science; Bachelor of Arts; Bachelor of Science in Business Administration; Associate in Arts; Associate in Science.

Program Mission Statement/Description: University College shares in the traditions of Creighton University, extending the commitments and resources of the university beyond customary academic boundaries. University College serves the educational needs and interests of diverse populations, providing access to Creighton's academic environment for adults. University College classes are offered during late afternoon and early evening hours for adult part-time students. However, University College students are also allowed to register for daytime courses and as full-time students.

Accreditation: North Central Association of Colleges and Schools; the American Assembly of Collegiate Schools of Business; National Council for Accreditation of Teacher Education.

Admission Requirements:

Undergraduate	Graduate
HS/GED Diploma	Undergraduate Degree
Prior Credits	Interview
Recommendations	GRE

Other Admission Requirements: Any student who has been dismissed from any educational institution in the previous calendar year will normally not be admitted to University College of Creighton. Graduate degrees are not awarded by University College but by the Creighton University Graduate School.

Credit Awards for Prior Learning: ACE Military Recommendations; ACE/PONSI Recommendations; Transfer Credit; Department Recommendation.

Limits to Credit Awards for Prior Learning: Normally the amount of transfer credit accepted is limited to 80 hours.

Credit Awards for Examinations: CLEP Subject Exams; College Board AP Exams; DANTES Subject Tests; Departmental Exams.

Limits to Credit Awards for Examinations: Amount of credit awarded is limited by the number of options available.

Estimated Average Completion Time: Associates' Degrees: 4-5 years (part-time); Bachelors' Degrees: 7-10 years (part-time).

Caveats Regarding Time Estimates: Time estimates assume no transfer hours and registration for 6 hours per semester, including summer.

Credit Hour Requirements:

Degree	Total Hours	Academic Residency*
Associate	64	32
Bachelor's	128	48-64

*Hours that must be earned at the institution exclusive of credit-by-exam, portfolio assessment, etc.

Distance Learning Options: Correspondence Courses; Independent Study; Supervised Fieldwork.

Student Support Services Available: Academic Advising; Career Counseling; Counseling/Testing; Financial Aid; Job Placement Assistance; Orientation; Tutoring.

Informational Materials Available: Institutional Catalog; Program Brochure.

Other Information Available: Counseling Center programs on how to study and test taking. Library use course on writing research papers. Interest Inventory, Myers-Briggs, and other tests at Counseling Center.

Program Age, Enrollment, and Degrees Conferred:

Degree	Year Est.	Current Enrollment	Degrees Conferred
BA	1983	123	33
BS	1983	64	41
BS in Bus. Admin.	1983	21	6
AA	1990	0	0
AS	1985	0	3

Percentage of Bachelor's Degree Holders Admitted to Graduate School: Information not available.

Geographic Admission Restrictions: None.

Tuition and Fees: In-State Tuition $250.00 per credit; Out-of-State Tuition $250.00 per credit; Application Fee $25.00; Credit-by-Exam Fee $10.00 per credit.

Other Fees: Special fees for labs and studio materials; University fee (for activities, etc.)—$140.00 for full-time students; $14.00 for part-time students.

107. Hastings College

22 PLUS Program
P.O. Box 269
Hastings, NE 68902

Degrees Offered: Bachelor of Arts; Bachelor of Music; Master of Arts in Teaching.

Program Mission Statement/Description: The 22-PLUS Program is for persons who are at least 22 years of age, who have not been a full-time student in an educational institution for at least 4 years, and who have not yet completed a bachelor's degree. Students may complete their first 60 semester hours of credit at Hastings College with a half-tuition scholarship.

Accreditation: North Central Association of Colleges and Schools; the National Council for the Accreditation of Teacher Education; and the National Association of Schools of Music.

Admission Requirements:

Undergraduate	Graduate
HS/GED Diploma	Undergraduate Degree
Recommendations	Recommendations
	GRE

Credit Awards for Prior Learning: ACE Military Recommendations; ACE/PONSI Recommendations; Portfolio Assessment; Transfer Credit.

Limits to Credit Awards for Prior Learning: Last 30 hours must be taken in residence.

Credit Awards for Examinations: CLEP Subject Exams; College Board AP Exams; Departmental Exams.

Limits to Credit Awards for Examinations: 20 semester hour limit on credit by examination.

Estimated Average Completion Time: Bachelors' Degrees: 8 years (part-time), 4 years (full-time); Graduate Degrees: MAT 3 years (part-time), 1 year (full-time).

Credit Hour Requirements:

Degrees	Total Hours	Academic Residency*
Bachelor's	130	30
Graduate	33	27

*Hours that must be earned at the institution exclusive of credit-by-exam, portfolio assessment, etc.

Distance Learning Options: Independent Study; Supervised Fieldwork.

Student Support Services Available: Academic Advising; Career Counseling; Counseling/Testing; Financial Aid; Job Placement Assistance; Orientation; Tutoring.

Informational Materials Available: Institutional Catalog; Program Brochure.

Program Age, Enrollment, and Degrees Conferred:

Degree	Year Est.	Current Enrollment	Degrees Conferred
22-PLUS	1986	89	21

Percentage of Bachelor's Degree Holders Admitted to Graduate School: Information not available.

Geographic Admission Restrictions: None.

Tuition and Fees:

	Undergraduate	Graduate
In-State Tuition	$297.00/credit	$109.00/credit
Out-of-State Tuition	$297.00/credit	$109.00/credit
Application Fee	$20.00	$20.00
Graduation Fee	$60.00	$60.00

108. Nebraska Wesleyan University

Wesley Institute for Lifelong Learning
5000 St. Paul Ave.
Lincoln, NE 68504

Degrees Offered: Bachelor of Science in Nursing; Bachelor of Arts; Bachelor of Science; Associate of Science in Business Administration; Associate of Arts in Paralegal Studies; Associate of Science in Massage Therapy; Associate of Arts in Art.

Program Mission Statement/Description: The Wesleyan Institute for Lifelong Learning extends the resources of Nebraska Wesleyan University to adults in the community through evening credit and noncredit programs.

Accreditation: North Central Association of Colleges and Schools.

Admission Requirements: HS/GED Diploma. The day program has selective admissions; the evening program has open admissions.

Credit Awards for Prior Learning: Transfer Credit.

Credit Awards for Examinations: ACT Proficiency Exams; CLEP Subject Exams.

Estimated Average Completion Time: Associates' Degrees: 4 years (part-time), 2 years (full-time); Bachelors' Degrees: 7 years (part-time), 4 years (full-time).

Caveats Regarding Time Estimates: This assumes no previous academic work—which is unusual.

Credit Hour Requirements:

Degree	Total Hours	Academic Residency*
Associate	65	30
Bachelor's	126	30

*Hours that must be earned at the institution exclusive of credit-by-exam, portfolio assessment, etc.

Distance Learning Options: Independent Study; Supervised Fieldwork.

Student Support Services Available: Academic Advising; Career Counseling; Counseling/Testing; Financial Aid; Job Placement Assistance; Orientation; Tutoring.

Informational Materials Available: Institutional Catalog; Program Brochure.

Program Age, Enrollment, and Degrees Conferred:

Degree	Year Est.	Current Enrollment	Degrees Conferred
Bachelor's and Associate's	1978	220	150

Percentage of Bachelor's Degree Holders Admitted to Graduate School: Information not available.

Geographic Admission Restrictions: None.

Tuition and Fees: In-State Tuition $110.00 per credit; Out-of-State Tuition $110.00 per credit; Application Fee $40.00; Library Fee per semester $5.00.

Other Pertinent Information: Although evening tuition is $110.00 per credit hour, current tuition in the day program is $312.00 per credit hour.

109. University of Nebraska at Omaha

College of Continuing Studies
208 Arts and Science Hall
60th and Dodge
Omaha, NE 68182

Degrees Offered: Bachelor of General Studies.

Program Mission Statement/Description: The Bachelor of General Studies degree requires 125 semester hours and features two options: Option I requires a 45 semester hour liberal arts core, a 30 semester hour area of concentration (38 to choose from), two 12 semester hour secondary fields, and 26 semester hours of elective credit. Option II requires a 45 semester hour liberal arts core, three 15 semester hour areas of emphasis, and 35 semester hours of elective credit.

Accreditation: North Central Association of Colleges and Schools.

Admission Requirements: HS/GED Diploma.

Credit Awards for Prior Learning: ACE Military Recommendations; ACE/PONSI Recommendations; Transfer Credit.

Other Options: College policies allow credit for hospital-based nursing programs; Licensed Radiologic, Cytotechnology, FAA pilots, and Insurance Industry programs.

Limits to Credit Awards for Prior Learning: 64 semester hours from an accredited 2-year junior college program. 65 semester hours from all noncollegiate sponsored instruction from all sources.

Credit Awards for Examinations: CLEP General Exams; CLEP Subject Exams; College Board AP Exams; DANTES Subject Tests; Departmental Exams.

Estimated Average Completion Time: 8 years (part-time), 4 years (full-time).

Credit Hour Requirements:

Degree	Total Hours	Academic Residency*
Bachelor's	125	24

*Hours that must be earned at the institution exclusive of credit-by-exam, portfolio assessment, etc.

Distance Learning Options: Cooperative Education; Correspondence Courses; Independent Study; Newspaper Courses; Television Courses.

Student Support Services Available: Academic Advising; Career Counseling; Counseling/Testing; Financial Aid; Job Placement Assistance; Orientation; Tutoring.

Informational Materials Available: Program Brochure.

Program Age, Enrollment, and Degrees Conferred:

Degree	Year Est.	Current Enrollment	Degrees Conferred
BGS	1950	1400	18000

Percentage of Bachelor's Degree Holders Admitted to Graduate School: Information not available.

Geographic Admission Restrictions: Must be admitted to College of Continuing Studies, University of Nebraska at Omaha, attending in residence and taking UNO academic courses.

Tuition and Fees: In-State Tuition $47.50 per credit; Out-of-State Tuition $128.25 per credit; Application Fee $10.00; Credit-by-Exam Fee varies. University program and facilities fee and ID card fee $55.00 a semester. Graduation fee if not attending ceremony $5.00.

New Hampshire

110. University System of New Hampshire

School for Lifelong Learning
Dunlap Center
Durham, NH 03824

Degrees Offered: Associate of Arts in General Studies; Bachelor of General Studies; Bachelor of Professional Studies.

Program Mission Statement/Description: The mission of the University System School for Lifelong Learning is to serve the higher educational needs of the adult population of New Hampshire. The school strives through innovative programming to create and assure the availability of high quality, adult-learner-oriented higher education opportunities to all New Hampshire citizens and to provide quality leadership in adult degree programming for the state and region. It seeks to develop the skills required for lifelong learning.

Accreditation: New England Association of Schools and Colleges, Inc.

Admission Requirements: Employment/Experience: 2 years for bachelor's program; Essay/Written Work; HS/GED Diploma; Interview.

Credit Awards for Prior Learning: ACE Military Recommendations; ACE/PONSI Recommendations; Portfolio Assessment; Transfer Credit; Validation/Local Version of ACE/PONSI Recommendations.

Credit Awards for Examinations: ACT Proficiency Exams; CLEP General Exams; CLEP Subject Exams; College Board AP Exams; DANTES Subject Tests; Departmental Exams.

Estimated Average Completion Time: Associates' Degrees: 4 years (part-time), 2 years (full-time); Bachelors' Degrees: 4 years (part-time), 2 years (full-time).

Credit Hour Requirements:

Degree	Total Hours	Academic Residency*
Associate	64	16
Bachelor's	124	30

*Hours that must be earned at the institution exclusive of credit-by-exam, portfolio assessment, etc.

Distance Learning Options: A/V Cassettes; Correspondence Courses; Independent Study; Television Courses.

Student Support Services Available: Academic Advising; Career Counseling; Counseling/Testing; Financial Aid; Job Placement Assistance; Tutoring.

Informational Materials Available: Institutional Catalog; Prior Learning Guides; Program Brochure.

Program Age, Enrollment, and Degrees Conferred:

Degree	Year Est.	Current Enrollment	Degrees Conferred
AAGS	1972	808	1222
BGS	1972	67	1442
BPS	1985	755	357

Percentage of Bachelor's Degree Holders Admitted to Graduate School: Information not available.

Geographic Admission Restrictions: None.

Tuition and Fees: In-State Tuition $95.00 per credit; Out-of-State Tuition $105.00 per credit; Application Fee $35.00; Graduation Fee $35.00.

New Jersey

111. Caldwell College

9 Ryerson Ave.
Caldwell, NJ 07006-6195

Degrees Offered: Bachelor of Arts; Bachelor of Science.

Program Mission Statement/Description: Caldwell College has a tradition and a commitment to assist adult learners in their pursuit of lifelong learning. Responsive to the adult's quest for ongoing study, creative self-development, and preprofessional training, the college provides flexible degree programming geared to meet the specific goals of men and women of different ages, backgrounds, interests, and goals.

Accreditation: Middle States Association of Colleges and Schools.

Admission Requirements: HS/GED Diploma; Interview.

Credit Awards for Prior Learning: ACE Military Recommendations; ACE/PONSI Recommendations; Portfolio Assessment; Transfer Credit.

Limits to Credit Awards for Prior Learning: Maximum of 75 credits from other sources; 45 credits must be taken at Caldwell.

Credit Awards for Examinations: ACT Proficiency Exams; CLEP General Exams; CLEP Subject Exams; DANTES Subject Tests.

Estimated Average Completion Time: 5-7 years (part-time), 4 years (full-time).

Credit Hour Requirements: 120 hours total; 45 hours academic residency (hours that must be earned at the institution exclusive of credit-by-exam, portfolio assessment, etc.).

Distance Learning Options: Cooperative Education; Independent Study.

Student Support Services Available: Academic Advising; Career Counseling; Counseling/Testing; Financial Aid; Orientation; Tutoring.

Informational Materials Available: Exam Preparation Guides; Institutional Catalog; Prior Learning Guides; Program Brochure.

Program Age, Enrollment, and Degrees Conferred:

Degree	Year Est.	Current Enrollment	Degrees Conferred
BA, BS	1969	340	Unknown

Percentage of Bachelor's Degree Holders Admitted to Graduate School: Information not available.

Geographic Admission Restrictions: None.

Tuition and Fees: In-State Tuition: $200.00 per credit; Out-of-State Tuition: $200.00 per credit; Application Fee: $25.00; Graduation Fee: $75.00; Credit-by-Exam Fee: Varies.

112. Georgian Court College

Evening Division
900 Lakewood Ave.
Lakewood, NJ 08701-2697

Degrees Offered: Bachelor of Arts in Art; Bachelor of Arts in Art History; Bachelor of Arts in Chemistry; Bachelor of Arts in Humanities; Bachelor of Arts in Mathematics; Bachelor of Arts in Physics; Bachelor of Arts in Psychology; Bachelor of Arts in Sociology; Bachelor of Arts in Special Education; Bachelor of Science in Accounting; Bachelor of Science in Biology; Bachelor of Science in Business Administration.

Program Mission Statement/Description: The mission of the Evening Division is to provide an academic alternative for men and women to pursue a high quality liberal arts education within the context of the Georgian Court College approach to learning, community, and service.

Accreditation: Middle States Associations of Colleges and Schools.

Admission Requirements: HS/GED Diploma, Interview, Recommendations.

Credit Awards for Prior Learning: ACE Military Recommendations; ACE/PONSI Recommendations; Transfer Credit.

Limits to Credit Awards for Prior Learning: Transfer credits are evaluated on an individual basis.

Credit Awards for Examinations: ACT Proficiency Exams; CLEP General Exams; CLEP Subject Exams; College Board AP Exams; DANTES Subject Tests.

Estimated Average Completion Time: Varies with each student (part-time), 5 years (full-time).

Credit Hour Requirements: 30 hours total; 50 hours academic residency (hours that must be earned at the institution exclusive of credit-by-exam, portfolio assessment, etc.).

Distance Learning Options: Cooperative Education; Independent Study; Supervised Fieldwork.

Student Support Services Available: Academic Advising; Career Counseling; Counseling/Testing; Financial Aid; Job Placement Assistance; Orientation; Tutoring.

Informational Materials Available: Institutional Catalog; Program Brochure.

Program Age, Enrollment, and Degrees Conferred:

Degree	Year Est.	Current Enrollment	Degrees Conferred
Art	1983	11	5
Art History	1983	4	0
Chemistry	1985	6	0
Humanities	1988	51	12
Mathematics	1982	5	10
Physics	1985	4	0
Psychology	1982	43	40
Sociology	1980	27	31
Special Education	1981	23	24
Accounting	1985	87	68
Biology	1985	15	3
Business Administration	1979	188	239
Social Work	1986	20	23

Percentage of Bachelor's Degree Holders Admitted to Graduate School: Information not available.

Geographic Admission Restrictions: None.

Tuition and Fees:

	Undergraduate
In-State Tuition	$195.00
Out-of-State Tuition	$195.00
Application Fee	$20.00
Graduation Fee	$110.00
Registration Fee	$10.00
Parking Fee	$40.00 per semester

113. Rutgers University

University College-New Brunswick
35 College Ave.
New Brunswick, NJ 08901

Degrees Offered: Bachelor of Arts; Bachelor of Science.

Program Mission Statement/Description: Established in 1934, University College is the unit of Rutgers University in New Brunswick that serves adult, part-time students.

Accreditation: Middle States Association of Schools and Colleges.

Admission Requirements: HS/GED Diploma.

Other Admission Requirements: In some cases, an interview and test are required. Applicants must also supply transcripts of previous college work.

Credit Awards for Prior Learning: Transfer Credit.

Credit Awards for Examinations: CLEP General Exams; CLEP Subject Exams; College Board AP Exams; Departmental Exams.

Estimated Average Completion Time: It is difficult to arrive at a "typical" amount of time, because most University College students are transfers, with widely differing amounts of transfer credits.

Credit Hour Requirements: 120 hours total; 30 hours academic residency (hours that must be earned at the institution exclusive of credit-by-exam, portfolio assessment, etc.).

Distance Learning Options: None.

Student Support Services Available: Academic Advising; Career Counseling; Counseling/Testing; Financial Aid; Job Placement Assistance; Orientation; Tutoring; Health Service.

Informational Materials Available: Institutional Catalog; Program Brochure.

Program Age, Enrollment, and Degrees Conferred:

Degree	Year Est.	Current Enrollment	Degrees Conferred
Bachelor's	1934	3100	16000

Percentage of Bachelor's Degree Holders Admitted to Graduate School: Information not available.

Geographic Admission Restrictions: None.

Tuition and Fees: In-State Tuition $93.00 per credit; Out-of-State Tuition $188.00 per credit; Application Fee $30.00; Credit-by-Exam Fee $30.00; Student Fee $48.00.

Other Pertinent Information: Courses and degree programs are available days and evenings. Most students are over age 25, most have previous college work, and most have full-time jobs and family obligations.

New York

114. City University of New York Baccalaureate Program

Graduate Center North,
25 W. 43 St., Ste. 300
New York, NY 10036

Degrees Offered: Bachelor of Arts; Bachelor of Science.

Program Mission Statement/Description: The City University of New York (CUNY) Baccalaureate Program has 3 goals: to allow self-directed, motivated, academically able students to design, under faculty guidance, an individualized program of undergraduate study that complements their academic, professional, and personal goals; to foster intellectual exploration and responsible educational innovation by permitting students to use a variety of learning strategies; to encourage students to avail themselves of the extraordinary resources and learning opportunities available at the City University's 17 undergraduate colleges and at the Graduate School.

Accreditation: Middle States Association of Colleges and Schools.

Admission Requirements: Essay/Written Work; HS/GED Diploma; Interview; Prior Credits: 15; Recommendations; Passing Scores on CUNY Skills Assessment Tests in Reading, Writing, and Mathematics; At least a 2.5 grade-point index; Matriculation at a CUNY College.

Credit Awards for Prior Learning: ACE Military Recommendations*; ACE/PONSI Recommendations; Portfolio Assessment; Transfer Credit.

Limits to Credit Awards for Prior Learning: Limit of 15 credits prior experiential learning; limit of 90 transfer credits, of which only 68 can come from community colleges; limit of 30 nonclassroom credits.

Credit Awards for Examinations: ACT Proficiency Exams*; CLEP Subject Exams; College Board AP Exams*; DANTES Subject Tests*; Departmental Exams*.

Other Exam Options: New York State Regents College Credit earned in high school.

Estimated Average Completion Time: 4 years part-time, 2 years full-time.

Caveats Regarding Time Estimates: Because students enter the program with from 15 to 90 earned credits, it is not uncommon for a full-time student to graduate after 1.5 years, a part-time student after 2-3 years.

Credit Hour Requirements: 120 hours total; 30 hours academic residency (hours that must be earned at the institution exclusive of credit-by-exam, portfolio assessment, etc.).

Distance Learning Options: None.

Student Support Services Available: Academic Advising; Career Counseling†; Counseling/Testing†; Financial Aid†; Job Placement Assistance†; Orientation; Tutoring†; Two Faculty Mentors; CUNY BA/BS coordinators at each campus.

Informational Materials Available: Institutional Catalog; Prior Learning Guides; Program Brochure; Individual information/guidance from admissions staff.

Program Age, Enrollment, and Degrees Conferred:

Degree	Year Est.	Current Enrollment	Degrees Conferred
BA, BS	1971	568	3866

Percentage of Bachelor's Degree Holders Admitted to Graduate School: About 40 percent.

Geographic Admission Restrictions: None.

Tuition and Fees:

	Undergraduate
In-State Tuition	$97.00/credit
Out-of-State Tuition	$202.00/credit
Application Fee	$25.00

†At college of matriculation.
*If transcripted by an accredited college.

115. Columbia University

School of General Studies
414 Lewisohn Hall
New York, NY 10027

Degrees Offered: Bachelor of Arts; Bachelor of Science; Master of Arts in Liberal Studies.

Program Mission Statement/Description: The School of General Studies is the liberal arts division at Columbia University for adult men and women (and for younger students who are prevented by their work from attending school full-time). The school is dedicated to the belief that highly motivated students who meet its standards should have full access to the quality education offered by the university.

Accreditation: Middle States Association of Colleges and Schools.

Admission Requirements:

Undergraduate	Graduate
HS/GED Diploma	Undergraduate Degree
Interview	Interview
Essay/Written Work	Essay/Written Work

Other Admission Requirements: Admissions Examination. Undergraduates must submit SAT or ACT results no older than one year, or take the school's nonadmission exam.

Credit Awards for Prior Learning: Transfer Credit.

Limits to Credit Awards for Prior Learning: BA/BS 124 points required for degree; no more than 64 in transfer. MALS 36 points required: No more than 6 graduate points on transfer permitted.

Credit Awards for Examinations: ACT Proficiency Exams; College Board AP Exams; Departmental Exams.

Estimated Average Completion Time: Bachelors' Degrees: 4-5 years (part-time), 4 years (full-time); Graduate Degrees: 4-5 years (part-time), 1.5 years (full-time).

Caveats Regarding Time Estimates: Most undergraduates bring on average somewhere around 40 points in transfer. Students also study in 2 terms of summer session; therefore a variety of patterns prevails. There is no upper limit on the bachelor's degree. People have completed the BA/BS over 20 or more years. For the master's, 5 years is the stated period.

Credit Hour Requirements:

Degree	Total Hours	Academic Residency*
Bachelor's	124	64
Graduate	36	30

*Hours that must be earned at the institution exclusive of credit-by-exam, portfolio assessment, etc.

Distance Learning Options: Independent Study.

Student Support Services Available: Academic Advising; Career Counseling; Counseling/Testing; Financial Aid; Job Placement Assistance; Orientation; Tutoring; Preprofessional and Graduate Advisory/Placement; Learning Center Computer Access.

Informational Materials Available: Institutional Catalog.

Program Age, Enrollment, and Degrees Conferred:

Degree	Year Est.	Current Enrollment	Degrees Conferred
BA/BS	1974	1200	270
MALS	1987	110	12
Nondegree credit students	1910	1250	

Percentage of Bachelor's Degree Holders Admitted to Graduate School: 60-65 percent.

Geographic Admission Restrictions: None.

Tuition and Fees:

	Undergraduate	Graduate
Out-of-State Tuition	$442.00/credit	$442.00/credit
Application Fee	$30.00	$30.00
Credit-by-Exam Fee	$20.00/point	

Other Fees: Some course fees in laboratory science, film, and art studies courses. Student activities fee of $12.00/term.

Other Pertinent Information: General Studies students take "regular" courses with other degree candidates at Columbia College or the Graduate School of Arts and Sciences, courses taught by the same faculty that serves the other Arts and Sciences Schools. Therefore, we have 1300 or more courses in the academic year, about 400 in the summer terms. About 20 percent of the courses are available in the evening, but in many disciplines, it is not possible to complete the degree exclusively in courses beginning after 5:00 p.m.

116. Dominican College

Weekend and Accelerated Evening Programs
10 Western Hwy.
Orangeburg, NY 10962

Degrees Offered: Bachelor of Science in Nursing; Bachelor of Science in Occupational Therapy; Bachelor of Arts in Humanities; Associate of Arts; Bachelor of Science in Business; Bachelor of Science in Accounting; Bachelor of Science in Management; Bachelor of Science in Computer Information Systems; Bachelor of Science in Business Administration.

Program Mission Statement/Description: Both Weekend and Accelerated Evening programs are tailored for the working adult. They offer opportunities for full-time study while a full-time working schedule is maintained. Both programs operate on a trimester basis and provide for individualized and personal counseling.

Accreditation: Middle States Association; Council on Social Work; National League for Nursing; American Occupational Therapy Association.

Admission Requirements: HS/GED Diploma; Interview.

Other Admission Requirements: For BSN, an RN is required. For BS in Occupational Therapy an interview and letters of recommendation are required.

Credit Awards for Prior Learning: ACE Military Recommendations; ACE/PONSI Recommendations; Portfolio Assessment; Transfer Credit.

Limits to Credit Awards for Prior Learning: Transfer credits from a 2-year college maximum of 60 credits; from a 4-year college maximum of 90 credits.

Credit Awards for Examinations: ACT Proficiency Exams; CLEP General Exams; CLEP Subject Exams; College Board AP Exams; DANTES Subject Tests; Departmental Exams.

Estimated Average Completion Time: Associates' Degrees: 3 1/3 years (part-time), 2 1/3 (full-time); Bachelors' Degrees: 6 1/2 years (part-time), 4 years (full-time).

Caveats Regarding Time Estimates: Trimester system equals 9 credits or 27 credits per year for Weekend College. For Accelerated Evening program, 36 credits per year is possible.

Credit Hour Requirements:

Degree	Total Hours	Academic Residency*
Associate	7	30
Bachelor's	12	30

*Hours that must be earned at the institution exclusive of credit-by-exam, portfolio assessment, etc.

Distance Learning Options: Independent Study; Supervised Fieldwork (bachelor only).

Student Support Services Available: Academic Advising; Career Counseling; Counseling/Testing; Financial Aid; Job Placement Assistance; Orientation; Tutoring.

Other Student Services: Accounting, Computer, and Math labs held in the evening. Learning Resource Center available to students who need help organizing and/or writing research papers. Library orientation available.

Informational Materials Available: Exam Preparation Guides; Institutional Catalog; Program Brochure; Student Guide.

Program Age, Enrollment, and Degrees Conferred:

Degree	Year Est.	Current Enrollment	Degrees Conferred
OT (Weekend)	1984	75	140
Nursing (Weekend)	1987	318	184
Business (Weekend)	1980	318	184
Accelerated (Business)	1990	35	0

Percentage of Bachelor's Degree Holders Admitted to Graduate School: 60 percent estimated.

Geographic Admission Restrictions: None.

Tuition and Fees: In-State Tuition $220.00 per credit; Out-of-State Tuition $220.00 per credit; Application Fee $15.00; Graduation Fee $75.00; Credit-by-Exam Fee $15.00.

Other Pertinent Information: Weekend College is a program designed for working adults who wish to complete their education and continue to work full-time. It gives an individual the option of a trimester schedule in which classes meet every third weekend. The degree offered may be completed on weekends; a student does not have to take a day or evening class to graduate.

117. Fordham University

College at Lincoln Center
School of General Studies
113 W. 60th St., Rm. 804
New York, NY 10023

Degrees Offered: Bachelor of Arts—the College at Lincoln Center; Bachelor of Arts—the School of General Studies; Bachelor of Science—the School of General Studies.

Program Mission Statement/Description: Fordham's oldest academic tradition, carried on through the College at Lincoln Center and the School of General Studies, is its commitment to educate talented men and women in the liberal arts and basic sciences. This commitment emphasizes a rigorous intellectual formation; it stresses humanistic and cultural values and provides not only the opportunity for mastery of intellectual disciplines but also the possibility of studying them in an environment where religious values have a vital and respected presence on the campuses.

Accreditation: Middle States Association of Colleges and Schools.

Admission Requirements: Essay/Written Work; HS/GED Diploma; Interview.

Other Admission Requirements: Excel entrance exam in lieu of HS/GED at the College at Lincoln Center only.

Credit Awards for Prior Learning: ACE Military Recommendations; ACE/PONSI Recommendations; Portfolio Assessment; Transfer Credit; Life Experience Program.

Limits to Credit Awards for Prior Learning: Maximum of 80 transfer credits; maximum of 40 Life Experience Credits; students must complete 48 credits in residence at the College at Lincoln Center.

Credit Awards for Examinations: ACT Proficiency Exams; CLEP General Exams; CLEP Subject Exams; College Board AP Exams; Departmental Exams.

Estimated Average Completion Time: 3-6 years (part-time), 2-4 years (full-time).

Credit Hour Requirements:

	Total Hours	Academic Residency*
Bachelor College at Lincoln Center	128	48
Bachelors' Degrees General Studies	128	60

*Hours that must be earned at the institution exclusive of credit-by-exam, portfolio assessment, etc.

Distance Learning Options: A/V Cassettes; Independent Study; Newspaper Courses; Supervised Fieldwork; Television Courses.

Student Support Services Available: Academic Advising; Career Counseling; Counseling/Testing; Financial Aid; Job Placement Assistance; Orientation; Tutoring.

Informational Materials Available: Exam Preparation Guides; Institutional Catalog; Prior Learning Guides; Program Brochure; Complete Orientation Packet Student Handbook.

Program Age, Enrollment, and Degrees Conferred:

Degree	Year Est.	Current Enrollment	Degrees Conferred
BA School of General Studies		500	0
BA College at Lincoln Center	1968	2100	0

Percentage of Bachelor's Degree Holders Admitted to Graduate School: Information not available.

Geographic Admission Restrictions: None.

Tuition and Fees: In-State Tuition $306.00 per course; Application Fee $35.00; Graduation Fee $60.00; Credit-by-Exam Fee $125.00; Orientation Fee $15.00; Activity Fee $17.00; Life Experience Fee $200.00.

118. Marymount College

Weekend College
Tarrytown, NY 10591

Degrees Offered: Weekend College offers 6 major programs toward the baccalaureate degree: business, economics, English, history, information science, and psychology. Within the business major, there are concentrations in accounting, management, marketing, computer management, finance, international business, and training and development.

Program Mission Statement/Description: Developing the potential of its learners for academic excellence and for assuming leadership roles in a rapidly changing technological society is the hallmark of a Marymount education. The Weekend College is dedicated to providing this opportunity to men and women in a format that accommodates their complex personal and professional lives. The Elisa Carrillo Scholars program extends the opportunity to adult women who wish to study in the Weekend Program.

Accreditation: Middle States Association of Colleges and Schools; Council on Social Work Education.

Admission Requirements: HS/GED Diploma; Interview.

Credit Awards for Prior Learning: ACE Military Recommendations; ACE/PONSI Recommendations; Portfolio Assessment; Transfer Credit.

Credit Awards for Examinations: CLEP Subject Exams; College Board AP Exams; DANTES Subject Tests; Departmental Exams; NY State Proficiency Exams.

Estimated Average Completion Time: 5 years (part-time).

Caveats Regarding Time Estimates: Maximum number of credits awarded through the various means of assessing prior noncollegiate sponsored learning is 60.

Credit Hour Requirements: 120 hours total; 45 hours academic residency (hours that must be earned at the institution exclusive of credit-by-exam, portfolio assessment, etc.).

Distance Learning Options: Independent Study; Supervised Fieldwork.

Student Support Services Available: Academic Advising; Career Counseling; Counseling/Testing; Financial Aid; Job Placement Assistance; Orientation; Tutoring.

Informational Materials Available: Exam Preparation Guides; Institutional Catalog; Prior Learning Guides; Program Brochure.

Program Age, Enrollment, and Degrees Conferred:

Degree	Year Est.	Current Enrollment	Degrees Conferred
Weekend College	1975	440	891

Percentage of Bachelor's Degree Holders Admitted to Graduate School: Information not available.

Geographic Admission Restrictions: None.

Tuition and Fees: In-State Tuition $190.00 per credit; Out-of-State Tuition $190.00 per credit; Application Fee $30.00; Graduation Fee $75.00; Credit-by-Exam Fee Varies.

Other Fees: Lab fees $50.00; Portfolio Assessment Fee $100.00 per portfolio.

119. Mount Saint Mary College

Powell Ave.
Newburgh, NY 12550

Degrees Offered: Bachelor of Arts; Bachelor of Science.

Program Mission Statement/Description: The program is designed to provide an educational alternative to adults who desire an accelerated college experience during the week without sacrificing weekend time with the family and in leisure activities. An adult may earn a degree, gain skills for a professional advancement, prepare for a career change or pursue a personal interest in accounting, business management, computer science, nursing, and public relations and human services.

Accreditation: Middle States Association of Colleges and Schools; National League for Nursing.

Admission Requirements: HS/GED Diploma; Interview; Prior Credits. If not taken during previous college experience, Math and English Placement Tests.

Credit Awards for Prior Learning: ACE Military Recommendations; ACE/PONSI Recommendations; Portfolio Assessment; Transfer Credit.

Limits to Credit Awards for Prior Learning: Transfer credits—up to 60 from 2-year school, up to 90 from 4-year school. Portfolio Assessment—up to 30 credits. Military, ACE/PONSI—included in total transfer allowed.

Credit Awards for Examinations: CLEP General Exams; CLEP Subject Exams; College Board AP Exams; Departmental Exams.

Limits to Credit Awards for Examinations: Credit-by-exam—up to 45 credits.

Estimated Average Completion Time: 5 years or more (part-time), 2.5 years (full-time).

Caveats Regarding Time Estimates: Under the Accelerated Program, student could take 2 3-credit courses each 6-week session which would take 2.5 years for the 4-year degree. Taking one 3-credit course each 6-week session would take 5 years for the 4-year degree.

Credit Hour Requirements: 120 hours total; 30 hours academic residency (hours that must be earned at the institution exclusive of credit-by-exam, portfolio assessment, etc.).

Distance Learning Options: Cooperative Education; Independent Study; Supervised Fieldwork; Internships.

Student Support Services Available: Academic Advising; Career Counseling; Counseling/Testing; Financial Aid; Job Placement Assistance; Tutoring.

Informational Materials Available: Institutional Catalog; Prior Learning Guides; Program Brochure; Tuition Reimbursement Brochure; Military Incentive Grant Brochure.

Program Age, Enrollment, and Degrees Conferred:

Degree	Year Est.	Current Enrollment	Degrees Conferred
BA, BS	1987-1988	400	113

Percentage of Bachelor's Degree Holders Admitted to Graduate School: Information not available.

Geographic Admission Restrictions: None.

Tuition and Fees: In-State Tuition $234.00 per credit; Out-of-State Tuition $234.00 per credit; Application Fee $20.00; Graduation Fee $50.00; Registration Fee each session $15.00.

120. Nyack College

Adult Degree Completion Program
Nyack, NY 10960

Degrees Offered: Bachelor of Science in Organizational Management.

Program Mission Statement/Description: Nyack College's Adult Degree Completion Program provides an alternative to the traditional method of obtaining a college degree. The program is tailored to the unique needs of the adult student who wants to balance both work and study. In as little as 14 months, students who successfully complete the prescribed credits can earn a BS degree in Organizational Management from Nyack College.

Accreditation: Middle States Association of Colleges and Schools.

Admission Requirements: Employment/Experience; Essay/Written Work; Prior Credits: 60; Recommendations.

Credit Awards for Prior Learning: ACE Military Recommendations; ACE/PONSI Recommendations; Portfolio Assessment; Transfer Credit.

Limits to Credit Awards for Prior Learning: Portfolio assessment. Maximum of 30 credits.

Credit Awards for Examinations: ACT Proficiency Exams; CLEP General Exams; CLEP Subject Exams; College Board AP Exams; DANTES Subject Tests; Departmental Exams.

Limits to Credit Awards for Examinations: No more than 60 credits.

Estimated Average Completion Time: One year (full-time).

Caveats Regarding Time Estimates: Only full-time study is permitted.

Credit Hour Requirements: 120 hours total; 32 hours academic residency (hours that must be earned at the institution exclusive of credit-by-exam, portfolio assessment, etc.).

Distance Learning Options: Cooperative Education; Correspondence Courses; Independent Study; Phone/Mail Instruction; Supervised Fieldwork.

Student Support Services Available: Academic Advising; Career Counseling; Financial Aid; Orientation; Tutoring; Learning Styles Inventory Services; On-site Registration; Textbooks delivered to the student.

Informational Materials Available: Exam Preparation Guides; Institutional Catalog; Prior Learning Guides; Program Brochure.

Program Age, Enrollment, and Degrees Conferred:

Degree	Year Est.	Current Enrollment	Degrees Conferred
BS in Org. Mgmt.	1989	130	40

Percentage of Bachelor's Degree Holders Admitted to Graduate School: Information not available.

Geographic Admission Restrictions: Students need to be able to attend class within a 50-mile radius of campus.

Tuition and Fees: In-State Tuition $3700.00 per semester; Out-of-State Tuition $3700.00 per semester; Application Fee $25.00; Graduation Fee $20.00 Portfolio Assessment Fee $20.00 per credit; Phase I Fee $250.00.

Other Pertinent Information: Classes are designed for the adult student and incorporate discussion and exercises which maximize student participation: minimal lecturing, maximum discussion. The program consists of a noncredit phase of 8 weeks and a credit phase of 32 credits taken in weekly 4-hour sessions over a period of 52 weeks. In the classes—more like business seminars—the student will explore, discuss, research, and solve practical problems relevant to individual careers. The student will learn from and with peers and share ideas and experiences with other business and management professionals. The student will become part of a small, cohesive learning group that remains together throughout the entire program.

121. Pace University

Division of General Studies
1 Pace Plaza
New York, NY 10038

Degrees Offered: Bachelor of Arts in Liberal Studies; Bachelor of Science in General Studies.

Program Mission Statement/Description: The BA in Liberal Studies and the BS in General Studies are degree programs specifically designed to meet the needs of adult students who are returning to school after several years in the workplace. These individuals often have accumulated considerable knowledge as a result of their life experience learning. Where such knowledge can be demonstrated, documented, evaluated, and deemed to be in accordance with the curriculum and standards of the university, students may receive up to 36 college credits toward either degree. A maximum of 32 business credits may be applied, as electives only, to either degree. Electives may not be used to accumulate more than 18 credits of advanced coursework in any one discipline.

Accreditation: Middle States Association of Colleges and Schools.

Admission Requirements: HS/GED Diploma.

Credit Awards for Prior Learning: ACE Military Recommendations; ACE/PONSI Recommendations; Portfolio Assessment; Transfer Credit.

Limits to Credit Awards for Prior Learning: 36 credits for Portfolio Assessment. All others depend on degree program, fitting in core requirements.

Credit Awards for Examinations: CLEP General Exams; CLEP Subject Exams; College Board AP Exams; DANTES Subject Tests; Departmental Exams.

Estimated Average Completion Time: 8 years (part-time), 4 years (full-time).

Credit Hour Requirements:

Degree	Total Hours	Academic Residency*
Bachelor's	128	32

*Hours that must be earned at the institution exclusive of credit-by-exam, portfolio assessment, etc.

Distance Learning Options: None.

Student Support Services Available: Academic Advising; Career Counseling; Counseling/Testing; Financial Aid; Job Placement Assistance; Orientation; Tutoring.

Informational Materials Available: Exam Preparation Guides; Institutional Catalog; Prior Learning Guides; Program Brochure.

Program Age, Enrollment, and Degrees Conferred: Information not available.

Percentage of Bachelor's Degree Holders Admitted to Graduate School: Information not available.

Geographic Admission Restrictions: None.

Tuition and Fees: In-State Tuition $268.00 per credit; Out-of-State Tuition $268.00 per credit; Application Fee $25.00; Graduation Fee $70.00; Credit-by-Exam Fee variable.

Other Fees: Some courses have additional instructional fees. They vary from $10.00-85.00.

122. Queens College

Adult Collegiate Education Program
City University of New York
Flushing, NY 11367

Degrees Offered: Bachelor of Arts.

Program Mission Statement/Description: The Adult Collegiate Education Program (ACE), offered through the School of General Studies at Queens College, is designed to provide highly motivated adult students 25 years or older who have at least a high school diploma or GED with an opportunity to earn a full baccalaureate degree from Queens College/CUNY at an accelerated pace.

Accreditation: Middle States Association of Colleges and Schools.

Admission Requirements: Employment/Experience; Essay/Written Work; HS/GED Diploma; Interview. Minimum age 25.

Credit Awards for Prior Learning: Portfolio Assessment; Transfer Credit.

Limits to Credit Awards for Prior Learning: 36 credits for life achievement credits (maximum) as evaluated by academic departments.

Credit Awards for Examinations: College Board AP Exams.

Estimated Average Completion Time: 5 years (part-time), 4 years (full-time).

Caveats Regarding Time Estimates: ACE students may work at their own pace during regular fall and spring semesters. They may also take courses during Future Session (June) and Summer Session (July). Students may attend part-time or full-time.

Credit Hour Requirements: 128 hours total; 45 hours academic residency (hours that must be earned at the institution exclusive of credit-by-exam, portfolio assessment, etc.).

Distance Learning Options: Cooperative Education; Independent Study; Supervised Fieldwork.

Student Support Services Available: Academic Advising; Career Counseling; Counseling/Testing; Financial Aid; Job Placement Assistance; Orientation; Tutoring; Scholarships; Student Association; Alumni Association.

Informational Materials Available: Exam Preparation Guides; Institutional Catalog; Program Brochure.

Program Age, Enrollment, and Degrees Conferred:

Degree	Year Est.	Current Enrollment	Degrees Conferred
Baccalaureate	1963	1500	3000

Percentage of Bachelor's Degree Holders Admitted to Graduate School: 30 percent.

Geographic Admission Restrictions: None.

Tuition and Fees: In-State Tuition $60.00 per credit; Out-of-State Tuition $170.00 per credit; Application Fee $30.00; Student Activity Fee evening and part-time $58.60, day full-time $91.35, day part-time $60.60.

Other Pertinent Information: The ACE Program, which began in 1963, has graduated nearly 3000 students. Some 1500 are currently enrolled. ACE students are older than the "typical" 18-year-old college student. Many are coming back to get the college education they missed or were denied earlier. Most have careers, families, and commitments, but they have placed their college degrees high on their priority list. Some are changing careers, empowering themselves with new skills and information. Many are seeking goal of a college degree, and the ACE Program is designed to help them to meet that challenge.

123. Saint Francis College

180 Remsen St.
Brooklyn, NY 11201

Degrees Offered: Bachelor of Science; Bachelor of Arts; Associate in Applied Science; Associate in Science.

Program Mission Statement/Description: The above-mentioned degree programs are offered in the evening to accommodate nontraditional college-age students who wish to study full-time or part-time.

Accreditation: Middle States Association of Colleges and Schools.

Admission Requirements: HS/GED Diploma; Interview; Recommendations.

Credit Awards for Prior Learning: ACE Military Recommendations; ACE/PONSI Recommendations; Portfolio Assessment; Transfer Credit.

Limits to Credit Awards for Prior Learning: 98 credits.

Credit Awards for Examinations: CLEP General Exams; CLEP Subject Exams; College Board AP Exams; DANTES Subject Tests.

Limits to Credit Awards for Examinations: 98 credits.

Estimated Average Completion Time: Associates' Degrees: 5 years (part-time), 2 years (full-time); Bachelors' Degrees: 8 years (part-time), 4 years (full-time).

Credit Hour Requirements:

Degree	Total Hours	Academic Residency*
Associate	63	30
Bachelor's	128	30

*Hours that must be earned at the institution exclusive of credit-by-exam, portfolio assessment, etc.

Distance Learning Options: Independent Study; Supervised Fieldwork.

Student Support Services Available: Academic Advising; Career Counseling; Counseling/Testing; Financial Aid; Job Placement Assistance; Orientation; Tutoring.

Informational Materials Available: Institutional Catalog; Program Brochure.

Program Age, Enrollment, and Degrees Conferred: Information not available.

Percentage of Bachelor's Degree Holders Admitted to Graduate School: Information not available.

Geographic Admission Restrictions: None.

Tuition and Fees: In-State Tuition $180.00 per credit; Out-of-State Tuition $180.00 per credit; Application Fee $20.00; Graduation Fee $65.00.

---

124. State University of New York College at Plattsburgh

Center for Lifelong Learning
Kehoe 413
Plattsburgh, NY 12901

Degrees Offered: Master of Arts in Liberal Studies.

Program Mission Statement/Description: The Master of Arts in Liberal Studies (MALS) is designed to provide adults learners with a high quality, flexible program of study that responds to their specific educational, personal development, and professional needs. Through the MALS Program, students may choose from 5 challenging master's degree operations: Administration and Leadership, Educational Studies, English Language and Literature, Historical Studies, Natural Sciences. Broadly based courses drawn from a variety of academic disciplines enable MALS students to investigate new ideas, to expand their knowledge and professional skills, and to rediscover the challenge of learning. Students may complete only one degree in the Master of Arts in Liberal Studies program.

Accreditation: Middle States Association of Colleges and Schools.

Admission Requirements: GRE, or GMAT or MAT; Recommendations; Undergraduate Degree.

Other Admission Requirements: Students may enroll in the program at any time during the calendar year. Admission decisions are based not only on past academic records but also taking into consideration such factors as work experience and demonstrated success and motivation. In general, the following requirements are adhered to a bachelor's degree from an accredited institution with a grade point average of 2.5 or higher (or Graduate Management Aptitude Test (GMAT). Three letters of reference indicating ability to successfully pursue graduate studies.

Credit Awards for Prior Learning: ACE Military Recommendations; Transfer Credit.

Limits to Credit Awards for Prior Learning: Students who have taken graduate courses at Plattsburgh or at other institutions may transfer up to 12 semester hours of A and B quality work into the MALS program. Credit can be granted for the successful completion of certain military training programs such as the Air Command and Staff Nonresident Seminar Program. Nonmatriculated students are urged to apply for formal matriculation to the program prior to the completion of 12 credit hours.

Credit Awards for Examinations: None.

Estimated Average Completion Time: 4 years (part-time), 1.5 years (full-time).

Caveats Regarding Time Estimates: MALS students may complete the program on either a part-time or full-time basis. Students proceed at their own rates and normally enroll for between 3 and 12 hours of coursework per semester. Students may take up to 10 years to complete their programs of study.

Credit Hour Requirements: 30 credits total; 18 credits academic residency (hours that must be earned at the institution exclusive of credit-by-exam, portfolio assessment, etc.).

Distance Learning Options: Independent Study.

Student Support Services Available: Academic Advising; Career Counseling; Counseling/Testing; Financial Aid; Job Placement Assistance; Tutoring.

Informational Materials Available: Institutional Catalog; Program Brochure.

Program Age, Enrollment, and Degrees Conferred:

Degree	Year Est.	Current Enrollment	Degrees Conferred
MA Liberal Studies	1974	80	1200

Geographic Admission Restrictions: None.

Tuition and Fees: In-State Tuition $102.50 per credit; Out-of-State Tuition $242.50 per credit; Application Fee $35.00.

Other Pertinent Information: MALS courses are offered during convenient evening hours on campus, at Plattsburgh Air Force Base and at several additional sites in northern New York.

North Carolina

125. Gardner-Webb College

Greater Opportunity of Adult Learners Program
Boiling Springs, NC 28017

Degrees Offered: Bachelor of Science in Business Administration; Bachelor of Science in Business Management; Bachelor of Science in Health Management; Bachelor of Science in Accounting; Bachelor of Science in Management Information Systems; Bachelor of Science in Social Science—Concentration in Criminal Justice or Bachelor of Science in Human Services; Bachelor of Science in Nursing; Bachelor of Art in Religion.

Program Mission Statement/Description: Gardner-Webb College provides comprehensive special studies programs consisting primarily of the Greater Opportunity for Adult Learners (GOAL) program, to meet specialized education needs of adult learners. The GOAL program provides opportunities for working adults who possess an associate's degree or equivalent to earn a Bachelor's Degree during evening hours. In addition to the Gardner-Webb campus, GOAL program are provided in the following regional locations in North Carolina: Charlotte, Dallas, Dobson, Valdese, Newton, Rockingham, Statesville, Troy, Wilkesboro, and Winston-Salem.

Accreditation: Southern Association of Colleges and Schools; National League for Nursing.

Admission Requirements: HS/GED Diploma; Prior Credits: 64 semester hours; specific prerequisites for the desired major and a 2.0 GPA on the 64 semester hours of transfer work.

Credit Awards for Prior Learning: ACE Military Recommendations; Transfer Credit.

Limits to Credit Awards for Prior Learning: 64 semester hours from 2-year institutions (regionally accredited); 98 semester hours from 4-year institutions (regionally accredited).

Credit Awards for Examinations: ACT Proficiency Exams; CLEP Subject Exams.

Limits to Credit Awards for Examinations: No more than 64 semester hours.

Estimated Average Completion Time: Varies (part-time); 24 months (full-time).

Credit Hour Requirements: 128 hours total; 30 hours academic residency (hours that must be earned at the institution exclusive of credit-by-exam, portfolio assessment, etc.).

Distance Learning Options: Independent Study; Supervised Fieldwork.

Student Support Services Available: Academic Advising; Financial Aid; Job Placement Assistance.

Informational Materials Available: Institutional Catalog; Program Brochure.

Program Age, Enrollment, and Graduates:

Degree	Year Est.	Current Enrollment	Degrees Conferred
BS	1978	720	Unknown
BA	1988	10	Unknown

Percentage of Bachelor's Degree Holders Admitted to Graduate School: Information not available.

Geographic Admission Restrictions: None.

Tuition and Fees: In-State Tuition $115.00 per credit; Out-of-State Tuition $115.00 per credit; Application Fee $15.00; Graduation Fee $45.00.

126. Guildford College

Center for Continuing Education
5800 W. Friendly Ave.
Greensboro, NC 27410

Degrees Offered: Bachelor in Arts; Bachelor of Science; Bachelor in Fine Arts; Bachelor of Arts in Administrative Science.

Program Mission Statement/Description: The Center for Continuing Education is designed to meet the special needs of adult and working students.

Accreditation: Southern Association of Colleges and Schools.

Admission Requirements: Essay/Written Work; HS/GED Diploma; Interview.

Credit Awards for Prior Learning: Transfer Credit.

Limits to Credit Awards for Prior Learning: A maximum of 64 credits may be transferred from 2-year technical colleges and up to 48 credits from 2-year technical colleges which are accredited by the Commission on Colleges of the Southern Association of Colleges and Schools (or one of its 5 regional equivalents). Up to 32 credits may be transferred from 2-year community colleges, technical colleges or other 2-year institutions not so accredited.

Credit Awards for Examinations: CLEP General Exams; CLEP Subject Exams; College Board AP Exams.

Limits to Credit Awards for Examinations: CLEP, AP—Maximum 16 hours may be earned with appropriate scores.

Estimated Average Completion Time: The bulk of Guildford College's students are transfer students, so the length of time to degree completion depends on the credit hours already earned. New continuing education students can complete their degrees by attending full-time at night and in summer school.

Credit Hour Requirements: 128 hours total; 32 hours academic residency (hours that must be earned at the institution exclusive of credit-by-exam, portfolio assessment, etc.).

Distance Learning Options: Independent Study; Supervised Fieldwork.

Student Support Services Available: Academic Advising; Career Counseling; Financial Aid; Job Placement Assistance; Orientation; Tutoring; Baby Sitting, Family Housing; Adult Student Government.

Informational Materials Available: Institutional Catalog; Program Brochure.

Program Age, Enrollment, and Graduates: Information not available.

Percentage of Bachelor's Degree Holders Admitted to Graduate School: Information not available.

Geographic Admission Restrictions: None.

Tuition and Fees: Out-of-State Tuition $168.00 per credit; Application Fee $25.00; Graduation Fee $30.00; Registration Fee $15.00; Student Activity Fee $15.00; Parking Fee $20.00.

Other Pertinent Information: The Center for Continuing Education (CCE) provides academic support services including admission, registration, comprehensive academic advising, financial aid assistance, an adult transitions course, study skills assistance, and an active adult student government association. Also available are an adult student-lounge, baby-sitting services, senior citizen discounts, limited low-cost family housing, and ample parking. CCE offices are open 8:30 a.m.-9:00 p.m. weekdays, and 3 class periods are available from 6:00-10:00 p.m. Monday through Friday with 7 majors available at night. Guildford College is the third oldest coed college in the nation. Founded in 1837, its continuing education program is the oldest in the Greensboro area. Founded by a special committee of the chamber of commerce, it was acquired in 1949 by the Guildford Board of Trustees.

127. Shaw University

Centers for Alternative Programs of Education (CAPE)
118 E. South St.
Raleigh, NC 27611

Degrees Offered: Bachelor of Arts; Bachelor of Science.

Program Mission Statement/Description: CAPE exist to provide opportunities for deserving students to participate in a college-level program who could not otherwise be able to do so because of the following reasons: jobs, family obligations, military status, incarceration, distance from other campuses or other special limitations. The program is designed primarily for the experienced adult and affords such students the opportunity to receive credit for their prior learning that may be gained through work experiences, enrichment courses, workshops, seminars, military training, community work, etc. The program (CAPE) is implemented through the establishment of learning centers and units in selected locations throughout the state of North Carolina.

Accreditation: Southern Association of Schools and Colleges.

Admission Requirements: HS/GED Diploma; Recommendations.

Credit Awards for Prior Learning: ACE Military Recommendations; ACE/PONSI Recommendations; Portfolio Assessment; Transfer Credit.

Limits to Credit Awards for Prior Learning: 27 semester hours for portfolio assessment; 70 semester hours from 2-year institution; 90 semester hours from 4-year institution. No limits on ACE recommendations.

Credit Awards for Examinations: ACT Proficiency Exams; CLEP General Exams; CLEP Subject Exams; College Board AP Exams; DANTES Subject Tests; Departmental Exams.

Estimated Average Completion Time: Bachelors' Degrees: 4 years (part-time), 3 years (full-time).

Credit Hour Requirements: 120 hours total; 30 hours academic residency (hours that must be earned at the institution exclusive of credit-by-exam, portfolio assessment, etc.).

Distance Learning Options: None.

Student Support Services Available: Academic Advising; Career Counseling; Counseling/Testing; Financial Aid; Job Placement Assistance; Orientation; Tutoring.

Informational Materials Available: Institutional Catalog; Prior Learning Guides; Program Brochure.

Program Age, Enrollment, and Graduates:

Degree	Year Est.	Current Enrollment	Degrees Conferred
BA	1970	700	1051
BS	1970	700	1051

Percentage of Bachelor's Degree Holders Admitted to Graduate School: 40 percent.

Geographic Admission Restrictions: North Carolina and persons who can commute to one of the instructional sites in the state.

Tuition and Fees: In-State Tuition $182.00 per credit; Application Fee $25.00; Graduation Fee $75.00; Credit-by-Exam Fee $450.00.

North Dakota

128. North Dakota State University

College of University Studies
Box 5103
Fargo, ND 58105

Degrees Offered: Bachelor of University Studies.

Program Mission Statement/Description: The Bachelor of University Studies (BUS) degree is a tailored degree program. Each candidate for this degree prepares a degree plan proposal for review and approval by the Program Review Committee of the college. The primary objective of the BUS degree is the same as that of all bachelors' degrees. It is a 4-year program of study that should aid the student in enjoying a better life in the future. A Program Review Committee judges the appropriateness of each degree plan for each individual. The Committee must compare each proposal with its view of the nature of a bachelor's degree and the aspirations of each student.

Accreditation: North Central Association of Colleges and Schools.

Admission Requirements: High School diploma with a minimum of 17 units, including 4 English and 2 mathematics; GED Diploma.

Credit Awards for Prior Learning: ACE Military Recommendations; ACE/PONSI Recommendations; Portfolio Assessment; Transfer Credit.

Credit Awards for Examinations: ACT Proficiency Exams; CLEP General Exams; CLEP Subject Exams; College Board AP Exams; Departmental Exams; International Baccalaureate.

Estimated Average Completion Time: 4 years (full-time).

Caveats Regarding Time Estimates: Most average 15.25 credits.

Credit Hour Requirements: 183 hours total; 45 hours academic residency (hours that must be earned at the institution exclusive of credit-by-exam, portfolio assessment, etc.).

Distance Learning Options: Cooperative Education; Correspondence Courses; Independent Study; Supervised Fieldwork; Television Courses.

Student Support Services Available: Academic Advising; Career Counseling; Counseling/Testing; Financial Aid; Job Placement Assistance; Orientation; Tutoring.

Informational Materials Available: Institutional Catalog; Program Brochure; Guide to BUS degree.

Program Age, Enrollment, and Degrees Conferred:

Degree	Year Est.	Current Enrollment	Degrees Conferred
BUS	1972	60	814

Percentage of Bachelor's Degree Holders Admitted to Graduate School: Information not available.

Geographic Admission Restrictions: None.

Tuition and Fees: In-State Tuition $46.25 per credit; Out-of-State Tuition $116.25 per credit; Application Fee $20.00.

Other Fees: Member of Western Institute Consortium of Higher Education, residents from those states pay 1.5 percent of resident tuition; Minnesota students with reciprocity pay 1.25 percent of resident tuition.

Other Pertinent Information: The College of University Studies grants experiential learning credit toward a degree. The college also provides a home for undecided students and thus enrollment may exceed 750, but less than 10 percent are upperclass students actively seeking a BUS

degree. The BUS program was designed to be flexible and to appeal to individuals with no previous college experience, to those with transfer credits from other institutions, or to unclassified students already attending the university. Students can attend day or evening classes and choose from the varied courses offered by the undergraduate colleges and schools.

129. Valley City State University

Alternate Learning Program
Valley City, ND 58072

Degrees Offered: Bachelor of Arts; Bachelor of Science; Bachelor of Science in Education; Bachelor of University Studies; Associate of Arts.

Program Mission Statement/Description: The Alternate Learning Program (ALP) is designed to offer adult learners the opportunity to apply learning received from life and work experience toward a university degree.

Accreditation: North Central Association of Colleges and Schools; National Council for Accreditation of Teacher Education.

Admission Requirements: HS/GED Diploma; Interview.

Credit Awards for Prior Learning: ACE Military Recommendations; Portfolio Assessment; Transfer Credit.

Limits to Credit Awards for Prior Learning: There is presently no upper or lower limit, but 36 quarter hours of residence credit is required.

Credit Awards for Examinations: CLEP General Exams; CLEP Subject Exams.

Estimated Average Completion Time: Associates' Degrees: 7 years (part-time), 2 years (full-time); Bachelors' Degrees: 7-8 years (part-time), 4-5 years (full-time).

Credit Hour Requirements:

Degree	Total Hours	Academic Residency*
Associate (quarter hours)	96	24
Bachelor's (quarter hours)	192	36

*Hours that must be earned at the institution exclusive of credit-by-exam, portfolio assessment, etc.

Minimum Campus Time Required: Same as academic residency above.

Distance Learning Options: Cooperative Education; Independent Study; Newspaper Courses.

Student Support Services Available: Academic Advising; Career Counseling; Counseling/Testing; Financial Aid; Job Placement Assistance; Orientation; Tutoring.

Informational Materials Available: Exam Preparation Guides; Institutional Catalog; Prior Learning Guides; Program Brochure.

Program Age, Enrollment, and Graduates: Information not available.

Percentage of Bachelor's Degree Holders Admitted to Graduate School: 5 percent.

Geographic Admission Restrictions: None.

Tuition and Fees: In-State Tuition $45.50 per credit; Out-of-State Tuition $114.17 per credit; Application Fee $20.00; Credit-by-Exam Fee $22.75.

Other Pertinent Information: In the 1992-93 school year, Valley City State University will change from a quarter-hour system to a semester-hour system.

Ohio

130. Antioch University

Weekend College
School for Adult & Experiential Learning
800 Livermore St.
Yellow Springs, OH 45387

Degrees Offered: Bachelor of Arts in Human Development; Bachelor of Arts in Human Services Administration; Bachelor of Arts in Humanities; Bachelor of Arts in Management.

Program Mission Statement/Description: Antioch University's Weekend College is designed to meet the needs of working adults. All administrative services and all courses needed for the degree are offered on Saturdays throughout the year. Classes are small, averaging fewer than 20 students. Four majors are offered: Human Development, Human Services Administration, Humanities, and Management. In addition, students may pursue the year-long World Classics Curriculum, which introduces the great literary, religious, and philosophical works of the major civilizations of human history. Antioch values intellectual debate, the seeking of truth, and the need to act upon what one learns and, thus, improve community life and the democracy. The curriculum makes central the integration of work and study. A student's life experience, past and present, is brought into the academic program in a variety of ways. Antioch asks students to be active in, and responsible for, their own education and to be active and responsible as leaders in the institutions and communities in which they work and live.

Accreditation: North Central Association of Colleges and Schools.

Admission Requirements: Employment/Experience: 20 hours/week; Essay/Written Work; HS/GED Diploma; Interview; Prior Credits: 40; Recommendations; Age 25 or older.

Credit Awards for Prior Learning: ACE Military Recommendations; ACE/PONSI Recommendations; Portfolio Assessment; Transfer Credit.

Limits to Credit Awards for Prior Learning: Maximum 112 nonresidential credits (all categories above). Maximum 45 nonclassroom credits. Maximum 90 lower-division credits.

Credit Awards for Examinations: ACT Proficiency Exams; CLEP General Exams; CLEP Subject Exams; DANTES Subject Tests; Departmental Exams.

Estimated Average Completion Time: 3 years (part-time), 1.5-2 years (full-time).

Caveats Regarding Time Estimates: These estimates are for a student entering with about 90 quarter credits.

Credit Hour Requirements: 180 hours total; 68 hours academic residency (hours that must be earned at the institution exclusive of credit-by-exam, portfolio assessment, etc.).

Distance Learning Options: Independent Study; Supervised Fieldwork.

Student Support Services Available: Academic Advising; Career Counseling; Counseling/Testing; Financial Aid; Orientation; Prior Experiential Learning Portfolio Preparation.

Informational Materials Available: Institutional Catalog; Program Brochure.

Program Age, Enrollment, and Degrees Conferred:

Degree	Year Est.	Current Enrollment	Degrees Conferred
Bachelor of Arts	1986	240	220

Percentage of Bachelor's Degree Holders Admitted to Graduate School: Information not available.

Geographic Admission Restrictions: None.

Tuition and Fees: In-State Tuition $155.00; Out-of-State Tuition $155.00; Application Fee $35.00; Graduation Fee $35.00.

Other Fees: Assessment of experiential learning (per packet, regardless of number of credits awarded or evaluated) is $300.00.

Other Pertinent Information: Students particularly value the convenience of the Saturday-only class schedule, the small classes, the discussion seminar style of teaching, and the respect accorded to the experience of adults.

131. Baldwin-Wallace College

Continuing Education Program
275 Eastland Rd.
Berea, OH 44017

Degrees Offered: Bachelor's Degree; Master of Business Administration; Master of Arts in Education.

Program Mission Statement/Description: Baldwin-Wallace is committed to the development of an exemplary continuing education program that can provide adult students with a rigorous curriculum and support services designed especially for them. Students may earn a degree by attending the Evening College and/or Weekend College programs where course formats are designed to accommodate the special time constraints of working adults. Students may enter the programs as degree candidates or take a course for credit or audit to find out how the programs operate. New students, both transfer and those just beginning college work, are provided advice and counseling to assist their entry into and progression through B-W's Continuing Education Program.

Accreditation: North Central Association of Colleges and Schools; National Council for Accreditation of Teacher Education.

Admission Requirements:

Undergraduate	Graduate
HS/GED Diploma	Undergraduate Degree
Recommendations	Essay/Written Work
Employment/Experience:	Recommendations
2 years	GMAT

Credit Awards for Prior Learning: ACE Military Recommendations; ACE/PONSI Recommendations; Portfolio Assessment; Transfer Credit.

Limits to Credit Awards for Prior Learning: Maximum transfer credit from all community college coursework is 93 quarter hours.

Credit Awards for Examinations: CLEP General Exams; CLEP Subject Exams; College Board AP Exams.

Estimated Average Completion Time: Bachelors' Degrees: 6-8 years (part-time), 4 years (full-time); Graduate Degrees: MBA 2 years (part-time); MAE 2 years (part-time).

Caveats Regarding Time Estimates: Graduate programs are offered on a part-time basis only. Both evening and weekend courses are available.

Credit Hour Requirements:

Degree	Total Hours	Academic Residency*
Bachelor's per quarter	186	48
Graduate (MBA)	80	70
Graduate (MA in Ed)	50	44

*Hours that must be earned at the institution exclusive of credit-by-exam, portfolio assessment, etc.

Distance Learning Options: Independent Study; Supervised Fieldwork.

Student Support Services Available: Academic Advising; Career Counseling; Counseling/Testing; Financial Aid; Job Placement Assistance; Orientation; Tutoring.

Informational Materials Available: Institutional Catalog; Program Brochure.

Program Age, Enrollment, and Degrees Conferred:

Degree	Year Est.	Current Enrollment	Degrees Conferred
Evening College	1965	930	Unknown
Weekend College	1978	560	Unknown
MBA	1975	560	Unknown
MEd	1975	160	Unknown

Percentage of Bachelor's Degree Holders Admitted to Graduate School: Approximately 10 percent; however, many do not pursue graduate school options immediately following graduation. Some attend graduate school several years after receiving their bachelor's degree.

Geographic Admission Restrictions: None.

Tuition and Fees:

	Undergraduate	Graduate
In-State Tuition	$147.00/credit	$240.00/credit
Application Fee	$15.00	$15.00

132. The Defiance College

Accelerated Business Management Program
701 N. Clinton St.
Defiance, OH 43512

Degrees Offered: Bachelor of Science in Business Administration; Bachelor of Science in Management.

Program Mission Statement/Description: The Accelerated Business Management program is for persons working in supervisory or managerial positions. It is an accelerated program (10-week modules, offered on Saturday morning and afternoon, 3 modules per year, but none in summer).

Accreditation: North Central Association of Colleges and Schools.

Admission Requirements: Employment/Experience; HS/GED Diploma; Recommendations.

Credit Awards for Prior Learning: ACE Military Recommendations; ACE/PONSI Recommendations; Portfolio Assessment; Transfer Credit.

Limits to Credit Awards for Prior Learning: 60 semester hours of credit from an AA degree from an approved (accredited) community college or other institutions of higher learning; 4 semester hours of credit for past learning experience; course-by-course evaluation for transfer credit.

Credit Awards for Examinations: CLEP General Exams; CLEP Subject Exams; College Board AP Exams; DANTES Subject Tests; Departmental Exams.

Estimated Average Completion Time: 6-8 years (part-time).

Credit Hour Requirements: 120 hours total; 30 hours academic residency (hours that must be earned at the institution exclusive of credit-by-exam, portfolio assessment, etc.).

Distance Learning Options: Cooperative Education; Independent Study.

Student Support Services Available: Academic Advising; Career Counseling; Counseling/Testing; Financial Aid; Job Placement Assistance; Tutoring.

Informational Materials Available: Institutional Catalog; Program Brochure; Cooperative Education Information; Yearly Schedules of Classes.

Program Age, Enrollment, and Degrees Conferred:

Degree	Year Est.	Current Enrollment	Degrees Conferred
BS	1982	42	Unknown

Percentage of Bachelor's Degree Holders Admitted to Graduate School: Information not available.

Geographic Admission Restrictions: None.

Tuition and Fees: In-State Tuition $155.00 per credit; Out-of-State Tuition $155.00 per credit; Application Fee $20.00; Credit-by-Exam Fee $25.00.

133. Edison State Community College

1973 Edison Dr.
Piqua, OH 45356

Degrees Offered: Associate of Arts; Associate of Science; Associate of Applied Science; Associate of Applied Business; Associate of Technical Study.

Program Mission Statement/Description: Edison State Community College, as the institution of higher education serving Darke, Miami, and Shelby counties, exists to assist individuals, firms, and communities in achieving their greatest potential. University transfer: associates' degrees that prepare students to transfer to 4-year colleges and universities. Career programs: associates' degrees, certificates, and other programs that prepare students for immediate employment for responsible positions in skilled and knowledge-based fields. Economic development: college-business partnerships and programs designed to assist area employers and individuals in developing a workforce with the knowledge and skills required to function in a changing economy and global marketplace. Lifelong learning: courses and programs which permit adults to pursue personal and professional goals throughout their lives.

Accreditation: North Central Association of Colleges and Schools.

Admission Requirements: HS/GED Diploma.

Credit Awards for Prior Learning: ACE Military Recommendations; ACE/PONSI Recommendations; Portfolio Assessment; Transfer Credit.

Limits to Credit Awards for Prior Learning: 45-credit limit. Total program credits minus the 30-hour residency.

Credit Awards for Examinations: CLEP Subject Exams; College Board AP Exams; Departmental Exams.

Estimated Average Completion Time: 6 (part-time), 3 (full-time).

Caveats Regarding Time Estimates: Programs are designed to be completed in 2 years of full-time attendance.

Credit Hour Requirements: 94 hours total; 30 hours academic residency (hours that must be earned at the institution exclusive of credit-by-exam, portfolio assessment, etc.).

Distance Learning Options: A/V Cassettes; Cooperative Education; Independent Study; Supervised Fieldwork; Television Courses.

Student Support Services Available: Academic Advising; Career Counseling; Counseling/Testing; Financial Aid; Job Placement Assistance; Orientation; Tutoring; Special Services for Handicapped.

Informational Materials Available: Institutional Catalog; Prior Learning Guides; Program Brochure.

Program Age, Enrollment, and Degrees Conferred:

Degree	Year Est.	Current Enrollment	Degrees Conferred
Associate's	1973	3400	300

Geographic Admission Restrictions: None.

Tuition and Fees: In-State Tuition $32.00 per credit; Out-of-State Tuition $64.00 per credit; Application Fee $10.00; Graduation Fee $10.00; Credit-by-Exam Fee $38.00; General Fee $3.00.

134. Hiram College

Weekend College
Hinsdale Hall
Hiram, OH 44234

Degrees Offered: Bachelor of Arts.

Program Mission Statement/Description: The Weekend College at Hiram College was established to offer Hiram's traditional undergraduate courses to adults. It was clear from the outset that a program designed for adults had to be serious and rigorous, while at the same time it had to be responsive to the specific needs of the adult learners. Classes meet on alternate weekends between Friday evening and Sunday morning. The structure of the Weekend College has proven to be an attractive alternative to evening programs as it has responded directly to both the demands and capabilities of adults for concentrated learning.

Accreditation: North Central Association of Colleges and Schools.

Admission Requirements: HS/GED Diploma; Interview.

Credit Awards for Prior Learning: ACE Military Recommendations; Portfolio Assessment; Transfer Credit.

Credit Awards for Examinations: CLEP Subject Exams.

Estimated Average Completion Time: 6 years (part-time), 4 years (full-time).

Credit Hour Requirements: 180 hours total; 90 hours academic residency (hours that must be earned at the institution exclusive of credit-by-exam, portfolio assessment, etc.).

Distance Learning Options: None.

Student Support Services Available: Academic Advising; Career Counseling; Counseling/Testing; Financial Aid; Orientation; Tutoring.

Informational Materials Available: Institutional Catalog; Program Brochure.

Program Age, Enrollment, and Degrees Conferred:

Degree	Year Est.	Current Enrollment	Degrees Conferred
BA	1977	450	700

Percentage of Bachelor's Degree Holders Admitted to Graduate School: 40 percent.

Geographic Admission Restrictions: None.

Tuition and Fees: Tuition per quarter $165.00; Activity Fee $10.00.

135. Lourdes College

Bachelor of Individualized Studies
Weekend College Program
6832 Convent Blvd.
Sylvania, OH 43560

Degrees Offered: Bachelor of Arts in Business, Bachelor of Arts in Gerontology.

Program Mission Statement/Description: Lourdes College addresses the needs of the nontraditional learner through innovative programs to provide an adult-learner centered environment and to recognize an individual's prior learning.

Accreditation: North Central Association of Colleges and Schools; National League for Nursing (NLN).

Admission Requirements: Employment/Experience: 45 semester hours; Essay/Written Work; HS/GED Diploma; Interview; Prior Credits: 96 semester hours.

Credit Awards for Prior Learning: ACE Military Recommendations; ACE/PONSI Recommendations; Portfolio Assessment; Transfer Credit; NLN validation.

Limits to Credit Awards for Prior Learning: Portfolio 45 semester hours. All prior learning maximum 96 semester hours.

Credit Awards for Examinations: ACT Proficiency Exams; CLEP General Exams; CLEP Subject Exams; College Board AP Exams; DANTES Subject Tests; Departmental Exams; NLN Exams.

Limits to Credit Awards for Examinations: CLEP 30 semester hours.

Estimated Average Completion Time: Associates' Degrees: 4 years (part-time), 2 years (full-time); Bachelors' Degrees 3-4 years (part-time), 2 years (full-time).

Caveats Regarding Time Estimates: Average bachelor's degree student transfers in about half in prior learning credits (sponsored and nonsponsored) across the institution.

Credit Hour Requirements: 128 hours total; 32 hours academic residency (hours that must be earned at the institution exclusive of credit-by-exam, portfolio assessment, etc.).

Distance Learning Options: Cooperative Education; Independent Study; Supervised Fieldwork.

Student Support Services Available: Academic Advising; Career Counseling; Counseling/Testing; Financial Aid; Job Placement Assistance; Orientation; Tutoring.

Informational Materials Available: Institutional Catalog; Prior Learning Guides; Program Brochure.

Program Age, Enrollment, and Degrees Conferred:

Degree	Year Est.	Current Enrollment	Degrees Conferred
BIS	1983	350	100

Percentage of Bachelor's Degree Holders Admitted to Graduate School: Information not available.

Geographic Admission Restrictions: None.

Tuition and Fees: In-State Tuition $170.00 per credit; Out-of-State Tuition $170.00 per credit; Application Fee $20.00; Graduation Fee $15.00; Portfolio Assessment Fee half regular tuition; Noncollegiate Sponsored Instruction Credit $10.00 per semester hour.

Other Pertinent Information: Approximately 7% of students participate in Portfolio Assessment. Average student age is 32 years. Average number of colleges used in transfer is 2.

---

136. Malone College

515 25th St., NW
Canton, OH 44709

Degrees Offered: Bachelor of Arts in Management.

Program Mission Statement/Description: The Bachelor of Arts in Management is an accelerated, intensive, degree completion program designed to provide the student with knowledge and skills in management.

Accreditation: North Central Association of Colleges and Schools.

Admission Requirements: Essay/Written Work; Prior Credits: 60 semester hours; Recommendations; Minimum age 25.

Credit Awards for Prior Learning: ACE Military Recommendations; ACE/PONSI Recommendations; Portfolio Assessment; Transfer Credit; Accredited Correspondence Credits.

Limits to Credit Awards for Prior Learning: Malone will accept up to 28 semester credits for portfolio-type assessment and no more than 20 semester hours toward a degree from either or both of the CLEP/PEP programs.

Credit Awards for Examinations: ACT Proficiency Exams; CLEP General Exams; CLEP Subject Exams; College Board AP Exams; DANTES Subject Tests; Departmental Exams.

Limits to Credit Awards for Examinations: A total of 63 semester hours may be earned through credit by examination.

Estimated Average Completion Time: 1.5 years (full-time).

Caveats Regarding Time Estimates: BA in Management program only available full-time.

Credit Hour Requirements: 124 hours total; 30 hours academic residency (hours that must be earned at the institution exclusive of credit-by-exam, portfolio assessment, etc.).

Distance Learning Options: Cooperative Education; Independent Study.

Student Support Services Available: Academic Advising; Career Counseling; Counseling/Testing; Financial Aid; Job Placement Assistance; Orientation; Tutoring.

Informational Materials Available: Institutional Catalog; Prior Learning Guides; Program Brochure.

Program Age, Enrollment, and Degrees Conferred:

Degree	Year Est.	Current Enrollment	Degrees Conferred
BA	1984	224	520

Percentage of Bachelor's Degree Holders Admitted to Graduate School: Information not available.

Geographic Admission Restrictions: None.

Tuition and Fees: In-State Tuition: $207.00 per credit; Application Fee $20.00; Credit-by-Exam Fee half tuition; Administration Fee $15.00.

Other Fees: Books/Materials/Administration—$150.00 per trimester; transcripting fee for CLEP, etc. $15.00; transcripting fee for PLA (Prior Learning Assessment) $25.00.

Other Pertinent Information: In a BA program, a group or class of 20 students go through the entire 36-hour program together. (They must take the entire program.) The retention rate is above 90 percent.

---

137. Northwestern College

Accelerated Degree Program
1441 N. Cable Rd.
Lima, OH 45805

Degrees Offered: Associate of Applied Business.

Program Mission Statement/Description: Our accelerated degree program is designed for the nontraditional student who has had some previous college work or who can gain credit for experiential learning. If the student enters with 45 credits, he or she can complete the degree in a year going full-time.

Accreditation: North Central Association of Colleges and Schools.

Admission Requirements: Employment/Experience: 45 credit hours; Essay/Written Work; HS/GED Diploma; Interview; Prior Credits: 45 credit hours.

Credit Awards for Prior Learning: Portfolio Assessment; Transfer Credit.

Limits to Credit Awards for Prior Learning: We will transfer just 45 credit hours (quarter) from other institutions. No more than half of these credits may be in major courses.

Credit Awards for Examinations: Departmental Exams.

Estimated Average Completion Time: 2.5-3 years if they do not get the 45 credit transfer hours.

Credit Hour Requirements: 108 hours total; 63 hours academic residency (hours that must be earned at the institution exclusive of credit-by-exam, portfolio assessment, etc.).

Distance Learning Options: Cooperative Education; Independent Study.

Student Support Services Available: Academic Advising; Career Counseling; Counseling/Testing; Financial Aid; Job Placement Assistance; Orientation; Tutoring.

Informational Materials Available: Institutional Catalog; Prior Learning Guides; Program Brochure.

Program Age, Enrollment, and Degrees Conferred:

Degree	Year Est.	Current Enrollment	Degrees Conferred
Associate's Degree	1989	2	0

Geographic Admission Restrictions: None.

Tuition and Fees: In-State Tuition $61.00 per credit; Application Fee $50.00; Credit-by-Exam Fee $35.00; In-State Tuition Computer Classes Fee $3.00; Portfolio Assessment Fee $20.00 per quarter hour.

---

138. Sinclair Community College

College Without Walls
444 W. 3rd St.
Dayton, OH 45402

Degrees Offered: Associate of Individualized Study; Associate of Technical Study.

Program Mission Statement/Description: The Associate of Technical Studies (ATS) degree is open to any student whose technical degree goals cannot be met through enrollment in one of Sinclair's existing degree programs. You may design a degree which combines 2 or more technical areas and results in a unique educational plan. As an alternative, part of your degree requirements may include credit that has been awarded through articulation agreements with other community education providers. In both cases, Sinclair faculty will help you plan the most appropriate course of study. College Without Walls (CWW) is a self-paced adult degree program that gives you flexibility in terms of how you use your time and where you study. CWW is directed independent study that gives you an alternative to structured classroom settings (classroom participation is an option). It offers you new opportunities for combining theoretical and experiential learning personalized to your learning style.

Accreditation: North Central Association of Colleges and Schools.

Admission Requirements: Employment/Experience: variable; Essay/Written Work; Interview.

Credit Awards for Prior Learning: ACE Military Recommendations; ACE/PONSI Recommendations; Portfolio Assessment; Transfer Credit; Articulation Agreements; Proficiency Examinations.

Credit Awards for Examinations: ACT Proficiency Exams; CLEP General Exams; CLEP Subject Exams; DANTES Subject Tests; Departmental Exams.

Estimated Average Completion Time: 3 (part-time), 2 (full-time).

Credit Hour Requirements: 90 hours total; 30 hours academic residency (hours that must be earned at the institution exclusive of credit-by-exam, portfolio assessment, etc.).

Distance Learning Options: A/V Cassettes; Cooperative Education; Independent Study; Television Courses; Learning Contract.

Student Support Services Available: Academic Advising; Career Counseling; Counseling/Testing; Financial Aid; Job Placement Assistance; Orientation; Tutoring.

Informational Materials Available: Institutional Catalog; Program Brochure.

Program Age, Enrollment, and Degrees Conferred:

Degree	Year Est.	Current Enrollment	Degrees Conferred
All CWW degrees	1975	120	150
ATS	1989	40	10

Geographic Admission Restrictions: Only students who reside within a 35-mile radius are accepted at Sinclair College.

Tuition and Fees: In-State Tuition $29.00 per credit; Out-of-State Tuition $39.00 per credit; Application Fee $10.00; Graduation Fee $10.00; Credit-by-Exam Fee varies.

---

139. University of Toledo

University College
Adult Liberal Studies
2801 W. Bancroft St.
Toledo, OH 43606

Degrees Offered: Bachelor of Arts; Bachelor of Science; Individualized Program of Study.

Program Mission Statement/Description: Adult Liberal Studies is a program of study that embodies the elements of a traditional general education curriculum. The program is for students age 25 and older who either have little or no previously earned college credit or attended college some years previously. Coursework includes 9 special topical seminars and a capstone thesis. It is also possible for a student to complete a discipline concentration. The Individualized Program of Study is a program that permits students to design their unique baccalaureate interdisciplinary intercollegiate curricula. Programs are written to meet specific educational goals. Students have their programs approved by faculty representing several undergraduate colleges of the university.

Accreditation: North Central Association of Schools and Colleges.

Admission Requirements: HS/GED Diploma; Prior Credits.

Other Admission Requirements: For Adult Liberal Studies, no prior credit is required. For the Individualized Program of Study, a minimum of 30 quarter hours of prior credit is required.

Credit Awards for Prior Learning: ACE Military Recommendations; ACE/PONSI Recommendations; Portfolio Assessment; Transfer Credit.

Limits to Credit Awards for Prior Learning: Transfer credit: 103 quarter hours from 2-year institutions; 141 quarter hours from 4-year institutions; Portfolio-type assessment: a maximum of 45 quarter hours of credit; ACE/PONSI, ACE and NY Regents: a maximum of 141 quarter hours of credit.

Credit Awards for Examinations: CLEP General Exams; CLEP Subject Exams; College Board AP Exams; DANTES Subject Tests; Departmental Exams; NY Regents; Nursing Diploma.

Estimated Average Completion Time: 1-6 years (part-time). 1/2-3 years (full-time).

Caveats Regarding Time Estimates: A student must earn at least 45 quarter hours enrolled as a student of University College.

Credit Hour Requirements: 186 hours total; 45 hours academic residency (hours that must be earned at the institution exclusive of credit-by-exam, portfolio assessment, etc.).

Distance Learning Options: Independent Study; Supervised Fieldwork.

Student Support Services Available: Academic Advising; Career Counseling; Counseling/Testing; Financial Aid; Job Placement Assistance; Orientation; Tutoring.

Informational Materials Available: Institutional Catalog; Prior Learning Guides; Program Brochure.

Program Age, Enrollment, and Degrees Conferred:

Degree	Year Est.	Current Enrollment	Degrees Conferred
ALS	1971	266	Unknown
Individualized Program	1971	2414	Unknown

Percentage of Bachelor's Degree Holders Admitted to Graduate School: 20-35 percent.

Geographic Admission Restrictions: None.

Tuition and Fees: In-State Tuition $56.00 per credit; Out-of-State Tuition $147.00 per credit; Application Fee $30.00; Graduation Fee $10.00; Credit-by-Exam Fee $15.00; General Fee per quarter hour $14.60.

140. Wittenberg University

Liberal Studies Program
P.O. Box 720
Springfield, OH 45501

Degrees Offered: Bachelor of Arts in liberal studies with concentrations in organization management; culture and technology; human services.

Program Mission Statement/Description: The Liberal Studies Program emphasizes the development of critical processes of thought, skills in writing and speaking, and a fundamental understanding of the principles underlying the student's chosen concentration.

Accreditation: North Central Association of Colleges and Schools.

Admission Requirements: HS/GED Diploma; Prior Credits: 30 semester hours.

Other Admission Requirements: Transfer GPA in the 3.0 range. Math equivalent to 3 years of college preparation math; Interview.

Credit Awards for Prior Learning: Transfer Credit.

Limits to Credit Awards for Prior Learning: Maximum from a 2-year school: 75 credits; Maximum overall: 112 credits; 1 Wittenberg credit: 0.84 semester hours; BA degree requires 150 Wittenberg credits.

Credit Awards for Examinations: ACT Proficiency Exams; CLEP Subject Exams; College Board AP Exams; Departmental Exams.

Estimated Average Completion Time: 6 years (part-time), 4 years (full-time).

Caveats Regarding Time Estimates: Most adults enter as transfer students, so the typical completion time is 3-5 years.

Credit Hour Requirements: 150 hours total; 32 hours academic residency (hours that must be earned at the institution exclusive of credit-by-exam, portfolio assessment, etc. one Wittenberg credit: 0.84 semester hours.)

Distance Learning Options: Independent Study (maximum 3 courses).

Student Support Services Available: Academic Advising; Financial Aid; Job Placement Assistance; Orientation; Tutoring.

Informational Materials Available: Institutional Catalog; Program Brochure.

Program Age, Enrollment, and Degrees Conferred:

Degree	Year Est.	Current Enrollment	Degrees Conferred
BA	1982	65	28

Percentage of Bachelor's Degree Holders Admitted to Graduate School: 35 percent.

Geographic Admission Restrictions: None.

Tuition and Fees: In-State Tuition $145.00 per credit; Application Fee $30.00; Credit-by-Exam Fee $356.00; Registration Fee $15.00.

Other Pertinent Information: Probably the most important feature is access of adults to the Wittenberg Day Program and its choice of over 30 majors.

Oregon

141. George Fox College

Human Resources Management Degree
  Completion Program
Department of Continuing Studies
Newberg, OR 97137

Degrees Offered: Bachelor of Arts in Human Resources Management.

Program Mission Statement/Description: Through its Human Resources Management Degree Completion Program, George Fox College's Department of Continuing Studies serves the needs of adult learners and helps them assess personal values, develop interpersonal skills, and enhance professional competencies to influence the quality of work within their organizations. The goals of the Human Resources Management Degree Completion Program are to improve and further develop interpersonal and leadership skills; written and oral communication skills; problem-solving and decision-making skills; understanding of the research process and its application; self-knowledge and self-image; learner independence and self-reliance.

Accreditation: Northwest Association of Schools and Colleges.

Admission Requirements: 2 years of college credit, including 35 semester hours of general education; Writing sample; Recommendations.

Credit Awards for Prior Learning: ACE Military Recommendations; ACE/PONSI Recommendations; Portfolio Assessment; Transfer Credit.

Limits to Credit Awards for Prior Learning: Credit needed/ 30 hours maximum.

Credit Awards for Examinations: ACT Proficiency Exams; CLEP General Exams; CLEP Subject Exams; DANTES Subject Tests.

Limits to Credit Awards for Examinations: Limit for CLEP/DANTES is 32 semester credits.

Estimated Average Completion Time: 15-month program (full-time).

Caveats Regarding Time Estimates: About 78 percent finish the program.

Credit Hours Requirements: 126 hours total; 34 hours academic residency (hours that must be earned at the institution exclusive of credit-by-exam, portfolio assessment, etc.).

Distance Learning Options: Cooperative Education; Independent Study.

Student Support Services Available: Academic Advising; Career Counseling; Financial Aid; Job Placement Assistance; Tutoring.

Informational Materials Available: Program Brochure; Student Handbook.

Program Age, Enrollment, and Degrees Conferred:

Degree	Year Est.	Current Enrollment	Degrees Conferred
BA	1986	222	317

Percentage of Bachelor's Degree Holders Admitted to Graduate School: Approximately 2-5 percent. All who have applied have been accepted.

Geographic Admission Restrictions: None.

Tuition and Fees: $7995.00 for entire program; $25.00 per credit for life experience learning credit earned through Portfolio Assessment; Application Fee $20.00; Graduation Fee $40.00

142. Northwest Christian College

Degree Completion Program
828 E. 11th Ave.
Eugene, OR 97401

Degrees Offered: Bachelor of Science in Managerial Leadership.

Program Mission Statement/Description: The purpose of the degree completion program is to provide an alternative to the traditional method of pursuing a degree. The program is designed for the working adult with at least 2 years of college and significant life experiences who wants to earn a college degree while continuing to work. The delivery system for the curriculum is based on course modules taught in the evenings and some Saturdays. This educational model assumes a level of experience that will serve to produce college credit for prior learning that is validated by means of the portfolio assessment process. This experience also plays a key role in the curriculum which integrates past and present work and life experiences in a learning process that emphasizes student participation and interaction.

Accreditation: Northwest Association of Schools and Colleges.

Admission Requirements: HS/GED Diploma; Interview; Recommendations; Employment/Experience: 5 years; Prior Credits: 75 quarter credits; 1-2 Autobiographic sketches.

Credit Awards for Prior Learning: ACE Military Recommendations; ACE/PONSI Recommendations; Portfolio Assessment; Transfer Credit.

Limits to Credit Awards for Prior Learning: Maximum of 46 credits awarded through the portfolio assessment process.

Credit Awards for Examinations: CLEP General Exams; CLEP Subject Exams; College Board AP Exams; DANTES Subject Tests.

Limits to Credit Awards for Examinations: 27 quarter credits.

Estimated Average Completion Time: 15 months (full-time).

Caveats Regarding Time Estimates: All enrolled students are full-time.

Credit Hour Requirements: 186 hours total; 45 hours academic residency (hours that must be earned at the institution exclusive of credit-by-exam, portfolio assessment, etc.).

Distance Learning Options: None.

Student Support Services Available: Academic Advising; Career Counseling; Financial Aid; Orientation.

Informational Materials Available: Institutional Catalog; Prior Learning Guides; Program Brochure.

Program Age, Enrollment, and Degrees Conferred:

Degree	Year Est.	Current Enrollment	Degrees Conferred
Managerial Leadership	1989	55	19

Percentage of Bachelor's Degree Holders Admitted to Graduate School: Information not available.

Geographic Admission Restrictions: None.

Tuition and Fees: In-State Tuition $125.00 per credit; Out-of-State Tuition $125.00 per credit; Application Fee $25.00; Credit-by-Exam Fee; $23.00 Prior Learning Credit $414.00 maximum.

Other Pertinent Information: Students are required to have 18 hours in Bible studies to earn a degree. These credits are included in the 60-hour Managerial Leadership curriculum.

143. Oregon State University

Office of Continuing Education
327 Snell Hall
Corvallis, OR 97331

Degrees Offered: Bachelor of Arts or Bachelor of Science in Liberal Studies; Master of Education in Training and Development.

Program Mission Statement/Description: The mission of the Office of Continuing Higher Education is to extend the academic resources, programs, and support services of Oregon State University to meet student needs that are not ordinarily met by traditional university programs. The Bend Liberal Studies Degree Program provides access to a bachelor's degree for placebound central Oregonians and is offered in conjunction with the Central Oregon Consortium for Higher Education. The Master of Education Program in Training and Development is designed to prepare Portland-area residents for work as design and delivery specialists in business, industrial, community, governmental, or educational settings.

Accreditation: Western Association of Schools and Colleges.

Admission Requirements:

Undergraduate	Graduate
HS/GED Diploma	Undergraduate Degree
Prior Credits: 90	Interview
Recommendations	

Credit Awards for Prior Learning: Transfer Credit.

Limits to Credit Awards for Prior Learning: Limit of 108 credits from community college; last 45 of BA/BS must be from Oregon State University; Training and Development program limits transfer (off-campus) credits to 27.

Credit Awards for Examinations: CLEP General Exams; CLEP Subject Exams; College Board AP Exams; Departmental Exams.

Estimated Average Completion Time: Bachelors' Degrees: 3-6 years (part-time); Graduate Degrees: Ed.M. 2-4 years (part-time).

Credit Hour Requirements:

Degree	Total Hours	Academic Residency*
Bachelor's quarter hour	192	45
Graduate Training and Development	45	18

*Hours that must be earned at the institution exclusive of credit-by-exam, portfolio assessment, etc.

Distance Learning Options: Independent Study; Supervised Fieldwork; Television Courses.

Student Support Services Available: Academic Advising; Career Counseling; Counseling/Testing; Financial Aid; Job Placement Assistance; Orientation.

Informational Materials Available: Institutional Catalog; Program Brochure.

Program Age, Enrollment, and Degrees Conferred:

Degree	Year Est.	Current Enrollment	Degrees Conferred
BA/BS Liberal Studies	1981	34	27
MEd. Educational Admin.	1989	21	0

Percentage of Bachelor's Degree Holders Admitted to Graduate School: Information not available.

Geographic Admission Restrictions: See Program Mission Statement/Description.

Tuition and Fees:

	Undergraduate	Graduate
In-State Tuition per quarter	$75.00	$495.00
Application Fee	$40.00	$40.00

Other Pertinent Information: Master of Education in Training and Development is a closed enrollment program.

Pennsylvania

144. Albright College

Evening Program
P.O. Box 15234
Reading, PA 19612

Degrees Offered: Bachelor of Science in Accounting; Bachelor of Science in Business Administration; Bachelor of Science in Computer Science.

Program Mission Statement/Description: To provide an academic program characterized by a common sense of purpose, integration and balance of breadth and specialization, intellectual challenges that demand the full use of one's abilities, and the basis for a liberal education.

Accreditation: Middle States Association of Colleges and Schools.

Admission Requirements: HS/GED Diploma.

Credit Awards for Prior Learning: Transfer Credit.

Limits to Credit Awards for Prior Learning: Transfer students must complete 50 percent of their degree course work at Albright. Only courses in which a grade of C or better has been earned will be transferred to Albright. Students may submit credits to a limit of 7 courses (3 courses in the concentration and related areas; 4 courses in general studies or electives).

Credit Awards for Examinations: CLEP Subject Exams; Departmental Exams.

Limits to Credit Awards for Examinations: A student must receive a score of 55 or above in CLEP or Challenge Tests or projects.

Estimated Average Completion Time: 8 years (part-time), 4 years (full-time).

Credit Hour Requirements: 32 hours total; 16 hours academic residency (hours that must be earned at the institution exclusive of credit-by-exam, portfolio assessment, etc.).

Distance Learning Options: None.

Student Support Services Available: Academic Advising; Career Counseling; Financial Aid; Job Placement Assistance; Tutoring.

Informational Materials Available: Exam Preparation Guides; Institutional Catalog; Program Brochure.

Program Age, Enrollment, and Degrees Conferred:

Degree	Year Est.	Current Enrollment	Degrees Conferred
BS Accounting	1960	45	9
BS Business Admin.	1960	66	15
BS Computer Science	1960	44	7

Percentage of Bachelor's Degree Holders Admitted to Graduate School: Information not available.

Geographic Admission Restrictions: None.

Tuition and Fees: In-State Tuition course unit $650.00; Out-of-State Tuition course unit $650.00; Credit-by-Exam Fee $105.00.

145. Alvernia College

Continuing Education Program
400 Saint Bernardine St.
Reading, PA 19607

Degrees Offered: Associate of Science in Accounting; Associate of Science in Banking and Finance; Associate of Science in Personnel Management; Bachelor of Arts in Accounting; Bachelor of Arts in Banking and Finance; Bachelor of Arts in Communications; Bachelor of Arts in Business Management and Administration; Bachelor of Arts in Marketing; Bachelor of Science in Computer Information Systems/Business Emphasis.

Program Mission Statement/Description: The Continuing Education Program at Alvernia College is sensitive to the needs of working adults who wish to pursue a college education. For professional reasons, most adults are eager to earn their degrees in a timely manner. For that reason, the program was designed to allow students to earn 6 credits (2 classes) every 8 weeks by attending only 2 nights per week. Hence, when the Continued Education program is maximized, a first-time student can earn an associate's degree in as little as 2 years or a bachelor's degree in as little as 4 years. In addition, a modified weekend schedule allows students to supplement their evening program and further accelerate progress toward a degree. Of course, students may work toward degrees at the pace that best fits their personal schedules and goals.

Accreditation: Middle States Association of Colleges and Schools.

Admission Requirements: HS/GED Diploma; Interview; Prior Credits: 12.

Other Admission Requirements: First-time students must earn 12 credits, with a cumulative GPA of 2.0 or better before they may apply for official admission to the college. An official copy of their high school transcript or GED will allow their registration to be processed initially. Transfer students apply immediately.

Credit Awards for Prior Learning: ACE Military Recommendations; ACE/PONSI Recommendations; Transfer Credit.

Limits to Credit Awards for Prior Learning: Maximum of 90 credits toward a bachelor's degree may be transferred (30 of which may be CLEP/ACE/PONSI). Maximum of 36 credits toward an associate's degree may be transferred (30 of which may be CLEP/ACE/PONSI).

Credit Awards for Examinations: CLEP General Exams; CLEP Subject Exams; DANTES Subject Tests; Departmental Exams.

Limits to Credit Awards for Examinations: Same as prior learning limits.

Estimated Average Completion Time: Associates' Degrees: 2 years or more (part-time), 2 years (full-time). Bachelors' Degrees: 4 years or more (part-time), 4 years (full-time).

Credit Hour Requirements:

Degree	Total Hours	Academic Residency*
Associate	66	30
Bachelor's	120	30

*Hours that must be earned at the institution exclusive of credit-by-exam, portfolio assessment, etc.

Distance Learning Options: None.

Student Support Services Available: Academic Advising; Career Counseling; Counseling/Testing; Financial Aid; Job Placement Assistance; Tutoring.

Informational Materials Available: Program Brochure.

Program Age, Enrollment, and Degrees Conferred:

Degree	Year Est.	Current Enrollment	Degrees Conferred
BA Business	1985	157	Unknown
BSCS	1985	48	Unknown
AS Business	1985	87	Unknown
BA Communications	1987	9	Unknown

Percentage of Bachelor's Degree Holders Admitted to Graduate School: Information not available.

Geographic Admission Restrictions: None.

Tuition and Fees: In-State Tuition $180.00 per credit; Out-of-State Tuition $180.00 per credit; Application Fee $25.00; Graduation Fee $80.00; Credit-by-Exam Fee $20.00; plus $25.00 per credit if passing score is achieved.

---

146. Edinboro University of Pennsylvania

Specialized and Liberal Studies Program
Edinboro, PA 16444

Degrees Offered: Bachelor of Arts Degree in Specialized Studies; Associate of Arts Degree in Liberal Studies.

Program Mission Statement/Description: The Bachelor of Arts Degree in Specialized Studies curriculum is designed to provide breadth and does not require the typical major area of specialization. This program is designed for those whose career goals are so unusual that they cannot be met by taking any of the traditional majors offered by the university. The Associate of Arts Degree in Liberal Studies is designed to meet the needs of those persons seeking to gain a 2-year program of higher education and accompanying credentials.

Accreditation: Middle States Association of Colleges and Schools; National Council for Accreditation of Teacher Education.

Admission Requirements: HS/GED Diploma; Interview.

Credit Awards for Prior Learning: ACE Military Recommendations; ACE/PONSI Recommendations; Portfolio Assessment; Transfer Credit.

Limits to Credit Awards for Prior Learning: Usually not beyond 16 credits.

Credit Awards for Examinations: ACT Proficiency Exams; CLEP General Exams; CLEP Subject Exams; College Board AP Exams; DANTES Subject Tests; Departmental Exams.

Estimated Average Completion Time: Associates' Degrees: 4 years (part-time), 2 years (full-time); Bachelors' Degrees: 7 years (part-time), 4 years (full-time).

Credit Hour Requirements:

Degree	Total Hours	Academic Residency*
Associate	60	16
Bachelor's	128	32

*Hours that must be earned at the institution exclusive of credit-by-exam, portfolio assessment, etc.

Distance Learning Options: Independent Study; Supervised Fieldwork.

Student Support Services Available: Academic Advising; Career Counseling; Counseling/Testing; Financial Aid; Job Placement Assistance; Orientation; Tutoring.

Informational Materials Available: Institutional Catalog; Program Brochure.

Program Age, Enrollment, and Degrees Conferred:

Degree	Year Est.	Current Enrollment	Degrees Conferred
AA Liberal Studies	1985	28	7
BA Specialized Studies	1976	25	19

Percentage of Bachelor's Degree Holders Admitted to Graduate School: Information not available.

Geographic Admission Restrictions: None.

Tuition and Fees: In-State Tuition: $95.00; Out-of-State Tuition: $180.00; Application Fee: $20.00; Credit-by-Exam Fee: $25.00 per credit hours.

Other Pertinent Information: The university's Opportunity College services the working adult with 13 degree programs that can be completed through weekend and evening classes.

147. Gannon University

Open University and Weekend Programs
University Square
Erie, PA 16541

Degrees Offered: Associate of Arts in Liberal Arts; Associate of Science in Business Administration; Associate of Science in Early Childhood Education; Associate of Science for the Multiskilled Medical Assisting Practitioner; Associate's Degree in Nursing; Bachelor of Science in Management; Bachelor of Science in Administrative Studies.

Program Mission Statement/Description: Gannon is a Catholic, Diocesan, student-centered university that provides for the holistic development of undergraduate and graduate students in the Judeo-Christian tradition. As such, it offers each student outstanding teaching and a value-centered education in both liberal arts and professional specializations to prepare students for leadership roles in their careers, society, and church. The university faculty and staff are committed to excellence and continuous improvement in teaching, learning, scholarship, research, and service. The university's environment is one of inclusiveness and cultural diversity.

Accreditation: Middle States Association of Colleges and Schools.

Admission Requirements: HS/GED Diploma.

Other Admission Requirements: For Associate's Degree in Nursing—Prerequisite Coursework.

Credit Awards for Prior Learning: ACE Military Recommendations; Transfer Credit.

Limits to Credit Awards for Prior Learning: Students must complete 60 percent upper-level major.

Credit Awards for Examinations: CLEP General Exams; CLEP Subject Exams; College Board AP Exams; Departmental Exams.

Estimated Average Completion Time: Associates' Degrees: 4.5-6 years (part-time), 2 years (full-time); Bachelors' Degrees: 4 years (full-time).

Credit Hour Requirements:

Degree	Total Hours	Academic Residency*
Associate	68	Unknown
Bachelor's	128	Unknown

Distance Learning Options: Correspondence Courses.

Student Support Services Available: Academic Advising; Career Counseling; Counseling/Testing; Financial Aid; Job Placement Assistance; Orientation; Tutoring.

Informational Materials Available: Institutional Catalog; Program Brochure.

Program Age, Enrollment, and Degrees Conferred:

Degree	Year Est.	Current Enrollment	Degrees Conferred
AA	1978	0	0
ADN	1987	63	38
AS	1987	9	1
BS	1990	27	0

Percentage of Bachelor's Degree Holders Admitted to Graduate School: Information not available.

Geographic Admission Restrictions: None.

Tuition and Fees: In-State Tuition $275.00 per credit; Out-of-State Tuition $275.00 per credit; Application Fee $25.00; Graduation Fee $80.00; Credit-by-Exam Fee $38.00.

148. La Salle University

La Salle School of Continuing Studies and Graduate Programs
Philadelphia, PA 19141

Degrees Offered: Bachelor of Arts in Computer and Information Science; Bachelor of Arts in Economics; Bachelor of Arts in Education; Bachelor of Arts in English; Bachelor of Arts in History; Bachelor of Arts in Humanities; Bachelor of Arts in Political Science/Public Administration; Bachelor of Arts in Psychology; Bachelor of Arts in Sociology and Criminal Justice; Bachelor of Science in Applied Math; Bachelor of Science in Business Administration; Bachelor of Science in Nursing; Associate in Arts in Liberal Arts; Master of Science in Nursing; Master of Arts in Bilingual/Bicultural Studies; Master of Arts in Education; Master of Arts in Human Services Psychology; Master of Science in Business Administration (MBA).

Program Mission Statement/Description: La Salle is a liberal arts university. The School of Continuing Studies and Graduate Programs is devoted to offering programs of intense study in academic and professional fields. La Salle is known for teaching excellence and individual attention to students. La Salle is committed to a tradition that views education as the free search for truth. The university is committed to providing an environment that cultivates in students the desire to develop the skills necessary for truth and knowledge.

Accreditation: Middle States Association of Colleges and Schools; Council on Social Work Education, National League for Nursing.

Admission Requirements:

Undergraduate	Graduate
HS/GED Diploma	Undergraduate Degree
Interview	Interview
Essay/Written Work	Essay/Written Work
Recommendations	Recommendations
Employment/Experience	Employment/Experience
Prior Credits	GRE, GMAT

Credit Awards for Prior Learning: ACE Military Recommendations; ACE/PONSI Recommendations; Portfolio Assessment; Transfer Credit.

Credit Awards for Examinations: ACT Proficiency Exams; CLEP General Exams; CLEP Subject Exams; College Board AP Exams; DANTES Subject Tests; Departmental Exams.

Estimated Average Completion Time: Associates' Degrees: 4 years (part-time); Bachelors' Degrees: 6-8 years (part-time); Graduate Degrees: 6-8 years (part-time).

Credit Hour Requirements:

Degree	Total Hours	Academic Residency*
Associate	60	Unknown
Bachelor's	120	Unknown

*Hours that must be earned at the institution exclusive of credit-by-exam, portfolio assessment, etc.

Distance Learning Options: Cooperative Education; Independent Study; Phone/Mail Instruction.

Student Support Services Available: Academic Advising; Career Counseling; Counseling/Testing; Financial Aid; Job Placement Assistance; Orientation; Tutoring.

Informational Materials Available: Exam Preparation Guides; Institutional Catalog; Program Brochure.

Program Age, Enrollment, and Degrees Conferred:

Degree	Year Est.	Current Enrollment	Degrees Conferred
BA/BS	1943	2000	200
AA	1975	300	80
MBA	1976	500	50
MEd.	1982	219	0
MA Bilingual/Bicultural Studies	1982	50	0
MA Human Services/MSN	1987	65	0

Percentage of Bachelor's Degree Holders Admitted to Graduate School: 20 percent.

Geographic Admission Restrictions: None.

Tuition and Fees:

	Undergraduate	Graduate
In-State Tuition	$202.00/credit	$315.00/credit
Out-of-State Tuition	$202.00/credit	$315.00/credit
Application Fee	$20.00	$20.00
Credit-by-Exam Fee	$30.00	
MBA tuition		$335.00/credit

149. Lafayette College

Office of Special Programs
201 Alumni Gym
Easton, PA 18042

Degrees Offered: Bachelor of Science in Electrical Engineering; Bachelor of Science in Mechanical Engineering; Bachelor of Science in Chemistry; Bachelor of Arts in Engineering; Bachelor of Arts in Economics; Bachelor of Arts in Business.

Program Mission Statement/Description: Evening and summer courses for nontraditional students.

Accreditation: Middle States Association of Colleges and Schools; Accreditation Board of Engineering and Technology, Inc.

Admission Requirements: HS/GED Diploma; Interview.

Credit Awards for Prior Learning: Transfer Credit.

Limits to Credit Awards for Prior Learning: Maximum of 60 transfer credits (half of number for degree—120) must be earned on campus.

Credit Awards for Examinations: College Board AP Exams.

Estimated Average Completion Time: 8-10 years (part-time).

Caveats Regarding Time Estimates: Part-time program. No associates' or graduate degrees.

Credit Hour Requirements: 120 hours total; 60 hours academic residency (hours that must be earned at the institution exclusive of credit-by-exam, portfolio assessment, etc.).

Distance Learning Options: None.

Student Support Services Available: Academic Advising; Career Counseling; Financial Aid; Job Placement Assistance; Orientation; Tutoring.

Informational Materials Available: Institutional Catalog; Program Brochure.

Program Age, Enrollment, and Degrees Conferred:

Degree	Year Est.	Current Enrollment	Degrees Conferred
BSEE	1953	82	Unknown
BSME	1953	83	Unknown
AB Engineering	1974	23	Unknown
BS Chemistry	1968	15	14
AB Economics	1971	34	46
Other degree candidates			32

Percentage of Bachelor's Degree Holders Admitted to Graduate School: Information not available.

Geographic Admission Restrictions: None.

Tuition and Fees: In-State Tuition $200.00 per credit; Out-of-State Tuition $200.00 per credit; Application Fee $25.00.

150. Lincoln University

Master, Human Services Program
Lincoln University, PA 19352

Degrees Offered: Master of Human Services.

Program Mission Statement/Description: The Master of Human Services (MHS) Program is a full-time graduate program for adult human service practitioners.

Accreditation: Middle States Association of Colleges and Schools.

Admission Requirements: Employment/Experience: 5 years minimum; Essay/Written Work; Interview; Recommendations. Must be employed full-time in a human-service position while in the MHS Program.

Credit Awards for Prior Learning: Students do prepare a portfolio of professional skills during their first semester but do not earn credit for prior learning because the BA/BS is not a requirement for entry.

Credit Awards for Examinations: None.

Estimated Average Completion Time: Master of Human Services—2 years (full-time).

Caveats Regarding Time Estimates: Only full-time study permitted.

Credit Hour Requirements: 54 total hours.

Distance Learning Options: Supervised Fieldwork.

Student Support Services Available: Academic Advising; Career Counseling; Counseling/Testing; Financial Aid; Job Placement Assistance; Orientation; Tutoring.

Informational Materials Available: Exam Preparation Guides; Institutional Catalog; Program Brochure; Pregraduate Semester in Writing and Critical Thinking Skills.

Program Age, Enrollment, and Degrees Conferred:

Degree	Year Est.	Current Enrollment	Degrees Conferred
MHS	1977	200	Unknown

Geographic Admission Restrictions: All students must travel to Lincoln's campus for Saturday classes; current students come from NY, PA, DC, and MD.

Tuition and Fees: In-State Tuition $160.00 per credit; Out-of-State Tuition $240.00 per credit; Application Fee $25.00; Graduation Fee $50.00; General Fees $13.00 per credit in-state, $18.00 per credit out-of-state.

Other Pertinent Information: All students must be employed full-time in a human-service job prior to and after admission; students may be accepted without undergraduate degree if they meet eligibility and test requirements. Applicants without a bachelor's degree must have a minimum of 3 years' experience in the human service field; applicants with a BA/BS must have a minimum of one year of work experience. Classes are held on Saturday at Lincoln's main campus; students also attend one evening class at various locations close to their home or work. The program is competency-based, applying relevant academic theory to problems encountered in agency practice. All students continue to work full-time while enrolled in the program. The curriculum follows a performance-based approach to education that organizes skills and theory into 5 basic competency units: self-directed learning, helping skills, group skills, community organization and program management, and social change.

151. Neumann College

Liberal Studies Program
Aston, PA 19014

Degrees Offered: Bachelor of Arts; Bachelor of Science in Liberal Studies; Associate of Arts in Liberal Studies.

Program Mission Statement/Description: The Liberal Studies major is designed to respond to the special needs, circumstances, and strengths of students pursuing a college degree while they maintain the full-time commitment of adult life. Offers concentrations in accounting, computer and information management, elementary education, humanities, marketing, business administration, early childhood education, health care administration, human resource development, and psychology.

Accreditation: Middle States Association of Colleges and Schools.

Admission Requirements: HS/GED Diploma; Interview.

Credit Awards for Prior Learning: ACE Military Recommendations; ACE/PONSI Recommendations; Portfolio Assessment; Transfer Credit

Limits to Credit Awards for Prior Learning: Portfolio—60 credits; Transfer Credits—64 from 2-year college, 90 from 4-year college/university.

Credit Awards for Examinations: ACT Proficiency Exams; CLEP General Exams; CLEP Subject Exams; College Board AP Exams; DANTES Subject Tests; Departmental Exams.

Limits to Credit Awards for Examinations: CLEP—30 credits; Challenge Exams—can challenge up to 25 percent of total coursework and up to 50 percent of coursework in concentration or major.

Estimated Average Completion Time: Associates' Degrees: 4 years (part-time), 2 years (full-time); Bachelors' Degrees: 8 years (part-time), 4 years (full-time).

Credit Hour Requirements:

Degree	Total Hours	Academic Residency*
Associate	60	30
Bachelor's	120	30

*Hours that must be earned at the institution exclusive of credit-by-exam, portfolio assessment, etc.

Distance Learning Options: Cooperative Education; Independent Study; Supervised Fieldwork.

Student Support Services Available: Academic Advising; Career Counseling; Counseling/Testing; Financial Aid; Job Placement Assistance; Orientation; Tutoring.

Informational Materials Available: Institutional Catalog; Prior Learning Guides; Program Brochure.

Program Age, Enrollment, and Degrees Conferred:

Degree	Year Est.	Current Enrollment	Degrees Conferred
BS/BA Liberal Studies	1974	600	680
AA Liberal Studies	1988	50	20

Percentage of Bachelor's Degree Holders Admitted to Graduate School: 20 percent.

Geographic Admission Restrictions: None.

Tuition and Fees: In-State Tuition $3666.00 per semester; Out-of-State Tuition $3666.00 per semester; Application Fee $25.00; Graduation Fee $80.00; Credit-by-Exam Fee varies.

152. University of Scranton

Dexter Hanley College
Gallery Building
Scranton, PA 18510-4582

Degrees Offered: Nineteen degree programs offered in the evening leading toward a baccalaureate degree; 2 designed specifically for adult students are BSN (for RNs) and liberal studies. There are 10 programs leading toward an associate's degree.

Program Mission Statement/Description: Dexter Hanley College is committed to carrying out the Jesuit tradition by offering quality programs, quality services, and the opportunity for adult students to accomplish their educational, professional, and personal goals.

Accreditation: Middle States Association of Colleges and Schools; National Council for the Accreditation of Teacher Education; National League for Nursing; American Physical Therapy Association.

Admission Requirements: HS/GED Diploma; Interview.

Credit Awards for Prior Learning: ACE Military Recommendations; ACE/PONSI Recommendations; Portfolio Assessment; Transfer Credit.

Limits to Credit Awards for Prior Learning: 60 transfer credits; 30 all other.

Credit Awards for Examinations: ACT Proficiency Exams; CLEP General Exams; CLEP Subject Exams; College Board AP Exams; DANTES Subject Tests; Departmental Exams.

Estimated Average Completion Time: Associates' Degrees: 4 years (part-time); Bachelors' Degrees: 10 years (part-time).

Credit Hour Requirements:

Degree	Total Hours	Academic Residency*
Associate	60	Unknown
Bachelor's	123	Unknown

*Hours that must be earned at the institution exclusive of credit-by-exam, portfolio assessment, etc.

Distance Learning Options: A/V Cassettes; Independent Study; Supervised Fieldwork; Television Courses.

Student Support Services Available: Academic Advising; Career Counseling; Counseling/Testing; Financial Aid; Job Placement Assistance; Orientation; Tutoring.

Informational Materials Available: Institutional Catalog; Prior Learning Guides; Program Brochure.

Program Age, Enrollment, and Degrees Conferred: Information not available.

Percentage of Bachelor's Degree Holders Admitted to Graduate School: 7 percent.

Geographic Admission Restrictions: None.

Tuition and Fees: In-State Tuition $258.00 per credit; Application Fee $10.00; Graduation Fee $115.00; Credit-by-Exam Fee $30.00; University Fee $225.00 full-time, $30.00 part-time; Recreational Fee $50.00; Orientation Fee $30.00.

153. Villanova University

University College
Villanova, PA 19085

Degrees Offered: Associate of Arts; Bachelor of Arts in General Studies; Bachelor of Arts in Human Services; Bachelor of Arts in Communication Arts; Bachelor of Arts in Philosophy; Bachelor of Arts in History; Bachelor of Arts in English; Bachelor of Science in Mathematics; Bachelor of Science in Computer Science; Bachelor of Science in Secondary Education; Bachelor of Science in Accountancy; Bachelor of Science in Business Administration; Bachelor of Science in Electrical Engineering; Bachelor of Science in Mechanical Engineering.

Program Mission Statement/Description: Villanova University, through the courses offered by University College, fulfills educational needs of men and women who are unable to pursue regular full-time day programs. In addition to its extensive offerings of courses and programs, University College provides comprehensive counseling services to assist adult students in planning their educational careers. One of the university's 5 undergraduate colleges, University College, is an integral part of the university structure. The program requirements and degrees earned are commensurate with those offered by the full-time colleges of the university.

Accreditation: Middle States Association of Colleges and Schools; Accreditation Board for Engineering and Technology, Inc.; American Assembly of Collegiate Schools of Business.

Admission Requirements:

Undergraduate	Graduate
HS/GED Diploma	Undergraduate Degree

Credit Awards for Prior Learning: Transfer Credit.

Limits to Credit Awards for Prior Learning: Maximum transfer credits accepted is 60.

Credit Awards for Examinations: CLEP Subject Exams; College Board AP Exams; Departmental Exams.

Estimated Average Completion Time: Associates' Degrees: 4 years (part-time), 2 years (full-time); Bachelors' Degrees: 7 years (part-time), 4 years (full-time).

Credit Hour Requirements:

Degree	Total Hours	Academic Residency*
Associate	60	30
Bachelor's	122	62

*Hours that must be earned at the institution exclusive of credit-by-exam, portfolio assessment, etc.

Distance Learning Options: Independent Study.

Student Support Services Available: Academic Advising; Career Counseling; Counseling/Testing; Financial Aid; Job Placement Assistance; Orientation; Tutoring.

Informational Materials Available: Institutional Catalog; Program Brochure.

Program Age, Enrollment, and Degrees Conferred: Villanova University has offered degree programs to part-time students through University College for over 60 years. No other information available.

Percentage of Bachelor's Degree Holders Admitted to Graduate School: Information not available.

Geographic Admission Restrictions: None.

Tuition and Fees: Tuition $230.00 per credit; Application Fee $25.00; Credit-by-Exam Fee $35.00 per credit; Registration Fee $15.00.

154. Widener University

Weekend College
Rm. 137 Kapelski
Chester, PA 19013

Degrees Offered: Bachelor of Science in Nursing; Bachelor of Science in Business Administration; Bachelor of Arts in Psychology.

Program Mission Statement/Description: Weekend College offers adults who cannot attend day or evening classes the opportunity to complete degrees through weekend study. They spend half the traditional class time in class with an instructor (about 21 hours for a 3-credit course). Classroom instruction is augmented by extensive out-of-class independent study.

Accreditation: Middle States Association of Colleges and Schools; National League for Nursing.

Admission Requirements: HS/GED Diploma; Interview.

Credit Awards for Prior Learning: ACE Military Recommendations; ACE/PONSI Recommendations; Portfolio Assessment; Transfer Credit.

Limits to Credit Awards for Prior Learning: The last 30 credits must be taken in classroom instruction at Widener University.

Credit Awards for Examinations: CLEP General Exams; CLEP Subject Exams; DANTES Subject Tests; Departmental Exams.

Estimated Average Completion Time: Associates' Degrees: 5 years (part-time), 2.5 years (full-time); Bachelors' Degrees: 7-9 years (part-time), 5 years (full-time).

Caveats Regarding Time Estimates: The above assumes no transfer credit from previous institutions attended.

Credit Hour Requirements:

Degree	Total Hours	Academic Residency*
Associate	60	15
Bachelor's	120	30

*Hours that must be earned at the institution exclusive of credit-by-exam, portfolio assessment, etc.

Distance Learning Options: Independent Study; Supervised Fieldwork.

Student Support Services Available: Academic Advising; Career Counseling; Financial Aid; Job Placement Assistance; Orientation; Tutoring.

Informational Materials Available: Institutional Catalog; Prior Learning Guides; Program Brochure.

Program Age, Enrollment, and Degrees Conferred:

Degree	Year Est.	Current Enrollment	Degrees Conferred
BSN	1984	200	105
BBA	1980	125	120
BA	1986	60	20

Percentage of Bachelor's Degree Holders Admitted to Graduate School: Information not available.

Geographic Admission Restrictions: None.

Tuition and Fees: In-State Tuition $180.00 per credit; Out-of-State Tuition $180.00 per credit; Credit-by-Exam Fee $50.00. New student fee payable at registration $10.00.

Rhode Island

155. Rhode Island College

Bachelor of General Studies Program
600 Mount Pleasant Ave.
Providence, RI 02908

Degrees Offered: Bachelor of General Studies.

Program Mission Statement/Description: The mission of the Bachelor of General Studies Program is to give students the flexibility to plan a unique undergraduate degree program that can be directed toward achieving specific career and academic goals.

Accreditation: New England Association of Schools and Colleges, Inc.

Admission Requirements: HS/GED Diploma; Interview.

Credit Awards for Prior Learning: ACE Military Recommendations; ACE/PONSI Recommendations; Portfolio Assessment; Transfer Credit.

Limits to Credit Awards for Prior Learning: Half of degree requirements (60/120 credits) for ACE, portfolio, and examinations. College has a 30 credit residency requirement.

Credit Awards for Examinations: ACT Proficiency Exams; CLEP General Exams; CLEP Subject Exams; College Board AP Exams; DANTES Subject Tests; Departmental Exams.

Estimated Average Completion Time: 6 years (part-time), 2 years (full-time).

Credit Hour Requirements:

Degree	Total Hours	Academic Residency*
Bachelor's	120	30

*Hours that must be earned at the institution exclusive of credit-by-exam, portfolio assessment, etc.

Distance Learning Options: Cooperative Education; Independent Study.

Student Support Services Available: Academic Advising; Career Counseling; Counseling/Testing; Financial Aid; Job Placement Assistance; Orientation; Tutoring.

Informational Materials Available: Institutional Catalog; Program Brochure.

Program Age, Enrollment, and Degrees Conferred:

Degree	Year Est.	Current Enrollment	Degrees Conferred
BGS	1975	100	250

Percentage of Bachelor's Degree Holders Admitted to Graduate School: 15 percent.

Geographic Admission Restrictions: None.

Tuition and Fees: In-State Tuition $70.00 per credit; Out-of-State Tuition $175.00 per credit; Credit-by-Exam Fee $40.00; Activity/Union/Arts $140.00 for full-time students.

156. University of Rhode Island

College of Continuing Education
199 Promenade St.
Providence, RI 02908

Degrees Offered: Bachelor of General Studies.

Program Mission Statement/Description: The Bachelor of General Studies (BGS) program is designed for adults who have been out of school for 5 or more years. The BGS program offers 2 majors: Human Studies and Business Institutions. The Human Studies major is the ideal avenue for the student who has special needs or special interests in working in some aspect of the broad field of human services. The Business Institutions major is a structured program designed to meet the needs of the general business student. Both majors are broadly interdisciplinary, offering student opportunities to study problems from a range of disciplinary approaches. The Human Studies major is also quite flexible, allowing students to select courses that focus on their particular concerns.

Accreditation: New England Association of Schools and Colleges, Inc.

Admission Requirements: HS/GED Diploma. Performance-based admission allows new students to use their first 15 credits to demonstrate their ability to do college-level work.

Credit Awards for Prior Learning: Transfer Credit.

Limits to Credit Awards for Prior Learning: Up to 90 credits may be transferred.

Credit Awards for Examinations: CLEP General Exams; CLEP Subject Exams; College Board AP Exams.

Limits to Credit Awarded for Examinations: A maximum of 21 CLEP General Exams (social science, natural science, humanities, English composition), not to exceed a total of 45 credits when combined with transfer credits.

Estimated Average Completion Time: 7 years (part-time), 4 years (full-time).

Credit Hour Requirements: 118 total hours.

Distance Learning Options: Independent Study; Supervised Fieldwork; Television Courses

Student Support Services Available: Academic Advising; Career Counseling; Counseling/Testing; Financial Aid; Job Placement Assistance; Orientation; Tutoring.

Informational Materials Available: Institutional Catalog; Program Brochure.

Program Age, Enrollment, and Degrees Conferred:

Degree	Year Est.	Current Enrollment	Degrees Conferred
BGS	1977	540	135

Percentage of Bachelor's Degree Holders Admitted to Graduate School: 100 percent of those who applied have been accepted; 33 percent have applied.

Geographic Admission Restrictions: None.

Tuition and Fees: Undergraduate: In-State Tuition $93.00/credit; Out-of-State Tuition: $298.00/credit; Credit-by-Exam Fee: $38.00 CLEP; Registration fee $10.00 each semester; Student Activities Fee $10.00.

South Carolina

157. Central Wesleyan College

Leadership Education for Adult Professionals
Box 497, CWC
Central, SC 29630

Degrees Offered: Associate of Science in General Business (ASGB); Bachelor of Science in Management of Human Resources; Master of Arts in Organizational Management; Master of Arts in Christian Ministries.

Program Mission Statement/Description: The mission of the Central Wesleyan College Leadership Education for Adult Professionals (LEAP) Program is to provide diverse, high-quality, undergraduate and graduate education. The program is guided by a Christian worldview and is designed for adult learners with previous college work. The program allows working adults to advance their personal and professional educational goals while maintaining a career. Adult learners use their everyday professional experience as the basis for promoting and stimulating the integration of theoretical knowledge and Christian principles with the demands of the workplace.

Accreditation: Southern Association of Colleges and Schools.

Admission Requirements:

Undergraduate	Graduate
HS/GED Diploma	Undergraduate Degree
Essay/Written Work	Essay/Written Work
Recommendations	Recommendations
Employment/Experience: 2 years	Employment/Experience: 2 years
Prior Credits: 60	GRE

Other Admission Requirements: No prior credits are required for AS-GB; GRE, MAT, or GMAT score must be submitted for graduate admission.

Credit Awards for Prior Learning: ACE Military Recommendations; ACE/PONSI Recommendations; Portfolio Assessment; Transfer Credit.

Limits to Credit Awards for Prior Learning: Maximum for nontraditional credits is 68 semester hours.

Credit Awards for Examinations: CLEP General Exams; CLEP Subject Exams; College Board AP Exams; DANTES Subject Tests; Departmental Exams.

Estimated Average Completion Time: Associates' Degrees: 20 months (full-time); Bachelors' Degrees: 18 months (full-time); Graduate Degrees: MA 18 months (full-time).

Caveats Regarding Time Estimates: The programs are all considered full-time and are lock-step, one night per week (plus one study group meeting per week).

Credit Hour Requirements:

Degree	Total Hours	Academic Residency*
Associate	64	30
Bachelor's	128	30
Graduate (MA)	33 or 36	27

*Hours that must be earned at the institution exclusive of credit-by-exam, portfolio assessment, etc.

Distance Learning Options: Independent Study.

Other Options: Many courses are held off-campus in locations convenient to students.

Student Support Services Available: Academic Advising; Career Counseling; Counseling/Testing; Financial Aid; Orientation; Tutoring.

Informational Materials Available: Exam Preparation Guides; Institutional Catalog; Prior Learning Guides; Program Brochure.

Program Age, Enrollment, and Degrees Conferred:

Degree	Year Est.	Current Enrollment	Degrees Conferred
BS	1986	225	275
AS	1988	150	10
MA	1990	0	0

Percentage of Bachelor's Degree Holders Admitted to Graduate School: 5 percent (Most are interested in BS as final degree).

Geographic Admission Restrictions: None.

Tuition and Fees:

	Undergraduate	Graduate
In-State Tuition	$185.00/credit	Unknown
Application Fee	$25.00	$25.00
Graduation Fee	$40.00	$80.00
Credit-by-Exam Fee	$30.00 per hour	

Other Fees: In-State and Out-of-State tuition for AS—$120.00, BS $160.00 per credit; Application Fee $25.00; Undergraduate Graduation Fee $40.00; Graduate Graduation Fee $80.00; Credit-by-Exam Fee $30.00 per credit. Information not available for Graduate Tuition. Educational Resources (all books and other materials $1000.00—Master's, $107.00—Bachelor's, $915.00—Associate's).

158. Coker College

Evening and Summer School
Hartsville, SC 29550

Degrees Offered: Bachelor of Science in Business Administration; Bachelor of Arts in Education; Bachelor of Arts in Sociology.

Program Mission Statement/Description: Coker College addresses the higher educational needs of nontraditional students living in its geographical region. The college's business and sociology majors may be completed entirely at night within a 4-year period, summers included. The education major requires some course-related internships in the public schools and one semester of student teaching in addition to the night courses. The business administration major offers concentrations in accounting, finance, operations management, and marketing. The sociology major offers concentrations in criminology and social work. The education major leads to certification in elementary education or special education.

Accreditation: Southern Association of Colleges and Schools.

Admission Requirements: HS/GED Diploma; Recommendations.

Credit Awards for Prior Learning: ACE Military Recommendations; ACE/PONSI Recommendations; Portfolio Assessment; Transfer Credit.

Limits to Credit Awards for Prior Learning: No more than 64 credit hours from a 2-year college.

Credit Awards for Examinations: CLEP General Exams; CLEP Subject Exams; College Board AP Exams; DANTES Subject Tests; Departmental Exams.

Estimated Average Completion Time: 6 years (part-time), 5 years (full-time).

Caveats Regarding Time Estimates: We have a program that can be completed in 4 years if the student attends year-round (5 8-week sessions, with 6 semester hours per session). Many of our students skip summer sessions; many others attend them and graduate in 4 years.

Credit Hour Requirements:

Degree	Total Hours	Academic Residency*
Bachelor's	120	30

*Hours that must be earned at the institution exclusive of credit-by-exam, portfolio assessment, etc.

Distance Learning Options: Cooperative Education; Independent Study; Supervised Fieldwork.

Student Support Services Available: Academic Advising; Career Counseling; Counseling/Testing; Financial Aid; Job Placement Assistance; Orientation; Tutoring.

Informational Materials Available: Institutional Catalog; Program Brochure.

Program Age, Enrollment, and Degrees Conferred: BS and BA information not available.

Percentage of Bachelor's Degree Holders Admitted to Graduate School: An estimated 85 percent of education majors go on to some graduate study to maintain their certification. Other figures are unavailable.

Geographic Admission Restrictions: See Program Mission Statement.

Tuition and Fees: In-State Tuition $341.00 per credit; Out-of-State Tuition $341.00 per credit; Application Fee $15.00; Graduation Fee $25.00; Credit-by-Exam Fee $38.00 for CLEP; Activity Fee $2.50 per hour.

Other Fees: $2.50 per hour activity fee.

159. Converse College

Converse II Program
580 E. Main St.
Spartanburg, SC 29302

Degrees Offered: Bachelor of Arts; Bachelor of Fine Arts; Bachelor of Music.

Program Mission Statement/Description: Converse II is an innovative program established by Converse College to encourage adult women 24 years old and up to return to school to pursue their undergraduate studies. Through the program, a student may work toward any of the undergraduate degrees offered at Converse—Bachelor of Arts, Bachelor of Fine Arts, or Bachelor of Music—or she may take courses on a nondegree basis for personal enrichment. Special features of CII program are simplified application procedure, reduced fee schedule, financial aid, flexible scheduling, individualized advisement, and career counseling.

Accreditation: Southern Association of Colleges and Schools.

Admission Requirements: HS/GED Diploma; Interview; Application. Attend an orientation session. If previous college work, the official transcripts must be sent for evaluation. If less than 20 hours college work, high school/GED diploma must also be presented.

Credit Awards for Prior Learning: Portfolio Assessment; Transfer Credit. Students may exempt courses in art on basis of portfolio or may exempt courses in theater or music on basis of performance/experience—but no academic credit given for experiential learning.

Credit Awards for Examinations: CLEP General Exams; CLEP Subject Exams.

Limits to Credit Awards for Examinations: CLEP—30 hours. Converse will grant no more than 30 semester hours of credit by examination to any student.

Estimated Average Completion Time: 6–8 years (part-time), 4 years (full-time).

Credit Hour Requirements:

Degree	Total Hours	Academic Residency*
Bachelor's	120	42

*Hours that must be earned at the institution exclusive of credit-by-exam, portfolio assessment, etc.

Distance Learning Options: Independent Study; Supervised Fieldwork.

Student Support Services Available: Academic Advising; Career Counseling; Counseling/Testing; Financial Aid; Job Placement Assistance; Orientation; Tutoring; Writing Skills, Study Skills Workshops; Converse II Association.

Informational Materials Available: Institutional Catalog; Program Brochure; Fee Schedule; Academic Calendar and Map; Class Schedules.

Program Age, Enrollment, and Degrees Conferred:

Degree	Year Est.	Current Enrollment	Degrees Conferred
Bachelor's	1983	139	173

Percentage of Bachelor's Degree Holders Admitted to Graduate School: 3 percent.

Geographic Admission Restrictions: There are no geographical restrictions for acceptance of out-of-state students. Though most usually reside off campus, they are now allowed to board on campus. No foreign students who require an I-20 may be admitted.

Tuition and Fees: In-State Tuition $134.00 per credit; Out-of-State Tuition $134.00 per credit; Application Fee $25.00; Graduation Fee $110.00; Credit-by-Exam Fee $10.00 per credit.

Other Fees: Directed Independent Studies $160.00; Registration Fee $15.00; Audit Fee $60.00 per credit; Applied Music Fee $250.00 one hour/week long term, $125.00 one hour/week winter term, $140.00 half hour/week long term, $70.00 half hour/week winter term.

160. Francis Marion College

Bachelor of General Studies Program
P.O. Box 100547
Florence, SC 29501-0547

Degrees Offered: Bachelor of General Studies.

Program Mission Statement/Description: The Bachelor of General Studies Program is offered for the benefit of certain students who, for specific reasons, are unable to complete a regular program in the academic disciplines within normal time limits. These students will normally fit into one of 2 categories: (1) those students who have earned many college credits at various institutions and in various disciplines over a long period of time but have not met specific requirements for a major; and (2) those students who are transfers to Francis Marion College from an associate's degree program earning many credits not applicable to bachelor of arts or bachelor of science majors.

Accreditation: Southern Association of Colleges and Schools.

Admission Requirements: HS/GED Diploma; Prior Credits; normally, mature adults over 25 years of age.

Credit Awards for Prior Learning: ACE Military Recommendations; Transfer Credit.

Limits to Credit Awards for Prior Learning: Normally, up to 90 transfer semester hours.

Credit Awards for Examinations: CLEP General Exams; CLEP Subject Exams; College Board AP Exams.

Estimated Average Completion Time: 6-7 years (part-time), 3 years (full-time).

Credit Hour Requirements:

Degree	Total Hours	Academic Residency*
Bachelor's	120	30

*Hours that must be earned at the institution exclusive of credit-by-exam, portfolio assessment, etc.

Distance Learning Options: Correspondence Courses; Independent Study; Newspaper Courses; Television Courses.

Student Support Services Available: Academic Advising; Career Counseling; Counseling/Testing; Financial Aid; Job Placement Assistance; Orientation; Tutoring.

Informational Materials Available: Institutional Catalog.

Program Age, Enrollment, and Degrees Conferred:

Degree	Year Est.	Current Enrollment	Degrees Conferred
BGS	1972	56	123

Percentage of Bachelor's Degree Holders Admitted to Graduate School: About 10 percent.

Geographic Admission Restrictions: None.

Tuition and Fees: In-State Tuition $107.00 per credit; Out-of-State Tuition $214.00 per credit; Application Fee $25.00; Graduation Fee $22.00; Credit-by-Exam Fee $15.00; Vehicle Fee $10.00; ID Card Fee $15.00; Transcript Fee $2.00.

161. Limestone College

Block Program
1115 College Dr.
Gaffney, SC 29340

Degrees Offered: Bachelor of Science; Bachelor of Arts; Associate of Arts.

Program Mission Statement/Description: The Block Program offers evening and Saturday classes to adults. Evening classes run 3 nights a week. At end of 11 class periods, class is complete. Can take 4 classes like this in course of semester.

Accreditation: Southern Association of Colleges and Schools.

Admission Requirements: HS/GED Diploma.

Credit Awards for Prior Learning: ACE Military Recommendations; ACE/PONSI Recommendations; Transfer Credit.

Limits to Credit Awards for Prior Learning: Limit 74 from 2-year school.

Credit Awards for Examinations: CLEP General Exams; CLEP Subject Exams; College Board AP Exams; DANTES Subject Tests; Departmental Exams.

Estimated Average Completion Time: Bachelors' Degrees: 6 years (part-time), 4 years (full-time).

Credit Hour Requirements:

Degree	Total Hours	Academic Residency*
Associate	62	30
Bachelor's	120	30

*Hours that must be earned at the institution exclusive of credit-by-exam, portfolio assessment, etc.

Distance Learning Options: None.

Student Support Services Available: Academic Advising; Counseling/Testing; Financial Aid.

Informational Materials Available: Institutional Catalog; Program Brochure.

Program Age, Enrollment, and Degrees Conferred:

Degree	Year Est.	Current Enrollment	Degrees Conferred
B.S.	1976	900	180/year

Percentage of Bachelor's Degree Holders Admitted to Graduate School: 30 percent seeking; 98 percent admitted.

Geographic Admission Restrictions: None.

Tuition and Fees: In-State Tuition $100.00 per credit; Out-of-State Tuition $100.00 per credit; Application Fee $15.00; Graduation Fee $20.00.

South Dakota

162. Sioux Falls College

Bachelor of Arts Organization and Management Program
1501 S. Prairie Ave.
Sioux Falls, SD 57105

Degrees Offered: Bachelor of Arts in Organizational Behavior and Management.

Program Mission Statement/Description: Working adults with 2–3 years of transferable college credit can complete a Bachelor of Arts in Organizational Behavior and Management in 17 months attending class one evening per week. Education that works for working adults.

Accreditation: North Central Association of Colleges and Schools.

Admission Requirements: Employment/Experience: 3 years; Essay/Written Work; HS/GED Diploma; Interview; Prior Credits: 64 semester hours; Recommendations.

Other Admission Requirements: English composition. 2.0 cumulative GPA for transfer, writing sample, 2 references.

Credit Awards for Prior Learning: ACE Military Recommendations; ACE/PONSI Recommendations; Transfer Credit Portfolio Assessment; American Institute of Banking Courses; Vo-Tech Programs (accredited) up to 15 semester hours.

Limits to Credit Awards for Prior Learning: No more than one third of a student credit for graduation can be nontraditional credit (ACE, military, workshops for credit, portfolio assessment, CLEP) 42 semester hours total.

Credit Awards for Examinations: CLEP Subject Exams; Departmental Exams.

Limits to Credit Awards for Exams: CLEP 42 total semester hours.

Estimated Average Completion Time: 17 months (full-time).

Caveats Regarding Time Estimates: Admitted with a minimum of 64 semester hours (major program is 36 semester hours) remaining credit can be earned through nontraditional areas.

Credit Hour Requirements:

Degree	Total Hours	Academic Residency*
Bachelor's	128	36 (Last 36 semester hours in the major.)

*Hours that must be earned at the institution exclusive of credit-by-exam, portfolio assessment, etc.

Distance Learning Options: A/V Cassettes.

Student Support Services Available: Academic Advising; Career Counseling; Counseling/Testing; Financial Aid; Job Placement Assistance; Orientation; Tutoring.

Informational Materials Available: Exam Preparation Guides; Institutional Catalog; Prior Learning Guides; Program Brochure; Activity Card; Campus Calendar; Campus Newsletter.

Program Age, Enrollment, and Degrees Conferred:

Degree	Year Est.	Current Enrollment	Degrees Conferred
BA Org. Behav. Mgmt.	1988	84	57

Percentage of Bachelor's Degree Holders Admitted to Graduate: 10 percent.

Geographic Admission Restrictions: None.

Tuition and Fees: In-State Tuition $183.00 per credit; Graduation Fee $50.00.

Other Fees: Books $450.00, CLEP $38.00; Assessment of Prior Learning $40.00 per credit hour.

163. South Dakota State University

College of Arts and Science
Adm 122
Brookings, SD 57007

Degrees Offered: Bachelor of General Studies, Bachelor of Science or Bachelor of Arts.

Program Mission Statement/Description: To extend the student's perspectives and to offer the student additional challenges not permitted within the restrictions and limitations of a traditional major program. It allows students to construct a program of advanced credits to meet their special needs.

Accreditation: North Central Association of Colleges and Schools.

Admission Requirements: HS/GED Diploma.

Other Admission Requirements: ACT of 21; upper half of high school class; must have taken 4 years of high school English, 3 years math, 3 years science, 3 years social science, half year art, and half year computers.

Credit Awards for Prior Learning: Transfer Credit.

Limits to Credit Awards for Prior Learning: We accept a maximum of 64 credits from community college Associate programs. Must have a C or better in any course that is transferred in. Academic Amnesty allows students, under strict condition, to drop previous work that is over 5 years old.

Credit Awards for Examinations: CLEP Subject Exams; Departmental Exams.

Limits to Credit Awards for Examinations: No more than 34 credits may be obtained by examination.

Estimated Average Completion Time: Information not available.

Credit Hour Requirements:

Degree	Total Hours	Academic Residency*
Bachelor's	128	32

*Hours that must be earned at the institution exclusive of credit-by-exam, portfolio assessment, etc.

Distance Learning Options: Cooperative Education; Correspondence Courses; Independent Study; Newspaper Courses; Supervised Fieldwork; Television Courses.

Student Support Services Available: Academic Advising; Career Counseling; Counseling/Testing; Financial Aid; Job Placement Assistance; Orientation; Tutoring.

Informational Materials Available: Institutional Catalog; Program Brochure.

Program Age, Enrollment, and Degrees Conferred:

Degree	Year Est.	Current Enrollment	Degrees Conferred
Nonmajors	1971	6	30
General Studies	1980	68	120

Percentage of Bachelor's Degree Holders Admitted to Graduate School: Information not available.

Geographic Admission Restrictions: None.

Tuition and Fees: In-State Tuition $39.20 per credit; Out-of-State Tuition $89.30 per credit; Application Fee $15.00; Credit-by-Exam Fee $5.00 per credit; Institutional Fee $12.85 per credit; Student Fee $11.25 per credit; Lab Fee $12.50 per credit.

Tennessee

164. East Tennessee State University

School of Continuing Studies
P.O. Box 22270A
Johnson City, TN 37617

Degrees Offered: Bachelor of General Studies (BGS).

Program Mission Statement/Description: The School of Continuing Studies offers the BGS degree to provide older adults an alternative to traditional degree programs that do not meet their needs. It allows students to develop a program of study in more than one academic area specifically tailored to their individual interests.

Accreditation: Southern Association of Colleges and Schools.

Admission Requirements: Essay/Written Work; HS/GED Diploma; Interview.

Credit Awards for Prior Learning: ACE Military Recommendations; Portfolio Assessment; Transfer Credit.

Limits to Credit Awards for Prior Learning: Up to 43 semester hours of credit may be awarded through the portfolio process.

Credit Awards for Examinations: ACT Proficiency Exams; CLEP General Exams; CLEP Subject Exams; Departmental Exams.

Estimated Average Completion Time: Information not available.

Credit Hour Requirements:

Degree	Total Hours	Academic Residency*
Bachelor's	128	34

*Hours that must be earned at the institution exclusive of credit-by-exam, portfolio assessment, etc.

Distance Learning Options: Correspondence Courses; Independent Study; Supervised Fieldwork; Television Courses.

Student Support Services Available: Academic Advising; Career Counseling; Counseling/Testing; Financial Aid; Job Placement Assistance; Orientation.

Informational Materials Available: Institutional Catalog; Program Brochure.

Program Age, Enrollment, and Degrees Conferred:

Degree	Year Est.	Current Enrollment	Degrees Conferred
BGS	1989	40	4

Percentage of Bachelor's Degree Holders Admitted to Graduate School: Information not available.

Geographic Admission Restrictions: None.

Tuition and Fees: In-State Tuition $62.00 per credit; Out-of-State Tuition $140.00 per credit; Application Fee $5.00; Graduation Fee $25.00; Credit-by-Exam Fee $5.00.

Other Pertinent Information: Courses are available at 2 off-campus centers.

165. Maryville College

Office of Continuing Education
Maryville, TN 37801

Degrees Offered: Bachelor of Arts in Management; Bachelor of Arts in Humanities; Bachelor of Arts in Social Science; Bachelor of Arts in Human Services; Bachelor of Arts in General Studies.

Program Mission Statement/Description: The Office of Continuing Education works to implement the college's goal of offering education to adults of all ages. The office facilitates adult admissions and advising, collaborates with faculty to design programs and courses of study especially for adults, and makes staffing needs known to the academic department chairpersons so that qualified teachers may be assigned to evening school classes. Additionally, the office staff communicates the needs of adult students to the institution and the traditions of Maryville College to the students.

Accreditation: Southern Association of Colleges and Schools.

Admission Requirements: Employment/Experience: 2 years; HS/GED Diploma.

Credit Awards for Prior Learning: ACE Military Recommendations; ACE/PONSI Recommendations; Portfolio Assessment; Transfer Credit.

Limits to Credit Awards for Prior Learning: Military—12 semester hours. Portfolio—12 semester hours.

Credit Awards for Examinations: ACT Proficiency Exams; CLEP General Exams; CLEP Subject Exams; DANTES Subject Tests; Departmental Exams.

Other Exam Options: Independent (correspondence) study with a limit of 6 semester hours.

Limits to Credit Awards for Examinations: 32 semester hours.

Estimated Average Completion Time: 4 years (part-time).

Caveats Regarding Time Estimates: Only part-time (11 credit hours or less) is permitted.

Credit Hour Requirements:

Degree	Total Hours	Academic Residency*
Bachelor's	128	32

*Hours that must be earned at the institution exclusive of credit-by-exam, portfolio assessment, etc.

Distance Learning Options: Phone/Mail Instruction; Supervised Fieldwork.

Student Support Services Available: Academic Advising; Career Counseling; Counseling/Testing; Financial Aid; Job Placement Assistance; Orientation; Tutoring; Alpha Sigma Lambda Honor Society; Evening hours for support services.

Informational Materials Available: Exam Preparation Guides; Institutional Catalog; Prior Learning Guides; Program Brochure.

Program Age, Enrollment, and Degrees Conferred:

Degree	Year Est.	Current Enrollment	Degrees Conferred
Humanities	1978	5	5
Business	1978	16	14
Social Science	1978	26	32
Management	1982	62	26
Nursing	1986	10	21
Human Services	1991	0	0
Liberal Studies	1991	0	0

Percentage of Bachelor's Degree Holders Admitted to Graduate School: Information not available.

Geographic Admission Restrictions: None.

Tuition and Fees: In-State Tuition $114.00 per credit; Out-of-State Tuition $114.00 per credit; Application Fee $15.00; Graduation Fee $40.00; Credit-by-Exam Fee $195.00; LEP $38.00; Departmental Exams $40.00. ACT/PEP varies.

Other Pertinent Information: The BA in Management program is a time-intensive program allowing students to complete 11 semester hours of coursework in one semester with classes meeting 2 evenings per week for the 11 credit hours.

166. Memphis State University

University College
Memphis, TN 38152

Degrees Offered: Bachelor of Professional Studies; Bachelor of Liberal Studies.

Program Mission Statement/Description: University College offers academic and professional degree programs responsive to the needs of adults and other nontraditional students by virtue of being interdisciplinary, individualized, and open to experiential learning. In addition, it is the purpose of University College to offer these studies through a degree process that responds to the needs of these students and enhances their educational experience.

Accreditation: Southern Association of Colleges and Schools.

Admission Requirements: HS/GED Diploma; Satisfactory ACT or SAT score if no previous college (special admission category for those over 21); Essay application; Recommendations.

Credit Awards for Prior Learning: ACE Military Recommendations; ACE/PONSI Recommendations; Portfolio Assessment; Transfer Credit.

Other Options: Credit for Advanced Placement, Correspondence Extension.

Limits to Credit Awards for Prior Learning: 33 hours.

Credit Awards for Examinations: CLEP Subject Exams; College Board AP Exams; DANTES Subject Tests; Departmental Exams.

Estimated Average Completion Time: Bachelors' Degrees: 3-4 years (part-time), 2-3 years (full-time).

Credit Hour Requirements:

Degree	Total Hours	Academic Residency*
Bachelor's	132	33 of last 66

*Hours that must be earned at the institution exclusive of credit-by-exam, portfolio assessment, etc.

Distance Learning Options: Telecourses using A/V Cassettes; Independent Study; Phone/Mail Instruction; Study Guides; Supervised Fieldwork; Compressed Video Instruction.

Student Support Services Available: Academic Advising; Career Counseling; Counseling/Testing; Financial Aid; Job Placement Assistance; Orientation; Tutoring.

Informational Materials Available: Institutional Catalog; Prior Learning Guides; Program Brochure; Guidelines for certain program areas.

Program Age, Enrollment, and Degrees Conferred:

Degree	Year Est.	Current Enrollment	Degrees Conferred
BPS, BLS	1975	724	719

Percentage of Bachelor's Degree Holders Admitted to Graduate School: 50 percent of University College Graduates.

Geographic Admission Restrictions: None.

Tuition and Fees:

	Undergraduate
In-State Tuition	$70.00/credit
Out-of-State Tuition	$227.00/credit
Application Fee	$5.00
Contract/Advising Fee	$25.00
Credit-by-Exam Fee	$45.00
Credit for Experiential Learning	$30.00/semester hour

Other Pertinent Information: Degree program guidelines are available in the following areas: Alcohol and Drug Abuse Services, Aviation Administration, Biomedical Illustration, Commercial Aviation, Fire Administration, Fire Prevention Technology, Health Services Administration, Human Services, Judaic Studies, Organizational Leadership, Orthotics/Prosthetics and Related Fields, Paralegal Services, Printing Management, and Services for the Aging.

Texas

167. Amber University

1700 Eastgate Dr.
Garland, TX 75041

Degrees Offered: Bachelor of Arts; Bachelor of Science; Bachelor of Business Administration; Master of Arts; Master of Science; Master of Business Administration.

Program Mission Statement/Description: The purpose of Amber University is to provide working adults with a relevant education through convenient scheduling within an innovative teaching/learning environment.

Accreditation: Southern Association of Colleges and Schools.

Admission Requirements:

Undergraduate	Graduate
Prior Credits: 30	Undergraduate Degree
Minimum age 21 years	

Credit Awards for Prior Learning: ACE Military Recommendations; Portfolio Assessment; Transfer Credit.

Credit Awards for Examinations: CLEP General Exams; CLEP Subject Exams.

Estimated Average Completion Time: Bachelors' Degrees: 3 years (part-time), 2 years (full-time); Graduate Degrees: MA, MS, MBA—3 years (part-time), 2 years (full-time).

Credit Hour Requirements:

Degree	Total Hours	Academic Residency*
Bachelor's	126	30
Graduate (MS, MBA)	36	24
Graduate (MA Counseling)	48	24

*Hours that must be earned at the institution exclusive of credit-by-exam, portfolio assessment, etc.

Distance Learning Options: Independent Study; Supervised Fieldwork (graduate only).

Student Support Services Available: Academic Advising; Financial Aid.

Informational Materials Available: Institutional Catalog; Program Brochure; Degree Program Preparation Guide.

Program Age, Enrollment, and Degrees Conferred:

Degree	Year Est.	Current Enrollment	Degrees Conferred
BBA	1980	299	500
BA	1983	118	50
BS	1980	215	200
MBA	1981	319	1200
MA	1983	233	48
MS	1980	123	300

Percentage of Bachelor's Degree Holders Admitted to Graduate School: 53 percent

Geographic Admission Restrictions: None.

Tuition and Fees:

	Undergraduate	Graduate
In-State Tuition	$125.00/credit	$125.00/credit
Out-of-State Tuition	$125.00/credit	$125.00/credit
Application Fee	$25.00	$25.00
Graduation Fee	$50.00	$50.00

Other Pertinent Information: Amber University is an upper-level and graduate institution designed for adult students. Students are offered a convenient schedule plan with 4 10-week sessions per year. All classes meet once a week for 10 weeks in the evenings and on weekends.

168. Howard Payne University

Bachelor of General Studies Program
HPU Station
Brownwood, TX 76801

Degrees Offered: Bachelor of General Studies.

Program Mission Statement/Description: A degree program designed for nontraditional students who are interested in a broad spectrum program for personal enrichment or for obtaining a degree acceptable in special fields that do not require traditional degrees.

Accreditation: Southern Association of Colleges and Schools.

Admission Requirements: Employment/Experience: Complete Portfolio; Essay/Written Work; HS/GED Diploma; Interview; Prior Credits: 60 hours.

Credit Awards for Prior Learning: ACE Military Recommendations; ACE/PONSI Recommendations; Portfolio Assessment; Transfer Credit.

Limits to Credit Awards for Prior Learning: No more than 42 semester hours may be accepted for this program by a combination of correspondence, extension, and/or work experience, with a limit of 30 semester hours credit for work experience. Technical/Vocational courses will be accepted per action of the BGS committee.

Credit Awards for Examinations: ACT Proficiency Exams; CLEP Subject Exams; College Board AP Exams; DANTES Subject Tests; Departmental Exams.

Estimated Average Completion Time: 6-8 years (part-time), 4 years (full-time).

Credit Hour Requirements:

Degree	Total Hours	Academic Residency*
Bachelor's	128	32

*Hours that must be earned at the institution exclusive of credit-by-exam, portfolio assessment, etc.

Distance Learning Options: Correspondence Courses.

Student Support Services Available: Academic Advising; Career Counseling; Counseling/Testing; Financial Aid; Job Placement Assistance; Tutoring.

Informational Materials Available: Institutional Catalog.

Program Age, Enrollment, and Degrees Conferred:

Degree	Year Est.	Current Enrollment	Degrees Conferred
BGS	1974	6	89

Percentage of Bachelor's Degree Holders Admitted to Graduate School: Information not available.

Geographic Admission Restrictions: None.

Tuition and Fees: In-State Tuition $132.00 per credit; Out-of-State Tuition $132.00 per credit; Graduation Fee $35.00; Credit-by-Exam Fee as required by each testing agency; Activity Fee $85.00; Entertainment Fee $15.00 for students taking 12 or more hours.

169. Our Lady of the Lake University

Weekend College
411 SW 24th St.
San Antonio, TX 78207

Degrees Offered: Bachelor of Applied Science and Bachelor of Arts in Management, Computer Information Management, Computer Information Systems, Liberal Studies; Bachelor of Business Administration in General Management; Business Administration in Human Resource Management; Business Administration in Marketing Management; Business Administration in Computer Information Systems; Master of Business Administration in General Management; Master of Business Administration in Health Care Administration.

Program Mission Statement/Description: Scheduling alternative for working adults to complete academic programs with minimal career interruption. Required courses are offered for a select group of undergraduate degrees on weekends with the full university support.

Accreditation: Southern Association of Schools and Colleges.

Admission Requirements:

Undergraduate	Graduate
HS/GED Diploma	Undergraduate Degree
Essay/Written Work	Recommendations
Employment/Experience: (3–5 years)	GRE, GMAT, or MAT

Other Admission Requirements: Undergraduate: Nelson/Denny assessment exam for applicants who have not taken either the ACT or SAT; Graduate: Resume.

Credit Awards for Prior Learning: ACE Military Recommendations; ACE/PONSI Recommendations; Portfolio Assessment; Transfer Credit.

Limits to Credit Awards for Prior Learning: 30-hour resident requirement in classroom.

Credit Awards for Examinations: ACT Proficiency Exams; CLEP General Exams; CLEP Subject Exams; College Board AP Exams; DANTES Subject Tests; Departmental Exams.

Estimated Average Completion Time: Bachelors' Degrees 4–5 years (part-time), 2.5–3 years (full-time). Graduate Degrees: MBA—2 years (part-time).

Caveats Regarding Time Estimates: Many students "stop-out" from time to time which influences time needed for degree completion. Some return after absence of 5–7 years.

Credit Hour Requirements:

Degree	Total Hours	Academic Residency*
Bachelor's	128	30
Graduate	36	30

*Hours that must be earned at the institution exclusive of credit-by-exam, portfolio assessment, etc.

Distance Learning Options: Independent Study.

Student Support Services Available: Academic Advising; Career Counseling; Counseling/Testing; Financial Aid; Job Placement Assistance; Orientation; Tutoring.

Informational Materials Available: Exam Preparation Guides; Institutional Catalog; Prior Learning Guides; Program Brochure.

Program Age, Enrollment, and Degrees Conferred:

Degree	Year Est.	Current Enrollment	Degrees Conferred
Undergraduate Weekend College-San Antonio	1978	400	200
MBA Weekend College	1983	130	227
Undergraduate Weekend College-Houston	1986	300	68

Percentage of Bachelor's Degree Holders Admitted to Graduate School: Information not available.

Geographic Admission Restrictions: None.

Tuition and Fees:

	Undergraduate	Graduate
In-State Tuition	$194.00/credit	$201.00/credit
Out-of-State Tuition	$194.00/credit	$201.00/credit
Application Fee	$15.00	$15.00
Graduation Fee	$35.00	$35.00
Credit-by-Exam Fee	$38.00	

170. Southwest Texas State University

Southwest Texas State Degree Program
San Marcos, TX 78666

Degrees Offered: Bachelor of Applied Arts and Sciences.

Program Mission Statement/Description: The Southwest Texas State Degree Program is established to provide the nontraditional learner skills to face the ever-changing world by offering a wide selection of choices in numerous disciplines. Additionally, Southwest Texas State (SWT) is dedicated to offering nontraditional methods to assist the adult learner in his/her quest for higher education.

Accreditation: Southern Association of Colleges and Schools.

Admission Requirements: HS/GED Diploma.

Credit Awards for Prior Learning: ACE Military Recommendations; ACE/PONSI Recommendations; Portfolio Assessment; Transfer Credit.

Limits to Credit Awards for Prior Learning: Transfer Junior College—66 hours; Noncollegiate (ACE—30 hours; Work Life Credit—24 hours.

Credit Awards for Examinations: ACT Proficiency Exams; CLEP General Exams; CLEP Subject Exams; DANTES Subject Tests.

Limits to Credit Awards for Examinations: 30 hours.

Estimated Average Completion Time: 2 year (part-time), 1-1.5 years (full-time).

Caveats Regarding Time Estimates: All estimates differ because of highly individualized programs.

Credit Hour Requirements: Bachelors' Degrees: 128 total hours, 30 academic residency hours (hours that must be earned at the institution exclusive of credit-by-exam, portfolio assessment, etc.). 24 of last 30 hours must be with Southwest Texas State. Must take 24 advance hours with SWT.

Distance Learning Options: Cooperative Education; Correspondence Courses; Supervised Fieldwork.

Student Support Services Available: Academic Advising; Career Counseling; Counseling/Testing; Financial Aid; Job Placement Assistance; Orientation; Tutoring.

Informational Materials Available: Institutional Catalog; Program Brochure.

Program Age, Enrollment, and Degrees Conferred:

Degree	Year Est.	Current Enrollment	Degrees Conferred
BAAS	1973	687	4000

Percentage of Bachelor's Degree Holders Admitted to Graduate School: Information not available.

Geographic Admission Restrictions: None.

Tuition and Fees: Tuition Fees for academic courses are 3 hours—$209.00, 6 hours—$283.00, 9 hours—$397.00, 12 hours—$481.00 and 15 hours—$565.00.

Utah

171. Brigham Young University

Degrees by Independent Study Program
305 Harman Building
Provo, UT 84602

Degrees Offered: Bachelor of Independent Study (BIS).

Program Mission Statement/Description: The Degrees by Independent Study (DIS) Program involves a wide range of subjects designed for adult students who are involved in professions that encourage additional general studies education; have a thirst for knowledge, a variety of interests, and a desire to continue their development toward the "whole person" are devoted to a program of study that will provide a broad and extensive general education; are self-starters who have inquiring minds with wide interests and who enjoy studying on an organized and continuing basis; and have the motivation to commit themselves to completing a specially designed program of independent studies.

Accreditation: Northwest Association of Schools and Colleges.

Admission Requirements: HS/GED Diploma; Recommendations; Students adhere to the Student Honor Code while attending on-campus seminars. Students must be 21 years of age or older.

Credit Awards for Prior Learning: ACE Military Recommendations; ACE/PONSI Recommendations; Transfer Credit.

Limits to Credit Awards for Prior Learning: 91 semester hours of credit can be awarded.

Credit Awards for Examinations: CLEP General Exams; CLEP Subject Exams.

Estimated Average Completion Time: 5–6 years (part-time), 4.5 years (full-time).

Caveats Regarding Time Estimates: Every student enrolls for study areas comprising 24 semester hours. The length of time to complete the program really depends on the amount of time the student is willing to devote to the program.

Credit Hour Requirements:

Degree	Total Hours	Academic Residency*
Bachelor's	128	24

*Hours that must be earned at the institution exclusive of credit-by-exam, portfolio assessment, etc.

Distance Learning Options: A/V Cassettes; Correspondence Courses; Independent Study; Study Guides.

Student Support Services Available: Academic Advising; Career Counseling; Counseling/Testing; Financial Aid; Job Placement Assistance; Orientation.

Informational Materials Available: Institutional Catalog; Program Brochure.

Program Age, Enrollment, and Degrees Conferred:

Degree	Year Est.	Current Enrollment	Degrees Conferred
BIS	1971	322	219

Percentage of Bachelor's Degree Holders Admitted to Graduate School: 63 percent.

Geographic Admission Restrictions: None.

Tuition and Fees: $550.00 for Final Senior Research Paper and Closure Seminar. In-state Tuition $625.00 per Growth Phase study area (24-semester-hour block), $53.00 per credit hour when taking 11 hours or less in a Growth Phase study area. Out-of-state Tuition $450.00 per on-campus seminar (3 semester hours). $200.00 when a study area is waived through CLEP exam. Fee covers cost of credit and syllabus used to prepare for the seminar. Application Fee: $15.00.

Other Pertinent Information: The DIS program is divided into 3 basic phases: (1) the Preparation Phase, (2) the Growth Phase, and (3) the Closure Phase. These phases are in turn subdivided into a combined total of 6 study areas: Foundations; Man and the Meaning of Life; Man and Society; Man and Beauty; Man and the Universe; and Closure. The study areas comprise blocks of related courses. A 2-week, on-campus seminar will follow each area of study. (If 15 or more semester hours are transferred into a study area, the accompanying seminar will be waived.)

Virginia

172. Averett College

Adult and Continuing Education
420 W. Main St.
Danville, VA 24541

Degrees Offered: Bachelor of Business Administration; Master of Business Administration.

Program Mission Statement/Description: To provide business degrees, based in the liberal arts and humanities, that will prepare adult students for the business world in which they now find themselves and for a future world of business. It is also the mission of adult education at Averett College to provide this education in a format and time schedule conducive to the adult learning experience. Averett's Adult Curriculum for Excellence (AACE) offers Bachelor of Business Administration and Master of Business Administration degree programs. AACE is a highly structured, lock-step, modular program. It is an accelerated program that enables adult students to plan their academic programs from the beginning to the end without interruption. Other bachelor's degree programs are offered by Averett's Individually Developed Education for Adult Learners (IDEAL). IDEAL is a self-paced program, without the schedule structure, that enables students to take longer to complete the program and with a less specific and structured methodology.

Accreditation: Southern Association of Colleges and Schools.

Admission Requirements:

Undergraduate	Graduate
HS/GED Diploma	Undergraduate Degree
Interview	Interview
Recommendations	Essay/Written Work
Employment/Experience:	Recommendations
(3 years)	Employment/Experience:
	(3 years)

Credit Awards for Prior Learning: ACE Military Recommendations; ACE/PONSI Recommendations; Portfolio Assessment; Transfer Credit.

Credit Awards for Examinations: CLEP General Exams; CLEP Subject Exams; DANTES Subject Tests; Departmental Exams.

Estimated Average Completion Time: Bachelors' Degrees: 24 months (full-time); Graduate Degrees: 21 months (full-time).

Credit Hour Requirements:

Degree	Total Hours	Academic Residency*
Bachelor's	123	42
Graduate	36	6

*Hours that must be earned at the institution exclusive of credit-by-exam, portfolio assessment, etc.

Distance Learning Options: Cooperative Education (bachelor only); Correspondence Courses (bachelor only); Independent Study; Study Guides; Supervised Fieldwork (bachelor only).

Student Support Services Available: Academic Advising; Career Counseling; Counseling/Testing; Financial Aid; Job Placement Assistance; Orientation; Tutoring.

Informational Materials Available: Exam Preparation Guides; Institutional Catalog; Prior Learning Guides; Program Brochure.

Program Age, Enrollment, and Degrees Conferred:

Degree	Year Est.	Current Enrollment	Degrees Conferred
BS-AACE	1987	300	125
MBA	1987	218	130
BS-IDEAL	1984	21	11

Percentage of Bachelor's Degree Holders Admitted to Graduate School: 10–15 percent.

Geographic Admission Restrictions: None.

Tuition and Fees:

	Undergraduate	Graduate
In-State Tuition	$165.00/credit	$195.00/credit
Application Fee	$20.00	$20.00
Graduation Fee	$50.00	$50.00
Credit-by-Exam Fee	$38.00 (CLEP)	
Challenge	$50.00	

173. George Mason University

Individualized Study Program
4400 University Dr.
Fairfax, VA 22030

Degrees Offered: Bachelor of Individualized Studies; Master of Arts in Interdisciplinary Studies.

Program Mission Statement/Description: The Bachelor of Individualized Study Program is designed to provide a flexible option for adult students to earn a baccalaureate degree. Adults, who are at least 8 years past their high school graduation dates, have completed at least 30 semester hours of transferrable college credits, and have a proposed program of study which is interdisciplinary and/or nontraditional are encouraged to apply. The Master of Arts in Interdisciplinary Studies Program is designed to (a) provide an opportunity for graduate students to earn an interdisciplinary master's degree, and (b) allow George Mason University to experiment with new and interdisciplinary master's programs.

Accreditation: Southern Association of Colleges and Schools.

Admission Requirements:

Undergraduate	Graduate
HS/GED Diploma	Undergraduate Degree
Interview	Interview
Prior Credits: 30 hours	Recommendations

Other Admission Requirements: Undergraduate admission requires prior admission to George Mason University. Both programs require a program application form in addition to the generic university application forms. Both programs include orientation within the required interview.

Credit Awards for Prior Learning: ACE Military Recommendations; ACE/PONSI Recommendations; Portfolio Assessment; Transfer Credit.

Limits to Credit Awards for Prior Learning: Portfolio assessment credit is limited to 12 hours at the undergraduate level and 6 hours at the master level.

Credit Awards for Examinations: CLEP General Exams; CLEP Subject Exams; College Board AP Exams; DANTES Subject Tests; Departmental Exams.

Estimated Average Completion Time: The Bachelor of Individualized Study Program has no time limits to complete the program. Completion time is entirely determined by the number of transfer credits and speed at which a student completes courses in the program. The Master of Arts in Interdisciplinary Studies Program requires that students complete the program within 6 years of admission. Either full-time or part-time enrollment is allowed.

Credit Hour Requirements:

Degree	Total Hours	Academic Residency*
Bachelor's	120	30
Graduate	36	24

*Hours that must be earned at the institution exclusive of credit-by-exam, portfolio assessment, etc.

Distance Learning Options: Cooperative Education (bachelor only); Independent Study; Supervised Fieldwork; Television Courses (bachelor only).

Student Support Services Available: Academic Advising; Career Counseling; Counseling/Testing; Financial Aid; Job Placement Assistance; Orientation.

Informational Materials Available: Institutional Catalog; Program Brochure.

Program Age, Enrollment, and Degrees Conferred:

Degree	Year Est.	Current Enrollment	Degrees Conferred
BA Indiv. Studies	1975	500	1000
MA Inter. Studies	1982	200	75

Percentage of Bachelor's Degree Holders Admitted to Graduate School: 30–40 percent.

Geographic Admission Restrictions: None.

Tuition and Fees:

	Undergraduate	Graduate
In-State Tuition	$123.00/credit	$123.00/credit
Out-of-State Tuition	$306.00/credit	$306.00/credit
Application Fee	$25.00	$25.00
Graduation Fee	$25.00	$25.00

Other Fees: George Mason uses the services of Thomas A. Edison College, Trenton, NJ, for undergraduate portfolio evaluation. Students pay Edison fees.

Other Pertinent Information: George Mason University does not offer an external degree program. All courses that Bachelor of Individualized Study students take are the ones offered to all George Mason University students. Students register with the rest of the George Mason University student population.

174. James Madison University

Harrisonburg, VA 22807

Degrees Offered: Bachelor of General Studies.

Program Mission Statement/Description: The Bachelor of General Studies degree is offered to provide returning adult students with the opportunity to pursue an education according to individualized needs, goals, and time requirements.

Accreditation: Southern Association of Colleges and Schools.

Admission Requirements: Essay/Written Work; HS/GED Diploma; Prior Credits: 30.

Other Admission Requirements: Three years out of school.

Credit Awards for Prior Learning: ACE Military Recommendations; ACE/PONSI Recommendations; Portfolio; Transfer Credit.

Other Options: Independent studies; Sponsored learning; Coursework; Credit by Examination; CLEP; Departmental Tests.

Limits to Credit Awards for Prior Learning: The amount of credit that can be earned through prior learning will be restricted only by its relativity to the degree proposal.

Credit Awards for Examinations: CLEP General Exams; CLEP Subject Exams; Departmental Exams.

Estimated Average Completion Time: 2 years (part-time).

Credit Hour Requirements:

Degree	Total Hours	Academic Residency*
Bachelor's	128	32

*Hours that must be earned at the institution exclusive of credit-by-exam, portfolio, etc.

Distance Learning Options: Independent Study; Supervised Fieldwork.

Student Support Services Available: Academic Advising; Career Counseling; Counseling/Testing; Financial Aid; Job Placement Assistance; Orientation; Tutoring; Portfolio Preparation.

Informational Materials Available: Institutional Catalog; Prior Learning Guides; Program Brochure; Handbook.

Program Age, Enrollment, and Degrees Conferred:

Degree	Year Est.	Current Enrollment	Degrees Conferred
BGS	1977	139	120

Percentage of Bachelor's Degree Holders Admitted to Graduate School: 39 percent.

Geographic Admission Restrictions: None.

Tuition and Fees: In-State Tuition $69.33 per credit; Out-of-State Tuition $176.33 per credit; Application Fee $20.00; Credit-by-Exam Fee $25.00; Prior Learning Assessment Fee $75.00.

---

175. Mary Washington College

Center for Graduate and Continuing Education
Fredricksburg, VA 22401

Degrees Offered: Bachelor of Liberal Studies Program; Master of Arts in Liberal Studies.

Program Mission Statement/Description: Center for Graduate and Continuing Education serves the educational needs of adult part-time commuting students by providing access, flexibility, and quality in both credit and noncredit programs.

Accreditation: Southern Association of Colleges and Schools.

Admission Requirements:

Undergraduate	Graduate
HS/GED Diploma	Undergraduate Degree
Interview	Interview
Essay/Written Work	Essay/Written Work
Prior Credits: 15	

Credit Awards for Prior Learning: ACE Military Recommendations; ACE/PONSI Recommendations; Portfolio Assessment; Transfer Credit; Challenge Exams; Credit-by-Examination.

Limits to Credit Awards for Prior Learning: 90 credits.

Credit Awards for Examinations: CLEP General Exams; CLEP Subject Exams; DANTES Subject Tests; Departmental Exams.

Estimated Average Completion Time: Bachelors' Degrees: 4 years (part-time), 2 years (full-time); Graduate Degrees: 3 years (part-time).

Caveats Regarding Time Estimates: Graduate degree available only on part-time basis.

Credit Hour Requirements:

Degree	Total Hours	Academic Residency*
Bachelor's	120	30
Graduate	30	24

*Hours that must be earned at the institution exclusive of credit-by-exam, portfolio assessment, etc.

Distance Learning Options: Cooperative Education; Correspondence Courses; Independent Study (Bachelor and Graduate); Supervised Fieldwork.

Student Support Services Available: Academic Advising; Career Counseling; Counseling/Testing; Financial Aid; Job Placement Assistance; Orientation; Tutoring.

Informational Materials Available: Institutional Catalog; Prior Learning Guides; Program Brochure.

Program Age, Enrollment, and Degrees Conferred:

Degree	Year Est.	Current Enrollment	Degrees Conferred
BLS	1977	375	634
MA Liberal Studies	1980	55	53

Percentage of Bachelor's Degree Holders Admitted to Graduate School: 35 percent.

Geographic Admission Restrictions: 30 hours resident credit.

Tuition and Fees:

	Undergraduate	Graduate
In-State Tuition	$76.00/credit	$76.00/credit
Out-of-State Tuition	$176.00/credit	$176.00/credit
Application Fee	$20.00	$25.00
Credit-by-Exam Fee	$15.00 credit	

176. Radford University

Continuing Education Office
P.O. Box 6917
Radford, VA 24142

Degrees Offered: Bachelor of General Studies.

Program Mission Statement/Description: The program, which leads to the Bachelor of General Studies degree, offers liberal transfer of credit, credit by exam, portfolio assessment of demonstrated learning, credit by independent study, and a course of study designed to match the learning interests of the mature adult student. Coursework consists of a core of art and science courses—English composition, humanities, lab science and mathematics, and social sciences—an individualized concentration, i.e., major, and a wide range of electives.

Accreditation: Southern Association of Colleges and Schools.

Admission Requirements: Essay/Written Work; HS/GED Diploma; Prior Credits: 30.

Other Admission Requirements: Minimum GPA of 2.0 (4.0 scale) on all college work previously attempted. A minimum of 30 semester credits of college transferable work. All prospective students must attend an information session and must be 25 years or older.

Credit Awards for Prior Learning: ACE Military Recommendations; ACE/PONSI Recommendations; Portfolio Assessment; Transfer Credit; Correspondence Study.

Limits to Credit Awards for Prior Learning: Portfolio assessment—9 semester hours maximum. Independent study by correspondence—21 semester hours.

Credit Awards for Examinations: CLEP General Exams; CLEP Subject Exams; College Board AP Exams; Departmental Exams.

Estimated Average Completion Time: 1-3 years (part-time).

Credit Hour Requirements:

	Total Hours	Academic Residency*
Bachelors' Degrees	126	30

*Hours that must be earned at the institution exclusive of credit-by-exam, portfolio assessment, etc.

Distance Learning Options: Directed study by Radford University Faculty.

Student Support Services Available: Academic Advising; Career Counseling; Counseling/Testing; Financial Aid; Job Placement Assistance; Orientation; Tutoring; Study Workshops on Preparing Curriculum Plans and Final Project Proposals, Study Skills Workshop for Adult Students.

Informational Materials Available: Exam Preparation Guides; Institutional Catalog; Program Brochure; Guide Books on Preparing Curriculum Plans and Final Projects; Student Handbook.

Program Age, Enrollment, and Degrees Conferred:

Degree	Year Est.	Current Enrollment	Degrees Conferred
BGS	1986	160	26

Percentage of Bachelor's Degree Holders Admitted to Graduate School: 27 percent.

Geographic Admission Restrictions: None.

Tuition and Fees: In-State Tuition $91.00 per credit; Out-of-State Tuition $196.00 per credit; Application Fee $15.00; Graduation Fee $16.50; Credit-by-Exam Fee $15.00 per credit.

177. Virginia State University

Bachelor of Individualized Studies Program
P.O. Box FF
Petersburg, VA 23803

Degrees Offered: Bachelor of Individualized Studies (BIS).

Program Mission Statement/Description: Specifically designed for the adult student, the Bachelor of Individualized Studies (BIS) degree is a nontraditional degree program which recognizes credit transferred from other accredited institutions, from military education and experience, from examination, and from evaluation of life/work experience. A mature student, in conjunction with an academic advisor, may tailor a program to meet his/her educational goals.

Accreditation: Southern Association of Colleges and Schools.

Admission Requirements: HS/GED Diploma; Interview.

Other Admission Requirements: Applicants must meet admission requirements of the University. Persons are not eligible for admission to the BIS program until 4 years after graduation from high school or, if they possess a GED, 4 years after their high school class graduated. Persons with a baccalaureate degree from accredited institutions are not eligible. Persons may not be enrolled simultaneously in the BIS program and another baccalaureate program.

Credit Awards for Prior Learning: ACE Military Recommendations; Portfolio Assessment; Transfer Credit.

Limits to Credit Awards for Prior Learning: There is an overall limitation of 64 semester hours credit from nontraditional sources. Subcategory limitations are maximum 94 semester hours of transfer credits; maximum 30 semester hours military MOS credits.

Credit Awards for Examinations: CLEP General Exams; CLEP Subject Exams; DANTES Subject Tests; Departmental Exams.

Estimated Average Completion Time: 2-2.5 years (part-time), 1-1.5 years (full-time).

Credit Hour Requirements:

Degree	Total Hours	Academic Residency*
Bachelor's	124	24

*Hours that must be earned at the institution exclusive of credit-by-exam, portfolio assessment, etc.

Distance Learning Options: None.

Student Support Services Available: Academic Advising; Career Counseling; Counseling/Testing; Financial Aid; Job Placement Assistance; Orientation; Tutoring.

Informational Materials Available: Institutional Catalog; Program Brochure.

Program Age, Enrollment, and Degrees Conferred:

Degree	Year Est.	Current Enrollment	Degrees Conferred
BIS	1981	75	257

Percentage of Bachelor's Degree Holders Admitted to Graduate School: Surveys indicate that all graduates who have applied for graduate school have been accepted. Meaningful data are not available to determine the percentage of BIS graduates who have applied.

Geographic Admission Restrictions: None.

Tuition and Fees: In-State Tuition $68.00 per credit; Out-of-State Tuition $205.00 per credit; Application Fee $25.00; Graduation Fee $50.00; Credit-by-Exam Fee 50 percent tuition; Full-Time student comprehensive fee $524.00 per semester; Portfolio assessment fee $100.00.

Washington

178. Central Washington University

Ellensburg, WA 98926

Degrees Offered: Bachelor of Science in Accounting, Business Administration, and Electronic Engineering Technology; Bachelor of Arts in Law and Justice; Bachelor of Arts in Education with majors in Early Childhood and Special Education; Master of Education in Reading and in Education Administration.

Program Mission Statement/Description: One part of the mission of Central Washington University is to be responsive to educational needs of adults at sites away from Ellensburg. Off-campus degree and nondegree programs as well as continuing education offerings provide access to higher education at convenient times and places for part-time, placebound student populations.

Accreditation: Northwest Association of Schools and Colleges; National Council for the Accreditation of Teacher Education; Accreditation Board for Engineering and Technology, Inc.; National Association of Schools of Music; and National Accrediting Agency for Clinical Laboratory Sciences.

Admission Requirements:

Undergraduate	Graduate
HS/GED Diploma	Undergraduate Degree
Recommendations	Recommendations
	GRE

Other Admission Requirements: Each program has specific GPA requirements.

Credit Awards for Prior Learning: ACE Military Recommendations; Transfer Credit.

Limits to Credit Awards for Prior Learning: 90 credits can be transferred from community colleges.

Credit Awards for Examinations: College Board AP Exams; DANTES Subject Tests.

Estimated Average Completion Time: Bachelors' Degrees: 10 quarters (part-time); 8 quarters (full-time); Masters' Degrees: 2 years (part-time).

Caveats Regarding Time Estimates: Many external degree students are enrolled part-time.

Credit Hour Requirements: Bachelors' Degrees: 180 quarter hours; Graduate Degrees (total hours): 45 minimum.

Distance Learning Options: Cooperative Education; Independent Study; Supervised Fieldwork.

Student Support Services Available: Academic Advising; Career Counseling; Counseling/Testing; Financial Aid; Job Placement Assistance; Orientation; Tutoring.

Informational Materials Available: Institutional Catalog; Program Brochure.

Program Age, Enrollment, and Graduates: Information not available.

Percentage of Bachelor's Degree Holders Admitted to Graduate School: Information not available.

Geographic Admission Restrictions: None.

Tuition and Fees:

	Undergraduate	Graduate
In-State Tuition	$54.00/quarter	$87.00/quarter
Application Fee	$25.00	$25.00

Other Pertinent Information: All course requirements can be completed at 4 off-campus centers located on community college campuses.

179. Fairhaven College

Western Washington University
Bellingham, WA 98225

Degrees Offered: Bachelor of Arts; Bachelor of Arts in Education; Bachelor of Fine Arts; Bachelor of Music; Bachelor of Science.

Program Mission Statement/Description: The purpose of Fairhaven College is to offer students the opportunity to take a large responsibility for the structure and content of their education. The college curriculum helps students develop their writing and research skills, critical thought, creative expression, independent judgement and scholarship, self-evaluation, and assessment. The Fairhaven Interdisciplinary Concentration provides an opportunity for developing an individually designed major for the Bachelor of Arts, or Bachelor of Arts/Education (BA/ED) degrees. It combines college and university classes, independent studies, fieldwork, and other practical experiences relevant to the student's purpose.

Accreditation: Western Association of Schools and Colleges.

Admission Requirements: Essay/Written Work; HS/GED Diploma; Interview; Prior Credits (only transfers): 40 credits after high school; Recommendations. Students must satisfy entrance requirements to WWU as well as Fairhaven College.

Credit Awards for Prior Learning: ACE Military Recommendations; Transfer Credit.

Limits to Credit Awards for Prior Learning: Maximum of 90 credits from community colleges (total).

Credit Awards for Examinations: ACT Proficiency Exams; College Board AP Exams; Departmental Exams.

Estimated Average Completion Time: 5 years (transfers), 4.5 years (new students) all full-time.

Caveats Regarding Time Estimates: Part-time study is hard to estimate. A number of students either take only a few hours per quarter or take some time away from study—usually for financial reasons.

Credit Hour Requirements: 180 hours total; 45 hours academic residency (hours that must be earned at the institution exclusive of credit-by-exam, portfolio assessment, etc.).

Distance Learning Options: Independent Study; Supervised Fieldwork.

Student Support Services Available: Academic Advising; Career Counseling; Counseling/Testing; Financial Aid; Job Placement Assistance; Orientation; Tutoring; Disabled Student Services; Health Center Services; Day Care Coop Facilities; Drug Information; Legal Information; Veterans Outreach Center; Cross-Cultural Center; Multicultural Services Center; Men's and Women's Center.

Informational Materials Available: Institutional Catalog; Program Brochure; Student guide to Fairhaven College; Previous interdisciplinary concentration proposals; Selected publications by Fairhaven College students.

Program Age, Enrollment, and Graduates:

Degree	Year Est.	Current Enrollment	Degrees Conferred
BA	1967	0	994
BA/ED	1967	0	131
BS	1967	0	52
BM	1967	0	5
BFA	1967	0	2

Percentage of Bachelor's Degree Holders Admitted to Graduate School: Information not available.

Geographic Admission Restrictions: None.

Tuition and Fees: In-State Tuition $60.00 per credit under 9 credits/over 9 credits $600.00 per quarter; Out-of State Tuition $210.00 per credit under 9 credits, over 9 credits $2100.00 per quarter; Application Fee $25.00; Graduation Fee $8.00; Credit-by-Exam Fee $25.00. $50.00 deposit for admission confirmation; $20.00 Teacher Certification; $2.00 Career Placement Service Fee.

180. Heritage College

3240 Fort Rd.
Toppenish, WA 98948

Degrees Offered: Bachelor of Arts in business, social work, social science, science, and education. Master of Education.

Program Mission Statement/Description: Heritage College is a nonprofit, independent, nondenominational, accredited 4-year institution of higher education. Its mission is to provide quality, accessible higher education at the undergraduate and graduate levels to a multicultural population which has been educationally isolated. Within its liberal arts curriculum, Heritage College offers strong professional and career-oriented programs designed to enrich the quality of life for students and their communities. Heritage's unique educational programs are specifically tailored to the special needs of a rural constituency and are delivered by highly qualified and unusually dedicated faculty and staff, with a very low student-teacher ratio. As an independent institution with a Christian philosophy, Heritage College has embraced issues of national and international significance in an era when cooperation across cultural boundaries may be vital to human survival. The college attempts to live up to its motto "Knowledge Brings Us Together" by placing great importance on the dignity and potential of each student and by considering diverse cultural and ethnic backgrounds as assets to the educational process. The student body has significant proportions of Hispanics, Native Americans, and Caucasians, as well as Asians, African Americans, and International students.

Accreditation: Northwest Association of Schools and Colleges.

Admission Requirements:

Undergraduate	Graduate
HS/GED Diploma	Undergraduate Degree
Essay/Written Work	
Recommendations	

Credit Awards for Prior Learning: ACE Military Recommendations; ACE/PONSI Recommendations; Transfer Credit.

Limits to Credit Awards for Prior Learning: Maximum: 60 semester credits from a 2-year community college. Maximum: 50 semester credits of courses with a passing grade including a maximum of 30 credits by any single means such as LINK, credit by examination, etc.

Credit Awards for Examinations: ACT Proficiency Exams; CLEP General Exams; CLEP Subject Exams; College Board AP Exams; DANTES Subject Tests; Departmental Exams.

Other Exam Options: The LINK Program is for adults who wish to integrate significant learning acquired through business or professional activities with college classroom learning in a baccalaureate degree program.

Estimated Average Completion Time: Associates' Degrees: 4 years (part-time), 2 years (full-time); Bachelors' Degrees: 7-8 years (part-time), 4 years (full-time); Graduate Degrees: MEd 2 years (full-time).

Credit Hour Requirements:

Degree	Total Hours	Academic Residency*
Bachelor's	126	32 of last 42
Graduate	30-50	22-42

*Hours that must be earned at the institution exclusive of credit-by-exam, portfolio assessment, etc.

Distance Learning Options: Cooperative Education (associate and bachelor only); Independent Study; Supervised Fieldwork.

Student Support Services Available: Academic Advising; Career Counseling; Counseling/Testing; Financial Aid; Job Placement Assistance; Orientation; Tutoring.

Informational Materials Available: Institutional Catalog.

Program Age, Enrollment, and Graduates:

Degree	Year Est.	Current Enrollment	Degrees Conferred
AA	1983	0	66
BA, BS, BA-Ed	1983	429	263
MEd	1983	494	300

Percentage of Bachelor's Degree Holders Admitted to Graduate School: Information not available.

Geographic Admission Restrictions: None.

Tuition and Fees:

	Undergraduate	Graduate
In-State Tuition	$155.00/credit	$190.00/credit
Out-of-State Tuition	$155.00/credit	$190.00/credit
Application Fee	$25.00	
Graduation Fee	$50.00	$75.00
Credit-by-Exam Fee	50% of tuition	
Computer Use Fee	$70.00/year	$70.00/year

181. University of Washington

UW Extension, GH-21
Seattle, WA 98195

Degrees Offered: Bachelor of Arts in General Studies.

Program Mission Statement/Description: The program, which consists of upper-division courses in the social sciences and the humanities, emphasizes analytical, communication, and critical thinking skills. Students in this program will explore diverse political, social, and humanistic perspectives in the pursuit of their degrees. Coursework has been arranged to encourage greater understanding of issues, ideas, and themes in history and the contemporary world. The curriculum is comprised of courses designed to build on prior academic experiences.

Accreditation: Northwest Association of Schools and Colleges.

Admission Requirements: HS/GED Diploma; Prior Credits: 75 per quarter.

Credit Awards for Prior Learning: Transfer Credit.

Credit Awards for Examinations: None.

Estimated Average Completion Time: 3-4 years (part-time).

Caveats Regarding Time Estimates: It is very difficult to carry a full-time course load.

Credit Hour Requirements: 180 hours total; 45 hours academic residency (hours that must be earned at the institution exclusive of credit-by-exam, portfolio assessment, etc.).

Distance Learning Options: Correspondence Courses.

Student Support Services Available: Academic Advising; Career Counseling; Counseling/Testing; Financial Aid; Job Placement Assistance; Orientation; Tutoring.

Informational Materials Available: Institutional Catalog; Program Brochure.

Program Age, Enrollment, and Graduates:

Degree	Year Est.	Current Enrollment	Degrees Conferred
General Studies	1990	300	0

Percentage of Bachelor's Degree Holders Admitted to Graduate School: Information not available.

Geographic Admission Restrictions: Out-of-state students can be admitted but must pay out-of-state fees.

Tuition and Fees: In-State Tuition per credit $65.00; Out-of-State Tuition per credit $181.00; Application Fee $25.00; Credit-by-Exam Fee $25.00; Transcript Fee $3.00.

---

182. Western Washington University

University Extended Programs
516 High St.
Bellingham, WA 98225

Degrees Offered: Bachelor of Arts in Human Services; Bachelor of Science in Electronics Engineering Technology; Bachelor of Arts in Fashion Marketing; Master of Education.

Program Mission Statement/Description: Western Washington University Extended Programs offer educational opportunities for groups and individuals who wish to continue their personal and/or educational goals outside the regular curriculum schedule. Continuing education courses may be credit or noncredit, in the evening or weekends, on or off-campus.

Accreditation: Northwest Association of Schools and Colleges; National Council for the Accreditation of Teacher Education; Accrediting Board for Engineering and Technology, Inc.

Admission Requirements:

Undergraduate	Graduate
HS/GED Diploma	Undergraduate Degree
Interview	GRE; MAT for certain programs
Essay/Written Work	
Recommendations	

Other Admission Requirements: Must submit standard application to WWU, same as on-campus students. Graduate admission: 3.0 GPA from accredited bachelor's degree institution.

Credit Awards for Prior Learning: Transfer Credit.

Limits to Credit Awards for Prior Learning: Limit of 90 credits transferrable from community college. Students must earn a minimum of 45 credit hours through WWU for graduation. Transferrable credits must be earned from an accredited institution. Limit of 9 transfer credits for the graduate program.

Credit Awards for Examinations: None.

Estimated Average Completion Time: Bachelors' Degrees: 4 years (full-time); Graduate Degrees: 2-3 years (part-time) 1,5 years (full-time).

Credit Hour Requirements:

Degree	Total Hours	Academic Residency*
Bachelor's (quarters)	180	90
Graduate	45	36

*Hours that must be earned at the institution exclusive of credit-by-exam, portfolio assessment, etc.

Distance Learning Options: Correspondence Courses; Independent Study.

Student Support Services Available: Academic Advising; Career Counseling; Counseling/Testing; Financial Aid; Job Placement Assistance; Orientation.

Informational Materials Available: Exam Preparation Guides; Institutional Catalog; Program Brochure.

Program Age, Enrollment, and Graduates:

Degree	Year Est.	Current Enrollment	Degrees Conferred
BS Engineering	1986	60	80
MEd	1987	175	75
BA Human Services	1984	230	225
BA Fashion Marketing	1985	75	150

Percentage of Bachelor's Degree Holders Admitted to Graduate School: Information not available.

Geographic Admission Restrictions: None.

Tuition and Fees:

	Undergraduate	Graduate
In-State Tuition	$66-$100.00/credit	$87-$100.00/credit
Out-of-State Tuition	$66-$100.00/credit	$87-$100.00/credit
Application Fee	$25.00	$25.00
Graduation Fee	$8.00	$8.00

West Virginia

183. Marshall University

Regents Bachelor's Degree Program
400 Hal Greer Blvd.
Huntington, WV 25755

Degrees Offered: Bachelor of Arts.

Program Mission Statement/Description: A program that encourages adults to come back to finish a bachelor's degree by requiring fewer specific courses, counting all previous college credits, forgiving F's earned more than 4 years before entering the program and offering the possibility of earning college-equivalent credit for work or learning experiences outside the classroom that may have resulted in college-level learning.

Accreditation: North Central Association of Colleges and Schools.

Admission Requirements: HS/GED Diploma. Proof of graduation from high school at least 4 years previously. Anyone who has been enrolled on a full-time basis in another baccalaureate program will not be admitted until one calendar year has passed.

Credit Awards for Prior Learning: ACE Military Recommendations; ACE/PONSI Recommendations; Portfolio Assessment; Transfer Credit.

Limits to Credit Awards for Prior Learning: None, though the minimum of 15 hours of residence credit makes more than 113 hours unnecessary.

Credit Awards for Examinations: CLEP General Exams; CLEP Subject Exams; Departmental Exams.

Estimated Average Completion Time: 3-4 years (part-time), 2-3 years (full-time).

Caveats Regarding Time Estimates: Because most of our students come to us with 40-70 hours of credit (although a student with no college credit is not precluded from the Regents Bachelor of Arts) and many apply for college-equivalent credit, they typically finish within 2 years.

Credit Hour Requirements: 128 hours total; 15 hours academic residency (hours that must be earned at the institution exclusive of credit-by-exam, portfolio assessment, etc.).

Distance Learning Options: None.

Student Support Services Available: Academic advising and all usual university services.

Informational Materials Available: Institutional Catalog; Prior Learning Guides; Program Brochure.

Program Age, Enrollment, and Degrees Conferred:

Degree	Year Est.	Current Enrollment	Degrees Conferred
Regents BA	1975	1351	1155

Percentage of Bachelor's Degree Holders Admitted to Graduate School: Approximately 40 percent of those who responded to a recent graduate survey.

Geographic Admission Restrictions: None.

Tuition and Fees: In-State Annual Tuition $1538.00; Portfolio Assessment $100.00 regardless of number of hours requested or awarded.

Other Pertinent Information: Any credit awarded by portfolio assessment will not be placed on the student's permanent record until all other requirements for the degree are completed.

Wisconsin

184. Cardinal Stritch College

Adult and Professional Continuing Professional Education
6801 N. Yates Rd.
Milwaukee, WI 53217

Degrees Offered: Associate of Science in Business; Bachelor of Science in Management; Bachelor of Science in Business Administration; Master of Science in Management; Master of Science in Health Administration; Master of Business Administration.

Program Mission Statement/Description: Accelerated, concentrated programs of study in management designed for working adults. Class groups start programs any month of the year and stay together as a cohort group (normally). Classes meet for 4 hours a night once a week on Monday-Thursday. Each course is typically 5 to 8 weeks in length. Classes are given on campus. (Other groups are formed off-campus to meet geographic needs.) Faculty members are professionals who work during the day in the areas of expertise that they teach at night. They must have at least a master's degree.

Accreditation: North Central Association of Colleges and Schools.

Admission Requirements:

Undergraduate	Graduate
HS/GED Diploma	Undergraduate Degree
Essay/Written Work	Essay/Written Work
Recommendations	Employment/Experience:
Employment/Experience:	3 years
2 years	
Prior Credits: 0-AS, 50-BS	

Other Admission Requirements: GPA 2.0 in all prior college and high school work for BS, 2.5 in undergraduate work for MS.

Credit Awards for Prior Learning: ACE Military Recommendations; ACE/PONSI Recommendations; Portfolio Assessment; Transfer Credit; Credit for Prior Learning Essays.

Limits to Credit Awards for Prior Learning: Maximum of 32 technical credits can transfer for BS (16 for AS); Maximum of 36 credits for portfolio for BS (18 for AS).

Credit Awards for Examinations: ACT Proficiency Exams; CLEP General Exams; CLEP Subject Exams; DANTES Subject Tests; Departmental Exams; PEP Exams.

Limits to Credit Awards for Examinations: Associates' Degrees 30 credits; Bachelors' Degrees 60 credits.

Estimated Average Completion Time: Associates' Degrees: 1-1.5 years (full-time); Bachelors' Degrees: 1-1.5 years (full-time); Graduate Degrees: 1.5-2.5 years (full-time).

Caveats Regarding Time Estimates: Ranges listed depend on credits transferred in for the undergraduate degrees. The MS degrees vary depending upon program and prerequisites needed. Only full-time study is permitted.

Credit Hour Requirements:

Degree	Total Hours	Academic Residency*
Associate	64	42/43
Bachelor's	128	38
Graduate	42	42

*Hours that must be earned at the institution exclusive of credit-by-exam, portfolio assessment, etc.

Distance Learning Options: None.

Student Support Services Available: Academic Advising; Career Counseling; Counseling/Testing; Financial Aid; Job Placement Assistance; Orientation; Tutoring.

Informational Materials Available: Institutional Catalog; Prior Learning Guides; Program Brochure; Portfolio Handbook; Essay Handbook; Report/Thesis Preparation Guides; Library Use Guide.

Program Age, Enrollment, and Degrees Conferred:

Degree	Year Est.	Current Enrollment	Degrees Conferred
BS Management	1982	362	1236
AS	1986	572	144
BS Business Admin.	1986	461	280
MS Management	1982	173	1086
MS Health Admin.	1982	48	213
MBA	1987	327	101

Percentage of Bachelor's Degree Holders Admitted to Graduate School: All Stritch BS degree holders are admitted to Stritch graduate school programs. Information on admission to other graduate schools not available.

Geographic Admission Restrictions: None.

Tuition and Fees:

	Undergraduate	Graduate
In-State Tuition	$117-$200.50/credit	$193-$205.00/credit
Out-of-State Tuition	$127-$208.50/credit	$213.00/credit
Application Fee	$15.00	$15.00
Graduation Fee	$35.00	$35.00
Credit-by-Exam Fee	$30.00/credit	
Portfolio Assessment Fee	$100-$200.00	

185. Carroll College

Part-Time Studies Program
100 N. East Ave.
Waukesha, WI 53186

Degrees Offered: Bachelor of Science; Bachelor of Science in Nursing; Bachelor of Arts; Master of Education.

Program Mission Statement/Description: The Part-Time Studies Program offers the above degrees through classes taught during the day or in the evening. Thirty-six different majors are offered during the day; and majors in accounting, business, communication, computer science, education, nursing, and psychology can be earned exclusively in the evening. The purpose of the program is to provide the flexibility that working adults need.

Accreditation: North Central Association of Colleges and Schools; National League for Nursing; Council on Social Work Education; National Accrediting Agency for Clinical Laboratory Sciences.

Admission Requirements: Application; Official transcripts of previous work at all colleges and technical schools.

Credit Awards for Prior Learning: ACE Military Recommendations; Transfer Credit; Retroactive Credit for Foreign Language; Present Work Experience for Required Internship.

Credit Awards for Examinations: CLEP General Exams; CLEP Subject Exams; College Board AP Exams; Departmental Exams.

Limits to Credit Awards for Examinations: CLEP 48 hours.

Estimated Average Completion Time: Bachelors' Degrees: 6-7 years (part-time), 4 years (full-time).

Caveats Regarding Time Estimates: Part-time is difficult to determine length of time to complete degree because it depends on the number of credits the student takes each semester. It is very flexible.

Credit Hour Requirements:

Degree	Total Hours	Academic Residency*
Bachelor's	130	32
Graduate	33	

*Hours that must be earned at the institution exclusive of credit-by-exam, portfolio assessment, etc.

Distance Learning Options: Correspondence Courses; Independent Study; Supervised Fieldwork.

Student Support Services Available: Academic Advising; Career Counseling; Financial Aid; Orientation; Tutoring.

Informational Materials Available: Institutional Catalog; Program Brochure.

Program Age, Enrollment, and Degrees Conferred: Information not available.

Percentage of Bachelor's Degree Holders Admitted to Graduate School: Information not available.

Geographic Admission Restrictions: None.

Tuition and Fees:

	Undergraduate	Graduate
In-State Tuition	$145.00/credit	$175.00/credit
Out-of-State Tuition	$145.00/credit	$175.00/credit
Credit-by-Exam Fee	$125.00	

186. Columbia College of Nursing

2121 E. Newport
Milwaukee, WI 53271

Degrees Offered: Bachelor of Science in Nursing.

Program Mission Statement/Description: Based on its philosophy, the mission of Columbia College of Nursing is to prepare liberally educated persons for the profession of nursing and to a assist the student to develop into an intellectually responsive, self-directing, responsible member of society. This mission is founded in a commitment to excellence and on the belief that a personalized liberal education for all students develops the capability for adaptation in a changing complex society. This is a joint program between Carroll College and Columbia College of Nursing.

Accreditation: North Central Association of Colleges and Schools; National League for Nursing.

Admission Requirements: HS/GED Diploma; Interview.

Credit Awards for Prior Learning: Transfer Credit.

Limits to Credit Awards for Prior Learning: All transfer students must complete a minimum of 32 credits at Carroll. Two-year college transfer students with an Associate of Arts or Associate of Science degree from an accredited college-level institution may receive up to 64 semester hours of credit if they meet the conditions for transfer credit.

Credit Awards for Examinations: CLEP General Exams; CLEP Subject Exams; Departmental Exams.

Limits to Credit Awards for Examinations: Up to 4 credits for CLEP.

Estimated Average Completion Time: Associate degree holders: 6 semester (part-time), 4 semester (full-time).

Credit Hour Requirements: 128 hours total; 32 hours academic residency (hours that must be earned at the institution exclusive of credit-by-exam, portfolio assessment, etc.).

Distance Learning Options: Correspondence Courses; Independent Study; Study Guides; Supervised Fieldwork.

Student Support Services Available: Academic Advising; Financial Aid; Orientation.

Informational Materials Available: Exam Preparation Guides; Institutional Catalog; Prior Learning Guides; Program Brochure.

Program Age, Enrollment, and Degrees Conferred:

Degree	Year Est.	Current Enrollment	Degrees Conferred
BSN 8 yrs	1983	350	Unknown

Percentage of Bachelor's Degree Holders Admitted to Graduate School: Information not available.

Geographic Admission Restrictions: None.

Tuition and Fees: In-State Tuition $130.00 per credit; Application Fee $20.00; Credit-by-Exam Fee: Varies.

Other Pertinent Information: Students may attend evening classes (part-time) as well as day classes to earn the BSN. Part-time and full-time study options are available. There is also a BSN completion track for registered nurses.

187. Marquette University

Part-time Studies Division
1217 W. Wisconsin Ave.
Milwaukee, WI 53233

Degrees Offered: Bachelor of Arts in Criminology and Law Studies; Bachelor of Arts in Psychology; Bachelor of Arts in Advertising; Bachelor of Arts in Journalism; Bachelor of Arts in Public Relations; Bachelor of Arts in Communication and Rhetorical Studies; Bachelor of Science in Business Administration; Bachelor of Science in Civil Engineering; Bachelor of Science in Electrical Engineering; Bachelor of Science in Industrial Engineering; Bachelor of Science in Mechanical Engineering.

Program Mission Statement/Description: At the Part-Time Studies Division (PTSD), we are committed to the belief that an education pursued on a part-time basis should be equal in quality and value to one pursued full-time. Part-Time Studies Center was established to aid adult students whose family and job responsibilities limit the time they can spend on campus.

Accreditation: North Central Association of Colleges and Schools; Accreditation Board for Engineering and Technology, Inc.; Accrediting Council on Education in Journalism and Mass Communications; American Assembly of Collegiate Schools of Business.

Admission Requirements:

Undergraduate	Graduate
HS/GED Diploma	Undergraduate Degree
Essay/Written Work	
Recommendations	
GMAT, MAT	
SAT or ACT	

Credit Awards for Prior Learning: ACE/PONSI Recommendations; Transfer Credit.

Limits to Credit Awards for Prior Learning: ACE 30 credit hours; Transfer usually 64 credit hours, but could be higher in some units.

Credit Awards for Examinations: CLEP Subject Exams; College Board AP Exams; DANTES Subject Tests; Departmental Exams.

Limits to Credit Awards for Examinations: CLEP 30 credit hours.

Estimated Average Completion Time: Bachelors' Degrees: 7-10 years (part-time), 4 years (full-time).

Credit Hour Requirements:

Degree	Total Hours	Academic Residency*
Bachelor's	128-133	32

*Hours that must be earned at the institution exclusive of credit-by-exam, portfolio assessment, etc.

Distance Learning Options: Independent Study; Supervised Fieldwork - bachelor and graduate only.

Student Support Services Available: Academic Advising; Career Counseling; Counseling/Testing; Financial Aid; Job Placement Assistance; Orientation; Tutoring.

Informational Materials Available: Institutional Catalog; Program Brochure.

Other Information Available: Preadmission advisors.

Program Age, Enrollment, and Degrees Conferred:

Degree	Year Est.	Current Enrollment	Degrees Conferred
PTSD	1987	800	Unknown

Percentage of Bachelor's Degree Holders Admitted to Graduate School: Information not available.

Geographic Admission Restrictions: None.

Tuition and Fees: Full-time tuition is $4500.00 to $4770.00 for undergraduate. Part-time tuition for undergraduate is $215.00 for PTSD and $290.00 for others. Part-time graduate tuition is $300.00 to $390.00; Application Fee $25.00; Undergraduate Graduation Fee $20.00; Credit-by-Exam Fee $65.00 per credit.

188. Silver Lake College

Division of Career Directed Programs for Adult Learners
2406 S. Alverno Rd.
Manitowoc, WI 54220

Degrees Offered: Bachelor of Science.

Program Mission Statement/Description: The Division of Career Directed Programs for Adult Learners offers an integrated liberal arts core with management or manufacturing systems engineering technology major for working adults desiring to complete a Bachelor of Science or certificate. The aim of the Division is to share a high quality Silver Lake College learning experience, founded on Christian values, with students who need an alternative to the traditionally structured college program to complete degree requirements. This is accomplished by offering the integrated curriculum at sites throughout the state of Wisconsin.

Accreditation: North Central Association of Colleges and Schools.

Admission Requirements: HS/GED Diploma; Prior Credits: 30; Transfer GPA of 2.00 on 4.00 scale.

Credit Awards for Prior Learning: ACE Military Recommendations; ACE/PONSI Recommendations; Portfolio Assessment; Transfer Credit.

Limits to Credit Awards for Prior Learning: 60 credits maximum must be matched with earned credits at the college.

Credit Awards for Examinations: ACT Proficiency Exams; CLEP General Exams; CLEP Subject Exams; DANTES Subject Tests.

Estimated Average Completion Time: 3 year (part-time) 2 year (full-time).

Credit Hour Requirements: 128 hours total; 30 hours academic residency (hours that must be earned at the institution exclusive of credit-by-exam, portfolio assessment, etc.).

Distance Learning Options: Cooperative Education; Independent Study; Supervised Fieldwork.

Student Support Services Available: Academic Advising; Career Counseling; Counseling/Testing; Financial Aid; Job Placement Assistance; Orientation.

Informational Materials Available: Institutional Catalog; Program Brochure; Format for Written Work.

Program Age, Enrollment, and Degrees Conferred:

Degree	Year Est.	Current Enrollment	Degrees Conferred
BS in Management	1986	163	119
Certificate Management	1986	9	2
BS Manufacturing Systems Engineering Technology	1991	20	0

Percentage of Bachelor's Degree Holders Admitted to Graduate School: 4 percent (within one year after graduation).

Geographic Admission Restrictions: See Program Mission Statement.

Tuition and Fees: In-State Tuition $130.00 per credit; Application Fee $15.00; Graduation Fee $35.00; Credit-by-Exam Fee $37.50.

Other Pertinent Information: Cost of tuition for each course includes books and materials for it.

189. University of Wisconsin—Eau Claire

Satellite Nursing Program
Park and Garfield
Eau Claire, WI 54702

Degrees Offered: Bachelor of Science in Nursing.

Program Mission Statement/Description: The mission of the Satellite Nursing Program is to provide access to Baccalaureate Nursing Education for students who are geographically bound to the central Wisconsin area. The program is offered in cooperation with St. Joseph's Hospital in Marshfield, WI.

Accreditation: North Central Association of Colleges and Schools; National League for Nursing.

Admission Requirements: HS/GED Diploma; Prior Credits: 30.

Other Admission Requirements: Three of 5 required sciences with a GPA of 2.5 (4.0 scale); overall cumulative GPA of 2.75 (4.0 scale).

Credit Awards for Prior Learning: Transfer Credit.

Credit Awards for Examinations: CLEP General Exams; CLEP Subject Exams; College Board AP Exams; Departmental Exams; Confirming Course Option.

Limits to Credit Awards for Examinations: 32 credits (does not include credits earned by confirming course option).

Estimated Average Completion Time: 4 years and 1 summer (full-time)

Caveats Regarding Time Estimates: The time required for completion of the degree via part-time study varies.

Credit Hour Requirements: 128 hours total; 128 hours academic residency (hours that must be earned at the institution exclusive of credit-by-exam, portfolio assessment, etc.).

Distance Learning Options: Correspondence Courses; Independent Study; Supervised Fieldwork; Audio/Graphic Course.

Student Support Services Available: Academic Advising; Career Counseling; Counseling/Testing; Financial Aid; Job Placement Assistance; Orientation; Tutoring; Health Services.

Informational Materials Available: Institutional Catalog; Program Brochure.

Program Age, Enrollment, and Graduates:

Degree	Year Est.	Current Enrollment	Degrees Conferred
BSN	1986	46	17

Percentage of Bachelor's Degree Holders Admitted to Graduate School: Information not available.

Geographic Admission Restrictions: See Program Mission Statement.

Tuition and Fees: In-State Tuition $76.25 per credit; Out-of-State Tuition $228.25 per credit; Application Fee $10.00; Credit-by-Exam Fee varies.

190. University of Wisconsin—Oshkosh

Bachelor of Liberal Studies Degree Program
800 Algoma Blvd.
Oshkosh, WI 54901

Degrees Offered: Bachelor of Liberal Studies.

Program Mission Statement/Description: The Bachelor of Liberal Studies (BLS) Degree Program provides the opportunity for the working adult to acquire a quality education. The BLS is a 4-year program with an interdisciplinary, thematically linked curriculum offered on Friday evenings, Saturdays, and Sunday mornings. There are 2 major parts to the curriculum: the general education core curriculum and the advanced studies.

Accreditation: Northern Central Association of Colleges and Schools.

Admission Requirements: HS/GED Diploma; Interview.

Credit Awards for Prior Learning: ACE Military Recommendations; ACE/PONSI Recommendations; Portfolio Assessment; Transfer Credit.

Credit Awards for Examinations: CLEP General Exams; CLEP Subject Exams; College Board AP Exams; Departmental Exams.

Estimated Average Completion Time: Bachelors' Degrees: 4 years (full-time).

Credit Hour Requirements:

Degree	Total Hours	Academic Residency*
Bachelor's	128	30

*Hours that must be earned at the institution exclusive of credit-by-exam, portfolio assessment, etc.

Distance Learning Options: Correspondence Courses; Independent Study; Newspaper Courses; Study Guides; Television Courses.

Student Support Services Available: Academic Advising; Career Counseling; Counseling/Testing; Financial Aid; Job Placement Assistance; Orientation; Tutoring.

Informational Materials Available: Exam Preparation Guides; Institutional Catalog; Program Brochure.

Program Age, Enrollment, and Degrees Conferred:

Degree	Year Est.	Current Enrollment	Degrees Conferred
BLS	1978	185	98

Percentage of Bachelor's Degree Holders Admitted to Graduate School: 6 percent.

Geographic Admission Restrictions: None.

Tuition and Fees: In-State Tuition $77.34 per credit; Out-of-State Tuition $236.84 per credit; Application Fee $10.00; Graduation Fee $20.00; Credit-by-Exam Fee $33.00 per exam.

Other Pertinent Information: Each BLS class is 3 weekends. The Adult Center, with its own staff of director, coordinator/advisor, and program assistant, handles all advising, counseling, and registration. We use regular UW-Oshkosh faculty. Six members of the faculty have won all-university teacher-of-the-year awards. Ninety-five percent of students work full-time; 65 percent of students are female.

191. University of Wisconsin—River Falls

Business Evening Program
River Falls, WI 54022

Degrees Offered: Bachelor of Science in Accounting; Bachelor of Arts in Business Administration.

Program Mission Statement/Description: The mission is to provide working adults with the opportunity to complete their degrees or start a degree for employment advancement.

Accreditation: North Central Association of Colleges and Schools.

Admission Requirements: HS/GED Diploma.

Credit Awards for Prior Learning: Transfer Credit.

Credit Awards for Examinations: CLEP General Exams; College Board Advance Placement credit by department; Departmental Exams

Estimated Average Completion Time: 8-10 years (part-time), 4 years (full-time).

Credit Hour Requirements: 128 hours total; 32 hours academic residency (hours that must be earned at the institution exclusive of credit-by-exam, portfolio assessment, etc.).

Distance Learning Options: Independent Study.

Student Support Services Available: Academic Advising; Career Counseling; Counseling/Testing; Financial Aid; Job Placement Assistance; Orientation; Tutoring.

Informational Materials Available: Institutional Catalog; Program Brochure.

Program Age, Enrollment, and Degrees Conferred: Information not available.

Percentage of Bachelor's Degree Holders Admitted to Graduate School: Information not available.

Geographic Admission Restrictions: None.

Tuition and Fees: Annual In-State Tuition $1900.00.

PART II
External Degree Programs

Alabama

192. Auburn University

College of Engineering
202 Ramsay Hall
Auburn, AL 36849

Degrees Offered: Master of Aerospace Engineering, Chemical Engineering, Civil Engineering, Computer Science and Engineering, Electrical Engineering, Industrial Engineering, Materials Engineering, Mechanical Engineering, and Manufacturing Systems Engineering; and Master of Business Administration.

Program Mission Statement/Description: Auburn University, as a part of its land-grant tradition, is committed to meeting the needs of industry and individuals through its extension programs and inservice education and training programs.

Accreditation: Southern Association of Colleges and Schools.

Admission Requirements: GMAT is required for the MBA program. GRE is required for a master in an engineering discipline.

Credit Awards for Prior Learning: Transfer Credit.

Limits to Credit Awards for Prior Learning: 6 semester hours or 10 quarter hours.

Credit Awards for Examinations: None.

Estimated Average Completion Time: 4 years (part-time), 1 1/3 years (full-time).

Credit Hour Requirements:

Degree	Total Hours	Academic Residency*
Graduate (Masters in Engineering)	45-48	Unknown
Graduate (MBA)	60	Unknown

*Hours that must be earned at the institution exclusive of credit-by-exam, portfolio assessment, etc.

Minimum Campus Time Required: None.

Distance Learning Options: Television Courses.

Other Options: Graduate courses are taped in on-campus classrooms with tapes mailed to off-campus students. Off-campus students must maintain the same pace as on-campus students. All exams are monitored by a site coordinator and mailed to the professor.

Student Support Services Available: Academic Advising; Career Counseling; Job Placement Assistance.

Informational Materials Available: Institutional Catalog; Program Brochure.

Program Age, Enrollment, and Graduates:

Degree	Year Est.	Current Enrollment	Degrees Conferred
Master of Engineering	1984	130	15
MBA	1990	30	0

Geographic Admission Restrictions: Students must reside within a 750-mile radius of the campus.

Tuition and Fees: In-State Tuition $180.00 per credit; Out-of-State Tuition $180.00 per credit; Application Fee $15.00; Graduation Fee $15.00.

193. Judson College

Adult Education
Marion, AL 36756

Degrees Offered: Bachelor of Arts; Bachelor of Science; Bachelor of Social Science; Bachelor of Humanities; Bachelor of Natural Science.

Program Mission Statement/Description: This program is designed to provide an educational opportunity for adult women who cannot attend classes in the traditional manner.

Accreditation: Southern Association of Colleges and Schools.

Admission Requirements: Essay/Written Work; HS/GED Diploma; Recommendations.

Credit Awards for Prior Learning: ACE Military Recommendations; Portfolio Assessment; Transfer Credit.

Limits to Credit Awards for Prior Learning: 30 semester hours (nonattendance credit); 6 semester hours in any one area (nonattendance credit).

Credit Awards for Examinations: CLEP General Exams; CLEP Subject Exams; College Board AP Exams; Departmental Exams.

Limits to Credit Awards for Examinations: 30 semester hours (nonattendance credit); 6 semester hours in any one area.

Estimated Average Completion Time: 4 years (part-time); 2-3 years (full-time).

Caveats Regarding Time Estimates: Most of our students have transfer credit; therefore, it typically takes less time than the traditional 4 years. They can also work at their own pace. Some without prior credit have finished in 3 years.

Credit Hour Requirements: 128 hours total; 30 hours academic residency (hours that must be earned at the institution exclusive of credit-by-exam, portfolio assessment, etc.).

Minimum Campus Time Required: None.

Distance Learning Options: Directed study/tutorials.

Student Support Services Available: Academic Advising; Financial Aid; Orientation.

Informational Materials Available: Institutional Catalog; Prior Learning Guides; Program Brochure.

Program Age, Enrollment, and Graduates:

Degree	Year Est.	Current Enrollment	Degrees Conferred
BA	1981	19	10
BS	1982	9	22

Percentage of Bachelor's Degree Holders Admitted to Graduate School: Information not available.

Geographic Admission Restrictions: None.

Tuition and Fees: In-State Tuition $128.00 per credit; Out-of-State Tuition $128.00 per credit; Application Fee $20.00; Graduation Fee $40.00; Prior Learning Credit $128.00 per credit hour.

Other Pertinent Information: Judson College is a military Servicemembers Opportunity College institution. Only women may be graduated, but men are allowed to take courses for transfer.

194. Troy State University in Montgomery

External Degree Programs
P.O. Drawer 4419
Montgomery, AL 36103-4419

Degrees Offered: Bachelor of Science in Professional Studies; Bachelor of Arts in Professional Studies; Associate of Science in General Education.

Program Mission Statement/Description: The program is designed to meet the needs of adult students (22 years of age or older) who, though otherwise qualified for and desirous of pursuing undergraduate degree programs, are unable to attend regularly scheduled classes because of handicap, work, or family restrictions. The program combines traditional academic curricula and recognized evaluation and prior learning assessment techniques with a variety of delivery systems.

Accreditation: The Commission on Southern Association of Colleges and Schools.

Admission Requirements: Essay/Written Work; HS/GED Diploma; Prior Credits: 30 quarter hours; Recommendations.

Other Admission Requirements: Minimum "C" average on all college-level work completed. Two courses (minimum 9 quarter hours total) in English composition, with a minimum of a "C" grade in each.

Credit Awards for Prior Learning: ACE Military Recommendations; ACE/PONSI Recommendations; Portfolio Assessment; Transfer Credit.

Limits to Credit Awards for Prior Learning: None per se, but may be limited by degree requirements such as a minimum of 96 quarter hours of senior-college credit or 45 quarter hours of residency.

Credit Awards for Examinations: ACT Proficiency Exams; CLEP General Exams; CLEP Subject Exams; DANTES Subject Tests; Departmental Exams.

Estimated Average Completion Time: Information not available.

Credit Hour Requirements:

Degree	Total Hours	Academic Residency*
Associate's	95	25
Bachelor's	192	45

*Hours that must be earned at the institution exclusive of credit-by-exam, portfolio assessment, etc.

Minimum Campus Time Required: Baccalaureate—one day at end of program for senior project defense.

Distance Learning Options: Independent Study; Phone/Mail Instruction; Study Guides; Television Courses; Student-initiated Learning Contracts.

Student Support Services Available: Academic Advising; Career Counseling; Counseling/Testing; Financial Aid; Job Placement Assistance; Orientation; Tutoring.

Informational Materials Available: Exam Preparation Guides; Institutional Catalog; Prior Learning Guides; Program Brochure.

Program Age, Enrollment, and Graduates:

Degree	Year Est.	Current Enrollment	Degrees Conferred
BSPS	1987	92	6
BAPS	1987	92	6
AS	1989	5	0

Percentage of Bachelor's Degree Holders Admitted to Graduate School: 33 percent.

Geographic Admission Restrictions: None.

Tuition and Fees: In-State Tuition $45.00 per credit; Out-of-State Tuition $65.00 per credit; Application Fee $50.00; Graduation Fee $20.00.

Other Fees: $40.00 for former Troy State University students. $16.00 per quarter hour requested for experiential learning. $100.00 per year after first year annual participation fee.

Other Pertinent Information: Students who do not meet all criteria for unconditional admission may be admitted conditionally.

195. The University of Alabama

New College External Degree Program
P.O. Box 870182
Tuscaloosa, AL 35487

Degrees Offered: Bachelor of Arts; Bachelor of Science.

Program Mission Statement/Description: The purposes of the New College External Degree (EXD) Program of the University of Alabama are (1) to serve as a degree-granting unit that enables adult learners to meet their academic goals through a variety of educational resources; and (2) to share successful adult learning practices and approaches with the higher education community.

Accreditation: Southern Association of Colleges and Schools.

Admission Requirements: Essay/Written Work; HS/GED Diploma; student must have academic goals that can be met by the program.

Credit Awards for Prior Learning: ACE Military Recommendations; ACE/PONSI Recommendations; Portfolio Assessment; Transfer Credit.

Limits to Credit Awards for Prior Learning: Only 64 semester hours may transfer from any or all 2-year institutions previously attended; and only 30 semester hours of professional credit (e.g., education, engineering, business, home economics, nursing, and social work) may be applied toward a degree.

Credit Awards for Examinations: CLEP General Exams; CLEP Subject Exams; DANTES Subject Tests; Departmental Exams; Challenge Examinations.

Estimated Average Completion Time: The External Degree Program is primarily a distance-learning degree program. The extraordinary variety of students who enter with different amounts of transfer credits, who have widely varying schedules, who receive varying amounts of credit for prior learning, etc., makes it impossible to generalize the time it takes to complete a degree. Each student must complete one 3-hour learning contract per year. Students, however, may go at their own pace.

Credit Hour Requirements: 128 hours total; 32 hours academic residency (hours that must be earned at the institution exclusive of credit-by-exam, portfolio assessment, etc.). Residency is defined as work under the guidance of the University of Alabama faculty. Of the 32 hours, 2 hours is granted for the beginning seminar completion, and the final 12-hour senior project must be new learning hours by contract learning. All general education hours, depth study/major, and elective hours may be completed by prior learning, contract courses, etc.

Minimum Campus Time Required: One 2-day orientation seminar.

Distance Learning Options: A/V Cassettes; Correspondence Courses; Independent Study; Newspaper Courses; Phone/Mail Instruction; Study Guides; Supervised Fieldwork; Television Courses; Contract Learning; Weekend Courses, Summer Seminars, Cross-Cultural Travel.

Student Support Services Available: Academic Advising; Career Counseling; Financial Aid; Job Placement Assistance; Orientation; 3 Individual Courses on Career Development.

Informational Materials Available: Institutional Catalog; Prior Learning Guides; Program Brochure.

Other Information Available: Written materials on various tests. A Guide to Life/Work planning time management, study skills. Books published by EXD staff members: "Creating Your Future: A Guide For Adults Returning to College," "The EXD Program Handbook," "Prior Learning and Reflection: Analytical Thinking From Experience," and "The Contract Writer's Guide" (Kendall/Hunt Publisher).

Program Age, Enrollment, and Graduates:

Degree	Year Est.	Current Enrollment	Degrees Conferred
BS and BA	1974	Unknown	626

Percentage of Bachelor's Degree Holders Admitted to Graduate School: Informal evaluation, about 1/3 of graduate to graduate schools all over the country.

Geographic Admission Restrictions: Primarily limited to nonoverseas students.

Tuition and Fees: In-State Tuition $72.00 per credit; Out-of-State Tuition $72.00 per credit; Application Fee $25.00; Graduation Fee $20.00; Prior Learning Fee $75-$350.00 depending on the amount of credit awarded; Annual Participation Fee $65.00; Optional Preorientation Evaluation Fee $25.00.

Other Pertinent Information: Graduates of the External Degree Program receive the same diploma as residential students.

Arizona

196. University of Phoenix

Distance Education Program
4615 E. Elwood St.
P.O. Box 52069
Phoenix, AZ 85072-2069

Degrees Offered: Associate of Arts in Business; Bachelor of Arts in Management; Bachelor of Science in Business Administration; Bachelor of Science in Nursing; Master of Business Administration; Master of Arts in Organizational Management; Master of Nursing; Master of Counseling; Master of Arts in Education; Master of Science in Computer Information Systems.

Program Mission Statement/Description: The University of Phoenix is a private, postsecondary institution that provides education and professional renewal services designed specifically for working adults. The university identifies and develops programs which respond to the professional and career goals of its target population and the education and training needs of the organizations in which they are employed.

Accreditation: North Central Association of Colleges and Schools; National League for Nursing.

University Admission Requirements: HS/GED Diploma for undergraduate; Bachelor's degree for graduate; prior and current employment requirement, general education requirements; institutional exam; TOEFL, if primary language is not English.

Credit Awards for Prior Learning: ACE Military Recommendations; ACE/PONSI Recommendations; Portfolio Assessment; Transfer Credit.

Limits to Credit Awards for Prior Learning: Maximum lower division 60; University of Phoenix major course of study must be completed.

Credit Awards for Examinations: ACT Proficiency Exams; CLEP General Exams; CLEP Subject Exams; DANTES Subject Tests.

Estimated Average Completion Time: Associate's Degree 2 years (full-time); Bachelor's Degree 3 years (full-time); Graduate Degrees 1-2 years (full-time).

Caveats Regarding Time Estimates: Time to complete degrees varies depending on number of credits students transfer, prior learning assessments, and personal time commitment.

Credit Hour Requirements:

Degrees	Total Hours	Academic Residency
Associate's	60	39
Bachelor's (BSBA)	120	38
Bachelor's (BAM)	120	32
Bachelor's (BSN)	126	40
Graduate (MBA)	37	31
Graduate (MAOM)	40	31
Graduate (MAEd)	17	11
Graduate (MAEd with specialization)	35-38	29-32
Graduate (MC)	52	52
Graduate (MSCIS)	39	30

*Hours that must be earned at the university exclusive of credit by exam, portfolio, assessment, etc.

Distance Learning Options: Directed/Independent Study; Computer Conferencing (Online).

Student Support Services Available: Academic Advisement; Counseling/Testing; Financial Aid; Orientation.

Information Materials Available: Exam Preparation Guides; Institutional Catalog; Prior Learning Guides; Program Brochures.

Program, Enrollment and Degrees Conferred:

Degree	Year Est.	Enrollment	Degrees Conferred
AA	1990	*	3
BSBA/BAM	1978	*	64
BSN	1982	*	7
MBA	1979	*	10
MAOM	1988	*	4
MAEd	1988	*	1

*Breakout figures not available. Total current enrollment—2164.

Percentage of Bacehlor's Degree Holders Admitted to Graduate School: Information not available.

Geographic Admission Restrictions: Campuses located in Arizona, California, Colorado, Hawaii, New Mexico, Puerto Rico, and Utah. Distance Education options available.

California

197. California State University

Humanities External Degree Program
Dominguez Hills
1000 E. Victoria St.
Carson, CA 90747

Degrees Offered: Master of Arts in Humanities.

Program Mission Statement/Description: The Humanities External Degree program provides a quality education at the master level. The degree offers a broad interdisciplinary exposure to all of the humanities areas—history, literature, philosophy, music and art—and the establishment of an integrative perspective among them, with emphasis on their interrelating effects and influences. Students are provided with the opportunity to specialize in a particular discipline. The degree is offered entirely on an external degree basis. This means that there is no residency requirement and that students can complete all of the coursework without going to the campus. This kind of program is best for anyone who is unable to regularly attend classes on campus and/or anyone who prefers an individualized approach to advanced education rather than traditional classroom courses on college campuses.

Accreditation: Western Association of Schools and Colleges.

Admission Requirements: Undergraduate Degree.

Other Admission Requirements: Intellectual Biography; Transcripts (2 copies of each); GPA of last 90 quarter/60 semester units taken for BA or BS.

Credit Awards for Prior Learning: Transfer Credit.

Limits to Credit Awards for Prior Learning: Nine units of graduate courses in humanities, art, music, literature, philosophy, history, film/theater.

Credit Awards for Examinations: None.

Estimated Average Completion Time: 3-4 years (part-time); 2 years (full-time).

Caveats Regarding Time Estimates: 5-year limit.

Credit Hour Requirements: 30 semester hours.

Minimum Campus Time Required: None.

Distance Learning Options: A/V Cassettes; Correspondence Courses; Independent Study; Phone/Mail Instruction; Study Guides.

Student Support Services Available: Academic Advising; Counseling/Testing; Financial Aid.

Informational Materials Available: Program Brochure; Admission application and intellectual biography forms.

Program Age, Enrollment, and Graduates:

Degree	Year Est.	Current Enrollment	Degrees Conferred
MA in Humanities	1974	500	600

Geographic Admission Restrictions: None.

Tuition and Fees: In-State Tuition $110.00 per credit; Out-of-State Tuition $110.00 per credit; Application Fee $55.00; Graduation Fee $17.00. Students must purchase texts, but not tapes for courses, at $30.00 per course.

198. Loma Linda University

School of Public Health
Nichol Hall
Loma Linda, CA 92350

Degrees Offered: Master of Public Health in Health Promotion and Education; Master of Public Health in Health Administration.

Program Mission Statement/Description: The mission of the extended campus and other nontraditional programs is to offer graduate training in public health to individuals in midcareer whose professional responsibilities limit their attendance in the traditional classroom setting. The university is committed to providing quality education while allowing the students to continue their employment.

Accreditation: Western Association of Schools and Colleges; Council on Education for Public Health.

Admission Requirements: Undergraduate Degree; Interview; Recommendations.

Credit Awards for Prior Learning: Transfer Credit.

Other Options: Advanced standing granted for coursework deemed comparable to required courses. Hours do not need to be made up by other courses. Waiver may also be granted, but units must be made up by taking another course.

Limits to Credit Awards for Prior Learning: Up to 9 units may be transferred in. Credit may not have been applied to another degree and must have been taken within last 5 years. May not go below 48 units after advanced standing granted.

Credit Awards for Examinations: None.

Estimated Average Completion Time: 2-4 years (part-time); 1-1.5 years (full-time).

Caveats Regarding Time Estimates: Shorter estimates for on-campus only. Extended programs take 3-4 years depending on whether the student travels to various sites.

Credit Hour Requirements: 48 hours total; 48 hours academic residency (hours that must be earned at the institution exclusive of credit-by-exam, portfolio assessment, etc.).

Minimum Campus Time Required: None.

Distance Learning Options: A/V Cassettes; Independent Study; Supervised Fieldwork.

Other Options: Full quarter courses offered at various locations around the United States which meet for 3-5 days of lecture and student-teacher interaction. Precourse assignments given 6 weeks before lecture session with postcourse assignments due 10 weeks after class begins. Evening sessions (after 4:00 pm) allow qualified individuals to complete their academic programs in 2 years with minimal interruption of work schedules.

Student Support Services Available: Academic Advising; Financial Aid; Orientation.

Informational Materials Available: Institutional Catalog; Program Brochure.

Geographic Admission Restrictions: None.

Tuition and Fees: In-State Tuition $248.00 per credit; Out-of-State Tuition $248.00 per credit; Application Fee $25.00; Credit-by-Exam Fee $25.00; Personal Career Development Profile Fee $35.00 optional.

199. Saybrook Institute

1550 Sutter St.
San Francisco, CA 94109

Degrees Offered: Master of Arts in Psychology; Master of Arts in Human Science; Doctor of Philosophy in Psychology; Doctor of Philosophy in Human Science.

Program Mission Statement/Description: The mission of Saybrook Institute is to provide a unique and creative environment for graduate study, research, and communication in humanistic psychology and human science, focused on understanding and enhancing the human experience. Applying the highest standards of scholarship, the institute is dedicated to fostering the full expression of the human spirit and humanistic values in society. To accomplish this mission, Saybrook Institute offers an innovative, individualized, and rigorous at-a-distance learning opportunity. It also encourages ongoing research to develop more valid and effective methodologies for building a meaningful body of knowledge about human experience.

Accreditation: Western Association of Schools and Colleges.

Admission Requirements: Undergraduate Degree; Employment/Experience; Essay/Written Work; Recommendations.

Credit Awards for Prior Learning: Transfer Credit.

Limits to Credit Awards for Prior Learning: 27 semester units, graduate level, from accredited institutions.

Credit Awards for Examinations: Departmental Exams.

Estimated Average Completion Time: Graduate Degrees: MA 3 years ; PhD 5 years.

Caveats Regarding Time Estimates: All students are considered full-time.

Credit Hour Requirements: Graduate Degrees: MA 30 semester units; PhD 72 units.

Minimum Campus Time Required: 2 one-week residencies per year until dissertation proposal is accepted by the faculty committee.

Distance Learning Options: Electronic Mail; Independent Study; Phone/Mail Instruction; Study Guides.

Student Support Services Available: Academic Advising; Counseling/Testing; Financial Aid; Orientation; Bimonthly Newsletter.

Informational Materials Available: Institutional Catalog; Program Brochure.

Program Age, Enrollment, and Graduates:

Degree	Year Est.	Current Enrollment	Degrees Conferred
MA Psychology	1971	10	11
MA Human Science	1985	9	1
PhD Psychology	1971	144	224
PhD Human Science	1971	30	22

Geographic Admission Restrictions: None.

Tuition and Fees: In-State Tuition $6825.00 per year; Application Fee $55.00; Graduation Fee $350-$400.00.

Other Fees: Student Association dues $15.00; Nonmatriculated tuition $515.00/course.

200. University of Redlands

Alfred North Whitehead Center for Lifelong Learning
P.O. Box 3080
Redlands, CA 92373

Degrees Offered: Bachelor of Science in Business; Bachelor of Science in Management; Bachelor of Science in Information Systems; Master of Arts in Education; Master of Business Administration; Master of Arts in Management.

Program Mission Statement/Description: The Alfred North Whitehead Center for Lifelong Learning is dedicated to providing a quality education for adult students who are employed or otherwise engaged but who wish to pursue advanced undergraduate or graduate study.

Accreditation: Western Association of Schools and Colleges.

Admission Requirements:

Undergraduate	Graduate
HS/GED Diploma	Undergraduate Degree
Employment/Experience:	Essay/Written Work
(5 years professional)	Employment/Experience:
Recommendations	(5 years managerial)
Prior Credits: 40	

Other Admission Requirements: GPA 2.0 or above for undergraduates; GPA 3.0 or above for graduates.

Credit Awards for Prior Learning: ACE Military Recommendations; ACE/PONSI Recommendations; Portfolio Assessment; Transfer Credit.

Limits to Credit Awards for Prior Learning: A maximum of 120 semester credits minus the number of credits needed to complete degree requirements may be transferred. A maximum of 66 lower division transfer semester credits. A maximum of 30 credits may be certified through faculty assessment of prior experiential learning.

Credit Awards for Examinations: CLEP General Exams; CLEP Subject Exams; DANTES Subject Tests; Departmental Exams.

Limits to Credits Awarded for Examinations: A maximum of 15 credits may be awarded for successful department/institutional course challenge exams.

Estimated Average Completion Time: Bachelors' Degrees: 2 years full-time; Graduate Degrees: MA and MBA 2 years full-time.

Credit Hour Requirements:

Degree	Total Hours	Academic Residency*
Bachelor's	39-48	32
Graduate	45	39

*Hours that must be earned at the institution exclusive of credit-by-exam, portfolio assessment, etc.

Minimum Campus Time Required: None.

Distance Learning Options: Independent Study (bachelor only); Supervised Fieldwork (graduate only).

Student Support Services Available: Academic Advising; Counseling/Testing; Financial Aid; Orientation.

Informational Materials Available: Institutional Catalog; Prior Learning Guides; Program Brochure; Thesis and Practicum Guides.

Program Age, Enrollment, and Graduates:

Degree	Year Est.	Current Enrollment	Degrees Conferred
BS Bus. and Mgmt.	1987	1016	463
BS Info. System	1985	104	199
MAEd	1985	95	144
MBA	1987	445	201

Percentage of Bachelor's Degree Holders Admitted to Graduate School: Information not available.

Geographic Admission Restrictions: University of Redlands may offer adult programs within a radius of 150 miles from campus.

Tuition and Fees:

	Undergraduate	Graduate
In-State Tuition	$300.00/credit	$330.00/credit
Application Fee	$30.00	$30.00
Credit-by-Exam Fee	$100.00	

Other Fees: Matriculation Fee $125.00 and Thesis Fee $35.00.

Colorado

201. Colorado Northwestern Community College

Criminal Justice Program
500 Kennedy Dr.
Rangely, CO 81648

Degrees Offered: Associate in Applied Science in Criminal Justice; Associate of Arts in Criminal Justice.

Program Mission Statement/Description: The ultimate objective of the Colorado Northwestern Community College (CNCC) Criminal Justice Program's educational task is to provide a multidimensional approach to criminal justice education and training that exceeds established standards for certification. The student will be able to assume the required duties in his/her area of chosen emphasis. This is achieved by providing the appropriate social foundations to effectively comprehend and apply the complex concepts upon which the criminal justice system operates.

Accreditation: North Central Association of Colleges and Schools.

Admission Requirements: HS/GED Diploma; Asset Testing.

Credit Awards for Prior Learning: Portfolio Assessment; Transfer Credit; Criminal Justice Experience, Training; and Academy Completion.

Limits to Credit Awards for Prior Learning: There are no real limits on the criminal justice content-specific credit. However, students must take 15 credit hours from CNCC that specifically apply to the degree.

Credit Awards for Examinations: ACT Proficiency Exams; CLEP General Exams; CLEP Subject Exams; Departmental Exams.

Limits to Credits Awarded for Examinations: 12 credit hours.

Estimated Average Completion Time: 3-4 years part-time; 2 years full-time.

Credit Hour Requirements: 69-77 hours total; 15 hours academic residency (hours that must be earned at the institution exclusive of credit-by-exam, portfolio assessment, etc.).

Minimum Campus Time Required: None.

Distance Learning Options: Cooperative Education; Correspondence Courses; Independent Study; Phone/Mail Instruction; Study Guides; Supervised Fieldwork; Television Courses.

Student Support Services Available: Academic Advising; Career Counseling; Counseling/Testing; Financial Aid; Job Placement Assistance; Orientation; Tutoring.

Informational Materials Available: Exam Preparation Guides; Institutional Catalog; Program Brochure.

Program Age, Enrollment, and Degrees Conferred:

Degree	Year Est.	Current Enrollment	Degrees Conferred
Law Enforcement AAS	1985	40	70
Corrections AAS	1985	15	30
Crime Analysis AAS	1989	3	1
AA	1989	5	6

Geographic Admission Restrictions: None.

Tuition and Fees: In-State Tuition $25.00 per credit; Out-of-State Tuition $93.00 per credit; Application Fee $10.00; Credit-by-Exam Fee $25.00; College Fee $3.00 per credit in-state, $95.00 out of state.

202. Colorado State University

Division of Continuing Education
Spruce Hall
Fort Collins, CO 80523

Degrees Offered: Master of Business Administration; Master of Science in Management; Master of Science in Computer Science; Master of Science in Statistics; and a master of science in 8 fields of engineering.

Program Mission Statement/Description: The Colorado SURGE (State University Resources in Graduate Education) program is an innovative method of delivering graduate education to working professionals who cannot attend regular on-campus classes. It was established fall 1967 as the very first video-based graduate education program of its kind in the country. The Colorado SURGE program is administered through the Division of Continuing Education as part of the Statewide Extended Studies Program.

Accreditation: North Central Association of Colleges and Schools; Accrediting Board for Engineering and Technology, Inc.; American Assembly of Collegiate Schools of Business.

Admission Requirements: GRE; Recommendations; Undergraduate Degree; GMAT for the MBA Program.

Credit Awards for Prior Learning: None.

Credit Awards for Examinations: CLEP Subject Exams.

Other Exam Options: CLEP Subject Exams may be used to satisfy prerequisites in some cases for the MBA and MS in management.

Estimated Average Completion Time: SURGE students typically are working adults taking 2-4 years to complete. Most students take 3-6 credits per semester.

Credit Hour Requirements: Graduate Degrees: MBA 33 credits minimum; MS 30–32 credits.

Minimum Campus Time Required: None.

Distance Learning Options: A/V Cassettes; Television Courses.

Student Support Services Available: Academic Advising; Career Counseling; Financial Aid.

Informational Materials Available: Exam Preparation Guides; Institutional Catalog; Program Brochure.

Program Age, Enrollment, and Degrees Conferred:

Degree	Year Est.	Current Enrollment	Degrees Conferred
MS, MBA	1967	450	332

Geographic Admission Restrictions: None.

Tuition and Fees: In-State Tuition $250.00 per credit; Out-of-State Tuition $300.00 per credit; Application Fee $30.00.

Other Pertinent Information: The MBA program is available to out-of-state students via the Mind Extension University, Education Network. Dial 1-800-777-MIND.

203. Regis University

University Without Walls
W. 50th and Lowell Blvd.
Denver, CO 80221-1099

Degrees Offered: Bachelor of Arts; Master of Arts in Liberal Studies.

Program Mission Statement/Description: The University Without Walls program offers students the opportunity to complete individualized undergraduate or graduate degrees or teacher certification at their own pace in independent, experiential learning situations. Students, with assistance from program faculty, develop their courses in their own communities, scheduling them around work, family, and other commitments.

Accreditation: North Central Association of Colleges and Schools.

Admission Requirements:

Undergraduate	Graduate
HS/GED Diploma	Undergraduate Degree
Recommendations	Essay/Written Work
	Recommendations

Credit Awards for Prior Learning: ACE Military Recommendations, ACE/PONSI Recommendations, Portfolio Assessment, Transfer Credit (undergraduate only).

Limits to Credit Awards for Prior Learning: Undergraduate limit on portfolio credit is 63 semester credits.

Credit Awards for Examinations: Undergraduate: CLEP General Exams; CLEP Subject Exams; DANTES Subject Tests; Departmental Exams.

Estimated Average Completion Time: Bachelors' Degrees: 2 years (part-time) 1.5 years (full-time); Graduate Degrees: 2 years (part-time) 1.5 years (full-time).

Credit Hour Requirements:

Degree	Total Hours	Academic Residency*
Bachelor's	128	30
Graduate	36	30

*Hours that must be earned at the institution exclusive of credit-by-exam, portfolio assessment, etc.

Minimum Campus Time Required: Undergraduate—one day orientation and seminar; Graduate—one weekend (Friday and Saturday) per semester.

Distance Learning Options: Independent Study; Supervised Fieldwork.

Student Support Services Available: Academic Advising; Career Counseling*; Counseling/Testing*; Financial Aid; Job Placement Assistance*; Orientation; Tutoring.

*Fees are charged for these services.

Informational Materials Available: Exam Preparation Guides; Institutional Catalog; Prior Learning Guides; Program Brochure.

Program Age, Enrollment, and Degrees Conferred: Information not available.

Percentage of Bachelor's Degree Holders Admitted to Graduate School: 20 percent.

Geographic Admission Restrictions: None.

Tuition and Fees:

	Undergraduate	Graduate
In-State Tuition	$220.00/credit	$220.00/credit
Application Fee	$60.00	$75.00
Graduation Fee	$75.00	$75.00
Credit-by-Exam Fee	$38.00	
Portfolio Fee	$42.00	
Credit-By-Exam Fee		$42.00

204. University of Northern Colorado

College of Continuing Education
Greeley, CO 80639

Degrees Offered: Master of Arts with majors in 8 areas of education; Master of Arts in Agency Counseling; Master of Arts in Communication; Master of Science with majors in statistics, operations research, and secondary science teaching.

Program Mission Statement/Description: The mission of the Division of Continuing Education is to provide quality educational opportunities by extending the resources of the University of Northern Colorado beyond the campus.

Accreditation: North Central Association of Colleges and Schools.

Admission Requirements: Employment/Experience: (typically 3 years for education degrees); Essay/Written Work; GRE Miller's Analogy; Recommendations; Undergraduate Degree; Interview Required for MA in Agency Counseling.

Other Admission Requirements: Each program has particular departmental admissions requirements peculiar to its program.

Credit Awards for Prior Learning: None.

Credit Awards for Examinations: ACT Proficiency Exams; CLEP Subject Exams; Departmental Exams.

Estimated Average Completion Time: 18-24 months (part-time).

Caveats Regarding Time Estimates: Part-time study only.

Credit Hour Requirements: Graduate Degrees typically 30 semester hours, although some programs require 36-40. The Agency Counseling program requires 48 semester hours.

Minimum Campus Time Required: None.

Distance Learning Options: A/V Cassettes; Correspondence Courses; Electronic Mail; Independent Study; Phone/Mail Instruction; Study Guides; Supervised Fieldwork; Television Courses; Compressed Video.

Student Support Services Available: Academic Advising; Counseling/Testing; Financial Aid; Orientation.

Informational Materials Available: Institutional Catalog; Program Brochure.

Program Age, Enrollment, and Degrees Conferred: UNC has offered external degrees since the early 1970s. Enrollment and data on the number of degrees conferred is not available.

Geographic Admission Restrictions: None.

Tuition and Fees: In-State Tuition $89.00 per credit; Application Fee $30.00; Graduation Fee $15.00.

Other Fees: A $38.00 per semester-hour program fee is also required. The Comprehensive Examination Fee is $25.00. Self-supporting program tuition is $139.00 for graduate programs.

Connecticut

205. Charter Oak College

The Exchange, Ste. 171
270 Farmington Ave.
Farmington, CT 06032

Degrees Offered: Bachelor of Arts; Bachelor of Science; Associate in Arts; Associate in Science.

Program Mission Statement/Description: Charter Oak College is the State of Connecticut's external college degree program established by the 1973 legislature to serve those individuals who cannot complete a college degree program through conventional means because of family, job, and/or financial responsibilities. In addition to validating credits earned at traditional institutions, Charter Oak's faculty, through its formal evaluation and testing procedures, gives recognition to learning acquired through independent study, work experience, and programs of noncollegiate educational activity.

Accreditation: New England Association of Schools and Colleges, Inc.

Admission Requirements: Prior Credits: 9.

Credit Awards for Prior Learning: ACE Military Recommendations; ACE/PONSI Recommendations; Portfolio Assessment; Transfer Credit.

Credit Awards for Examinations: ACT Proficiency Exams; CLEP General Exams; CLEP Subject Exams; College Board AP Exams; DANTES Subject Tests; Departmental Exams.

Estimated Average Completion Time: Associates' Degrees: one year; Bachelors' Degrees: 2 years.

Caveats Regarding Time Estimates: Determined by how many credits a student transfers to Charter Oak and the motivation of the student to finish.

Credit Hour Requirements: Associates' Degrees: 60 hours total; Bachelor's Degree: 120 hours total.

Minimum Campus Time Required: None.

Distance Learning Options: Correspondence Courses; Independent Study; Television Courses.

Student Support Services Available: Academic Advising; Financial Aid.

Informational Materials Available: Exam Preparation Guides; Institutional Catalog; Program Brochure.

Program Age, Enrollment, and Graduates:

Degree	Year Est.	Current Enrollment	Degrees Conferred
AA	1973	30	227
AS	1973	141	962
BA	1977	104	438
BS	1977	611	1304

Percentage of Bachelor's Degree Holders Admitted to Graduate School: 33 percent.

Geographic Admission Restrictions: Persons who reside outside of New England must request a waiver of residence. Application will be reviewed to determine possibility of completing the degree from that location.

Tuition and Fees: Application Fee $25.00; Graduation Fee $80.00; Credit-by-Exam Fee $100.00 (or test agency's fee or Special Assessment Fee). Base Charge $150.00, then add $10.00 per credit attempted.

Other Fees: Enrollment Fee $250.00 in-state; $375.00 out-of-state. Baccalaureate Program Planning Fee $175.00. Annual Advisement and Records Maintenance $190.00 in-state; $305.00 out-of-state.

Florida

206. Embry-Riddle Aeronautical University

Department of Independent Study
600 S. Clyde Morris Blvd.
Daytona Beach, FL 32114

Degrees Offered: Associate in Science in Professional Aeronautics; Bachelor of Science in Professional Aeronautics; Bachelor of Science in Aviation Business Administration.

Program Mission Statement/Description: The mission of the Department of Independent Study is to provide high-quality independent study associate and bachelor's degree programs which will enable mature professional aviation-oriented adults an opportunity to fulfill their educational and career advancement goals.

Accreditation: Southern Association of Colleges and Schools.

Admission Requirements: Employment/Experience; HS/GED Diploma; Prior Credits: varies.

Credit Awards for Prior Learning: ACE Military Recommendations; ACE/PONSI Recommendations; Portfolio Assessment; Transfer Credit; FAA Aviation Licenses, Certificates and Ratings.

Limits to Credit Awards for Prior Learning: Credit may be awarded up to the limit of residency requirements.

Credit Awards for Examinations: ACT Proficiency Exams; CLEP General Exams; CLEP Subject Exams; College Board AP Exams; DANTES Subject Tests; Departmental Exams.

Estimated Average Completion Time: Associates' Degrees: 1-2 years (part-time); Bachelors' Degrees: 1-3 years (full-time)

Credit Hour Requirements:

Degree	Total Hours	Academic Residency*
Associate's	63	15
Bachelor's	126	30

*Hours that must be earned at the institution exclusive of credit-by-exam, portfolio assessment, etc.

Minimum Campus Time Required: None. Completion of independent study courses are considered residency credit.

Distance Learning Options: A/V Cassettes; Correspondence Courses; Electronic Mail (Bachelor only); Independent Study; Study Guides.

Student Support Services Available: Academic Advising; Career Counseling; Counseling/Testing; Financial Aid; Job Placement Assistance; Orientation.

Informational Materials Available: Exam Preparation Guides; Institutional Catalog; Program Brochure.

Program Age, Enrollment, and Graduates:

Degree	Year Est.	Current Enrollment	Degrees Conferred
AS Professional Aeronautics	1980	100	125
BS Professional Aeronautics	1980	1500	450
BS Aviation Business Admin.	1982	217	100

Percentage of Bachelor's Degree Holders Admitted to Graduate School: Information not available.

Geographic Admission Restrictions: None.

Tuition and Fees: In-State Tuition $130.00 per credit; Out-of-State Tuition $130.00 per credit; Application Fee $15.00; Credit-by-Exam Fee $100.00.

207. Southeastern College

Continuing Education Department
1000 Longfellow Blvd.
Lakeland, FL 33801

Degrees Offered: Bachelor of Arts with majors in Bible, Christian Education, Missions, and Pastoral Ministries.

Program Mission Statement/Description: The mission of the Continuing Education Department of Southeastern College is to provide to the adult learner the opportunity for personal or professional development as related to Biblical, ministerial, and theological studies utilizing independent study delivery systems and to provide means for recognizing measurable prior learning experiences, while maintaining standards of knowledge, competence, and intellectual attainment that are comparable to those established for resident programs.

Accreditation: Southern Association of Colleges and Schools.

Admission Requirements: Essay/Written Work; HS/GED Diploma; Interview; Recommendations.

Credit Awards for Prior Learning: ACE Military Recommendations; ACE/PONSI Recommendations; Portfolio Assessment; Transfer Credit.

Limits to Credit Awards for Prior Learning: Portfolio and Assessment—total of 30 credits.

Credit Awards for Examinations: ACT Proficiency Exams; CLEP General Exams; CLEP Subject Exams; College Board AP Exams; DANTES Subject Tests; Departmental Exams.

Estimated Average Completion Time: 3-4 years (full-time)

Caveats Regarding Time Estimates: The time required for completion of the degree via part-time study varies.

Credit Hour Requirements: 130 total hours.

Minimum Campus Time Required: None.

Distance Learning Options: Correspondence Courses; Phone/Mail Instruction; Study Guides; Supervised Fieldwork; Learning Contracts.

Student Support Services Available: Academic Advising; Career Counseling; Counseling/Testing; Orientation.

Informational Materials Available: Exam Preparation Guides; Institutional Catalog; Prior Learning Guides; Program Brochure.

Program Age, Enrollment, and Graduates: Information not available.

Percentage of Bachelor's Degree Holders Admitted to Graduate School: Information not available.

Geographic Admission Restrictions: None.

Tuition and Fees: In-State Tuition $55.00 per credit; Out-of-State Tuition $55.00 per credit; Application Fee $35.00; Graduation Fee $50.00; Credit-by-Exam Fee $55.00 per credit.

208. University of South Florida

Bachelor of Independent Studies External Degree Program
HMS 443
4202 E. Fowler Ave.
Tampa, FL 33620

Degrees Offered: Bachelor of Independent Studies.

Program Mission Statement/Description: University of South Florida offers an external undergraduate program of Interdisciplinary Studies (including social sciences, natural sciences, and humanities) for adult learners in careers who cannot readily attend traditional classes. Program goals include personal enrichment and career enhancement.

Accreditation: Southern Association of Colleges and Schools.

Admission Requirements: Essay/Written Work; HS/GED Diploma.

Other Admission Requirements: Foreign Language, acceptable CLAST scores (college level academic skills test) for transfer applicants. Acceptable SAT/ACT scores for first time in college applicants.

Credit Awards for Prior Learning: Transfer Credit.

Other Options: Waiver of a study area tutorial via successful completion of area comprehensive exam—no waiver of seminar requirement.

Limits to Credit Awards for Prior Learning: Applicants can transfer credit (60 hours) to validate completion of an associate in arts or an associate in science in selected health-related fields, such as nursing, radiologic technology, nuclear medicine technology, respiratory therapy, and dental hygiene.

Credit Awards for Examinations: CLEP Subject Exams.

Limits to Credit Awards for Examinations: Individuals can waive a maximum of 2 area tutorials by exam (a maximum of 30 semester hours). Those applying for articulation of a community college degree are not eligible to apply for waiver of area tutorials.

Estimated Average Completion Time: 4-8 years (part-time).

Caveats Regarding Time Estimates: 2 area curriculum contracts (comparable to 2 years of work) students complete within 1-4 years. 4 area curriculum contracts (comparable to four years of college work) students complete within 5-8 years.

Credit Hour Requirements: 120 total hours; 30/45 hours academic residency. Hours required in conjunction with BIS resident Seminars of 15 semester hours each (30 for 2 Area Contract; 45 for 4 Area Contract). Academic residency are hours that must be earned at the institution exclusive of credit-by-exam, portfolio, etc.

Minimum Campus Time Required: 2 area curriculum contract: 2 2-week seminars = 4-week physical residency. 4 area curriculum contract: 3 2-week seminars = 6-week physical residency.

Distance Learning Options: A/V Cassettes; Correspondence Courses; Independent Study; Phone/Mail Instruction; Study Guides; Television Courses.

Student Support Services Available: Academic Advising; Counseling/Testing; Financial Aid; Job Placement Assistance; Orientation; Tutoring.

Informational Materials Available: Institutional Catalog; Program Brochure; Introduction to Guide to Independent Study.

Program Age, Enrollment, and Graduates:

Degree	Year Est.	Current Enrollment	Degrees Conferred
BIS	1968	145	125

Percentage of Bachelor's Degree Holders Admitted to Graduate School: 35 percent.

Geographic Admission Restrictions: Out-of-state accepted in keeping with nonresident tuition schedule.

Tuition and Fees: In-State Tuition $43.03 per credit; Out-of-State Tuition $153.40 per credit; Application Fee $15.00.

Other Fees: Books, travel, room, and board for seminars.

Other Pertinent Information: BIS is a State University System of Florida External Degree Program currently available through the Florida State University (Tallahassee), the University of Florida (Gainesville), the University of North Florida (Jacksonville), and the University of South Florida (Tampa). The degree is awarded through the College of Arts and Sciences at USF, which also houses the central administration office for the program.

Idaho

209. Lewis-Clark State College

8th Ave. and 6th St.
Lewiston, ID 83501

Degrees Offered: Bachelor of Science in General Studies; Bachelor of Business Administration; Bachelor of Social Work; Bachelor of Science in Nursing.

Program Mission Statement/Description: To provide alternate pathways to degrees that enable adult students to complete programs while still meeting their family, society, and professional responsibilities.

Accreditation: Northwest Association of Schools and Colleges; National Council for Accreditation of Teacher Education; Council on Social Work Education.

Admission Requirements: HS/GED Diploma; Interview.

Credit Awards for Prior Learning: ACE Military Recommendations; Portfolio Assessment; Transfer Credit.

Limits to Credit Awards for Prior Learning: 32 credits (semester) maximum can be awarded for experiential or cooperative education.

Credit Awards for Examinations: CLEP Subject Exams; College Board AP Exams; Departmental Exams.

Limits to Credits Awarded for Examinations: 12 hours.

Estimated Average Completion Time: Bachelors' Degrees: 6-10 years (part-time); 5-9 years (full-time).

Caveats Regarding Time Estimates: Many degree (BA) students return after a long absence with previous credits.

Credit Hour Requirements: 128 total hours; 30 of last 40 hours academic residency (hours that must be earned at the institution exclusive of credit-by-exam, portfolio assessment, etc.).

Minimum Campus Time Required: None.

Distance Learning Options: A/V Cassettes; Cooperative Education (bachelor); Correspondence Courses (bachelor); Electronic Mail; Independent Study; Phone/Mail Instruction; Study Guides; Supervised Fieldwork (bachelor); Television Courses.

Student Support Services Available: Academic Advising; Counseling/Testing; Financial Aid; Job Placement Assistance; Tutoring.

Informational Materials Available: Exam Preparation Guides; Institutional Catalog; Prior Learning Guides; Program Brochure.

Program Age, Enrollment, and Degrees Conferred:

Degree	Year Est.	Current Enrollment	Degrees Conferred
BS General Studies	1986	200	75
BS Management	1984	400	150
BBA	1988	50	20
BSN	1988	30	6

Percentage of Bachelor's Degree Holders Admitted to Graduate School: 15-20 percent.

Geographic Admission Restrictions: Out-of-state tuition applies when carrying more than 10 credits per semester. Other restriction: out-reach largely for Northern part of state.

Tuition and Fees: In-State Tuition $60.00 per credit; Out-of-State Tuition $100.00 per credit; Graduation Fee $40.00; Credit-by-Exam Fee $60.00.

210. University of Idaho

Engineering Outreach Dept.
Moscow, ID 83843

Degrees Offered: Master in Computer Science, Computer Engineering, Civil Engineering, Electrical Engineering, Geological Engineering, Mechanical Engineering, Psychology (Human Factors), Interdisciplinary Studies.

Program Mission Statement/Description: The Engineering Outreach program is designed to provide continuing education to practicing professionals in engineering, computer science, and human factors.

Accreditation: Northwest Association of Schools and Colleges.

Admission Requirements: Undergraduate Degree; GRE for computer science, human factors, and interdisciplinary studies only.

Other Admission Requirements: GPA of 2.8 on 4.0 scale except 3.0 for computer science, human factors, and interdisciplinary studies.

Credit Awards for Prior Learning: Transfer credit from other graduate institutions.

Limits to Credit Awards for Prior Learning: 12 credits total from another graduate institution or from nonmatriculating transcripts.

Credit Awards for Examinations: None.

Estimated Average Completion Time: Graduate Degrees: MS, ME 5 years (part-time).

Caveats Regarding Time Estimates: Students are almost all working professionals who typically take only 3 credits. 14 percent take 6 credits; 1 percent take 9 credits.

Credit Hour Requirements: Graduate Degrees: MS, ME, 30-36 total hours.

Minimum Campus Time Required: For engineering graduate degrees, student must come to campus for 1-2 days to take comprehensive examination or defend thesis. For human factors program, thesis students must spend 6-9 months on campus; nonthesis students spend 2 weeks on campus to take comprehensive examination.

Distance Learning Options: A/V Cassettes; Television Courses.

Student Support Services Available: Academic Advising.

Informational Materials Available: Institutional Catalog; Program Brochure.

Program Age, Enrollment, and Degrees Conferred:

Degree	Year Est.	Current Enrollment	Degrees Conferred
MS, ME Electrical Engr.	1978	100	20
MS Computer Engr.	1980	70	10
MS, ME Mechanical Engr.	1980	70	10
MS Psych./Human Factors	1988	20	0
MS Inter. Studies	1987	0	0
MS, ME Geological Engr.	1988	15	
MS, ME Computer Engr.	1988	20	
MS, ME Civil Engr.	1988	30	

Geographic Admission Restrictions: Continental U.S., Alaska, Hawaii.

Tuition and Fees: In-State Tuition $242.00 per credit; Out-of-State Tuition $242.00 per credit; Application Fee $15.00; Graduation Fee $20.00; Credit-by-Exam Fee $15.00.

Illinois

211. Board of Governors of State Colleges and Universities

Board of Governors Bachelor of Arts Degree Program
200 Hilton Plaza
700 E. Adams
Springfield, IL 62701

Degrees Offered: Bachelor of Arts.

Program Mission Statement/Description: The Board of Governors Bachelor of Arts Degree Program is a systemwide degree program designed to meet the undergraduate educational needs of experienced adults in a manner compatible with career and family responsibilities. This nontraditional approach to education is available at each of the 5 universities constituting the Illinois Board of Governors of State Colleges and Universities system, which includes Chicago State, Eastern Illinois, Governors State, Northeastern Illinois, and Western Illinois Universities.

Accreditation: North Central Association of Colleges and Schools.

Admission Requirements: HS/GED Diploma.

Other Admission Requirements: The vice president for Academic Affairs may waive this requirement for individuals that do not hold a high school or GED diploma.

Credit Awards for Prior Learning: ACE Military Recommendations; ACE/PONSI Recommendations (through a prior learning portfolio process); Portfolio Assessment; Transfer Credit.

Credit Awards for Examinations: ACT Proficiency Exams; CLEP General Exams; CLEP Subject Exams; DANTES Subject Tests; Departmental Exams.

Estimated Average Completion Time: Bachelors' Degrees: 2.5 years (part-time).

Caveats Regarding Time Estimates: Completion time varies with the amount of work transferred, prior learning assessment, individual circumstances, etc. The range is as short as one term, and it is not unusual for the completion time to extend over several years.

Credit Hour Requirements:

Degree	Total Hours	Enrollment Requirement*
Bachelor's	120	15

*Hours that must be earned at the institution exclusive of credit-by-exam, portfolio assessment, etc.

Minimum Campus Time Required: None.

Distance Learning Options: A/V Cassettes; correspondence Courses; Electronic Mail; Independent Study; Newspaper Courses; Phone/Mail Instruction; Study Guides; Television Courses.

Student Support Services Available: Academic Advising; Career Counseling; Counseling/Testing; Financial Aid; Job Placement Assistance (services are available to those students who can come to campus); Orientation; Tutoring.

Informational Materials Available: Exam Preparation Guides; Institutional Catalog; Prior Learning Guides; Program Brochure.

Program Age, Enrollment, and Graduates:

Degree	Year Est.	Current Enrollment	Degrees Conferred
BA	1973	10,692	9357*

*Total of the five Board of Governors System universities.

Percentage of Bachelor's Degree Holders Admitted to Graduate School: 37 percent.

Geographic Admission Restrictions: None.

Tuition and Fees: In-State Tuition $65.50 per credit Lower Division, $66.50 per credit Upper Division; Application Fee $25.00 at one of the universities; Graduation Fee $5-$15.00; Portfolio Evaluation Fee $30.00.

212. City Colleges of Chicago

External Degree Program
226 W. Jackson Blvd.
Rm. 912
Chicago, IL 60606

Degrees Offered: Associate in Arts; Associate in Applied Science; Associate in General Studies.

Program Mission Statement/Description: To serve the educational needs of adults through innovative programs and services and nontraditional means of delivering instruction.

Accreditation: North Central Association of Colleges and Schools.

Admission Requirements: HS/GED Diploma. Adults are accepted for enrollment without high school or GED diplomas if they can demonstrate ability to do college-level work.

Credit Awards for Prior Learning: ACE Military Recommendations; ACE/PONSI Recommendations; Portfolio Assessment; Transfer Credit.

Other Options: Faculty evaluation of other noncollegiate programs—approval given if college-level and City Colleges of Chicago course-equivalent courses are offered.

Limits to Credit Awards for Prior Learning: 45 credit hours.

Credit Awards for Examinations: ACT Proficiency Exams; CLEP General Exams; CLEP Subject Exams; DANTES Subject Tests; Departmental Exams.

Limits to Credits Awarded for Examinations: 45 credits.

Estimated Average Completion Time: Information not available.

Credit Hour Requirements:

Degree	Total Hours	Academic Residency*
Associate's	60-62	15

*Hours that must be earned at the institution exclusive of credit-by-exam, portfolio assessment, etc.

Minimum Campus Time Required: None.

Distance Learning Options: Package Course/Study Guides; Television Courses; Video Cassettes.

Student Support Services Available: Academic Advising; Counseling/Testing; Financial Aid.

Informational Materials Available: Institutional Catalog; Prior Learning Guides; Program Brochure.

Program Age, Enrollment, and Graduates: Information not available.

Geographic Admission Restrictions: None.

Tuition and Fees: Information not available. There is a special reduced fee for distant students for video programs.

---

213. Roosevelt University

External Studies Program
430 S. Michigan Ave.
Chicago, IL 60605

Degrees Offered: Bachelor of General Studies.

Program Mission Statement/Description: The External Studies Program is a guided independent study program for adults 25 or older. Credit from external courses can be applied to a degree program. Students can sign up for external courses at any time and have up to 6 months to complete the courses. Students have direct access to regular university faculty who grade their courses through phone, mail, or in-person meetings. The external studies program is ideal for students with jobs or family responsibilities conflicting with regular schedules of classroom study.

Accreditation: North Central Association of Colleges and Schools.

Admission Requirements: HS/GED Diploma.

Credit Awards for Prior Learning: ACE Military Recommendations; ACE/PONSI Recommendations; Portfolio Assessment; Transfer Credit.

Credit Awards for Examinations: CLEP General Exams; CLEP Subject Exams; College Board AP Exams; DANTES Subject Tests; Departmental Exams.

Limits to Credit Awards for Examinations: Limited by need to complete the university residency requirements and the 300-level requirements.

Estimated Average Completion Time: 5 years (part-time), 2.5 years (full-time).

Credit Hour Requirements:

Degree	Total Hours	Academic Residency*
Bachelor's	81-90	30

*Hours that must be earned at the institution exclusive of credit-by-exam, portfolio assessment, etc.

Minimum Campus Time Required: None.

Distance Learning Options: Independent Study; Phone/Mail Instruction; Study Guides.

Student Support Services Available: Academic Advising; Career Counseling; Counseling/Testing; Financial Aid; Job Placement Assistance; Orientation; Tutoring.

Informational Materials Available: Institutional Catalog; Program Brochure.

Program Age, Enrollment, and Degrees Conferred: Information not available.

Percentage of Bachelor's Degree Holders Admitted to Graduate School: 65 percent of all BGS students go on for graduate work.

Geographic Admission Restrictions: None.

Tuition and Fees: In-State Tuition $262.00 per credit; Out-of-State Tuition $262.00 per credit; Application Fee $20.00; Graduation Fee $25.00.

Indiana

214. Indiana University-Purdue University at Indianapolis

University-Wide General Studies Degree Program
620 Union Dr., Rm. 543
Indianapolis, IN 46202

Bloomington
Director of Continuing Studies
Indiana University Bloomington
Owen Hall 202
Bloomington, IN 47405

Richmond
Director of Continuing Studies
Indiana University East
2325 Chester Blvd.
Richmond, IN 47374-9979

South Bend
Director of Extended Programs
Indiana University at South Bend
1700 Mishawaka Ave.
P.O. Box 7111
South Bend, IN 46634

Gary
Director of Continuing Studies
Indiana University Northwest
3400 Broadway
Gary, IN 46408

New Albany
Director of Continuing Studies
Indiana University Southeast
4201 Grant Line Rd.
New Albany, IN 47150

Fort Wayne
Director of General Studies Degree Programs
Indiana University-Purdue University at Fort Wayne
2101 Coliseum Blvd., E.
Fort Wayne, IN 46805

Kokomo

Director of Continuing Studies

Indiana University at Kokomo

P.O. Box 9003

2300 S. Washington St.

Kokomo, IN 46904-9003

Columbus

Assistant Director of Continuing Studies

IUPUI Columbus

4601 Central Ave.

Columbus, IN 47203

Degrees Offered: Associate of General Studies (AGS); Bachelor of General Studies (BGS).

Program Mission Statement/Description: The General Studies Degree Program brings a college education to those who have been prevented from beginning or completing work in a traditional degree program because of work schedules, domestic responsibilities, or logistical problems. The program enables students to complete a degree in general studies at their own pace and their own location.

Accreditation: North Central Association of Colleges and Schools.

Admission Requirements: HS/GED Diploma. In the absence of high school or GED, persons 21 or older whose experiential learning indicates fair prospect of success in college are given provisional admission. Must complete 12 credits with grade of "C" or better to fill admission requirement.

Credit Awards for Prior Learning: ACE Military Recommendations; ACE/PONSI Recommendations; Portfolio Assessment; Transfer Credit.

Limits to Credit Awards for Prior Learning: Portfolio 15 credits AGS, 30 credits BGS.

Credit Awards for Examinations: CLEP General Exams (Humanities); CLEP Subject Exams; College Board AP Exams; DANTES Subject Tests; Departmental Exams.

Estimated Average Completion Time: Associates' Degrees: 4 years (part-time, 2 years (full-time); Bachelors' Degrees: 8 years (part-time), 4 years (full-time).

Credit Hour Requirements:

Degree	Total Hours	Academic Residency*
Associate's	60	15
Bachelor's	120	30

*Hours that must be earned at the institution exclusive of credit-by-exam, portfolio assessment, etc. (All "residency" hours can be done via Independent Study by Correspondence.)

Minimum Campus Time Required: None.

Distance Learning Options: A/V Cassettes; Cooperative Education; Correspondence Courses; Independent Study; Study Guides; Television Courses.

Student Support Services Available: Academic Advising; Career Counseling; Counseling/Testing; Financial Aid; Job Placement Assistance; Orientation; Tutoring.

Informational Materials Available: Institutional Catalog; Prior Learning Guides; Program Brochure.

Program Age, Enrollment, and Graduates:

Degree	Year Est.	Current Enrollment	Degrees Conferred
AGS	1976	3970	4046
BGS	1976	3830	3635

Percentage of Bachelor's Degree Holders Admitted to Graduate School: Information not available.

Geographic Admission Restrictions: None.

Tuition and Fees: In-State Tuition $66.00 per credit; Application Fee $25.00; Credit-by-Exam Fee varies.

Other Pertinent Information: There are 2 kinds of students in the General Studies Degree Program: those who have access to an Indiana University (IU) campus and those who do not. Campus-based students attend classes and receive counseling and other services through the campus at which they are enrolled. Those who are not within commuting distance of an IU campus are admitted through the universitywide General Studies Degree Program. These students generally enroll in Independent Study by Correspondence courses to complete IU credit requirements. They can combine these credits with those acquired at other colleges and apply them toward graduation. Students receive counseling and other services through the universitywide office.

215. Vincennes University

1002 N. 1st St.

Vincennes, IN 47591

Degrees Offered: Associate of Science in General Studies.

Program Mission Statement/Description: Currently our goal is to offer sufficient courses to permit students to "complete" the Associate of Science degree. Credits earned via this program add onto transfer credits, military credits, etc., to achieve sufficient credits to meet graduation requirements. The university currently offers 15 courses for degree completion. Their goal is to gradually add course offerings until students may complete an entire degree via this program.

Accreditation: North Central Association of Colleges and Schools.

Admission Requirements: HS/GED Diploma.

Credit Awards for Prior Learning: ACE Military Recommendations; Portfolio Assessment; Transfer Credit.

Limits to Credit Awards for Prior Learning: No limit except that students must meet residency requirements.

Credit Awards for Examinations: ACT Proficiency Exams; CLEP General Exams; CLEP Subject Exams; College Board AP Exams; DANTES Subject Tests; Departmental Exams.

Other Exam Options: CCAF Exams; USAFI Exams.

Limits to Credit Awards for Examinations: 6 hours in each of the CLEP exams; others as per the ACE recommendations and within the residency requirement limits.

Estimated Average Completion Time: Information not available.

Caveats Regarding Time Estimates: The university currently offers 15 courses for degree completion. Their goal is to gradually add course offerings until students may complete an entire degree via this program.

Credit Hour Requirements:

Degree	Total Hours	Academic Residency*
Associate's	62	30

*Hours that must be earned at the institution exclusive of credit-by-exam, portfolio assessment, etc. Required hours are less for active duty military personnel. Consult the college catalog for details.

Minimum Campus Time Required: None.

Distance Learning Options: A/V Cassettes; Correspondence Courses; Independent Study; Study Guides; Television Courses.

Student Support Services Available: Academic Advising; Career Counseling; Counseling/Testing; Financial Aid; Job Placement Assistance; Tutoring.

Informational Materials Available: Institutional Catalog; Program Brochure.

Program Age, Enrollment, and Graduates:

Degree	Year Est.	Current Enrollment	Degrees Conferred
Associate of Science	1989	134	0

Geographic Admission Restrictions: None.

Tuition and Fees: Tuition $200.00 per 3-credit-hour course.

Iowa

216. The University of Iowa

Center for Credit Programs
116 International Center
Iowa City, IA 52242

Degrees Offered: Bachelor of Liberal Studies

Program Mission Statement/Description: The Bachelor of Liberal Studies (BLS) external degree program is designed to serve adults whose lifestyle or location prevents them from attending college on-campus. The BLS degree can be completed without ever visiting campus. The BLS degree does not have a traditional major. Instead, students concentrate in 3 out of 5 broad distribution areas. In this way, the multidisciplinary competence implied by a liberal arts degree is demonstrated.

Accreditation: North Central Association of Colleges and Schools.

Admission Requirements: Prior Credits: 62 semester hours; 2.25 GPA.

Credit Awards for Prior Learning: ACE Military Recommendations; Transfer Credit.

Credit Awards for Examinations: CLEP General Exams; CLEP Subject Exams; College Board AP Exams; DANTES Subject Tests.

Estimated Average Completion Time: 4 years (part-time); 2 years (full-time).

Caveats Regarding Time Estimates: Students enter the Bachelor of Liberal Studies degree program as juniors.

Credit Hour Requirements:

Degree	Total Hours	Academic Residency*
Bachelor's	124	45

*Hours that must be earned at the institution exclusive of credit-by-exam, portfolio assessment, etc. Note: Students must complete 30 semester hours after admission to the program.

Minimum Campus Time Required: None.

Distance Learning Options: Cooperative Education; Correspondence Courses; Independent Study; Television Courses.

Student Support Services Available: Academic Advising.

Informational Materials Available: Program Brochure.

Program Age, Enrollment, and Graduates:

Degree	Year Est.	Current Enrollment	Degrees Conferred
BLS	1977	350	190

Percentage of Bachelor's Degree Holders Admitted to Graduate School: Information not available.

Geographic Admission Restrictions: No geographic restrictions within the United States. American citizens in foreign countries are admissible, but not foreign students in foreign countries.

Tuition and Fees: In-State Tuition $68.00 per credit; Out-of-State Tuition $68.00 per credit; Application Fee $20.00; Correspondence Courses Tuition $57.00.

Other Pertinent Information: The University of Iowa offers more than 160 correspondence courses. All requirements for the BLS degree can be satisfied through correspondence courses from the university.

217. Upper Iowa University

Continuing Studies
Box 1861
Fayette, IA 52142

Degrees Offered: Bachelor of Science in Marketing; Bachelor of Science in Management; Bachelor of Science in Public Administration and Accounting.

Program Mission Statement/Description: Upper Iowa University provides postsecondary education to a widely diverse student clientele, including both recent high school graduates and mature learners. Because the educational needs of the university's constituency vary significantly, the university is committed to maintaining curricular flexibility to provide for these diverse needs.

Accreditation: North Central Association of Colleges and Schools.

Admission Requirements: HS/GED Diploma.

Credit Awards for Prior Learning: ACE Military Recommendations; ACE/PONSI Recommendations; Portfolio Assessment; Transfer Credit.

Other Options: Other training experiences based on contact hours and relevance to the degree.

Limits to Credit Awards for Prior Learning: Training credits limited to 30 semester hours; work experience credit limited to 24 semester hours; combined credit for work and training limited to 45 semester hours. 30 semester hours must be completed through coursework at Upper Iowa University.

Credit Awards for Examinations: CLEP Subject Exams; DANTES Subject Tests; Departmental Exams.

Estimated Average Completion Time: 6 years (part-time), 4 years (full-time).

Caveats Regarding Time Estimates: 6 months to complete each course allowed. An extension can be granted.

Credit Hour Requirements:

Degree	Total Hours	Academic Residency*
Bachelor's	120	30

*Hours that must be earned at the institution exclusive of credit-by-exam, portfolio assessment, etc.

Minimum Campus Time Required: 2-week summer residency with completion of minimum 3 hours for each 60 hours needed for degree.

Distance Learning Options: Correspondence Courses; Independent Study; Study Guides.

Student Support Services Available: Academic Advising; Financial Aid; Job Placement Assistance.

Informational Materials Available: Institutional Catalog; Prior Learning Guides; Program Brochure.

Program Age, Enrollment, and Graduates:

Degree	Year Est.	Current Enrollment	Degrees Conferred
BS Management	1979	217	1100
BS Marketing	1974	130	635
BS Public Admin.	1974	60	319
BS Accounting	1974	50	172

Percentage of Bachelor's Degree Holders Admitted to Graduate School: Information not available.

Geographic Admission Restrictions: None.

Tuition and Fees: In-State Tuition $98.00 per credit; Out-of-State Tuition $98.00 per credit; Graduation Fee $35.00; Credit-by-Exam Fee $5.00 per hour; Training/Life Experience Fee $50.00 per credit.

Kansas

218. Kansas State University

Division of Continuing Education
Distance Education
225 College Court
Manhattan, KS 66506

Degrees Offered: Bachelor of Interdisciplinary Social Science (BIS); Bachelor in Agriculture, Animal Sciences and Industry: Animal Products Option.

Program Mission Statement/Description: Kansas State University is a member of the National Universities Degree Consortium (NUDC). See Appendix G for NUDC mission and description.

Accreditation: North Central Association of Colleges and Schools.

Admission Requirements: HS/GED Diploma; 60 prior college credits recommended; Accumulative GPA of 2.0 in all college-level work attempted.

Credit Awards for Prior Learning: ACE Military Recommendations; ACE PONSI Recommendations; Portfolio Assessment; Transfer Credit; Approval courses for other NUDC institutions.

Limits to Credit Awards for Prior Learning: Academic policy to be determined on amount of credit awarded for prior learning.

Credit Awards for Examinations: ACT Proficiency Exams; CLEP Subject Exams; College Board AP Exams; CLEP General Exams; DANTES Subject Tests; Departmental Exams.

Limits to Credit Awards for Examinations: Up to 60 semester hours.

Estimated Average Completion Time: Varies.

Credit Hour Requirements: 120 total hours.

Minimum Campus Time Required: None.

Distance Learning Options: A/V Cassettes; Correspondence Courses; Independent Study; Study Guides; Television Courses; Voice Mail.

Student Support Services Available: Academic Advising; Orientation; Financial Aid.

Informational Materials Available: NUDC Program Brochure; Exam Preparation Guides; Institutional Catalog; Prior Learning Guide Book; NUDC Student Handbook.

Program Age and Enrollment:

Degree	Year Est.	Current Enrollment
BIS	1992	250
Bachelor in Agriculture	1992	250

Percentage of Bachelor's Degree Holders Admitted to Graduate School: Not applicable.

Geographic Admission Restrictions: None.

Tuition and Fees: $400.00 per 3-semester course; Application Fee $25.00; Graduation Fee $25.00; Credit-by-Exam Fee $127.00 In-State, and $132.00 Out-of-State.

---

219. Pittsburg State University

Division of Continuing Studies
215 Russ Hall
Pittsburg, KS 66762

Degrees Offered: Bachelor of General Studies; Bachelor of Science in Business Administration; Bachelor of Science in Education; Bachelor of Science in Technology; Bachelor of Science in Nursing; and Bachelor of Science in Vocational Technology Education; Master in Educational Administration; Master in Human Resource Development; Master in Technical Education; Master in Technology, and Master in Special Education.

Program Mission Statement/Description: The mission of Pittsburg State University's Division of Continuing Studies is to administer, facilitate, and provide quality graduate and undergraduate educational programs, courses, and noncredit programs for the professions, liberal arts, and vocational technical fields for all qualified students and members of area communities on an outreach basis.

Accreditation: North Central Association of Colleges and Schools; National League for Nursing.

Admission Requirements: Prior Credits: 55-64 maximum transfer.

Other Admission Requirements: Ready for junior status; prerequisites for courses.

Credit Awards for Prior Learning: Transfer Credit.

Credit Awards for Examinations: CLEP Subject Exams; College Board AP Exams; Departmental Exams.

Other Exam Options: English credit awarded for qualifying ACT composite scores.

Estimated Average Completion Time: Bachelors' Degrees: 4 years (part-time); Graduate Degrees: 4 years (part-time).

Caveats Regarding Time Estimates: Offerings limited to 2 degree courses off-campus per semester.

Credit Hour Requirements: Total hours: Bachelors' Degrees 124; Graduate Degrees 32.

Minimum Campus Time Required: None.

Distance Learning Options: A/V Cassettes; Independent Study; Supervised Fieldwork; Television Courses.

Student Support Services Available: Academic Advising; Orientation.

Informational Materials Available: Institutional Catalog.

Program Age, Enrollment, and Degrees Conferred:

Degree	Year Est.	Current Enrollment	Degrees Conferred
BS BA	1989	16	12
BS Technology	1989	15	4
BS Nursing	1985	55	150
BS VTE	1989	0	9
BGS	1987	0	1
MS Admin.	1988	30	20
MS HRD	1989	0	36
MS TED	1989	8	5

Percentage of Bachelor's Degree Holders Admitted to Graduate School: Information not available.

Geographic Admission Restrictions: None.

Tuition and Fees:

	Undergraduate	Graduate
In-State Tuition	$52.00/credit	$70.00/credit
Out-of-State Tuition	$52.00/credit	$70.00/credit

Kentucky

220. Murray State University

Murray, KY 42071

Degrees Offered: Bachelor of Independent Studies.

Program Mission Statement/Description: The Bachelor of Independent Studies (BIS) degree provides exposure to liberal arts supported by research methods and completion of a field of study project. At the completion of studies, the adult student will be one who has "learned how to continue learning" through exposure to liberal studies and by demonstrating methods for acquiring knowledge. The BIS degree represents the Murray State University philosophy of serving the adult learner with programs which circumvent barriers to participation in higher education.

Accreditation: Southern Association of Colleges and Schools.

Admission Requirements: HS/GED Diploma; Prior Credits 12.

Credit Awards for Prior Learning: ACE Military Recommendations; Portfolio Assessment; Transfer Credit.

Limits to Credit Awards for Prior Learning: 30 credit hours for the portfolio; 67 credit hours from a 2-year college.

Credit Awards for Examinations: CLEP General Exams; CLEP Subject Exams; College Board AP Exams; DANTES Subject Tests; Departmental Exams.

Estimated Average Completion Time: 1-5 years (full-time).

Caveats Regarding Time Estimates: The number of years to earn a BIS degree is dependent upon the number of hours students have when they enter the program.

Credit Hour Requirements: 128 total hours; 24 hours academic residency (hours that must be earned at the institution exclusive of credit-by-exam, portfolio assessment, etc.).

Minimum Campus Time Required: 2-day introductory BIS seminar held on the Murray State University campus or designated sites.

Distance Learning Options: A/V Cassettes; Correspondence Courses; Independent Study; Study Guides; Television Courses.

Student Support Services Available: Academic Advising; Career Counseling; Counseling/Testing; Financial Aid; Job Placement Assistance; Orientation; Tutoring.

Informational Materials Available: Institutional Catalog; Program Brochure.

Program Age, Enrollment, and Degrees Conferred:

Degree	Year Est.	Current Enrollment	Degrees Conferred
BIS	1986	324	28

Percentage of Bachelor's Degree Holders Admitted to Graduate School: 20 percent.

Geographic Admission Restrictions: None.

Tuition and Fees: In-State Tuition $53.00 per credit; Out-of-State Tuition $152.00 per credit; Application Fee $25.00; Graduation Fee $20.00; Credit-by-Exam Fee $5.00 per credit hour; Portfolio Assessment Fees: $25.00.

Louisiana

221. Grantham College of Engineering

34641 Grantham College Rd.
P.O. Box 5700
Slidell, LA 70469-5700

Degrees Offered: Associate of Science and Bachelor of Science in Engineering Technology with majors in Electronics and Computers.

Program Mission Statement/Description: The Grantham degree programs have been developed for adults who are employed in electronics and allied fields. The objective of these programs is to upgrade mature workers to higher-level, better-paying positions.

Accreditation: National Home Study Council.

Admission Requirements: Although not required, it is recommended that students have a high school diploma or the equivalent, and some related employment or experience, prior to admission.

Credit Awards for Prior Learning: ACE Military Recommendations; ACE/PONSI Recommendations; Transfer Credit.

Other Options: Proof of at least two years work experience in electronics, computers, or closely related fields is required prior to completion of the BSET degree (12 credit hours). Proof of laboratory proficiency in the use of state-of-the-art electronics equipment is required prior to completion of the ASET degree in electronics (6 credit hours).

Limits to Credit Awards for Prior Learning: Students are required to transfer in 21 semester hours of credits from other accredited institutions or through special examination programs such as CLEP courses, because some (e.g., English, history, etc.) are not offered by Grantham. No advanced standing is granted nor are any transfer credits allowed in lieu of Grantham courses.

Credit Awards for Examinations: ACT Proficiency Exams; CLEP General Exams; CLEP Subject Exams; College Board AP Exams; DANTES Subject Tests.

Limits to Credit Awards for Examinations: Credit awarded for examinations is limited to the 21 hours of required transfer courses.

Estimated Average Completion Time: Associates' Degrees: 3-4 years (part-time); 2 years (full-time); Bachelors' Degrees: 5-6 years (part-time); 4 years (full-time).

Credit Hour Requirements:

Degree	Total Hours
Associate's	60-66
Bachelor's	82-88

Minimum Campus Time Required: None.

Distance Learning Options: Correspondence Courses; Independent Study.

Student Support Services Available: Academic Advising.

Informational Materials Available: Institutional Catalog; Program Brochure.

Program Age, Enrollment, and Graduates:

Degree	Year Est.	Current Enrollment	Degrees Conferred
BSET Electronics	1973	675	225
BSET Computers	1988	300	2

Percentage of Bachelor's Degree Holders Admitted to Graduate School: Approximately 20 percent.

Geographic Admission Restrictions: None.

Tuition and Fees: In-State Tuition $2050.00 per phase (approximately one year); Out-of-State Tuition $2050.00 per phase.

Maryland

222. University of Maryland University College

National University Degree Consortium
University Blvd. at Adelphi Rd.
College Park, MD 20742

Degrees Offered: Bachelor of Arts; Bachelor of Science.

Program Mission Statement/Description: The University of Maryland University College is a member of the National Universities Degree Consortium. See Appendix G for information.

Accreditation: Middle States Association of Colleges and Schools.

Admission Requirements: HS/GED Diploma.

Credit Awards for Prior Learning: ACE Military Recommendations; ACE/PONSI Recommendations; Transfer Credit.

Limits to Credit Awards for Prior Learning: Up to 90 semester hours for 4-year institution transfer credits (only 60 semester hours from 2-year institutions). Up to 90 semester hours for ACE/PONSI and ACE Military.

Credit Awards for Examinations: ACT Proficiency Exams; CLEP General Exams; CLEP Subject Exams; College Board AP Exams; DANTES Subject Tests; Departmental Exams.

Estimated Average Completion Time: Information not available.

Credit Hour Requirements:

Degree	Total Hours	Academic Residency*
Bachelor's	120	30

*Hours that must be earned at the institution exclusive of credit-by-exam, portfolio assessment, etc.

Minimum Campus Time Required: None.

Distance Learning Options: A/V Cassettes; Cooperative Education; Correspondence Courses; Electronic Mail; Independent Study; Phone/Mail Instruction; Study Guides; Television Courses.

Student Support Services Available: Academic Advising; Financial Aid; Orientation; Tutoring.

Informational Materials Available: Institutional Catalog; Program Brochure.

Program Age, Enrollment, and Degrees Conferred:

Degree	Year Est.	Current Enrollment	Degrees Conferred
Bachelor of Arts/Sciences	1991	131	0

Percentage of Bachelor's Degree Holders Admitted to Graduate School: Information not available.

Geographic Admission Restrictions: None.

Tuition and Fees: In-State Tuition $160.00 per credit; Out-of-State Tuition $175.00 per credit; Application Fee $25.00; Graduation Fee $25.00; Credit-by-Exam Fee $127.00 In-State, and $132.00 Out-of-State.

Massachusetts

223. Atlantic Union College

Adult Degree Program
Main St.
South Lancaster, MA 01561

Degrees Offered: Bachelor of Science; Bachelor of Arts.

Program Mission Statement/Description: The Adult Degree Program is based on 2 beliefs held by the college faculty: that many adults whose college work has been interrupted by marriage, work, military service, or other personal circumstances should have the opportunity of completing their degrees; and that there are many ways of doing reputable academic work other than being enrolled in on-campus courses. The program was founded in 1972 for adults who wish to complete degrees started years before, for college graduates who are changing their professions, and for lifelong learners anywhere and any age.

Accreditation: New England Association of Schools and Colleges, Inc.; Council on Social Work Education; National League for Nursing.

Admission Requirements: HS/GED Diploma; Essay/Written Work; Recommendations; Prior Credits: 6 semester hours.

Other Admission Requirements: Applicants must be at least 25 years old. Applicants whose native language is not English must present a score of 550 or above on the test of English as a Foreign Language (TOEFL).

Credit Awards for Prior Learning: ACE Military Recommendations; ACE/PONSI Recommendations; Portfolio Assessment; Transfer Credit.

Limits to Credit Awards for Prior Learning: Transfer credits: must be from regionally accredited institutions (or foreign equivalents). No limit, but 2-unit (32 semester hours) minimum required in program. Portfolios: no more than 2 units (32 semester hours) of credit.

Credit Awards for Examinations: ACT Proficiency Exams; CLEP General Exams; CLEP Subject Exams; College Board AP Exams; Departmental Exams.

Limits to Credit Awards for Examinations: Maximum of 4 units (64 semester hours) for credit by exams. No more than half of requirements in a general education area may be met by examination.

Estimated Average Completion Time: 8 years (part-time), 4 years (full-time).

Caveats Regarding Time Estimates: Actually, a typical student has 2-3 years of college credit upon entering the program and receipt of experiential learning credit. A typical student takes about 1.5 years to graduate.

Credit Hour Requirements: 128 total hours; 32 hours academic residency (hours that must be earned at the institution exclusive of credit-by-exam, portfolio assessment, etc.).

Minimum Campus Time Required: Attendance at 2-week seminars in January or July for entering students. Afterward, attendance at one-week seminars for continuing students from a distance or at weekend seminars for commutting students.

Distance Learning Options: A/V Cassettes; Independent Study; Phone/Mail Instruction; Study Guides; Supervised Fieldwork; Television Courses.

Student Support Services Available: Academic Advising; Career Counseling; Counseling/Testing; Financial Aid; Job Placement Assistance; Orientation.

Informational Materials Available: Institutional Catalog; Prior Learning Guides; Program Brochure.

Program Age, Enrollment, and Graduates:

Degree	Year Est.	Current Enrollment	Degrees Conferred
BA/BS	1972	65	360

Percentage of Bachelor's Degree Holders Admitted to Graduate School: 35 percent.

Geographic Admission Restrictions: None. However, practical considerations prevent most residents of foreign countries outside the western hemisphere from attending.

Tuition and Fees: In-State Tuition $183.00 per credit; Out-of-State Tuition $183.00 per credit; Application Fee $15.00; Graduation Fee $15.00.

Michigan

224. Northwood Institute

External Plan of Study Program
3225 Cook Rd.
Midland, MI 48640

Degrees Offered: Associate's Degree in Accounting, Associate's Degree in Advertising, Associate's Degree in Automotive Marketing, Associate's Degree in Business Management, Associate's Degree in Retail Merchandising, Associate's Degree in Computer Science/Management, Associate's Degree in Fashion Marketing and Merchandising, Associate's Degree in Hotel and Restaurant Management, Associate's Degree in Automotive Aftermarket Management, and Associate's Degree in Executive Secretarial, Bachelor of Business Administration in Accounting, Bachelor of Business Administration in Management, Bachelor of Business Administration in Marketing and Management, Bachelor of Business Administration in Computer Science/Management, Bachelor of Business Administration in Management and Economics, and Bachelor of Business Administration in Computer Information Management.

Program Mission Statement/Description: Northwood's External Plan of Study Program is an off-campus program aimed at highly motivated men and women with specific business career goals and whose schedules preclude much traditional campus attendance.

Accreditation: North Central Association of Colleges and Schools.

Admission Requirements: Employment/Experience: 6-10 years minimum; Essay/Written Work; HS/GED Diploma; Interview.

Credit Awards for Prior Learning: ACE Military Recommendations; ACE/PONSI Recommendations; Portfolio Assessment; Transfer Credit.

Limits to Credit Awards for Prior Learning: 144 quarter hours (35 is average).

Credit Awards for Examinations: ACT Proficiency Exams; CLEP General Exams; CLEP Subject Exams; DANTES Subject Tests; Departmental Exams.

Estimated Average Completion Time: Associates' Degrees: 3 years (part-time) 2 years (full-time); Bachelors' Degrees: 3 years (part-time) 2 years (full-time).

Caveats Regarding Time Estimates: After the associate's degree, year-round work can shorten time frames.

Credit Hour Requirements:

Degree	Total Hours	Academic Residency*
Associate's	90	36
Bachelor's	180	36

*Hours that must be earned at the institution exclusive of credit-by-exam, portfolio assessment, etc.

Minimum Campus Time Required: 2 seminars, 3 days each and one day for a final oral/written comprehensive examination.

Distance Learning Options: Correspondence Courses; Independent Study.

Student Support Services Available: Academic Advising; Career Counseling; Counseling/Testing; Financial Aid; Job Placement Assistance; Tutoring.

Informational Materials Available: Institutional Catalog; Program Brochure; Writing Guides.

Program Age, Enrollment, and Graduates:

Degree	Year Est.	Current Enrollment	Degrees Conferred
BBA	1972	3775	5000

Percentage of Bachelor's Degree Holders Admitted to Graduate School: 20 percent.

Geographic Admission Restrictions: None.

Tuition and Fees: In-State Tuition $155.00/credit; Out-of-State Tuition $155.00/credit; Application Fee $15.00; Graduation Fee $25.00; Credit-by-Exam Fee $25.00/credit; Independent Study Courses $40/credit.

225. Spring Arbor College

Post House
Spring Arbor, MI 49283

Degrees Offered: Bachelor of Arts in Management of Human Resources; Bachelor of Arts in Health Sciences and Gerontology; Bachelor of Arts in Leadership in Business Administration.

Program Mission Statement/Description: Spring Arbor College (SAC) is a Christian liberal arts college whose mission is driven by the SAC concept. This philosophical underpinning drives all SAC programs and calls for a community of learners who are distinguished by their serious involvement in the study of the liberal arts, their total commitment to Jesus Christ as a perspective for learning, and their critical participation in the affairs of the contemporary world.

Accreditation: North Central Association of Colleges and Schools.

Admission Requirements: Employment/Experience: currently working; Essay/Written Work; HS/GED Diploma; Interview (off-campus); Prior Credits: 60 credits transferrable.

Credit Awards for Prior Learning: ACE Military Recommendations; ACE/PONSI Recommendations; Portfolio Assessment; Transfer Credit.

Limits to Credit Awards for Prior Learning: 40 technical transfer credits maximum; 30 portfolio assessment credits maximum.

Credit Awards for Examinations: ACT Proficiency Exams; CLEP General Exams; CLEP Subject Exams; College Board AP Exams; DANTES Subject Tests; TECEP.

Limits to Credit Awards for Examinations: 60 credits maximum; humanities CLEP exams only.

Estimated Average Completion Time: 2-3 years (part-time) one year (full-time).

Caveats Regarding Time Estimates: 42 percent take longer than the year.

Credit Hour Requirements: 124 total hours; 34-40 hours academic residency (hours that must be earned at the institution exclusive of credit-by-exam, portfolio assessment, etc.).

Minimum Campus Time Required: None.

Distance Learning Options: A/V Cassettes; Independent Study; Supervised Fieldwork; Television Courses.

Student Support Services Available: Academic Advising; Financial Aid; Orientation; Tutoring.

Informational Materials Available: Institutional Catalog; Prior Learning Guides; Program Brochure.

Program Age, Enrollment, and Graduates:

Degree	Year Est.	Current Enrollment	Degrees Conferred
BAMHR	1983	477	1052
BAHSG	1988	54	16
BALBA	1987	109	6

Percentage of Bachelor's Degree Holders Admitted to Graduate School: 10 percent.

Geographic Admission Restrictions: None.

Tuition and Fees: Tuition ranges from $2405.00 to $3807.00 per semester depending on program major and semester term; Application Fee $15.00; Graduation Fee $20.00; Credit-by-Exam Fee $37.00-$45.00 per exam; Assessment of Prior Learning Fee ranges from $15.00 to $300.00 depending on the number of credits granted. (Fee is for assessor's fees, not for credit per se).

Minnesota

226. Bemidji State University

Center for Extended Learning
1500 Birchmont Dr., WE #27
Bemidji, MN 56601

Degrees Offered: Associate in Arts/Associate in Science in Criminal Justice; Bachelor of Science in Industrial Technology; Bachelor of Science in Applied Psychology; Bachelor of Science in Business Administration; Bachelor of Science in Accounting; Bachelor of Arts/Bachelor of Science in Criminal Justice, Social Studies; Bachelor of Science in History.

Program Mission Statement/Description: External studies is both a concept and a method of delivering classes to persons unable to come to campus. It is a way of evaluating what students have already learned and assisting them with the completion of courses and/or degrees. It is not a separate program with its own curriculum.

Accreditation: North Central Association of Colleges and Schools.

Admission Requirements: HS/GED Diploma.

Credit Awards for Prior Learning: ACE Military Recommendations; ACE/PONSI Recommendations; Portfolio Assessment; Transfer Credit.

Credit Awards for Examinations: CLEP General Exams; CLEP Subject Exams; DANTES Subject Tests; Departmental Exams.

Estimated Average Completion Time: Associates' Degrees: 2-4 years (part-time); 2 years (full-time); Bachelors' Degrees: 6-7 years (part-time); 4 years (full-time).

Credit Hour Requirements:

Degree	Total Hours	Academic Residency*
Associate's (quarter hours)	96	32
Bachelor's (quarter hours)	192	45

*Hours that must be earned at the institution exclusive of credit-by-exam, portfolio assessment, etc. Note: External studies counts as residence credit.

Minimum Campus Time Required: None.

Distance Learning Options: Audiovisual Cassettes; Study Guides; Supervised Fieldwork.

Student Support Services Available: Academic Advising; Career Counseling; Counseling/Testing; Financial Aid; Job Placement Assistance; Orientation.

Informational Materials Available: Institutional Catalog; Program Brochure.

Program Age, Enrollment, and Graduates:

Degree	Year Est.	Current Enrollment	Degrees Conferred
BS Industrial Tech.	1975	35	70
BS Vocational Education	1976	24	67
BS Applied Psychology	1975	96	184
BS Elementary Education	1986	107	87
BS Criminal Justice	1976	92	70

Percentage of Bachelor's Degree Holders Admitted to Graduate School: Information not available.

Geographic Admission Restrictions: No international students.

Tuition and Fees: In-State Tuition $51.45 per credit; Out-of-State Tuition $99.20 per credit; Application Fee $15.00; Graduation Fee $10.00; Credit-by-Exam Fee Varies.

227. North Central Bible College

Carlson Institute
910 Elliot Ave. S.
Minneapolis, MN 55404

Degrees Offered: Bachelor of Arts/Bachelor of Science in Church Ministries and Christian Education; Associate of Arts in Bible Theology.

Program Mission Statement/Description: To educate students for ministry and to provide a special environment for higher education and spiritual development, using nontraditional education methods.

Accreditation: North Central Association of Colleges and Schools; American Association of Bible Colleges.

Admission Requirements: HS/GED Diploma; Recommendations.

Other Admission Requirements: Those consistent with a private religious college.

Credit Awards for Prior Learning: ACE Military Recommendations; ACE/PONSI Recommendations; Portfolio Assessment; Transfer Credit.

Limits to Credit Awards for Prior Learning: Portfolio limit of 30 semester credit.

Credit Awards for Examinations: ACT Proficiency Exams; CLEP General Exams; CLEP Subject Exams; DANTES Subject Tests.

Estimated Average Completion Time: Associates' Degrees: 4 years (part-time), 2 years (full-time); Bachelors' Degrees: 8 years (part-time), 4 years (full-time)

Credit Hour Requirements:

Degree	Total Hours	Academic Residency*
Associate's	65	27
Bachelor's	130	27

*Hours that must be earned at the institution exclusive of credit-by-exam, portfolio assessment, etc.

Minimum Campus Time Required: None.

Distance Learning Options: Correspondence Courses; Study Guides.

Student Support Services Available: Academic Advising; Career Counseling; Counseling/Testing; Job Placement Assistance; Orientation.

Informational Materials Available: Institutional Catalog; Prior Learning Guides; Program Brochure.

Program Age, Enrollment, and Graduates:

Degree	Year Est.	Current Enrollment	Degrees Conferred
BA	1991	1	0
BS	1991	17	0

Percentage of Bachelor's Degree Holders Admitted to Graduate School: Information not available.

Geographic Admission Restrictions: None.

Tuition and Fees: In-State Tuition $65.00 per credit; Out-of-State Tuition $65.00 per credit; Application Fee $25.00; Graduation Fee $50.00; Program Enrollment $50.00.

228. Saint Mary's College of Minnesota

St. Mary's College Graduate Center
2510 Park Ave.
Minneapolis, MN 55404

Degrees Offered: Master of Arts in Human Development; Master of Arts in Education; Bachelor of Science Completion in Telecommunications Management.

Program Mission Statement/Description: The Master of Arts programs in human development and education were established by Saint Mary's College in 1972. These are 32 credit hour programs that offer a high quality nontraditional approach. Students develop individualized program plans in consultation with program staff and a faculty advisor. The completion program was established in 1991. It is designed for professionals working in the field of information service who need the skills to manage the telecommunications function in a rapidly changing environment. Students learn key telecommunications concepts and key managerial concepts related to corporate telecommunications needs.

Accreditation: North Central Association of Colleges and Schools.

Admission Requirements:

Undergraduate	Graduate
HS/GED Diploma	Undergraduate Degree
Interview	Interview
Essay/Written Work	Essay/Written Work
Employment/Experience	Recommendations
Prior Credits: 60	

Other Admission Requirements: Undergraduate: DD214 (military credential, if applicable); CLEP or DANTES Scores, if applicable; Transcripts from accredited colleges attended.

Credit Awards for Prior Learning: (Undergraduate Only); ACE Military Recommendations; ACE/PONSI Recommendations; Portfolio Assessment; Transfer Credit.

Limits to Credit Awards for Prior Learning: 30 semester credit hours (undergraduate only).

Credit Awards for Examinations: ACT Proficiency Exams; CLEP General Exams; CLEP Subject Exams; College Board AP Exams; DANTES Subject Tests; Departmental Exams.

Limits to Credit Awards for Examinations: 30 semester credit hours (undergraduate only).

Estimated Average Completion Time: Bachelors' Degrees: 14-28 months (part-time); Graduate Degrees: 2.5 years (part-time); 20 months (full-time).

Caveats Regarding Time Estimates: Very few students enroll full-time.

Credit Hour Requirements:

Degree	Total Hours	Academic Residency
Bachelor's (semester hours)	122	
Graduate (semester hours)	32	1 course

Minimum Campus Time Required: A one-credit orientation course that lasts one weekend is required. Remainder of coursework is delivered in corporate setting.

Distance Learning Options: Independent Study; Supervised Fieldwork; Corporate Education.

Student Support Services Available: Academic Advising; Counseling/Testing; Financial Aid; Orientation.

Informational Materials Available: Exam Preparation Guides; Institutional Catalog; Prior Learning Guides; Program Brochure.

Program Age, Enrollment, and Graduates:

Degree	Year Est.	Current Enrollment	Degrees Conferred
MA Human Development	1972	250	*
MA Education	1972	40	*
BS Telecommunications Management	1991	0	

*The total combined number of degrees conferred is 475.

Percentage of Bachelor's Degree Holders Admitted to Graduate School: Information not available.

Geographic Admission Restrictions: Master of Arts in Human Development, 150 miles of Minneapolis, St. Paul, Rochester, and Winona, MN. Master of Arts in Education (external) Wisconsin.

Tuition and Fees:

	Undergraduate	Graduate
In-State Tuition	$200.00/credit	$175.00/credit
Out-of-State Tuition	$200.00/credit	$175.00/credit
Application Fee	$50.00	$20.00
Graduation Fee	$50.00	$25.00
CLEP Subject Exam	$38.00	
DANTES Subject Test	$25.00	
Portfolio Assessment Fee	$50.00/credit	

229. Walden University

415 1st Ave., N.
Minneapolis, MN 55401

Degrees Offered: Doctor of Philosophy in administration/ management; education; health and human services; and doctor of education.

Program Mission Statement/Description: Walden University's mission is to provide high-quality academic study for experienced professionals. The university's programs build upon professional and personal competence and seek to enhance that competence through scholarly inquiry and the advancement of knowledge in matters of societal significance. This century has seen unprecedented social, political, and technological changes; and more profound changes lie ahead. By seeking a better understanding of the potential and the problems of the future, we aspire to contribute to making it a more humane one.

Accreditation: North Central Association of Colleges and Schools.

Admission Requirements: Interview; Recommendations; Undergraduate Degree; Master's degree or equivalent plus 3 years professional experience.

Credit Awards for Prior Learning: Assessment is conducted and recognition given only for admissions requirements.

Credit Awards for Examinations: None.

Estimated Average Completion Time: 2-2.5 years (full-time).

Caveats Regarding Time Estimates: Continuous enrollment is required, service is provided on dispersed residency basis, program is self-paced independent study.

Credit Hour Requirements: 78 total hours.

Minimum Campus Time Required: Initial Admission/ Orientation Workshop (weekend); 3-week summer residence or cluster session of 8 weekends; 2 regional sessions per year (2 days each). Sessions dispersed throughout United States.

Distance Learning Options: Independent Study; Phone/ Mail Instruction.

Student Support Services Available: Academic Advising; Financial Aid; Orientation.

Informational Materials Available: Institutional Catalog; Prior Learning Guides; Program Brochure.

Program Age, Enrollment, and Graduates:

Degree	Year Est.	Current Enrollment	Degrees Conferred
Doctoral	1971	475	1500

Geographic Admission Restrictions: None.

Tuition and Fees: Annual Tuition and Fees $9900.00.

Other Pertinent Information: Specific educational objectives are (1) to create alternative graduate opportunities for adults; (2) to conduct the curriculum through competency assessments of learning outcomes; (3) to provide an adult learning environment based upon knowledge of adult development; (4) to enhance professional understanding with the knowledge of change; and (5) to provide doctoral-level education to professionals who want to enhance their understanding of change within their lives and within the areas of administration/management, education, health services and human services. Walden fosters scholar-practitioners who can both advance the state of knowledge and implement that knowledge in new applications. Walden seeks adult learners who want to develop new and renewed social commitments in their lives and professions.

Missouri

230. Berean College

1445 Boonville Ave.
Springfield, MO 65802

Degrees Offered: Bachelor of Arts with majors in Bible/ theology, Christian education, pastoral ministries, and Christian counseling; Associate of Arts with emphases in Bible/theology, and in church ministries.

Program Mission Statement/Description: The objectives of Berean College degrees include (1) the ministerial credential preparation required by the districts of the Assemblies of God; (2) the opportunity for pastors to implement intensive Bible study in their local churches; (3) the opportunity for systematic study of the Bible for individuals who could not attend a residential college; and (4) the nontraditional educational requirements of individual students of the residential colleges.

Accreditation: National Home Study Council.

Admission Requirements: HS/GED Diploma.

Credit Awards for Prior Learning: ACE Military Recommendations; Portfolio Assessment; Transfer Credit; Credit for Life Experience.

Limits to Credit Awards for Prior Learning: Credit for Life Experience up to 32 credits. Transfer of credit from other colleges but must complete at least 32 credits with Berean College.

Credit Awards for Examinations: ACT Proficiency Exams; CLEP General Exams; CLEP Subject Exams; DANTES Subject Tests.

Estimated Average Completion Time: Varies.

Caveats Regarding Time Estimates: Berean is a correspondence college so there are no full-time students. Students can take no more than 2 courses at a time. They are allowed up to 12 months to complete any course after enrollment.

Credit Hour Requirements:

Degree	Total Hours	Academic Residency*
Associate's	64	32
Bachelor's	128	32

*Hours that must be earned at the institution exclusive of credit-by-exam, portfolio assessment, etc.

Minimum Campus Time Required: None.

Distance Learning Options: A/V Cassettes; Correspondence Courses; Independent Study; Phone/Mail Instruction; Study Guides.

Student Support Services Available: Academic Advising.

Informational Materials Available: Exam Preparation Guides; Institutional Catalog; Program Brochure.

Program Age, Enrollment, and Graduates:

Degree	Year Est.	Current Enrollment	Degrees Conferred
BA	1985	750	10
AA	1985	82	2

Percentage of Bachelor's Degree Holders Admitted to Graduate School: Information not available.

Geographic Admission Restrictions: None.

Tuition and Fees: In-State Tuition $59.00 per credit; Out-of-State Tuition $59.00 per credit; Application Fee $25.00; Graduation Fee $40.00 ($25.00 without cap and gown); Credit-by-Exam Fee $40.00 per course; Credit for Life Experience $10.00 per credit hour.

231. Southwest Baptist University

1601 S. Springfield St.
Bolivar, MO 65613

Degrees Offered: Associate of Applied Science; Bachelor of Applied Science; Bachelor of Science in Nursing.

Program Mission Statement/Description: Southwest Baptist University is an institution of higher education providing lifelong learning opportunities of excellent quality in liberal arts and professional and vocational studies through traditional and nontraditional delivery systems to the church and society from the perspective of a Christian worldview and the Baptist tradition.

Accreditation: North Central Association of Colleges and Schools.

Admission Requirements: HS/GED Diploma; Recommendations.

Credit Awards for Prior Learning: ACE Military Recommendations; Portfolio Assessment; Transfer Credit.

Credit Awards for Examinations: ACT Proficiency Exams; CLEP General Exams; CLEP Subject Exams; College Board AP Exams; Departmental Exams.

Estimated Average Completion Time: There is no typical completion time that can be tracked because of the wide variety of academic backgrounds and work schedules.

Credit Hour Requirements:

Degree	Total Hours	Academic Residency*
Associate's	64	15
Bachelor's	128	30

*Hours that must be earned at the institution exclusive of credit-by-exam, portfolio assessment, etc.

Minimum Campus Time Required: 4-week summer term.

Distance Learning Options: A/V Cassettes; Cooperative Education; Correspondence Courses; Independent Study; Study Guides; Supervised Fieldwork.

Student Support Services Available: Academic Advising; Career Counseling; Financial Aid; Job Placement Assistance; Orientation; Tutoring.

Informational Materials Available: Institutional Catalog; Program Brochure

Program Age, Enrollment, and Graduates:

Degree	Year Est.	Current Enrollment	Degrees Conferred
BSN	1985	178	20
BAS	1989	17	1
AAS	1988	2	4

Percentage of Bachelor's Degree Holders Admitted to Graduate School: Information not available.

Geographic Admission Restrictions: None.

Tuition and Fees: In-State Tuition $80.00 per credit; Application Fee $25.00; Graduation Fee AAS $25.00; BAS $35.00; Credit-by-Exam Fee $16.00 per credit.

232. Stephens College Without Walls

Campus Box 2083
Stephens College
Columbia, MO 65215

Degrees Offered: Bachelor of Arts in Business Administration; Psychology (General or Clinical/Counseling); Child Study; Health Care Dual-Disciplinary majors and Student-initiated majors. Bachelor of Science in Health Information Management; Early Childhood and Elementary Education. Associate of Arts Degree.

Program Mission Statement/Description: Stephens College Without Walls is designed to meet the needs of the adult student, 23 years of age and older, with a curriculum that emphasizes issues concerning women and minorities. The program is dedicated to enhanced personal and professional development of adults through quality education and a commitment to life-long learning. Stephens College Without Walls fosters personal empowerment and leadership in students.

Accreditation: North Central Association of Colleges and Schools; American Medical Record Association, American Medical Association.

Admission Requirements: HS/GED Diploma; Recommendations.

Other Admission Requirements: Complete application; Pay application fee; Attend and satisfactorily complete the introductory course, The Changing Human Image; Arrange for official transcripts be sent to New Student Coordinator for all courses taken at other accredited colleges and universities.

Credit Awards for Prior Learning: ACE Military Recommendations; ACE/PONSI Recommendations; Portfolio Assessment; Transfer Credit.

Other Options: Technical training programs of 2 weeks or more duration for Registered Nurses specialization.

Limits to Credit Awards for Prior Learning: Portfolio assessment of experiential learning—limited to 30 semester hours and the experience must have occurred prior to attendance at the introductory course, The Changing Human Image.

Credit Awards for Examinations: CLEP General Exams; CLEP Subject Exams; College Board AP Exams; DANTES Subject Tests; Departmental Exams.

Limits to Credit Awards for Examinations: CLEP subject and general exams and DANTES subject tests are limited to total of 30 semester hours.

Estimated Average Completion Time: Associates' Degrees: 1-4 years (part-time), 2-2.5 years (full-time). Bachelors' Degrees: 1-10 years (part-time), 4-5 years (full-time).

Caveats Regarding Time Estimates: The student may progress at a rate of full-time or part-time. The first year a student should plan on a minimum of 3 courses (9 semester hours) with Stephens faculty. Every succeeding year, a minimum of 2 courses (6 semester hours) must be taken with Stephens faculty. A student who wishes to progress more rapidly is encouraged to do so. The student may also take approved courses concurrently at local colleges and transfer the credit to Stephens College.

Credit Hour Requirements:

Degree	Total Hours	Academic Residency*
Associate's	60	30
Bachelor's	120	30

*Hours that must be earned at the institution exclusive of credit-by-exam, portfolio assessment, etc.

Minimum Campus Time Required: Stephens College Without Walls prospective students must attend the introductory course, The Changing Human Image. This course is offered several times each year on the Stephens College campus in either an 8-day format or in a double weekend format. Assignments are done by the student prior to attendance on campus, during the course and a final assignment after returning home. Satisfactorily passing the course is necessary for admission into the college.

Distance Learning Options: A/V Cassettes; Correspondence Courses; Independent Study; Phone/Mail Instruction; Supervised Fieldwork (Bachelor only).

Student Support Services Available: Academic Advising; Career Counseling; Financial Aid; Job Placement Assistance; Orientation.

Informational Materials Available: Institutional Catalog; Prior Learning Guides; Program Brochure.

Program Age, Enrollment, and Graduates:

Degree	Year Est.	Current Enrollment	Degrees Conferred
BA/BS	1971	314	1067
AA	1971	Unknown	Unknown

Percentage of Bachelor's Degree Holders Admitted to Graduate School: 53.9 percent of Stephens College Without Walls students have attended graduate school.

Geographic Admission Restrictions: None.

Tuition and Fees: In-State Tuition $208.33 per credit; Out-of-State Tuition $208.33 per credit; Application Fee $50.00.

New Jersey

233. Thomas A. Edison State College

101 W. State St.
Trenton, NJ 08608-1176

Degrees Offered: Bachelor of Arts; Bachelor of Science in Business Administration; Applied Science and Technology, Human Services; Nursing; Associate of Arts; Associate of Science in Natural Sciences/Math; Management; Applied Science and Technology; Public and Social Services; and Associate in Applied Science in Radiologic Technology.

Program Mission Statement/Description: Thomas A. Edison State College was established by the State of New Jersey and chartered by the New Jersey Board of Higher Education in 1972. The college was founded for the purpose of providing diverse and alternative methods of achieving a collegiate education of the highest quality for mature adults.

Accreditation: Middle States Association of Colleges and Schools; National League for Nursing.

Admission Requirements: HS/GED Diploma.

Other Admission Requirements: Open admissions (expect students to be mature, self-directed).

Credit Awards for Prior Learning: ACE Military Recommendations; ACE/PONSI Recommendations; Portfolio Assessment; Transfer Credit; Licenses and Certificates.

Credit Awards for Examinations: ACT Proficiency Exams; CLEP General Exams; CLEP Subject Exams; College Board AP Exams; DANTES Subject Tests; Departmental Exams; TECEP.

Estimated Average Completion Time: Associates' Degrees: 1-2 years part-time; Bachelors' Degrees: 3-4 years part-time.

Credit Hour Requirements: Associates' Degrees 60 total hours; Bachelors' Degrees 120 total hours.

Minimum Campus Time Required: None.

Distance Learning Options: A/V Cassettes; Cooperative Education; Correspondence Courses; Electronic Mail; Independent Study; Newspaper Courses; Phone/Mail Instruction; Study Guides; Television Courses.

Student Support Services Available: Academic Advising; Career Counseling; Counseling/Testing; Financial Aid; Orientation; Nursing Peer Study Groups; Faculty Mentors in Thomas Edison's Guided Study Courses.

Informational Materials Available: Exam Preparation Guides; Institutional Catalog; Prior Learning Guides; Program Brochure; Program Planning Handbook; Orientation Video; Program Planning Video.

Program Age, Enrollment, and Degrees Conferred:

Degree	Year Est.	Current Enrollment	Degrees Conferred
BA	1974	2013	2424
BS Business Admin.	1973	2279	988
BS AST and HS	1977	2867	1075
BS Nursing	1983	195	52
AA	1973	906	2750
AS Management	1973	1114	581
AS AST, PSS, and NSM	1985	1465	581
AAS Radiologic Tech.	1974	35	36

Percentage of Bachelor's Degree Holders Admitted to Graduate School: 51 percent.

Geographic Admission Restrictions: None.

Tuition and Fees: Application Fee $75.00; Graduation Fee $90.00; Credit-by-Exam Fee (TECEP per exam) $25.00 New Jersey resident; $35.00 nonresident.

Other Fees:

	In-State	Out-of-State
Annual Enrollment	$220.00	$365.00
Assessment Tuition	$110.00	$165.00
Credit Transfer Evaluation	varies	varies
Portfolio/Practicum	$10.00/credit	$15.00/credit
Guided Study Tuition	$40.00/credit	$60.00/credit

Other Pertinent Information: Thomas A. Edison State College has a purpose distinct from that of other institutions of higher education. Created in response to a national need to provide educational opportunities to adults, Thomas Edison helps adult learners achieve their educational goals in every state. Students are not required to travel to the college to earn a degree.

New York

234. Empire State College/State University of New York

1 Union Ave.
Saratoga Springs, NY 12866

Degrees Offered: Associate of Arts; Associate of Science; Bachelor of Arts; Bachelor of Science; Bachelor of Professional Studies; Master of Arts.

Program Mission Statement/Description: Empire State College, a comprehensive College of Arts and Sciences within the State University of New York (SUNY), offers innovative models for higher education at the associate, baccalaureate, and master's degree levels throughout the State of New York and beyond. The college's central purpose is to expand access to higher education for students, primarily adults, who choose alternatives to the fixed schedule, place, program, and structure of campus-based education. This purpose is met through a variety of approaches to teaching and learning, including guided independent studies, group studies, applications of computer and video technologies, experiential learning, and collaboration with SUNY and other organizations. Empire State College does not offer traditional majors. Undergraduate students design individual degree programs with concentrations in any one of 11 broad areas of study: (1) arts; (2) business, management, and economics; (3) community and human services; (4) cultural studies; (5) educational studies; (6) historical studies; (7) human development; (8) science, mathematics, and technology; (9) social theory, social structure, and change; (10) labor studies (available only in New York City); and (11) interdisciplinary studies. Areas of study in the Master of Arts program are business and policy studies, culture and policy studies, and labor and policy studies.

Accreditation: Middle States Association of Colleges and Schools.

Admission Requirements:

Undergraduate	Graduate
HS/GED Diploma	Undergraduate Degree
Essay/Written Work	Essay/Written Work
	Recommendations

Other Admission Requirements: The ability of the college to meet the applicant's explicit and implicit educational needs and objectives.

Credit Awards for Prior Learning: Transfer Credit; Portfolio Assessment; ACE/PONSI Recommendation; ACE Military Recommendations.

Other Options: Generic evaluations are done for selected training programs that are not PONSI-evaluated. Review process is similar to PONSI.

Limits to Credit Awards for Prior Learning: Associates' degrees: 40 credits; Baccalaureate degrees: 96 credits.

Credit Awards for Examinations: ACT Proficiency Exams; CLEP General Exams; CLEP Subject Exams; DANTES Subject Tests; College Board AP Exams; Departmental Exams; Thomas A. Edison College Examinations.

Estimated Average Completion Time: Associates' Degrees: 3 years (part-time); 1.5 years (full-time); Bachelors' Degrees: 4 years (part-time); 2 years (full-time); Graduate Degrees: 3 years (part-time); 1.5 years (full-time).

Caveats Regarding Time Estimates: The estimates for completion assume enrollment year-round (equivalent of 3 semesters per year) and that the student brings in an average amount of prior learning credit for the level of degree.

Credit Hour Requirements:

Degree	Total Hours	Academic Residency*
Associate's	64	24**
Bachelor's	128	32**
Graduate	36	24

*Hours that must be earned at the institution exclusive of credit-by-exam, portfolio assessment, etc.

**Up to half of these may be taken, with approval, in cross-registration at other colleges. Note: Up to 12 semester hours of transfer credit may be accepted for graduate degrees.

Minimum Campus Time Required: Students study independently and meet weekly or biweekly with faculty mentors.

Distance Learning Options: Television Courses; Correspondence Courses; Newspaper Courses; Electronic Mail; A/V Cassettes; Study Guides; Supervised Fieldwork; Independent Study; Phone/Mail Instruction.

Other Options: Weekend residencies combined with independent study.

Student Support Services Available: Orientation; Academic Advising; Financial Aid; Counseling/Testing; Career Counseling; Tutoring; Prior Learning Portfolio Development Workshops.

Informational Materials Available: Program Brochures; Institutional Catalog; Prior Learning Guides; Distance Learning Course Catalog.

Program Age, Enrollment, and Graduates:

Degree	Year Est.	Current Enrollment	Degrees Conferred
Associate in Arts	1971	233	890
Associate in Science	1971	2024	3794
Bachelor of Arts	1971	1239	4176
Bachelor of Science	1971	1634	10,625
Bachelor of Professional Studies	1974	272	1822
Master of Arts	1984	195	101

Percentage of Bachelor's Degree Holders Admitted to Graduate School: 50 percent.

Geographic Admission Restrictions: None.

Tuition and Fees:

	Undergraduate	Graduate
In-State Tuition	$105.00/credit	$168.00/credit
Out-of-State Tuition	$274.00/credit	$308.00/credit

Other Fees: Orientation Fee $30.00; Assessment Fee $200.00; Student Activity Fee $6.00 per term; College Fee $6.25 per term part-time, $12.50 per term full-time.

Other Pertinent Information: Students design individualized degree programs in consultation with a faculty mentor. Students study in learning contracts that are individually planned and may incorporate, as appropriate, any of the resources and methods identified above.

235. Regents College

1450 Western Ave.
Albany, NY 12203

Degrees Offered: Associate in Arts; Bachelor of Arts; Associate in Science; Bachelor of Science; Associate in Science in General Business; Associate in Science in Nursing; Associate in Science in Electronic Technology; Associate in Science in Computer Software; and Associate in Science in Nuclear Technology; Associate in Applied Science in Nursing; Bachelor of Science in General Business; Bachelor of Science in Accounting; Bachelor of Science in Finance; Bachelor of Science in Management; Bachelor of Science in Human Resources; Bachelor of Science in Marketing; Bachelor of Science in Operations Management; Bachelor of Science in Nursing; Bachelor of Science in Electronics Technology; Bachelor of Science in Computer Technology; Bachelor of Science in Computer Software; Bachelor of Science in Nuclear Technology.

Program Mission Statement/Description: Regents College affirms that what individuals know is more important than how or where they acquire the knowledge. The college exists to advance the learning of students, primarily adults who, for personal, economic, family, or other reasons, choose to pursue their education in a flexible, self-paced manner. Although remaining open to all, the college ensures academic quality through rigorous programs, student-centered advisement, and careful assessment. By offering high-quality innovative educational opportunities to those desiring an alternative to traditional institutions of higher education, the college strives to broaden individual horizons, develop intellectual autonomy and respect for inquiry, expand career interests and options, and inspire a commitment to lifelong learning.

Accreditation: Middle States Association of Colleges and Schools; National League for Nursing.

Admission Requirements: Completely open admissions.

Credit Awards for Prior Learning: ACE Military Recommendations; ACE/PONSI Recommendations; Portfolio Assessment; Transfer Credit.

Other Options: Special Assessment—this program assesses students' prior learning through direct, in-person examination (oral and/or written as determined on a case-by-case basis) by 2 faculty members in the field or discipline of learning.

Credit Awards for Examinations: ACT Proficiency Exams; CLEP General Exams; CLEP Subject Exams; College Board AP Exams; DANTES Subject Tests; Departmental Exams; GRE and Other ACE-Approved Exam Programs; Other exam programs from regionally accredited colleges and universities.

Estimated Average Completion Time: Associate degree students typically finish within a year of registering. The average length of enrollment for baccalaureate students is 2 years.

Caveats Regarding Time Estimates: Regents College provides examinations and special assessments for its students; it evaluates transfer credit from other colleges, the military, and industry training. Depending upon educational background, students may move as quickly or as slowly as meet their needs.

Credit Hour Requirements: Associates' Degrees: 60 total hours; Bachelors' Degrees: 120 total hours.

Minimum Campus Time Required: Regents College is a college without walls—no residency is required.

Distance Learning Options: Independent Study; Study Guides.

Other Options: AB-Examinations are considered to be a form of guided independent study via exam study guides. Regents College accepts credit earned from regionally accredited colleges through all of the options above.

Student Support Services Available: Academic Advising; Career Counseling; Financial Aid; Orientation (print-based).

Informational Materials Available: Exam Preparation Guides; Institutional Catalog; Program Brochure. A self-assessment manual and videotapes about some of the exams are available.

Program Age, Enrollment, and Graduates:

Degree	Year Est.	Current Enrollment	Degrees Conferred
AA	1972	153	5762
BA	1974	797	3274
AS	1974	694	12917
BS	1974	3300	14102
AS General Business	1985	113	14102
BS General Business	1976	789	1193
BS Accounting	1972	306	203
BS Finance	1972	62	50
BS Management and Human Resources	1972	121	146
BS Marketing	1972	89	61
BS Operations Management	1972	55	26
AS Nursing	1975	2407	4407
AS Science in Nursing	1973	1017	1723
BS Nursing	1976	2241	2318
AS Electronics Technology	1985	76	7
BS in Electronics Technology	1985	277	73
BS in Computer Technology	1985	64	18
AS Computer Software	1985	23	3
BS Computer Software	1985	312	109
AS Nuclear Technology	1985	112	10
BS Nuclear Technology	1985	384	94

Percentage of Bachelor's Degree Holders Admitted to Graduate School: 25 percent go directly to graduate school.

Geographic Admission Restrictions: None. 20 percent of students are from New York; 80 percent are from the rest of the United States or are international students (10 percent are international). There are students from every state.

Tuition and Fees:

	Associate	Baccalaureate
Enrollment/Initial Evaluation Fee	$425.00	$425.00
Annual Advisement and Evaluation Fee	$220.00	$220.00
Program Completion Graduation Fee	$180.00	$205.00
Late Fee	$25.00	$25.00
Program Transfer Fee	$160.00	$160.00
Transcript Fee	$7.00	$7.00
Transcript Update Fee	$80.00	$80.00
Special Assessment Fee	$750.00	$750.00

Other Pertinent Information: The college has developed a DISTANCE LEARN database for use by students (and other organizations who license it) which lists all credit bearing regionally accredited courses that are available completely at a distance with no local or resident requirement attached. The database currently has video courses but will eventually include examinations and print-based (correspondence) courses.

---

236. Skidmore College

University Without Walls
Saratoga Springs, NY 12866

Degrees Offered: Bachelor of Arts; Bachelor of Science.

Program Mission Statement/Description: Skidmore University Without Walls (SUWW), the external degree program of Skidmore College. Founded in 1971, the program provides an alternative plan for undergraduate education, while continuing many of the traditions of conventional colleges and universities. It offers a unique opportunity for those who seek a rigorous, challenging academic program without matriculating at a residential 4-year college. The chief characteristic of SUWW is flexibility—the ability to adapt learning to a student's individual goals and to help a student find and use the variety of educational opportunities available. The University Without Walls provides a campus that is truly worldwide. There is no residency requirement, and students may study for their degree in whatever settings they find themselves.

Accreditation: Middle States Association of Colleges and Schools.

Admission Requirements: Autobiographical Essay; HS/GED Diploma; Interview; Recommendations; Transcripts of Previous College Work.

Credit Awards for Prior Learning: ACE Military Recommendations; ACE/PONSI Recommendations; Assessment of Experiential Learning; Transfer Credit.

Credit Awards for Examinations: ACT Proficiency Exams; CLEP General Exams; CLEP Subject Exams; College Board AP Exams; DANTES Subject Tests.

Estimated Average Completion Time: 3 years (part-time) 2 years (full-time).

Caveats Regarding Time Estimates: There is a wide range of completion time because students enroll with varying amounts of previous learning.

Credit Hour Requirements: 120 total semester hours, including prior learning hours; 6-hour final project, academic residency (hours that must be earned at the institution exclusive of credit-by-exam, portfolio assessment, etc.).

Minimum Campus Time Required: 3 one-day campus visits for admissions interview, initial advising session, and degree plan review.

Distance Learning Options: Correspondence Courses; Independent Study; Supervised Fieldwork.

Other Options: Credit-bearing courses offered by any accredited college.

Student Support Services Available: Academic Advising; Career Planning; Financial Aid.

Informational Materials Available: Institutional Catalog; Program Brochure.

Program Age, Enrollment, and Graduates:

Degree	Year Est.	Current Enrollment	Degrees Conferred
BA/BS	1971	350	Unknown

Percentage of Bachelor's Degree Holders Admitted to Graduate School: All who applied were admitted.

Geographic Admission Restrictions: None.

Tuition and Fees: All students pay an annual enrollment fee of $1850.00; Final Project Fee $150.00; Application Fee $30.00; Credit-by-Exam Fee $50.00; Independent Study Fee $250.00.

---

237. Syracuse University

Independent Study Degree Program
301 Reid Hall
610 E. Fayette St.
Syracuse, NY 13244

Degrees Offered: Bachelor of Science in liberal studies, business administration, food systems management, criminal justice; Master of Business Administration; Master of Social Science; Master of Arts in Advertising Design, and Illustration.

Program Mission Statement/Description: Founded in 1870, Syracuse University is a private university of 17,500 students with a long-standing commitment to adult education. Nowhere is this better evidenced than in the Independent Study Degree Program (ISDP). ISDP is offered through Syracuse University's continuing education division and reflects the university's response to the demands for innovative educational techniques and programs in a constantly changing society. The content of all ISDP programs is developed and carefully monitored by the schools and colleges of Syracuse University although the specific curriculum may vary slightly.

Accreditation: Middle States Association of Colleges and Schools; American Assembly of Collegiate Schools of Business; National Association of Schools of Art and Design.

Admission Requirements:

Undergraduate	Graduate
HS/GED Diploma	Undergraduate Degree
Essay/Written Work	Essay/Written Work
Recommendations	Recommendations
Employment/Experience: 3 years	
GMAT, TOEFL for non-English speakers	

Credit Awards for Prior Learning: Portfolio Assessment; Transfer Credit.

Limits to Credit Awards for Prior Learning: 90 transfer credits from accredited institutions of which 66 can be from junior college level work; 30 credits can be awarded for advanced credit exams or portfolio assessment—these are included within the 90-credit limit.

Credit Awards for Examinations: CLEP Subject Exams; College Board AP Exams; Departmental Exams—Syracuse University only; Advanced Credit Exams.

Limits to Credit Awards for Examinations: Credit awarded for some exams (e.g., CLEP) is limited or depends upon the examination score (e.g., AP Exams).

Estimated Average Completion Time: Bachelors' Degrees: 4 years (part-time); 2.5 years (full-time); Graduate Degrees: MA 3 years (part-time); MSS 2 years (part-time); MBA 3 years (part-time); 1.5 years (full-time).

Credit Hour Requirements:

Degree	Total Hours	Academic Residency*
Bachelor's	120-124	30
Graduate (MA/MSS)	30 hours	30 hours
Graduate (MBA)	54 hours	30 hours

*Hours that must be earned at the institution exclusive of credit-by-exam, portfolio assessment, etc.

Minimum Campus Time Required: BA, BS, MBA—one week per semester residence; MA—2 weeks residence in summer and 11 contact days; MSS—2 weeks residence in summer.

Distance Learning Options: Electronic Mail; Phone/Mail Instruction.

Student Support Services Available: Academic Advising; Career Counseling; Counseling/Testing; Financial Aid; Job Placement Assistance; Tutoring.

Informational Materials Available: Exam Preparation Guides; Institutional Catalog; Program Brochure; Program Newsletters.

Program Age, Enrollment, and Graduates:

Degree	Year Est.	Current Enrollment	Degrees Conferred
BA	1966	500	400
BS Business	1972	500	400
BS Food Service Mgmt.	1988	500	400
BS Criminal Justice	1990	500	400
MA	1973	100	200
MSSC	1975	100	100
MBA	1978	400	100

Percentage of Bachelor's Degree Holders Admitted to Graduate School: Information not available.

Geographic Admission Restrictions: None.

Tuition and Fees:

	Undergraduate	Graduate
In-State Tuition	$217.00/credit	$357.00/credit
Out-of-State Tuition	$217.00/credit	$357.00/credit
Application Fee	$40.00	$40.00
Credit-by-Exam Fee	$100.00	

Ohio

238. Capital University

Adult Degree Program
2199 E. Main St.
Columbus, OH 43209

Degrees Offered: Bachelor of General Studies; Bachelor of Arts; Bachelor of Fine Arts; Bachelor of Nursing.

Program Mission Statement/Description: As an integral component, Capital University is firmly committed to providing academic integrity. The Adult Degree Program (ADP) strives to maintain and extend excellence within the liberal arts tradition by providing quality higher education to adult learners. Through integrative advising and teaching, ADP provides flexible learning environments that encourage self-directed, proactive, and interdisciplinary approaches; a commitment to the values of experiential and lifelong learning; and a fostering of the development of each student's personal enrichment and social awareness.

Accreditation: North Central Association of Colleges and Schools.

Admission Requirements: Employment/Experience; Essay/Written Work; HS/GED Diploma; Interview.

Credit Awards for Prior Learning: ACE Military Recommendations; ACE/PONSI Recommendations; Portfolio Assessment; Transfer Credit.

Credit Awards for Examinations: CLEP Subject Exams; College Board AP Exams; Departmental Exams.

Estimated Average Completion Time: 3-4 years (part-time), 1-2 years (full-time).

Credit Hour Requirements: 124 total hours; 30 hours academic residency (hours that must be earned at the institution exclusive of credit-by-exam, portfolio assessment, etc.).

Minimum Campus Time Required: None.

Distance Learning Options: A/V Cassettes; Independent Study; Study Guides.

Student Support Services Available: Academic Advising; Career Counseling; Counseling/Testing; Financial Aid; Orientation; Tutoring.

Informational Materials Available: Institutional Catalog; Prior Learning Guides; Program Brochure.

Program Age, Enrollment, and Degrees Conferred:

Degree	Year Est.	Current Enrollment	Degrees Conferred
BA	1979	885	Unknown
BSW	1979	50	Unknown
BSN	1986	160	Unknown
BAM	1990	1	Unknown

Percentage of Bachelor's Degree Holders Admitted to Graduate School: 28 percent.

Geographic Admission Restrictions: None.

Tuition and Fees: In-State Tuition $210.00 per credit; Application Fee $15.00; Credit-by-Exam Fee $40.00 per credit.

---

239. Ohio University

External Student Program
309 Tupper Hall
Athens, OH 45701

Degrees Offered: Bachelor of Specialized Studies; Associate in Arts; Associate in Science; Associate in Individualized Studies.

Program Mission Statement/Description: The Ohio University External Student Program is designed to provide educational access to individuals who traditionally may not be able to gain access because of geographical or time restraints. It is a flexible academic program within the traditional administrative structure of a public 4-year institution.

Accreditation: North Central Association of Colleges and Schools.

Admission Requirements: HS/GED Diploma.

Credit Awards for Prior Learning: ACE Military Recommendations; ACE/PONSI Recommendations; Portfolio Assessment; Transfer Credit.

Limits to Credit Awards for Prior Learning: No limits; however, at least one-quarter of the degree must be made up of Ohio University credits.

Credit Awards for Examinations: CLEP Subject Exams; Departmental Exams.

Estimated Average Completion Time: It is impossible to provide typical completion times because the program is self-paced. Students come into the program with a range of transfer credits, and their completion time varies accordingly.

Credit Hour Requirements:

Degree	Total Hours	Academic Residency*
Associate's (quarter hours)	96	30
Bachelor's (quarter hours)	192	48

*Hours that must be earned at the institution exclusive of credit-by-exam, portfolio assessment, etc.

Minimum Campus Time Required: No on-campus time is required.

Distance Learning Options: A/V Cassettes; Correspondence Courses; Study Guides; Television Courses.

Student Support Services Available: Academic Advising; Career Counseling; Counseling/Testing.

Informational Materials Available: Institutional Catalog; Program Brochure; Independent Study Bulletin.

Program Age, Enrollment, and Degrees Conferred: The external student enrollment and graduation statistics are not differentiated from the campus figures.

Percentage of Bachelor's Degree Holders Admitted to Graduate School: Information not available.

Geographic Admission Restrictions: None.

Tuition and Fees: In-State Tuition $41.00 per quarter; Out-of-State Tuition $41.00 per quarter; Credit-by-Exam Fee: $22.00.

Other Fees: Program Application Fee $100.00; Prior Learning Assessment $89.00.

Oklahoma

240. Oklahoma Baptist University

500 W. University
Shawnee, OK 74801

Degrees Offered: Associate of Arts in Christian Studies; Bachelor of Arts in Christian Studies.

Program Mission Statement/Description: Oklahoma Baptist University, in cooperation with the Office of Ministerial Services of the Baptist General Convention of Oklahoma, offers college-level training for (1) vocational or bivocational ministers who are presently serving as pastors or staff members of local churches, (2) those persons who have responded to God's calling into such ministry but have not yet had the opportunity to serve in a local church, and (3) laypersons who desire to become better-equipped servants of God in their local churches. Ministry Training Institute centers are located in various locations around the state.

Accreditation: North Central Association of Colleges and Schools.

Admission Requirements: HS/GED Diploma.

Other Admission Requirements: A student must be a minimum of 26 years old to receive the associate's degree and a minimum of 30 years old to receive the bachelor's degree.

Credit Awards for Prior Learning: ACE Military Recommendations; Transfer Credit

Other Options: A limit of 16 hours of transfer credit from correspondence schools. A limit of half of the major or area of concentration can be taken in transfer credit.

Credit Awards for Examinations: ACT Proficiency Exams; CLEP Subject Exams; College Board AP Exams; DANTES Subject Tests; Departmental Exams

Limits to Credit Awards for Examinations: 32 semester hours for the BA degree.

Estimated Average Completion Time: Associates' Degrees: 5 years (part-time), 2 years (full-time); Bachelors' Degrees: 10 years (part-time), 4 years (full-time).

Caveats Regarding Time Estimates: Virtually all of our students in the external program take fewer than 6 hours (4 hours average) per semester.

Credit Hour Requirements:

Degree	Total Hours	Academic Residency*
Associate's	64	33
Bachelor's	128	33 of last 64

*Hours that must be earned at the institution exclusive of credit-by-exam, portfolio assessment, etc.

Minimum Campus Time Required: None at the moment; planning to change and require at least one week summer residence.

Distance Learning Options: Study Guides; Supervised Fieldwork.

Student Support Services Available: Academic Advising; Financial Aid.

Informational Materials Available: Program Brochure.

Program Age, Enrollment, and Graduates:

Degree	Year Est.	Current Enrollment	Degrees Conferred
BA	1989	12	1
AA	1983	262	3

Percentage of Bachelor's Degree Holders Admitted to Graduate School: Information not available.

Geographic Admission Restrictions: None.

Tuition and Fees: In-State Tuition $30.00 per credit; Out-of-State Tuition $35.00 per credit; Graduation Fee $30.00.

241. Oklahoma City University

Competency-Based Degree Program
2501 N. Blackwelder
Oklahoma City, OK 73106

Degrees Offered: Bachelor of Science; Bachelor of Arts.

Program Mission Statement/Description: The Competency-Based Degree Program (CBDP) is an alternative method of earning college-level credits and completing a BS or BA degree. CBDP allows the student to develop an individualized program for earning credits. The CBDP allows for credit, where applicable, the use of nontraditional college-level learning experience gained since high school to fulfill degree requirements as well as traditional college courses, specific independent new learning, or advanced standing credit.

Accreditation: North Central Association of Colleges and Schools.

Admission Requirements: Employment/Experience; HS/GED Diploma; Interview; Prior Credits.

Credit Awards for Prior Learning: ACE Military Recommendations; ACE/PONSI Recommendations; Portfolio Assessment; Transfer Credit.

Limits to Credit Awards for Prior Learning: 68 credits maximum from junior college; 60 credits maximum from any noncollege source; 94 credits maximum on combination, unless approved by director; 30 hours from OCU required.

Credit Awards for Examinations: ACT Proficiency Exams; CLEP General Exams; CLEP Subject Exams; DANTES Subject Tests.

Limits to Credit Awards for Examinations: 30 maximum for standardized tests.

Estimated Average Completion Time: 2.5 years (part-time).

Credit Hour Requirements: 124 total hours.

Minimum Campus Time Required: One day workshop.

Distance Learning Options: Study Guides.

Student Support Services Available: Academic Advising; Financial Aid; Orientation.

Informational Materials Available: Institutional Catalog; Prior Learning Guides; Program Brochure.

Program Age, Enrollment, and Graduates:

Degree	Year Est.	Current Enrollment	Degrees Conferred
BS or BA	1976	250	500

Percentage of Bachelor's Degree Holders Admitted to Graduate School: Information not available.

Geographic Admission Restrictions: None.

Tuition and Fees: Application Fee $25.00; Graduation Fee: $50.00; In-State Tuition $170.00 per credit nontraditional and $70.00 per credit traditional on-campus courses. Record Maintenance/Enrollment $45.00

242. Oral Roberts University

Center for Lifelong Education
7777 S. Lewis
Tulsa, OK 74171

Degrees Offered: Bachelor of Science with majors in Business Administration; Church Ministries; Christian Care and Counseling; and Elementary Christian School Education. The Master of Arts Degree is also offered with emphasis in Christian School Curriculum Specialist; Christian School Administrator; Christian School Teacher.

Program Mission Statement/Description: The mission of the Center for Lifelong Education is to provide innovative and comprehensive educational opportunities to mature learners seeking to achieve their fullest mental, physical, and spiritual potential. Recognizing that learning is an ongoing process, the center provides special instructional programs that offer quality learning experiences regardless of the student's geographic location or physical limitations.

Accreditation: North Central Association of Colleges and Schools.

Admission Requirements:

Undergraduate	Graduate
HS/GED Diploma	Undergraduate Degree
Essay/Written Work	Essay/Written Work
Recommendations	Recommendations
	GRE

Credit Awards for Prior Learning: ACE Military Recommendations; Portfolio Assessment; Transfer Credit.

Limits to Credit Awards for Prior Learning: Up to 30 hours may be granted for college-level learning experiences.

Credit Awards for Examinations: ACT Proficiency Exams; CLEP General Exams; CLEP Subject Exams; DANTES Subject Tests; Departmental Exams.

Limits to Credits Awarded for Examinations: Up to 30 hours may be granted by examination.

Estimated Average Completion Time: BA 6-7 years (part-time); Graduate Degrees: MA 3-4 years (part-time).

Credit Hour Requirements:

Degree	Total Hours	Academic Residency*
Bachelor's	129	12
Graduate (MA)	36	18

*Hours that must be earned at the institution exclusive of credit-by-exam, portfolio assessment, etc.

Minimum Campus Time Required: Bachelor's Degree: one week summer residence for every 30 hours completed. Master's Degree: Summer modules are offered lasting 2 weeks each whereby students may earn up to 6 credit hours each summer; 3 summer modules are required to meet the 18 hour requirements.

Distance Learning Options: A/V Cassettes (bachelor only); Cooperative Education; Correspondence Courses; Independent Study; Phone/Mail Instruction; Study Guides; Supervised Fieldwork.

Student Support Services Available: Academic Advising; Career Counseling; Counseling/Testing; Financial Aid; Job Placement Assistance; Orientation; Tutoring.

Informational Materials Available: Institutional Catalog; Prior Learning Guides; Program Brochure.

Program Age, Enrollment, and Graduates:

Degree	Year Est.	Current Enrollment	Degrees Conferred
Bachelor's	1989	150	0
Master's	1988	48	4

Percentage of Bachelor's Degree Holders Admitted to Graduate School: Information not available.

Geographic Admission Restrictions: None.

Tuition and Fees:

	Undergraduate	Graduate
In-State Tuition	$105.00/credit	$105.00/credit
Out-of-State Tuition	$105.00/credit	$105.00/credit
Application Fee	$25.00	$25.00
Graduation Fee	$10.00	$10.00
Credit-by-Exam Fee	$25.00	

Other Fees: A fee of one half the regular tuition rate is charged for recording credit earned by exam.

243. The University of Oklahoma

Dept. of Advanced Programs
1700 Asp Ave.
Norman, OK 73037-0001

Degrees Offered: Master of Arts with majors in economics and communication; Master of Education with a major in educational psychology; Master of Social Work; Master of Public Administration; Master of Human Relations.

Program Mission Statement/Description: The mission of Advanced Programs is to offer programs and new approaches that meet the special needs of individuals who seek retraining or upgrading of skills or who cannot spend an entire semester in residence. Such programs encourage highly talented individuals in and out of the state. The University of Oklahoma is also committed to offering more research-based degree programs for students in the state's urban areas and in assisting the state's economic development by making available knowledge from these programs.

Accreditation: North Central Association of Colleges and Schools; American Assembly of Collegiate Schools of Business; Council on Social Work Education.

Admission Requirements: Employment/Experience; GRE required for social work, recommended for other areas; Recommendations; Undergraduate Degree.

Other Admission Requirements: Please request the Advanced Programs Bulletin for limited provisional admission (hours of letter-granted coursework).

Credit Awards for Prior Learning: ACE Military Recommendations; Transfer Credit.

Limits to Credit Awards for Prior Learning: There is a 6-year limit on transfer credit applied to the degree; no more than 25 percent of the credit hours required for the master's degree may be transferred; and no credit counted toward completion of one degree may be applied toward a second degree.

Credit Awards for Examinations: None.

Estimated Average Completion Time: 48 months (part-time); 18-24 months (full-time)

Caveats Regarding Time Estimates: Refer to the Advanced Programs Bulletin.

Credit Hour Requirements: MPA 36; MSW 60; MHR 34; MA COM 32; MA ECON 32; MEd-Ed Psy 32.

Minimum Campus Time Required: None.

Distance Learning Options: Phone/Mail Instruction; Supervised Fieldwork; Television Courses.

Student Support Services Available: Academic Advising; Career Counseling; Financial Aid; Job Placement Assistance; Orientation.

Informational Materials Available: Exam Preparation Guides; Institutional Catalog; Program Brochure.

Other Information Available: Course outlines and study guides for each course. Student packet for preparing research perspectives. Home-study use of PBS series: Against All Odds: Inside Statistics. Military-Library enrichment of specific journals and publications.

Program Age, Enrollment, and Graduates:

Degree	Year Est.	Current Enrollment	Degrees Conferred
MPA	1964	446	1286
MHR	1970	262	1092
MA Economics	1968	102	511
MA Communications	1978	87	287
MEd Ed Psychology	1978	62	265
MSW	1982	28	107

Geographic Admission Restrictions: None.

Tuition and Fees: In-State Tuition $110.00 per credit; Out-of-State Tuition $203.00 per credit; Application Fee $30.00; Cap and Gown Rental $15.00.

Oregon

244. Portland State University

Statewide MBA
P.O. Box 751
Portland, OR 97207

Degrees Offered: Master of Business Administration.

Program Mission Statement/Description: To provide the Portland State University accredited MBA degree program on videotape to residents in the greater Oregon community who are unable to earn this degree in the traditional manner.

Accreditation: Northwest Association of Schools and Colleges; American Assembly of Collegiate Schools of Business.

Admission Requirements: Undergraduate Degree; GMAT; 2.75 Undergraduate GPA.

Credit Awards for Prior Learning: Transfer Credit.

Limits to Credit Awards for Prior Learning: 26 credits maximum can be transferred in.

Credit Awards for Examinations: Departmental Exams.

Estimated Average Completion Time: 3 years (part-time).

Caveats Regarding Time Estimates: Students take 6 credits per quarter, 4 quarters per year.

Credit Hour Requirements: Graduate Degrees (MBA): 72 quarter hours; 46 quarter hours academic residency.

Minimum Campus Time Required: No physical residency is required on campus.

Distance Learning Options: A/V Cassettes.

Student Support Services Available: Academic Advising; Career Counseling; Counseling/Testing; Financial Aid; Orientation; Tutoring.

Informational Materials Available: Exam Preparation Guides; Institutional Catalog; School of Business Graduate Catalog.

Program Age, Enrollment, and Graduates:

Degree	Year Est.	Current Enrollment	Degrees Conferred
MBA	1988	65	34

Geographic Admission Restrictions: None.

Tuition and Fees: In-State Tuition $175.00 per credit; Out-of-State Tuition $175.00 per credit; Application Fee $40.00.

Other Pertinent Information: It is the only advanced degree program offered via videocassette tape in the state of Oregon.

Pennsylvania

245. The American College

270 Bryn Mawr Ave.
Bryn Mawr, PA 19010

Degrees Offered: Master of Science in Financial Services; Master of Science in Management.

Program Mission Statement/Description: The American College is dedicated to the advancement of learning and professionalism in financial services by offering lifelong education through certification, graduate degrees, and specialized learning programs; utilizing professional examination and assessment resources and technology.

Accreditation: Middle States Association of Colleges and Schools.

Admission Requirements: Undergraduate Degree; Completion of 4-course certificate program.

Credit Awards for Prior Learning: Transfer Credit.

Limits to Credit Awards for Prior Learning: 9 credits.

Credit Awards for Examinations: Graduate-level courses from other accredited colleges.

Estimated Average Completion Time: 2.5-3 years (part-time).

Caveats Regarding Time Estimates: Students typically are fully employed adults who study and have full-time jobs.

Credit Hour Requirements: 40 credit hours total; 16 credit hours academic residency (hours that must be earned at the institution exclusive of credit-by-exam, portfolio assessment, etc.), plus 24 distance courses.

Minimum Campus Time Required: 2 one-week periods.

Distance Learning Options: Independent Study; Phone/Mail Instruction; Study Guides.

Student Support Services Available: Academic Advising.

Informational Materials Available: Exam Preparation Guides; Institutional Catalog; Program Brochure; Study Guides.

Program Age, Enrollment, and Graduates:

Degree	Year Est.	Current Enrollment	Degrees Conferred
MS Financial Services	1974	894	1284
MS Management	1982	212	244

Geographic Admission Restrictions: None.

Tuition and Fees: In-State Tuition $145.00 per credit; Out-of-State Tuition $145.00 per credit; Application Fee $250.00; Graduation Fee $75.00.

Other Fees: Residency $1200 Tuition, $700 Room and Board first week. Residency $1200 Tuition, $600 Room and Board second week.

246. ICS Center for Degree Studies

925 Oak St.
Scranton, PA 18515

Degrees Offered: Associate in Specialized Business with majors in Accounting, Business Management, Management, Finance, Marketing; Associate in Specialized Technology with majors in Civil, Electrical, Mechanical Engineering Technology; Electronics Technology.

Program Mission Statement/Description: The ICS Center for Degree Studies is a nontraditional proprietary institution offering postsecondary career education in business and technology. Established to provide a learning system based on guided independent study, the center offers, for those unable or unwilling to pursue their educational goals through traditional means, an opportunity to earn an ASB or AST degree. The center shares with other institutions of higher learning the belief that credentialed education should be available to all qualified adults who seek it. Specifically, the center aims to provide specialized education designed to fulfill practical needs—career, job advancement, self-improvement—without sacrificing the ultimate goals of education: personal growth and enrichment.

Accreditation: National Home Study Council.

Admission Requirements: HS/GED Diploma.

Credit Awards for Prior Learning: ACE/PONSI Recommendations; Portfolio Assessment; Transfer Credit.

Limits to Credit Awards for Prior Learning: 50 percent must be ICS coursework.

Credit Awards for Examinations: None.

Estimated Average Completion Time: 8-10 months (part-time).

Credit Hour Requirements: Associates' Degrees: 60 total hours.

Minimum Campus Time Required: A 2-week residency for the AST degree.

Distance Learning Options: Independent Study.

Student Support Services Available: Academic Advising.

Informational Materials Available: Institutional Catalog.

Program Age, Enrollment, and Graduates:

Degree	Year Est.	Current Enrollment	Degrees Conferred
Business Management	1975	8120	770
Accounting	1975	11625	295
Mechanical Engineering	1975	1734	230
Civil Engineering	1975	1348	126
Electronics	1975	1937	62
Electrical Engineering	1975	1372	179
Marketing	1982	1993	25
Finance	1982	2188	22

Geographic Admission Restrictions: None.

Tuition and Fees: In-State Tuition: $689.00-$789.00.

---

247. Marywood College

Undergraduate Off-Campus Degree Program
2300 Adams Ave.
Scranton, PA 18509

Degrees Offered: Bachelor of Science Degree with concentrations in Accounting and Business Administration.

Program Mission Statement/Description: The Undergraduate Off-Campus Degree Program (OCDP) was introduced in 1975 in anticipation of the demographic changes affecting higher education. The minimum degree graduation requirements—126 credits—are the same as the degree on campus. Current policy specifies that students must register for 2 2-week residencies of 6 credits each to complete the requirements for graduation. The purpose of residency is to offer each student the opportunity to experience an on-campus environment that allows for student-to-student and teacher-to-student interaction.

Accreditation: Middle States Association of Colleges and Schools.

Admission Requirements: HS/GED Diploma.

Other Admission Requirements: A student must be at least 21 years of age and reside more than 25 miles from campus. A score of 500 or above in the Test of English as a Foreign Language (TOEFL) is required of all applicants whose first language is not English.

Credit Awards for Prior Learning: ACE Military Recommendations; Transfer Credit.

Limits to Credit Awards for Prior Learning: A student must earn a minimum of 60 credits from Marywood College including 30 credits in the major area regardless of the number of advanced standing credits granted.

Credit Awards for Examinations: ACT Proficiency Exams; CLEP General Exams (500+); DANTES Subject Tests.

Limits to Credit Awards for Examinations: CLEP is not appropriate with prior college attendance.

Estimated Average Completion Time: 3-4 years (full-time).

Caveats Regarding Time Estimates: Students must register for 3 courses or 9 hours each semester. The expected timeframe to complete a semester's work is 6 months' or 2 months' study time per course.

Credit Hour Requirements: 126 total hours; 12 hours academic residency (hours that must be earned at the institution exclusive of credit-by-exam, portfolio assessment, etc.).

Minimum Campus Time Required: 2 2-week residencies.

Distance Learning Options: A/V Cassettes; Correspondence Courses; Electronic Mail; Independent Study; Phone/Mail Instruction; Study Guides.

Other Options: Fax.

Student Support Services Available: Academic Advising; Career Counseling; Financial Aid; Job Placement Assistance; Orientation.

Informational Materials Available: Exam Preparation Guides; Institutional Catalog; Program Brochure.

Program Age, Enrollment, and Graduates:

Degree	Year Est.	Current Enrollment	Degrees Conferred
BS	1975	150	350

Percentage of Bachelor's Degree Holders Admitted to Graduate School: 25 percent.

Geographic Admission Restrictions: Applicants must reside outside of a 25-mile radius from the campus.

Tuition and Fees: In-State Tuition $230.00 per credit; Out-of-State Tuition $230.00 per credit; Application Fee $40.00; Graduation Fee $60.00.

Other Fees: Registration Fee $60.00.

Other Pertinent Information: Marywood College is a Military Servicemembers Opportunity College, and the OCDP is approved for VA educational benefits.

248. Northampton Community College

College-at-Home Program
3835 Green Pond Rd.
Bethlehem, PA 18017

Degrees Offered: Associate in Arts in Business Administration.

Program Mission Statement/Description: Northampton's College-at-Home Program is an individualized program of instruction designed for individuals who cannot attend regularly scheduled on-campus courses because of commuting distance, physical handicaps, work schedule, family commitments, prison, or other reasons.

Accreditation: Middle States Association of Colleges and Schools.

Admission Requirements: HS/GED Diploma; Interview.

Credit Awards for Prior Learning: Transfer Credit.

Limits to Credit Awards for Prior Learning: Maximum of 45 transfer credits.

Credit Awards for Examinations: ACT Proficiency Exams; CLEP General Exams; CLEP Subject Exams; Departmental Exams.

Limits to Credit Awards for Examinations: Maximum of 45 credits.

Estimated Average Completion Time: 3 or 4 years (part-time).

Caveats Regarding Time Estimates: Students may enroll in one course at a time, complete it as quickly as possible, and enroll in another. Students may enroll in one College-at-Home Course and one on-campus course concurrently.

Credit Hour Requirements: Associates' Degrees 60-66 total hours.

Minimum Campus Time Required: 9 of the last 15 semester hours must be completed on campus.

Distance Learning Options: Independent Study; Study Guides; Television Courses.

Student Support Services Available: Academic Advising; Career Counseling; Counseling/Testing; Financial Aid; Job Placement Assistance; Tutoring.

Informational Materials Available: Institutional Catalog; Program Brochure.

Program Age, Enrollment, and Graduates: Information not available.

Geographic Admission Restrictions: Limited to Pennsylvania residents and nearby New Jersey.

Tuition and Fees: In-District Tuition $52.00 per credit; Out-of-State Tuition $150.00 per credit; Application Fee $15.00; $101.00 per credit for Out-of-District Pennsylvania student.

249. The Pennsylvania State University

Dept. of Independent Learning
115 Mitchell Bldg.
University Park, PA 16802

Degrees Offered: Associate's Degree in Dietetic Food Systems Management; Associate's Degree in Letters, Arts, and Sciences.

Program Mission Statement/Description: The associate's degree in dietetic food systems management is designed to prepare dietetic technicians. The program aims to broaden students' knowledge in food service management and nutrition and to deepen their understanding of many other subjects. Letters, Arts, and Sciences (LAS) provides a general education for students who want an associate's degree that will broaden their understanding, interests, and skills. It is an interdisciplinary program that includes study in the traditional arts, humanities, social and behavioral sciences, natural sciences, and quantification and writing/speaking skills. The LAS program is best characterized by its flexibility. In addition to its general education component, the degree program permits academic exploration through electives. (It can serve as a stepping-stone to many bachelor's degree programs.)

Accreditation: Middle States Association of Colleges and Schools; American Dietetic Association.

Admission Requirements: HS/GED Diploma; Prior Credits

Other Admission Requirements: First-year students—SAT or ACT scores; advanced standing—9 Penn State credits with a 2.00 GPA; 18 credits from a regionally accredited college or university (no SAT or ACT scores required).

Credit Awards for Prior Learning: ACE Military Recommendations; Transfer Credit.

Limits to Credit Awards for Prior Learning: 18 of the last 30 credits for an associate's degree must be earned through Penn State.

Credit Awards for Examinations: CLEP General Exams; CLEP Subject Exams; College Board AP Exams; DANTES Subject Tests; Departmental Exams.

Estimated Average Completion Time: 4 years (part-time); 2 years (full-time).

Credit Hour Requirements: Associates' Degrees 60 hours total.

Minimum Campus Time Required: None.

Distance Learning Options: A/V Cassettes; Correspondence Courses; Supervised Fieldwork; Television Courses.

Student Support Services Available: Academic Advising; Orientation.

Informational Materials Available: Institutional Catalog; Program Brochure.

Program Age, Enrollment, and Graduates: Information not available.

Geographic Admission Restrictions: None.

Tuition and Fees: In-State Tuition $66.00 per credit; Out-of-State Tuition $66.00 per credit; Credit-by-Exam Fee $30.00; Application Fee $35.00 one-time, nonrefundable.

Rhode Island

250. Roger Williams College

School of Continuing Education
Bristol, RI 02809

Degrees Offered: Bachelor of Arts in Historic Preservation; Bachelor of Science in Administration of Justice; Business Administration; Industrial Technology; Public Administration.

Program Mission Statement/Description: The program offers courses and degree programs to students who are unable to be served by traditional educational programs. It enables students to enroll not only in classroom courses but also in a variety of nonclassroom courses and to receive credit for nontraditional learning experiences. The program is offered throughout the year, and selected programs are offered to students who are geographically removed from the main campus.

Accreditation: New England Association of Schools and Colleges, Inc.; Accreditation Board for Engineering and Technology, Inc.; Council on Social Work Education.

Admission Requirements: HS/GED Diploma; Interview. Students must enter with advanced standing based on credits already acquired from previous college attendance, military training, creditable employment/life experience, and /or CLEP or other exams. Students must also have various educational resources available to them in the event such resources need to be incorporated into their programs.

Credit Awards for Prior Learning: ACE Military Recommendations; ACE/PONSI Recommendations; Portfolio Assessment; Transfer Credit.

Limits to Credit Awards for Prior Learning: 90 credits Transfer; 60 credits Portfolio Assessment; 60 credits ACE/PONSI; 90 credits ACE Military Recommendations.

Credit Awards for Examinations: CLEP General Exams; CLEP Subject Exams; DANTES Subject Tests; Departmental Exams.

Limits to Credit Awards for Examinations: 60 credits limit.

Estimated Average Completion Time: Bachelors' Degrees: 3.5 years (part-time), 1.5 years (full-time).

Caveats Regarding Time Estimates: Above estimates are based on the level of advanced standing of the typical student who enrolls in the program. Most students enter with 60 or more credits from a variety of sources.

Credit Hour Requirements: 120 hours total; 30 hours academic residency (hours that must be earned at the institution exclusive of credit-by-exam, portfolio assessment, etc.).

Minimum Campus Time Required: No required residency; on-campus interview and program assessment session.

Distance Learning Options: A/V Cassettes; Cooperative Education; Independent Study; Phone/Mail Instruction; Study Guides; Supervised Fieldwork.

Student Support Services Available: Academic Advising; Career Counseling; Counseling/Testing; Financial Aid; Job Placement Assistance; Orientation; Tutoring.

Informational Materials Available: Institutional Catalog; Prior Learning Guides; Program Brochure.

Program Age, Enrollment, and Graduates:

Degree	Year Est.	Current Enrollment	Degrees Conferred
Associate in Arts	1974	5	36
Associate in Science	1974	70	270
Bachelor of Fine Arts	1974	4	7
Bachelor of Arts	1974	28	81
Bachelor of Science	1974	590	1335

Percentage of Bachelor's Degree Holders Admitted to Graduate School: Depending upon the major, from 25-40 percent.

Tuition and Fees: Tuition $320.00 per credit; Application Fee $35.00; Graduation Fee $35.00.

251. Salve Regina College

Graduate Extension Study
Newport, RI 02840

Degrees Offered: Master of Arts in International Relations; Human Resource Management; Liberal Studies, Master of Science in: Management; Management/Information Systems Science.

Program Mission Statement/Description: Graduate Extension Study is a highly personalized alternative to the traditional classroom approach. It involves a one-on-one relationship with instructors who guide student learning and progress through the courses via the exchange of written comments and telephone conversations. Detailed study guides, prepared by faculty members, provide a structured step-by-step approach to learning while allowing the student the utmost flexibility in organizing study time.

Accreditation: New England Association of Schools and Colleges, Inc.

Admission Requirements: GRE or MAT; Recommendations; Undergraduate Degree.

Credit Awards for Prior Learning: ACE Military Recommendations; Transfer Credit.

Limits to Credit Awards for Prior Learning: The usual number of transfer credits is 6. Graduates of U.S. Military Colleges may transfer a maximum of 21 credits toward a degree in management or international relations.

Credit Awards for Examinations: None.

Estimated Average Completion Time: A student is allowed 6 months to complete each course. This time may be increased or decreased depending on the student's circumstances.

Credit Hour Requirements: Graduate Degrees 36 total semester hours.

Minimum Campus Time Required: None at the present time although a 2-week summer residence may be required in the future.

Distance Learning Options: Correspondence Courses; Independent Study; Phone/Mail Instruction; Study Guides.

Student Support Services Available: Academic Advising; Financial Aid; Counseling.

Informational Materials Available: Exam Preparation Guides; Institutional Catalog; Program Brochure; Course Syllabi.

Program Age, Enrollment, and Graduates:

Degree	Year Est.	Current Enrollment	Degrees Conferred
MA International Relations	1985	69	42
MS Management	1985	58	32
MS Management/Info. Systems Science	1989	2	0
MA Human Resource Management	1987	10	1
MA Liberal Studies	1985	0	0

Geographic Admission Restrictions: None.

Tuition and Fees: Tuition per 3 credits $900.00; Application Fee $25.00; Graduation Fee $100.00.

South Carolina

252. University of South Carolina

College of Engineering
Off-Campus Programs
3A01 Swearingen Engineering
Columbia, SC 29208

Degrees Offered: Master of Engineering; Master of Science.

Program Mission Statement/Description: The University of South Carolina College of Engineering offers off-campus graduate coursework toward the Master of Engineering and Master of Science degrees via a combination of videotapes and live closed-circuit television lectures featuring student talk-back capability. Degree programs are available in the chemical, civil, electrical and computer, and mechanical engineering departments.

Accreditation: Southern Association of Colleges and Schools; Accreditation Board for Engineering and Technology, Inc.

Admission Requirements: GRE; Recommendations; TOEFL-students whose native language is not English; Undergraduate Degree.

Other Admission Requirements: Students must have graduated from an Accreditation Board for Engineering and Technology, Inc., accredited undergraduate engineering program to be fully admitted to an off-campus graduate degree program.

Credit Awards for Prior Learning: Transfer Credit.

Limits to Credit Awards for Prior Learning: A maximum of 12 semester hours of transfer credit are permitted.

Credit Awards for Examinations: None.

Estimated Average Completion Time: 2.5-3 years (part-time), one year (full-time).

Credit Hour Requirements: 30 hours total.

Minimum Campus Time Required: None.

Distance Learning Options: A/V Cassettes; Television Courses.

Student Support Services Available: Academic Advising.

Informational Materials Available: Institutional Catalog; Program Brochure.

Program Age, Enrollment, and Graduates:

Degree	Year Est.	Current Enrollment	Degrees Conferred
MS, ME	1969	178	401

Geographic Admission Restrictions: None.

Tuition and Fees: In-State Tuition $155.00 per credit; Out-of-State Tuition $155.00 per credit; Application Fee $25.00; Graduation Fee $25.00.

253. University of South Carolina

College of Library and Information Science
Columbia, SC 29208

Degrees Offered: Master of Library and Information Science; Specialist in Library and Information Science.

Program Mission Statement/Description: As the state's only advanced program of education in the fields of library and information services, the College of Library and Information Science has basic goals and objectives related to the needs of South Carolina and the southeastern region. Among these goals is the provision of a master's degree program that ensures that graduates are able to perform competently in the library and information profession and the provision of a specialist's degree program with competitive and selective enrollment to serve the needs of librarians and information specialists needing advanced training.

Accreditation: Southern Association of Colleges and Schools; American Library Association; National Council for the Accreditation of Teachers.

Admission Requirements: GRE, MAT; Interview; Recommendations; Undergraduate Degree; TOEFL (for international students).

Credit Awards for Prior Learning: Transfer Credit.

Limits to Credit Awards for Prior Learning: 6 hours of transfer credit allowed. Credit may not be more than 6 years old. Grade must be B or above.

Credit Awards for Examinations: None.

Estimated Average Completion Time: 2.5 years (part-time); 12 months (full-time); 6 years maximum time allowed.

Credit Hour Requirements:

Degree	Total Hours	Academic Residency*
Graduate (MLIS)	36	30
Graduate (SLIS)	30	24

*Hours that must be earned at the institution exclusive of credit-by-exam, portfolio assessment, etc.

Minimum Campus Time Required: None.

Distance Learning Options: A/V Cassettes; Independent Study; Supervised Fieldwork; Television Courses.

Other Options: Courses are taught on the university's regional campuses throughout the state.

Student Support Services Available: Academic Advising; Career Counseling; Counseling/Testing; Financial Aid; Job Placement Assistance; Orientation.

Informational Materials Available: Exam Preparation Guides; Institutional Catalog; Program Brochure.

Program Age, Enrollment, and Graduates:

Degree	Year Est.	Current Enrollment	Degrees Conferred
MLIS	1972	235	1300
SLIS	1978	3	10

Geographic Admission Restrictions: No restrictions.

Tuition and Fees: In-State Tuition $122.00 per credit; Out-of-State Tuition $122.00 per credit; Application Fee $25.00; Graduation Fee $25.00.

Texas

254. Saint Edward's University

New College
3001 S. Congress
Austin, TX 78704

Degrees Offered: Bachelor of Liberal Studies.

Program Mission Statement/Description: The goals of the the New College program are to provide a high quality undergraduate degree program designed for adults; an academic program and support services that enable them to graduate within a reasonable time; a cost-effective program for adults; an educational program that emphasizes learning outcomes; learning opportunities that emphasize the formulation and application of a personal values system, as well as an understanding of the values of others; a liberal arts education that develops critical reasoning skills; and an academic program which stresses that learning is a continuous, lifelong process.

Accreditation: Southern Association of Colleges and Schools.

Admission Requirements: Essay/Written Work (resume); HS/GED Diploma; Interview.

Credit Awards for Prior Learning: ACE Military Recommendations; ACE/PONSI Recommendations; Portfolio Assessment; Transfer Credit; Southwestern's PONSI-Style Reviews.

Limits to Credit Awards for Prior Learning: 60 hours transfer credit from 2-year school.

Credit Awards for Examinations: CLEP General Exams; CLEP Subject Exams; DANTES Subject Tests; Departmental Exams.

Estimated Average Completion Time: 2 years (part-time).

Caveats Regarding Time Estimates: Most students have about 60 hours of transfer credit. If they have less, they need more time.

Credit Hour Requirements: 120 hours total.

Minimum Campus Time Required: 30 hours earned at St. Edward's, including campus courses, individualized studies, prior learning assessment.

Distance Learning Options: A/V Cassettes; Cooperative Education; Independent Study; Phone/Mail Instruction; Study Guides; Supervised Fieldwork.

Student Support Services Available: Academic Advising; Career Counseling; Counseling/Testing; Financial Aid; Job Placement Assistance; Orientation; Tutoring.

Informational Materials Available: Institutional Catalog; Prior Learning Guides; Program Brochure.

Program Age, Enrollment, and Graduates:

Degree	Year Est.	Current Enrollment	Degrees Conferred
BLS	1974	950	900

Percentage of Bachelor's Degree Holders Admitted to Graduate School: More than 50 percent.

Geographic Admission Restrictions: Students must be able to come to campus on a regular basis (minimum of about twice per semester).

Tuition and Fees: In-State Tuition $256.00 per credit; Out-of-State Tuition $256.00 per credit; Application Fee $25.00; Graduation Fee $50.00.

---

255. Southwestern Adventist College

Adult Degree Programs
Keene, TX 76059

Degrees Offered: Bachelor of Science; Bachelor of Arts; Bachelor of Business Administration; Associate of Science.

Program Mission Statement/Description: The Adult Degree Program (ADP) is designed to give the adult student an opportunity to learn and earn a degree in a nontraditional way. Requirements parallel the on-campus program academically but is flexible in delivery. The ADP enables the motivated individual with family and/or job responsibilities to pursue higher education through independent study. Individual guidance is provided for each student in determining education goals.

Accreditation: Southern Association of Colleges and Schools.

Admission Requirements: Essay/Written Work; HS/GED Diploma; 22 years or older.

Credit Awards for Prior Learning: ACE Military Recommendations; ACE/PONSI Recommendations; Portfolio Assessment; Transfer Credit.

Limits to Credit Awards for Prior Learning: Portfolio 33 hours. Must take at least 30 hours with our institution.

Credit Awards for Examinations: CLEP General Exams; CLEP Subject Exams; DANTES Subject Tests; Departmental Exams.

Estimated Average Completion Time: Associates' Degrees: 3-5 years (part-time); 3-4 years (full-time); Bachelors' Degrees: 4-7 years (part-time); 4-5 years (full-time).

Caveats Regarding Time Estimates: Depends on level of commitment of individual.

Credit Hour Requirements:

Degree	Total Hours	Academic Residency*
Associate's	64	18
Bachelor's	128	30

*Hours that must be earned at the institution exclusive of credit-by-exam, portfolio assessment, etc.

Minimum Campus Time Required: 8 days admission seminar, 3 days each year recommended.

Distance Learning Options: A/V Cassettes; Independent Study; Phone/Mail Instruction; Study Guides (Associate and Bachelor); Supervised Fieldwork.

Student Support Services Available: Academic Advising; Career Counseling; Counseling/Testing; Financial Aid; Orientation.

Informational Materials Available: Exam Preparation Guides; Institutional Catalog; Prior Learning Guides; Program Brochure.

Program Age, Enrollment, and Graduates:

Degree	Year Est.	Current Enrollment	Degrees Conferred
Bachelor's	1978	198	78

Percentage of Bachelor's Degree Holders Admitted to Graduate School: Information not available.

Geographic Admission Restrictions: None.

Tuition and Fees: Tuition $225.00 per credit; Graduation Fee $25.00; Credit-by-Exam Fee $35.00; Recording Fee $20.00.

---

256. Southwestern Assemblies of God College

1200 Sycamore
Waxahachie, TX 75165

Degrees Offered: Bachelor of Career Arts.

Program Mission Statement/Description: This program enables students to have direct, personal contact with campus services and then to complete course requirements without attending periodic class meetings. The program objectives are (1) to provide quality learning experiences to adults regardless of their residential location; (2) to assist students in obtaining support from the various college services; and (3) to bolster students through emotional, spiritual, and academic support.

Accreditation: Southern Association of Colleges and Schools; American Association of Bible Colleges.

Admission Requirements: HS/GED Diploma; Recommendations; Approved Christian Character; 23 years of age.

Credit Awards for Prior Learning: ACE Military Recommendations; ACE/PONSI Recommendations; Portfolio Assessment; Transfer Credit.

Limits to Credit Awards for Prior Learning: Portfolio experiential learning credit is limited to 35 semester hours. All Portfolio Experiential Learning credit must be applicable to the students degree plan.

Credit Awards for Examinations: ACT Proficiency Exams; CLEP General Exams; CLEP Subject Exams; College Board AP Exams; DANTES Subject Tests; Departmental Exams.

Estimated Average Completion Time: 4 years (part-time), 2 years (full-time).

Credit Hour Requirements: 126 semester hours; 30 hours academic residency (hours that must be earned through the external program exclusive of credit-by-exam, portfolio assessment, etc.).

Minimum Campus Time Required: One-week Enrollment Seminar; 2-day Registration Seminar each semester.

Distance Learning Options: A/V Cassettes; Cooperative Education; Correspondence Courses; Independent Study; Phone/Mail Instruction; Study Guides; Supervised Fieldwork; Full Library Services by Mail.

Student Support Services Available: Academic Advising; Career Counseling; Counseling/Testing; Financial Aid; Job Placement Assistance; Orientation; Tutoring.

Informational Materials Available: Exam Preparation Guides; Institutional Catalog; Program Brochure.

Program Age, Enrollment, and Graduates:

Degree	Year Est.	Current Enrollment	Degrees Conferred
BA Career Arts	1983	208	240

Percentage of Bachelor's Degree Holders Admitted to Graduate School: Approximately 15 percent.

Geographic Admission Restrictions: None.

Tuition and Fees: Tuition $110.00 per credit; Application Fee $30.00; Graduation Fee $17.00; Credit-by-Exam Fee $50.00; Portfolio Assessment Fee $150.00.

257. Trinity University

Health Care Administration
715 Stadium Drive
San Antonio, TX 78212

Degrees Offered: Master of Science in Health Care Administration.

Program Mission Statement/Description: Trinity University's Individual Study Program in Health Administration (ISPHA) allows individuals currently employed in a health care setting to pursue work toward a Master's Degree in Health Care Administration. Each semester begins with a 2-3 day intensive on-campus session followed by 5 months of home-study and regular teleconferences. The program generally involves 4 years of part-time study. Trinity's nontraditional MS program maintains the same "as the traditional, full-time" objectives program.

Accreditation: Southern Association of Colleges and Schools; Accrediting Commission on Education for Health Services Administration.

Admission Requirements: Employment/Experience: 3 years in HCF; Essay/Written Work; GRE, GMAT; Recommendations; Undergraduate Degree.

Credit Awards for Prior Learning: Transfer Credit.

Limits to Credit Awards for Prior Learning: Maximum of 10 semester hours.

Credit Awards for Examinations: None.

Estimated Average Completion Time: 4 years (part-time).

Caveats Regarding Time Estimates: Only part-time study is permitted in the nontraditional program. Students must maintain employment in the health services field.

Credit Hour Requirements: 45 hours total; 45 hours academic residency (hours that must be earned at the instituion exclusive of credit-by-exam, portfolio, etc.).

Minimum Campus Time Required: See Program Mission Statement.

Distance Learning Options: Correspondence Courses; Independent Study.

Student Support Services Available: Academic Advising; Job Placement Assistance.

Informational Materials Available: Institutional Catalog; Program Brochure.

Program Age, Enrollment, and Degrees Conferred:

Degree	Year Est.	Current Enrollment	Degrees Conferred
MS	1978	42	176

Geographic Admission Restrictions: None.

Tuition and Fees: In-State Tuition $425.00 per credit; Out-of-State Tuition $425.00 per credit; Application Fee $25.00; Graduation Fee $50.00; Teleconferencing Fee $25.00 per course.

Vermont

258. Goddard College

Plainfield, VT 05667

Degrees Offered: Bachelor of Arts; Master of Arts; Master of Fine Arts in Writing; Master of Arts in Social Ecology; Master of Arts in Psychology and Counseling; Master of Arts in School Guidance.

Program Mission Statement/Description: The mission is to help both younger and older adults develop their abilities to learn, to think, and to act with intelligence and responsibility, in such a way that they will be increasingly effective in improving the physical, social, cultural, and spiritual condition of persons everywhere and in restoring and creating a life-enhancing environment. Students attend an 8-day residency in Vermont at the beginning of each semester. Personal academic advisors are assigned and study plans formalized at that time. The remaining 19 weeks of the semester students communicate with advisors by mail, approximately every 3 weeks.

Accreditation: New England Association of Schools and Colleges, Inc.

Admission Requirements:

Undergraduate	Graduate
HS/GED Diploma	Undergraduate Degree
Interview	Interview
Essay/Written Work	Essay/Written Work
Recommendations	Recommendations

Other Admission Requirements: Written work for MA and MFA programs include personal statement and preliminary study plan.

Credit Awards for Prior Learning: Portfolio Assessment, BA only; Transfer Credit.

Limits to Credit Awards for Prior Learning: MA/MFA students must complete final 20 semester hours at Goddard; transfer credit up to 10 semester hours for MA; no other prior learning credit. BA students must complete 2 semesters at Goddard.

Credit Awards for Examinations: CLEP General Exams.

Estimated Average Completion Time: Bachelors' Degrees: 18 months (full-time); Graduate Degrees: 24 months (full-time).

Caveats Regarding Time Estimates: Only full-time study is permitted. Two sequential semesters on leave-of-absence requires reapplication.

Credit Hour Requirements: Bachelors' Degrees 120 total hours; Graduate Degrees (MA) 30 total hours; Graduate Degrees (MFA) 45 total hours; Graduate Degrees (MA in Psychology and Counseling) 45 total hours.

Minimum Campus Time Required: One week per semester (2 semesters per year).

Distance Learning Options: Independent Study.

Student Support Services Available: Academic Advising; Career Counseling; Financial Aid; Orientation.

Informational Materials Available: Institutional Catalog; Program Brochure.

Program Age, Enrollment, and Graduates:

Degree	Year Est.	Current Enrollment	Degrees Conferred
BA	1981	128	327
MA/MFA	1981	150	477

Percentage of Bachelor's Degree Holders Admitted to Graduate School: Information not available.

Geographic Admission Restrictions: None.

Tuition and Fees: MA/MFA Comprehensive Fee $3550.00 per semester; BA Comprehensive Fee $3100.00 per semester.

259. Johnson State College

External Degree Program
Johnson, VT 05656

Degrees Offered: Bachelor of General Studies, Biology, Physical Education, Art, Math, Management Information, Health Science, Music, Performing Arts, Health Education, Education, Psychology, Anthropology/Sociology, Political Science, Hotel/Hospitality Management, Liberal Studies, Business Management, and Environmental Studies; Bachelor of Fine Arts in Music, Theater, Writing.

Program Mission Statement/Description: The External Degree Program (EDP) began admitting students at Windham College, Castleton State College, and Johnson State College in the fall of 1977. Since 1980, Johnson alone has administered the program statewide. The External Degree Program invites adult learners to complete their college degrees through convenient studies in their own communities with the flexibility to work around job and family schedules. No campus residence is required, and credits in this upper-division junior and senior program may be gained through independent study or weekend, evening, or daytime classes sponsored by Johnson State College or other colleges available to the student. Each student works in continuing consultation with a local advisor called a "mentor," who is the student's link to Johnson State College, to educational resources for learning in the community, and to other students involved in the same challenging and rewarding process.

Accreditation: New England Association of Schools and Colleges, Inc.

Admission Requirements: HS/GED Diploma Essay/Written Work Prior Credits: 60.

Credit Awards for Prior Learning: ACE Military Recommendations; ACE/PONSI Recommendations; Portfolio Assessment; Transfer Credit.

Credit Awards for Examinations: ACT Proficiency Exams; CLEP General Exams; CLEP Subject Exams; College Board AP Exams; DANTES Subject Tests.

Estimated Average Completion Time: 4 years (part-time), 2 years (full-time).

Caveats Regarding Time Estimates: Three-quarters of our students enroll for part-time study. Full-time student numbers are sometimes inflated by students doing teaching practica.

Credit Hour Requirements: 122 hours total; 30 hours academic residency (hours that must be earned at the institution exclusive of credit-by-exam, portfolio assessment, etc.).

Distance Learning Options: Correspondence Courses; Independent Study; Study Guides; Supervised Fieldwork; Television Courses.

Other Options: Weekend intensive courses.

Student Support Services Available: Academic Advising; Counseling/Testing; Financial Aid; Orientation; Tutoring.

Informational Materials Available: Institutional Catalog; Program Brochure

Program Age, Enrollment, and Degrees Conferred:

Degree	Year Est.	Current Enrollment	Degrees Conferred
EDP	1977	200	470

Percentage of Bachelor's Degree Holders Admitted to Graduate School: Information not available.

Geographic Admission Restrictions: Only Vermont students, and limited New Hampshire students, are accepted to the program. Local mentors, instructors, and tutors prohibit students from other states.

Tuition and Fees:

	Undergraduate	Graduate
In-State Tuition	$105.00/credit	$105.00/credit
Out-of-State Tuition	$142.00/credit	$142.00/credit
Application Fee	$37.00	
Graduation Fee	$50.00	

Other Fees: EDP fee $50.00-$100.00 (part-time/full-time). Individual course fees vary.

260. Vermont College of Norwich University

Adult Degree Program
The Adult Center
Montpelier, VT 05602

Degrees Offered: Bachelor of Arts in Liberal Studies; Master of Arts in Writing, Art Therapy; MFA Visual Art.

Program Mission Statement/Description: Our mission is to offer high-quality, student-centered education involving independent study and brief, intensive periods of academic residence to adults unable to attend residence and campus-based institutions.

Accreditation: New England Association of Schools and Colleges, Inc.

Admission Requirements:

Undergraduate	Graduate
HS/GED Diploma	Undergraduate Degree
Essay/Written Work	Interview
Recommendations	Essay/Written Work
	Recommendations

Credit Awards for Prior Learning: Undergraduate program only: ACE Military Recommendations; ACE/PONSI Recommendations; Portfolio Assessment; Transfer Credit. Vermont College uses the ACE guidelines to evaluate other workshops and training programs that ACE has not already evaluated.

Limits to Credit Awards for Prior Learning: 30 credits maximum for assessment of prior learning (life experience); 30 credits maximum for college-level work completed at unaccredited institutions; 75 credits maximum allowed (i.e., 3 semester minimum to get BA degree).

Credit Awards for Examinations: CLEP General Exams; CLEP Subject Exams.

Limits to Credit Awards for Examinations: CLEP credit for first-year credit only (30 credits).

Estimated Average Completion Time: Bachelors' Degrees: 2-4 years (full-time); Graduate Degrees: MA: 12-18 months (full-time).

Credit Hour Requirements:

Degree	Total Hours	Academic Residency*
Bachelor's	120	45
Graduate	30	30

*Hours that must be earned at the institution exclusive of credit-by-exam, portfolio assessment, etc.

Minimum Campus Time Required: MA: no required residency, one week summer colloquium optional. BA: Adult Degree Program (ADP) cycle—9 day residency every 6 months; ADP weekend—6 weekends per semester.

Distance Learning Options: Correspondence Courses; Electronic Mail; Independent Study.

Student Support Services Available: Academic Advising; Career Counseling; Counseling/Testing; Financial Aid; Job Placement Assistance; Orientation; Tutoring.

Informational Materials Available: Institutional Catalog; Prior Learning Guides; Program Brochure.

Program Age, Enrollment, and Graduates:

Degree	Year Est.	Current Enrollment	Degrees Conferred
BA Liberal Studies	1963	305	527
Master's	1970	220	0

Percentage of Bachelor's Degree Holders Admitted to Graduate School: Approximately 50 percent.

Geographic Admission Restrictions: None.

Tuition and Fees:

	Undergraduate	Graduate
In-State Tuition	$5670.00/sem.	$7350.00/sem.
Out-of-State Tuition	$5670.00/sem.	$7350.00/sem.
Application Fee	$25.00	$25.00

Other Fees: Life Experience Fee $250.00-$500.00 (depending on credits given).

Virginia

261. Mary Baldwin College

Adult Degree Program
Staunton, VA 24401

Degrees Offered: Bachelor of Arts.

Program Mission Statement/Description: Mary Baldwin College Adult Degree Program, believing that a liberal arts education is valuable to people of all ages, serves adults who, because of family and work responsibilities, need an alternative method of obtaining a college education.

Accreditation: Southern Association of Colleges and Schools.

Admission Requirements: Essay/Written Work; HS/GED Diploma; Interview; Prior Credits: one semester more; Recommendations; Must be 21 Years or Older.

Credit Awards for Prior Learning: ACE Military Recommendations; ACE/PONSI Recommendations; Portfolio Assessment; Transfer Credit.

Credit Awards for Examinations: ACT Proficiency Exams; CLEP General Exams; CLEP Subject Exams; DANTES Subject Tests; Departmental Exams.

Estimated Average Completion Time: Depends on amount of transfer credit—average 2.5 years.

Credit Hour Requirements: 132 hours total; 33 hours academic residency (hours that must be earned at the institution exclusive of credit-by-exam, portfolio assessment, and transfer credit.).

Minimum Campus Time Required: 2-day orientation.

Distance Learning Options: A/V Cassettes; Cooperative Education; Correspondence Courses; Independent Study; Phone/Mail Instruction; Study Guides; Supervised Fieldwork; Television Courses.

Student Support Services Available: Academic Advising; Career Counseling; Counseling/Testing; Financial Aid; Job Placement Assistance; Orientation; Tutoring.

Informational Materials Available: Institutional Catalog; Prior Learning Guides; Program Brochure; Student Handbook.

Program Age, Enrollment, and Degrees Conferred:

Degree	Year Est.	Current Enrollment	Degrees Conferred
BA	1977	540	625

Percentage of Bachelor's Degree Holders Admitted to Graduate School: 40 percent.

Geographic Admission Restrictions: None.

Tuition and Fees: Tuition $230.00 per credit; Application Fee $20.00; Graduation Fee $35.00; Credit-by-Exam Fee $200.00.

262. Regents University

Center for Extended Learning
Virginia Beach, VA 23464

Degrees Offered: Master of Business Administration; Masters of Arts in Management.

Program Mission Statement/Description: The mission of the program is to disseminate the degree programs at Regent to individuals across the nation and around the world. The unique feature of Regent's curriculum is that it integrates the best practices in each discipline with traditional Judeo-Christian ethical principles.

Accreditation: Southern Association of Colleges and Schools.

Admission Requirements: Employment/Experience; Essay/Written Work; GRE, GMAT; Interview; Recommendations; Undergraduate Degree.

Credit Awards for Prior Learning: Transfer Credit.

Limits to Credit Awards for Prior Learning: Approximately 25 percent of the program.

Credit Awards for Examinations: Departmental Exams.

Limits to Credit Awards for Examinations: Approximately 25-30 percent of the program.

Estimated Average Completion Time: 2-3 years for MA; 3-4 years for MBA.

Credit Hour Requirements:

Degree	Total Hours
MBA	84 quarter hours *
MA	48 quarter hours

*A maximum of 36 quarter hours may be waived for prior, formal academic coursework in business.

Minimum Campus Time Required: A total of 2 weeks—one week early in the program and one week late.

Distance Learning Options: A/V Cassettes; Correspondence Courses; Electronic Mail; Independent Study; Phone/Mail Instruction; Study Guides; Supervised Fieldwork.

Student Support Services Available: Academic Advising; Career Counseling; Counseling/Testing; Financial Aid; Job Placement Assistance; Orientation; Tutoring.

Informational Materials Available: Institutional Catalog; Program Brochure.

Program Age, Enrollment, and Degrees Conferred:

Degree	Year Est.	Current Enrollment	Degrees Conferred
MBA	1990	50	2
MA Management	1990	25	0

Geographic Admission Restrictions: Regents operates in states only where the complete licensure procedures is waived or provisional approval status is granted.

Tuition and Fees: In-State Tuition per quarter hour $158.00; Application Fees $30.00; Graduation Fees $45.00; Materials and Book Fee $40.00 per quarter hour.

Other Pertinent Information: Both master programs have the following tracks: entrepreneurship, ministry management, mixed.

Washington

263. City University

Distance Learning Program
16661 Northup Way
Bellevue, WA 98008

Degrees Offered: Associate of Science in Accounting; Associate of Science in Aviation; Associate of Science in Management; Associate of Science in Health Care Management; and Associate of Science in Law and Justice. Bachelor of Science in Accounting; Bachelor of Science in Aviation Management; Bachelor of Science in Business Administration; Bachelor of Science in Health Care Administration; Bachelor of Science in Individual Financial Planning; Bachelor of Science in Legal Administration; Bachelor of Science in Construction Administration; Bachelor of Science in Fire Command Administration; Bachelor of Science in Hearing Health Care; Bachelor of Science in Law Enforcement Administration; Bachelor of Science in Military Technology Management; Bachelor of Science in Nursing Administration; Bachelor of Science in Sales Management; and Bachelor of Science in Telecommunications Management. Master of Business Administration in Financial Management; Master of Business Administration in Health Care Administration; Master of Business Administration in Individual Financial Planning; Master of Business Administration in Information Systems; Master of Business Administration in Managerial and Organizational Leadership; Master of Business Administration in Marketing; Master of Business Administration in Technology/Engineering Management; and Master of Business Administration in Telecommunications Management. Master of Public Administration in Criminal Justice; Master of Public Administration in Criminal Investigations and Procedures; and Master of Public Administration in Fire Command. Combined Master of Business Administration/Master of Public Administration.

Program Mission Statement/Description: Distance Learning is a part of City University's commitment to accessibility, as expressed by its willingness to attempt to tailor instruction to the changing real-world conditions of its students' lives.

Accreditation: Northwest Association of Schools and Colleges.

Admission Requirements: Undergraduate: HS/GED Diploma; Graduate: Undergraduate Degree.

Credit Awards for Prior Learning: ACE Military Recommendations; ACE/PONSI Recommendations; Portfolio Assessment; Transfer Credit.

Limits to Credit Awards for Prior Learning: Transfer Credit—Undergraduate 135, Graduate 12; ACE/PONSI—Per recommendations up to 135; Portfolio—45; ACE Military—Per recommendations up to 135.

Credit Awards for Examinations: ACT Proficiency Exams; CLEP General Exams; CLEP Subject Exams; DANTES Subject Tests; Departmental Exams.

Limits to Credit Awards for Examinations: ACT 90; CLEP Subject 45; CLEP General 45; DANTES 90.

Estimated Average Completion Time: Information not available.

Credit Hour Requirements:

Degree	Total Hours	Academic Residency*
Bachelor's	180	45
Graduate (MBA/MPA)	46	34

*Hours that must be earned at the institution exclusive of credit-by-exam, portfolio assessment, etc.

Minimum Campus Time Required: None.

Distance Learning Options: Electronic Mail; Independent Study; Phone/Mail Instruction; Study Guides.

Student Support Services Available: Academic Advising; Financial Aid; Job Placement Assistance.

Informational Materials Available: Institutional Catalog; Prior Learning Guides; Program Brochure.

Program Age, Enrollment, and Graduates: Information not available.

Percentage of Bachelor's Degree Holders Admitted to Graduate School: Information not available.

Geographic Admission Restrictions: None.

Tuition and Fees:

	Undergraduate	Graduate
In-State Tuition	$555.00/quarter	$670.00
Out-of-State Tuition	$555.00	$670.00
Application Fee	$50.00	$50.00
Graduation Fee	$100.00	$100.00
CLEP	$37.00 per examination	
Course Challenge Fee	Full Tuition	Full Tuition

264. Washington State University

Extended Academic Programs
202 Van Doren
Pullman, WA 99164

Degrees Offered: Bachelor of Social Science.

Program Mission Statement/Description: Washington State University is a member of the National Universities Degree Consortium. See Appendix G for NUDC mission and description.

Accreditation: North Central Association of Colleges and Schools.

Admission Requirements: HS/GED Diploma; 60 Prior college credits recommended; Accumulative GPA of 2.0 in all college-level work attempted.

Credit Awards for Prior Learning: ACE Military Recommendations; ACE PONSI Recommendations; Portfolio Assessment; Transfer Credit; Approval Courses for Other NUDC Institutions.

Limits to Credit Awards for Prior Learning: To be determined.

Credit Awards for Examinations: ACT Proficiency Exams; CLEP Subject Exams; College Board AP Exams; CLEP General Exams; DANTES Subject Tests; Departmental Exams.

Limits to Credit Awards for Examinations: Up to 60 semester hours.

Estimated Average Completion Time: Varies.

Credit Hour Requirements: Bachelors' Degrees 120 total hours; Graduate Degrees 30 total hours.

Minimum Campus Time Required: None.

Distance Learning Options: A/V Cassettes; Correspondence Courses; Independent Study; Study Guides; Television Courses; Voice Mail.

Student Support Services Available: Academic Advising; Orientation; Financial Aid.

Informational Materials Available: NUDC Program Brochure; Exam Preparation Guides; Institutional Catalog; Prior Learning Guide Book; NUDC Student Handbook.

Program Age, Enrollment, and Degrees Conferred:

Degree	Year Est.	Current Enrollment	Degrees Conferred
BA Social Science	1992	250	0

Percentage of Bachelor's Degree Holders Admitted to Graduate School: Not applicable.

Geographic Admission Restrictions: None.

Tuition and Fees: $400.00 per 3-semester course; Application Fee $25.00; Graduation Fee $25.00; Credit-by-Exam Fee $127.00 In-State and $132.00 Out-of-State.

West Virginia

265. Concord College

Regents Bachelor of Arts Degree Program
College Box 4
Athens, WV 24712

Degrees Offered: Bachelor of Arts.

Program Mission Statement/Description: The Regents Bachelor of Arts Degree Program is a nontraditional program at the baccalaureate degree-granting institutions in West Virginia. The program is designed for adults who are interested in obtaining a bachelor's degree. The program will be of high academic quality, and the holder of the Regents degree will have met comparable requirements for the more conventional degree. Each student entering the program will be judged on his or her own merit and may create a unique program suited for the person's needs.

Accreditation: North Central Association of Colleges and Schools.

Admission Requirements: HS/GED Diploma. Students must have graduated from high school at least 5 years before being admitted to the program.

Credit Awards for Prior Learning: ACE Military Recommendations; ACE/PONSI Recommendations; Portfolio Assessment; Transfer Credit; Statewide RBA Established Credit Awards.

Limits to Credit Awards for Prior Learning: No limits beyond the residency requirement that 15 hours of graded experiences must be taken from a state-supported college or university.

Credit Awards for Examinations: ACT Proficiency Exams; CLEP General Exams; CLEP Subject Exams; College Board AP Exams; Departmental Exams.

Other Exam Options: Statewide RBA Established Credit Awards.

Limits to Credit Awards for Examinations: 15 hours of graded experiences must be taken from a state-supported college or university.

Estimated Average Completion Time: 7 years (part-time) 5 years (full-time).

Caveats Regarding Time Estimates: Data difficult to ascertain because most students have already accumulated academic credit prior to entering program.

Credit Hour Requirements: 128 semester hours total; 15 hours academic residency (hours that must be earned at any West Virginia state-supported institution exclusive of credit-by-exam, portfolio assessment, etc.).

Minimum Campus Time Required: None.

Distance Learning Options: Correspondence Courses; Independent Study; Newspaper Courses; Supervised Fieldwork; Television Courses.

Student Support Services Available: Academic Advising; Career Counseling; Financial Aid (if full-time); Tutoring.

Informational Materials Available: Institutional Catalog; Prior Learning Guides; Program Brochure.

Program Age, Enrollment, and Graduates:

Degree	Year Est.	Current Enrollment	Degrees Conferred
CRBA	1975	50	100

Percentage of Bachelor's Degree Holders Admitted to Graduate School: Information not available.

Geographic Admission Restrictions: None.

Tuition and Fees: In-State Tuition $59.00 per credit; Out-of-State Tuition $141.00 per credit; Graduation Fee $15.00; Credit-by-Exam Fee $50.00 per class.

Other Fees: Portfolio Evaluation Fee $100.00.

266. Davis and Elkins College

Mentor-Assisted Program
100 Sycamore St.
Elkins, WV 26241

Degrees Offered: Associate in Arts in Business Administration; Hospital Management; Nursing; English; Office Administration; Psychology and Human Services; Ski Area Management; and individually designed contract majors. Bachelor of Arts, Bachelor of Science—a few selected majors.

Program Mission Statement/Description: The Mentor-Assisted Program (MAP) provides a degree completion or additional teacher certification or individually designed contract programs for nontraditional students to complete their college degree or additional study off campus.

Accreditation: North Central Association of Colleges and Schools; National League for Nursing.

Admission Requirements: HS/GED Diploma; Interview; Prior Credits: 28 semester hours or equivalent; Recommendations.

Other Admission Requirements: Approved application; transcript of prior college work and/or qualified postsecondary education, including prior military service; screening exam for students majoring in nursing.

Credit Awards for Prior Learning: ACE Military Recommendations; ACE/PONSI Recommendations; Portfolio Assessment; Transfer Credit.

Limits to Credit Awards for Prior Learning: 35 semester hours of portfolio credit is recorded on the transcript only after 15 hours of course credit is completed at Davis and Elkins.

Credit Awards for Examinations: ACT Proficiency Exams; CLEP Subject Exams; College Board AP Exams; Departmental Exams.

Estimated Average Completion Time: Associates' Degrees: 3 years (part-time), 2 years (full-time); Bachelors' Degrees: 6 years (part-time), 5 years (full-time).

Caveats Regarding Time Estimates: Includes partial summer study if desired by student.

Credit Hour Requirements:

Degree	Total Hours	Academic Residency*
Associate's	64	28
Bachelor's	124	28

*Hours that must be earned at the institution exclusive of credit-by-exam, portfolio assessment, etc.

Minimum Campus Time Required: Associates' degrees—one week of miniresidency spread throughout course program. Bachelors' degrees—2 weeks of miniresidency spread throughout course of study.

Distance Learning Options: A/V Cassettes; Correspondence Courses; Independent Study; Phone/Mail Instruction; Study Guides; Supervised Fieldwork.

Student Support Services Available: Academic Advising; Career Counseling; Counseling/Testing; Financial Aid; Job Placement Assistance; Orientation.

Informational Materials Available: Institutional Catalog; Prior Learning Guides; Program Brochure; Successful Portfolio Samples.

Program Age, Enrollment, and Graduates:

Degree	Year Est.	Current Enrollment	Degrees Conferred
Associate's	1986	5	3
Bachelor's	1986	120	28

Percentage of Bachelor's Degree Holders Admitted to Graduate School: 25-35 percent.

Geographic Admission Restrictions: None.

Tuition and Fees: In-State Tuition $235.00; Application Fee $25.00; Graduation Fee $50.00; Credit-by-Exam Fee $30.00 per credit; Life Learning Portfolio Fee $30.00 per credit hour awarded; Deposit for Financial Aid Package $100.00 (applies to tuition upon enrollment).

Other Pertinent Information: The program provides a good deal of attention to individual goals and needs through the mentor and faculty. Admission is via the MAP office with admission granted through the campus admissions office.

---

267. Fairmont State College

Regents Bachelor of Arts Degree Program
Locast Ave.
Fairmont, WV 26554

Degrees Offered: Bachelor of Arts.

Program Mission Statement/Description: The Regents Bachelor of Arts Degree Program (RBA) is a flexible nontraditional program designed for adults in the belief that they, in their maturity and responsibilities, are distinctly different in their educational needs. The program can be tailored to fit those who need a degree for career advancement, those who have an associate's degree in a field in which there is no corresponding baccalaureate degree available, or those who seek intellectual development and personal fulfillment. The RBA has particular appeal for persons who completed some college work in past years but did not obtain a degree.

Accreditation: North Central Association of Colleges and Schools.

Admission Requirements: HS/GED Diploma; Interview; Prior Credits.

Other Admission Requirements: If transfer, student must be eligible to return to previous institution. Applicants are eligible for admission 4 years after graduation from high school. Persons with high school equivalency may be admitted 4 years after their high school class graduated. There is no fee for admission to the program. If an applicant has previous college credit, grades of F received 4 years or more before admission to the Regents program are disregarded.

Credit Awards for Prior Learning: ACE Military Recommendations; ACE/PONSI Recommendations; Portfolio Assessment; Transfer Credit.

Limits to Credit Awards for Prior Learning: Maximum allowed would be all for which eligible but more practical would be 113 to allow for residence requirement of 15, and most practical would be less than 113 because of specific, though flexible, general education requirements.

Credit Awards for Examinations: ACT Proficiency Exams; CLEP General Exams; CLEP Subject Exams; DANTES Subject Tests; Departmental Exams.

Limits to Credit Awards for Examinations: 113 or less to allow for residence requirement and other program specifications.

Estimated Average Completion Time: 3-4 years (part-time), 2 years (full-time).

Credit Hour Requirements: 128 hours total; 15 hours academic residency (hours that must be earned at the institution exclusive of credit-by-exam, portfolio assessment, etc.).

Minimum Campus Time Required: 15 semester hours.

Distance Learning Options: Correspondence Courses; Independent Study; Newspaper Courses; Study Guides; Television Courses.

Student Support Services Available: Academic Advising; Career Counseling; Counseling/Testing; Financial Aid; Job Placement Assistance; Orientation; Tutoring.

Informational Materials Available: Institutional Catalog; Prior Learning Guides; Program Brochure.

Program Age, Enrollment, and Graduates:

Degree	Year Est.	Current Enrollment	Degrees Conferred
Regents BA	1975	660	590

Percentage of Bachelor's Degree Holders Admitted to Graduate School: Estimation of 35 percent or majority of those who seek admission.

Geographic Admission Restrictions: None.

Tuition and Fees: In-State Tuition $843.00 per semester (12 hours); Out-of-State Tuition $2003.00 per semester (12 hours); Graduation Fee $20.00; Credit-by-Exam Fee $4.00 if enrolled; Portfolio Assessment Fee $100.00.

268. West Liberty State College

Regents Bachelor of Arts Degree Program
West Liberty, WV 26074

Degrees Offered: Bachelor of Arts.

Program Mission Statement/Description: The Regents Bachelor of Arts degree is a nontraditional program designed for adults interested in obtaining a bachelor's degree.

Accreditation: North Central Association of Colleges and Schools.

Admission Requirements: HS/GED Diploma; Interview.

Credit Awards for Prior Learning: ACE Military Recommendations; ACE/PONSI Recommendations; Portfolio Assessment; Transfer Credit.

Credit Awards for Examinations: ACT Proficiency Exams; CLEP General Exams; CLEP Subject Exams; College Board AP Exams; DANTES Subject Tests; Departmental Exams.

Estimated Average Completion Time: 4.5 years (part-time), 2.5 years (full-time).

Credit Hour Requirements: 128 hours total; 15 hours academic residency (hours that must be earned at the institution exclusive of credit-by-exam, portfolio assessment, etc.).

Minimum Campus Time Required: 15 semester hours.

Distance Learning Options: Independent Study; Supervised Fieldwork; Television Courses.

Student Support Services Available: Career Counseling; Financial Aid Counseling/Testing; Job Placement Assistance; Orientation; Academic Advising; Tutoring.

Informational Materials Available: Institutional Catalog; Prior Learning Guides; Program Brochure.

Program Age, Enrollment, and Graduates:

Degree	Year Est.	Current Enrollment	Degrees Conferred
Regents BA	1975	225	490

Percentage of Bachelor's Degree Holders Admitted to Graduate School: 51 percent.

Geographic Admission Restrictions: None.

Tuition and Fees: In-State Tuition $56.41 per credit; Out-of-State Tuition $133.66 per credit.

Other Fees: Portfolio Assessment $100.00.

269. West Virginia Institute of Technology

Regents Bachelor of Arts Degree Program
Montgomery, WV 25136

Degrees Offered: Bachelor of Arts.

Program Mission Statement/Description: The program is designed for adults who wish to tailor their academic courses to meet their individual needs and preferences. The program accepts credit from any accredited college, has a short residency requirement of 15 hours, accepts credit by examination, and offers credit by petition for work-and-life experience.

Accreditation: North Central Association of Colleges and Schools; Accreditation Board for Engineering and Technology, Inc.; National Council for the Accreditation of Teacher Education.

Admission Requirements: HS/GED Diploma. Students are not eligible for admission to the Regents BA program until at least 4 years after graduation from high school.

Credit Awards for Prior Learning: ACE Military Recommendations; ACE/PONSI Recommendations; Portfolio Assessment; Transfer Credit.

Credit Awards for Examinations: CLEP General Exams; CLEP Subject Exams; College Board AP Exams; DANTES Subject Tests; Departmental Exams.

Estimated Average Completion Time: 4 years (part-time), 8 years (full-time).

Caveats Regarding Time Estimates: Most Regents BA candidates are part-time students and are adults with some previous college experience.

Credit Hour Requirements: 128 hours total; 15 hours academic residency (hours that must be earned at the institution exclusive of credit-by-exam, portfolio assessment, etc.).

Minimum Campus Time Required: 15 semester hours.

Distance Learning Options: Independent Study; Supervised Fieldwork; Television Courses.

Student Support Services Available: Academic Advising; Career Counseling; Counseling/Testing; Financial Aid; Job Placement Assistance.

Informational Materials Available: Institutional Catalog; Program Brochure.

Program Age, Enrollment, and Graduates:

Degree	Year Est.	Current Enrollment	Degrees Conferred
Regents BA	1975	50	234

Percentage of Bachelor's Degree Holders Admitted to Graduate School: Approximately 25 percent.

Geographic Admission Restrictions: All Regents BA candidates need at least 15 classroom hours in a West Virginia state-supported college or university.

Tuition and Fees: In-State Tuition $892.00 per semester (12 hours); Out-of-State Tuition $2000.00 per semester (12 hours); Graduation Fee $20.00; Credit-by-Exam Fee Varies.

Other Fees: Portfolio Evaluation Fee $100.00. In-State $316.50 for 6 hours, $714.00 for 12 hours.

Other Pertinent Information: The program is especially suited for adults who have attended several colleges and not graduated or who have significant work-and-life experience involving college-level learning.

270. West Virginia University

Regents Bachelor of Arts Degree Program
206 Student Services
Morgantown, WV 26506

Degrees Offered: Bachelor of Arts.

Program Mission Statement/Description: To provide a bachelor of arts degree program for nontraditional students. West Virginia University services and requirements are designed to assist adult learners.

Accreditation: North Central Association of Colleges and Schools.

Admission Requirements: Essay/Written Work; HS/GED Diploma; Interview.

Credit Awards for Prior Learning: ACE Military Recommendations; ACE/PONSI Recommendations; Portfolio Assessment; Transfer Credit.

Credit Awards for Examinations: CLEP General Exams; CLEP Subject Exams; College Board AP Exams; DANTES Subject Tests; Departmental Exams.

Estimated Average Completion Time: 8 years (part-time); 4 years (full-time).

Credit Hour Requirements: 128 semester hours; 15 hours academic residency (hours that must be earned at the institution exclusive of credit-by-exam, portfolio assessment, etc.).

Minimum Campus Time Required: No stated limit.

Distance Learning Options: Supervised Fieldwork; Television Courses.

Student Support Services Available: Academic Advising; Career Counseling; Counseling/Testing; Financial Aid; Orientation.

Informational Materials Available: Institutional Catalog; Prior Learning Guides; Program Brochure.

Program Age, Enrollment, and Graduates:

Degree	Year Est.	Current Enrollment	Degrees Conferred
Regents BA	1975	1500	800

Percentage of Bachelor's Degree Holders Admitted to Graduate School: Information not available.

Geographic Admission Restrictions: None.

Tuition and Fees: In-State Tuition $49.00 per credit; Out-of-State Tuition $154.00 per credit; Application Fee $10.00; Graduation Fee $20.00; Credit-by-Exam Fee $40.00; Portfolio Evaluation Fee $100.00.

Wisconsin

271. University of Wisconsin—River Falls

Extended Degree Program
College of Agriculture
River Falls, WI 54022

Degrees Offered: Bachelor of Science in Agricultural Business; Bachelor of Science in Broad Area Agriculture.

Program Mission Statement/Description: The College of Agriculture currently offers 2 degrees through an off-campus Extended Degree Program designed for the self-directed adult who is unable to attend classes on a day-to-day basis. The program allows persons to design a course of study around a core set of agricultural courses; students set their own time-table for course and degree completion. This program is available to persons statewide (including Minnesota residents on a reciprocity basis) who are unable to attend college in a traditional manner.

Accreditation: North Central Association of Colleges and Schools.

Admission Requirements: HS/GED Diploma.

Other Admission Requirements: Admission and re-entry standards are consistent with the standards required on campus, i.e., high school rank, transfer GPA, etc.

Credit Awards for Prior Learning: ACE Military Recommendations; Portfolio Assessment; Transfer Credit.

Limits to Credit Awards for Prior Learning: 72 semester or 108 quarter credits accepted in transfer from 2-year college programs; 56 semester credits in portfolio assessment.

Credit Awards for Examinations: CLEP General Exams; Departmental Exams.

Limits to Credit Awards for Examinations: CLEP General Exams 14 semester credits.

Estimated Average Completion Time: Depends on student.

Credit Hour Requirements: 128 hours total; 32 hours academic residency (hours that must be earned at the institution exclusive of credit-by-exam, portfolio assessment, etc.).

Minimum Campus Time Required: Periodic visits to campus depending on course(s) selected. Visits range from a half day to one full week.

Distance Learning Options: A/V Cassettes; Independent Study; Study Guides; Internship.

Student Support Services Available: Academic Advising; Career Counseling; Counseling/Testing; Financial Aid; Job Placement Assistance; Orientation; Tutoring. Students may have to come to campus for some of the services, i.e., specialized counseling or testing.

Informational Materials Available: Institutional Catalog; Prior Learning Guides; Program Brochure.

Program Age, Enrollment, and Graduates:

Degree	Year Est.	Current Enrollment	Degrees Conferred
BS Broad Area Agriculture	1979	80	20
BS Agriculture Business	1988	20	1

Percentage of Bachelor's Degree Holders Admitted to Graduate School: Information not available.

Geographic Admission Restrictions: Program only funded for Wisconsin and Minnesota residents with reciprocity. Nonresidents of Wisconsin and Minnesota accepted on a case-by-case basis.

Tuition and Fees: Tuition for Wisconsin and Minnesota residents $63.75 per credit; Out-of-State Tuition $215.75 per credit; Application Fee $10.00; Graduation Fee $15.00; Credit-by-Exam Fee Varies; Annual Service Fee $50.00; Portfolio Assessment Fee Varies.

---

272. University of Wisconsin—Superior

Extended Degree Program
1800 Grand Ave.
Superior, WI 54880

Degrees Offered: Bachelor of Science; Bachelor of Arts.

Program Mission Statement/Description: University of Wisconsin-Superior's Extended Degree Program is a baccalaureate degree program featuring the individualized major. The major includes competencies in at least 3 academic areas of the university curriculum and allows the student to design a unique program which reflects background, prior academic experience, personal preference, and/or career goals. All of the competencies identified relate directly to the student's personal or career goals. In addition to the individualized major, university general education and other degree requirements must be met.

Accreditation: North Central Association of Colleges and Schools.

Admission Requirements: HS/GED Diploma; Prior Credits: one semester.

Credit Awards for Prior Learning: ACE Military Recommendations; ACE/PONSI Recommendations; Portfolio Assessment; Transfer Credit.

Credit Awards for Examinations: CLEP General Exams; CLEP Subject Exams; College Board AP Exams; DANTES Subject Tests; Departmental Exams.

Limits to Credit Awards for Examinations: 32 credit limit on examinations.

Estimated Average Completion Time: Bachelors' Degrees: 8 years (part-time), 4 years (full-time).

Credit Hour Requirements: 128 hours total; 32 hours academic residency (hours that must be earned at the institution exclusive of credit-by-exam, portfolio assessment, etc.).

Minimum Campus Time Required: Some courses require one day or 1-2 weekend seminars.

Distance Learning Options: A/V Cassettes; Electronic Mail; Independent Study; Phone/Mail Instruction; Study Guides; Supervised Fieldwork.

Student Support Services Available: Academic Advising; Financial Aid; Job Placement Assistance; Orientation.

Informational Materials Available: Institutional Catalog; Prior Learning Guides; Program Brochure; Audio Tape.

Program Age, Enrollment, and Graduates:

Degree	Year Est.	Current Enrollment	Degrees Conferred
BS, BA	1978	500	185

Percentage of Bachelor's Degree Holders Admitted to Graduate School: 35-40 percent.

Geographic Admission Restrictions: Wisconsin residents or Minnesota with reciprocity approval.

Tuition and Fees: In-State Tuition $64.00 per credit; Application Fee $10.00; Graduation Fee $35.00; Credit-by-Exam Fee $20.00 per exam; Annual Fee $50.00.

Appendix A
Principles of Good Practice for Alternative and External Degree Programs for Adults

Prepared by
The ACE Alliance Task Force on
the Principles of Good Practice for Alternative and External Degree Programs
Eugene Sullivan, Chair

"True partnership presupposes a contribution, freedom and initiative from both sides; otherwise there is no partnership."
Edward Schillebeeck

Background

During the past two decades, postsecondary education has increasingly recognized a growing population of students: adult learners. Many institutions have responded by developing alternative and external degree programs. These often include a variety of special features ranging from flexible scheduling, individualized majors, and prior learning assessment to instruction at the work place, instruction delivered via various technologies (distance learning), and self-directed independent study.

Programs designed for adults vary in format, methodology, intended audience, and name. Among the frequently used names are external, alternative, special, off-campus, weekend, individualized, and general studies. Some degree programs adapt course content to the characteristics of their students (e.g., executive MBA programs) whereas others focus on different modes of instructional delivery and learning opportunities. Although specific elements vary from program to program, all are centered around meeting the needs of adult students.

Whatever the format, title, or other characteristic, the central issue for these programs has been balancing quality and access within the academic context of each institution. Each program and institution has given special attention to the unique policies and practices necessary to serve adult students.

The American Council on Education (ACE) and the Alliance: An Association for Alternative Degree Programs for Adults recognized the critical need to establish principles by which programs designed for adult students could be implemented, evaluated, and improved. From 1987 to 1990, an ACE/Alliance task force, composed of faculty, administrators, and academic professionals in consultation with colleagues across the country, was created to develop a set of principles, which were then published as the *Principles of Good Practice for Alternative and External Degree Programs for Adults*. The *Principles* focus on eight areas related to quality degree programs: institutional mission, learning outcomes, assessment of learning, personnel—faculty and academic professionals, learning experiences, student services, program administration, and program evaluation.

Although the *Principles* are applicable to all degree programs, they are intended for those specifically structured to serve adults. Because of this central purpose, the *Principles* stress consideration of the special conditions, experiences, needs, and responsibilities of adult students. Included are matters such as scheduling and accessibility of courses, the work and community environments of the adult learner, and the relevance of prior learning to academic expectations.

Principles and Program Expectations

You should not expect to find yourself in the traditional role of student in either an alternative or external degree program. You should, instead, find a relationship that might well be characterized as a partnership-in-learning. The *Principles* provide a framework for developing a partnership where you are an active, inquiring, and reflective coparticipant in the learning process. Some of the key activities constituting that process include the following:

- identifying your learning goals
- developing a program to achieve those goals
- establishing the means to assess your learning
- recognizing the learning you have achieved before coming into the program
- connecting the concurrent learning you achieve in your job or other settings outside the program with your degree work.

The *Principles* provide the basis for dialogue and reflection between you and program persons on these process activities.

In contrast to the traditional student role where you have little or nothing to say about what you will be learning, you should expect to participate more actively in shaping the details of your learning. Principle 3 on learning outcomes is an example of where active participation should occur. This principle states that the student's goals should be incorporated in framing learning outcomes for both the general, comprehensive curriculum as well as for more specific, individualized learning outcomes. Although the final responsibility for determining both general and specific learning outcomes rests with the faculty and academic professionals, you need to participate in that determination.

Active student participation in the process of education enhances the student-teacher relationship. There is a growing realization on college and university campuses that students who actively participate in the learning process are better able to apply new learning in their lives; they are more likely to become lifelong learners by learning how to learn.

Using the Principles to Make a Program Decision

As you begin to explore a possible degree program, you can use the principles as a basis for inquiry and for collecting information. You might start by asking whether the program cites the *Principles*. If it does, you will need to determine the extent to which the *Principles* are actually applied in the program(s) you are considering. In making this determination, you may find the following illustrative questions helpful:

Principle 1: Mission Statement

Does the program or institution have a mission statement? If so, does it state in clear terms why the program exists? Does the statement seem appropriate to your educational goals?

Principle 2: Personnel: Faculty and Academic Professionals

Have faculty and academic professionals had experience in teaching and working with adult learners? Are they actively involved in establishing academic standards for the program and in evaluating program effectiveness? Are the criteria, standards, and expectations for part-time or adjunct faculty clearly stated?

Principle 3: Learning Outcomes

Will there be opportunities for you to participate in the determination of expected learning outcomes? Will it be possible for you to modify these outcomes or develop new ones if there are changes in your circumstances and/or academic goals? How will you be helped to connect learning outcomes and learning experiences for individual courses with the learning outcomes for your curriculum as a whole?

Principle 4: Learning Experiences

How will the learning experiences you have in the program contribute to both your short-term educational goals and to your being an effective lifelong learner? How will the learning that you already have achieved be recognized and applied to degree requirements? Will you be actively involved in designing and planning your learning experiences?

Principle 5: Assessment of Student Learning

Will you be taught to assess your own learning progress and develop new goals based on what you have accomplished? How will assessment be built into your learning experiences? What can you expect by way of feedback on your learning?

Principle 6: Student Services

Are student services designed to meet needs unique to adult learners? When you begin the program, will you be helped to assess your academic skills and to identify areas that need improvement? Will you be helped to deal with the responsibilities of being a student while dealing with other responsibilities in your life?

Principle 7: Program Administration

Will learning resources such as library materials and services be readily available to you? Do the criteria used to determine tuition and fees reflect the purposes, practices, services, and outcomes of the program? Are there standards and methods for managing and maintaining the quality of faculty, students, courses, and program design?

Principle 8: Program Evaluation

Is the program evaluated on a continuing and systematic basis? How are the results of program evaluation used to improve the program? What information on graduates of the program is available to you?

These questions are illustrative of the inquiries you may wish to make as you consider a degree program. Other questions may occur to you as you relate the *Principles* to your degree planning explorations.

The *Principles* should be viewed as benchmark ideals for any alternative or external degree program. It is unlikely any program will meet every major principle and subprinciple perfectly. However, the *Principles* can be useful to you in determining how closely the program(s) you are considering meet these ideals.

The *Principles* are not intended to be prescriptive for those institutions offering alternative and external degree programs. Rather, they are intended to foster processes that promote, sustain, and strengthen quality programs. The *Principles* provide a new means for establishing, evaluating, and maintaining quality programs.

Continuing Questions

There are two questions that you and your program need to ask throughout your academic work: How is the program doing as your partner-in-learning? How are you doing as a partner in your learning enterprise? The *Principles* provide the context for joint reflection on these two questions vital to the successful realization of your academic goals and plans. This is especially important in programs that emphasize independent, self-directed study, and various distance learning technologies.

> *Note:* I hope you will find the *Principles* helpful in selecting a program and in working toward your degree. I would appreciate learning of your experiences in using the *Principles*. Please send your comments to Eugene Sullivan, The Center for Adult Learning and Educational Credentials, American Council on Education, One Dupont Circle, Washington, DC 20036-1193. Thanks.

OVERVIEW OF THE PRINCIPLES OF GOOD PRACTICE FOR ALTERNATIVE AND EXTERNAL DEGREE PROGRAMS FOR ADULTS

Principle 1: Mission Statement

The program has a mission statement that reflects an educational philosophy, goals, purposes, and general intent and that clearly complements the institutional mission.

Principle 2: Personnel - Faculty and Academic Professionals

Faculty and academic professionals working in alternative and external degree programs share a commitment to serve adult learners and have the attitudes, knowledge, and skills required to teach, advise, counsel, and assist such students.

Principle 3: Learning Outcomes

Clearly articulated programmatic learning outcomes frame the comprehensive curriculum as well as specific learning experiences; in developing these outcomes, the program incorporates general student goals.

Principle 4: Learning Experiences

The program is designed to provide diverse learning experiences that respond to the characteristics and contexts of adult learners while meeting established academic standards.

Principle 5: Assessment of Student Learning

The assessment of a student's learning is based on the achievement of comprehensive and specific learning outcomes.

Principle 6: Student Services

The policies, procedures, and practices of the program take into account the conditions and circumstances of adult learners and promote the success of those students.

Principle 7: Program Administration

The administrative structures and the human, fiscal, and learning resources are sufficient, appropriate, and stable for accomplishing the program mission.

Principle 8: Program Evaluation

Evaluation of the program involves faculty, academic professionals, administrators, and students on a continuing, systematic basis to assure quality and standards and to stimulate program improvement.

PRINCIPLES OF GOOD PRACTICE FOR ALTERNATIVE AND EXTERNAL DEGREE PROGRAMS FOR ADULTS

Principle 1: Mission Statement

The program has a mission statement that reflects an educational philosophy, goals, purposes, and general intent and that clearly complements the institutional mission.

Rationale

A well-defined program mission statement has a guiding, vitalizing, and unifying effect on all those who develop and operate the program. In addition to describing the fundamental goals and purposes of the program, the mission statement presents a commitment to the constituencies it endeavors to serve, and it provides key parameters for evaluating the program. Although the mission statement reflects common goals and values, it allows for a diversity of viewpoints and directions within the program by which the goals may be reached and values expressed.

For a program that is a part of an institution, the mission statement establishes the internal relationship of the program to the institution's mission. Alternative and external degree programs for adults are, by their very nature, dynamic and evolving; therefore, a clear mission statement serves to ensure continuity of purpose despite programmatic and personnel changes.

Subprinciples

1.1 The program mission statement is congruent with, extends from, or is a part of the institutional mission.
1.2 The program mission statement is reflected in program planning, goal setting, decision making, and in program policies.

1.3 The program mission statement is included in the institution's catalog and program materials.
1.4 The program mission statement is reviewed periodically and revised, as necessary, to reflect changes in the program, institution, and the larger community.

Principle 2: Personnel—Faculty and Academic Professionals

Faculty and academic professionals working in alternative and external degree programs share a commitment to serve adult learners and have the attitudes, knowledge, and skills required to teach, advise, counsel, and assist such students.

Rationale

Faculty and academic professionals who work in degree programs for adult learners have common characteristics, although their titles and responsibilities may vary. Their tasks may be wide ranging, encompassing the characteristics of teacher, administrator, advisor, counselor, broker, and student personnel provider. Although certain positions will emphasize certain tasks over others, most positions will involve a general mix of roles. In terms of the overall program, the combination of these various roles, whether within an individual or among the program staff, provides an integration of attitudes and abilities central to serving adult learners.

The academic competencies of the faculty must be complemented by their understanding of adult learners and the goals and nature of the adult degree program. Likewise, part-time or adjunct faculty, who often provide special perspectives, resources, and expertise, need similar orientation and development. Meeting the needs of these part-time faculty members and integrating them into degree programs for adults are issues for the future.

In addition to fulfilling their other leadership responsibilities, all academic professionals in alternative and external degree programs serve as advocates for adult learners within their institutions. Their responsibilities include speaking for this population and increasing the institution's understanding of adult learners.

Subprinciples

2.1 In addition to academic or professional expertise, faculty and academic professionals have an understanding of adult learning and development and other characteristics and needs of adult students.
2.2 Professional development is systematically planned and implemented for all personnel involved in the

program to improve understanding of adult learners and to enhance academic and professional expertise.

2.3 Faculty and academic professionals actively participate in establishing, implementing, and evaluating the curricular and academic standards of their programs.

2.4 Criteria, rationale, and procedures for the selection and evaluation of faculty and academic professionals in the program are congruent with the standards of the institution.

2.5 Specific criteria, standards, and expectations for the role of part-time or adjunct faculty are clearly articulated.

2.6 Faculty and academic professionals in the program participate in the institution's systems for evaluation, incentive, and reward, e.g., promotion and tenure.

Principle 3: Learning Outcomes

Clearly articulated programmatic learning outcomes frame the comprehensive curriculum as well as specific learning experiences; in developing these outcomes, the program incorporates general student goals, and, in implementing them, it accommodates individual goals.

Rationale

Learning outcomes provide a focus for teaching, for what is to be learned, and for assessment of that learning; they also serve as a foundation for program evaluation. A distinction is made between programmatic learning outcomes that are comprehensive or programwide in scope and programmatic learning outcomes that are identified for a specific learning experience (course, tutorial, independent project, etc.). Faculty and academic professionals determine both types of outcomes but seek the involvement of students in that determination. Some specific learning experiences may involve students in the identification of their own individual outcomes for those experiences.

Adult learners enroll in degree programs for various reasons often with specific personal or career goals in mind. It is both reassuring and motivating to them if programmatic outcomes clearly relate to their individual goals. The interrelationships among comprehensive outcomes, specific outcomes of learning experiences, and students' goals reinforce the learning process. The direct participation of the students in the identification of specific outcomes for a learning experience further supports their achievement and recognition of academic progress.

As part of the comprehensive outcomes, programs have a responsibility to assist students in the acquisition of the depth and breadth of knowledge requisite for their specific degrees. They are also responsible for aiding students in the development of skills and abilities in critical thinking, communication, problem solving, learning resource utilization, and analysis and integration of knowledge. The development of these skills and abilities encourages students to become more autonomous, self-directed lifelong learners.

Subprinciples

3.1 The faculty and other academic professionals determine the program's learning outcomes to form a coherent curriculum.

3.2 Learning outcomes reflect the core values and standards of the program and institution and the general learning goals of their students.

3.3 The achievement of learning outcomes for the specific learning experiences can be demonstrated and assessed.

3.4 Programmatic learning outcomes are described so that students can relate the specific learning outcomes of each learning experience to the comprehensive outcomes of the program.

3.5 Learning outcomes for specific experiences are framed in consultation with students.

3.6 Learning outcomes provide a context for faculty/student discussions of academic progress and help guide student program implementation and modification.

3.7 Learning outcomes are clearly described so that external audiences (graduate schools, employers, etc.) understand both comprehensive and specific programmatic outcomes.

3.8 Programmatic learning outcomes are periodically revised to reflect changes in the program, institution, student population, and larger community.

Principle 4: Learning Experiences

The program is designed to provide diverse learning experiences that respond to the characteristics and contexts of adult learners while meeting established academic standards.

Rationale

Learning experiences in adult degree programs recognize the social environments, experiences, backgrounds, motivations, and learning styles of adult students. Program designs might employ a variety of methods: didactic presentation, small group discussion, interactive sessions, internships, or independent study. The experiences take into account the increasing use of technology to achieve learning goals. In addition to the mastery of academic subject matter, learning experiences should be designed to facilitate and enhance the learning skills, capabilities, and strengths of the learner.

American society abounds in resources for learning. Public and private colleges, universities, and proprietary institutions exercise the central, but not exclusive, responsibility for providing postsecondary education. Associations, businesses, government, industry, military, labor, and other groups offer formal instruction, much of it at the postsecondary level. In addition, independent study and reading, career and voluntary work, the mass media, community involvement, and social interaction contribute to each individual's learning.

Given that college-level learning occurs in many places and at many times, college and university faculty have a responsibility to assess and accommodate extrainstitutional as well as institutional learning as part of their credentialing function. Through reliable and valid assessment of extrainstitutional learning, new learning is encouraged, past learning is renewed, and theory becomes integrated with practice. Faculty involved in degree programs for adults have the special responsibility of determining with the individual how this learning contributes to the goal of becoming an effective lifelong learner.

Subprinciples

4.1 Specific learning experiences are determined by faculty and academic professionals in consultation with students to facilitate the achievement of learning outcomes, to use and extend the strengths of the individual's learning style, and to develop the student's social and work environment as a learning resource.

4.2 Learning experiences equip learners to develop progressively those habits, skills, and values necessary for lifelong learning.

4.3 Learning experiences make use of current research and theory about how adults learn.

4.4 Learning experiences are offered in a variety of ways, settings, and time frames to accommodate individual learning styles and life situations.

4.5 Learning experiences are designed to provide feedback to learners regarding their progress in achieving the specific learning outcomes.

4.6 Program design and specific learning experiences recognize an individual's prior and current extrainstitutional postsecondary learning.

4.7 Learners are assisted in examining the relationship of prior and current institutional and extrainstitutional learning to their learning abilities, learning outcomes, and overall degree goals.

Principle 5: Assessment of Student Learning

The assessment of a student's learning is based on the achievement of comprehensive and specific learning outcomes.

Rationale

The progress of students and their achievement of outcomes require assessment that has direct, personal links to the teaching-learning process. Because the assessment of learning is complex, programs use multiple methods of assessment including written and oral examinations, case study methods, interviews, portfolio and project review, and other means to determine that learning goals are achieved. Forms of assessment selected are appropriate for the particular learning experience and assist students in their learning.

Just as the learner's involvement in identifying learning experiences and learning outcomes is essential, so too is the learner's involvement in the assessment process. Assessment grows from a partnership of faculty or academic professional and student that is committed to a process of helpful dialogue and feedback. Student participation in assessment contributes significantly to the goal of developing more self-managing, autonomous learners. Without the capacity for assessing one's own learning, the accomplishment of this goal is unlikely to be realized.

In addition to serving the individual student, assessment of students' progress provides essential information regarding the teaching and learning processes of the program. Individual student assessment is an integral part of the general program assessment and evaluation plan and contributes to the accountability of the program and the institution.

Subprinciples

5.1 Assessment is designed to be an integral and active part of each learning experience.

5.2 Student learning is evidenced by what the student knows and can do through demonstrations of knowledge and skill.

5.3 The assessment criteria, methods, techniques, or strategies are developed by faculty and academic professionals on the basis of how effectively they might determine the extent to which the specific learning outcomes are achieved.

5.4 The assessment process for student learning provides ongoing feedback between teacher and learner regarding the acquisition of both knowledge and skills.

5.5 The development of student self-assessment skills is an integral part of the learning process and is critical to the growth of self-managing, autonomous learning.

5.6 The program has policies and procedures for assessing and recognizing extrainstitutional learning, as well as learning that takes place at accredited postsecondary institutions.

5.7 Program policy for recognizing prior or current extrainstitutional learning specifies standards or criteria, administrative and faculty responsibility, means of assessment, recording of results on transcripts, and the maximum number of credits or other forms of recognition allowable.

Principle 6: Student Services

The policies, procedures, and practices of the program take into account the conditions and circumstances of adult learners and promote the success of those students.

Rationale

Student success in alternative and external degree programs for adults is enhanced not only by the academic quality of the program but also by well-designed and appropriately delivered services that recognize the particular needs and circumstances of adult learners. Student services policies and practices support student academic and personal success in the form of student achievement and student development. Student achievement is identified as learning at the highest possible level consistent with program standards, one's interests and abilities, and the personal constraints experienced in making progress toward one's goals. Student achievement is demonstrated by such evidence as course completion, satisfaction with goal attainment, improved learning or self-management skills, and degree completion. Student development fosters personal characteristics such as self-esteem, self-directedness, autonomy, and the ability to formulate clear goals.

Adult and external degree programs are essentially student centered. Their student services enable learners to succeed from admission to graduation by recognizing, responding to, and honoring student diversity in preparedness, ethnicity, work and family commitments, goals, age, race, gender, and other characteristics.

Initial services focus on successful entry to the college, including useful program materials that inform students about educational options and procedures and an admissions process that is responsive to adult learners. Subsequently, transition into the education realm is eased and focused by providing meaningful orientation services and assessment of academic and learning skills. Support services to promote student success while pursuing degree work include financial aid, counseling, advising, life/career planning, placement, child care, and academic tutoring. These services, which need to be accessible to adults, are directed at focusing student goals and options and overcoming obstacles to goal achievement.

Subprinciples

6.1 Promotional materials present a clear, comprehensive, and accurate description of the educational program and the services offered, including information concerning admission requirements, degree(s) awarded, curriculum, costs, learning formats, assessment methods, graduation requirements, policies regarding the recognition of extrainstitutional learning, and accreditation.

6.2 Admission and retention policies take into account qualitative as well as quantitative data that reflect the student's current motivation and ability.

6.3 Financial arrangements and student financial assistance policies and procedures for adult students are equitable with those for other students at the institution.

6.4 Program entry services help students assess and understand their academic and learning skills as a basis for undertaking the program; students are assisted to strengthen these skills.

6.5 Orientation services are provided to help students understand themselves as learners and their new learning environment.

6.6 Academic progress of students is monitored, and intervention strategies geared to adult learners are developed to improve student success.

6.7 A program plan is developed for student achievement and retention; follow-up research is conducted to ascertain reasons for problems and success of students and graduates.

6.8 Students in the program are included in the various institutional policies and practices with regard to awards, recognition, and honors.

6.9 Student support services of the institution are available, accessible, and appropriate for the adult learner; such services are designed to assist the student from admission through graduation.

Principle 7: Program Administration

Rationale

The administrative structures and the human, fiscal, and learning resources are sufficient, appropriate, and stable for accomplishing the program mission.

Rationale

Central to the success of degree programs serving adults is the institutional commitment to the program. This commitment is reflected in the fundamental administrative structure, the financial and budgetary arrangements, the academic systems, and other resource arrangements that support the program. The administrative structure of the program has equitable status with other academic units within its institution. At the same time, just as the program as a whole needs to be dynamic, open, innovative, and responsive, its administration also must possess these characteristics.

The administrative structure of adult degree programs varies; it may involve a program within a college or university; a separate college, school, or division within a larger institution; or a freestanding institution. Regardless of structure, administrators provide leadership in designing and implementing policies and procedures to serve adult learners in the program, while remaining consistent with the general policies, procedures, and standards of the institution.

Financial and other resources need to be sufficient to achieve the goals of the program. Particular attention is given to ensuring that proper library, media, laboratory, and computer support is available to students and faculty. The program's academic systems must also provide recognized, acceptable, and equitable strategies for a broad range of issues, including hiring, training, and evaluating faculty; developing and evaluating curricula; admitting students and assessing their learning; and evaluating overall program success.

Subprinciples

7.1 Administrators provide leadership to assure that program operation grows out of an integration of administrative, academic, and student support commitments to the adult learner.

7.2 Criteria, standards, and expectations are clearly articulated for the roles of faculty and academic professionals in the program; specific requirements are delineated for part-time faculty.

7.3 Faculty and academic professionals participate in the development, review, and revision of program policies, procedures, and practices.

7.4 Funding and fiscal policies of a program are consistent with its own mission and with the general fiscal directions, purposes, and goals of the institution as a whole.

7.5 Adequate learning resources, including but not limited to computer support, laboratories, and library materials and services are available to students, faculty, and academic professionals.

7.6 Academic systems provide clearly stated standards and methods for managing and maintaining the quality of faculty, students, curricula, and program design.

7.7 Administrative arrangements are reviewed periodically to determine the extent to which they support program and institutional goals, purposes, and values.

7.8 The administrative structure and governance system provide ongoing planning and analysis of program directions and practices.

7.9 Criteria used to determine tuition and fees reflect the purposes, practices, services, and outcomes of the program.

Principle 8: Program Evaluation

Evaluation of the program involves faculty, academic professionals, administrators, and students on a continuing, systematic basis to assure standards and quality and to stimulate program improvement.

Rationale

Continuous evaluation of a program and its components is vital to the maintenance of quality, the assurance of accountability, and the development and improvement of the program. The program administrator provides leadership for evaluation with the involvement of faculty, academic professionals, students, and others who contribute to the process.

The participation of faculty and academic professionals from other academic units provides valuable perspectives for the review of degree programs for adults. Likewise, the viewpoints of professionals from the nonacademic community and from other educational programs for adults are beneficial to the evaluative process.

Program evaluation results, shared widely, inform all those involved in the program and guide them in determining future program direction. The results also become a part of an external review process by being linked directly or indirectly to the institutional accreditation procedure.

Subprinciples

8.1 In the context of the program and institutional missions, program evaluation focuses on both the attainment of goals and objectives and the processes designed to attain them.

8.2 Program evaluation provides for the inclusion of information from various constituencies, including faculty, academic professionals, administrators, students, graduates, and other appropriate groups.

8.3 Program evaluation processes encourage the participation of professionals from outside the program or the institution.

8.4 Results of program evaluation are reported to the institution's chief administrator and to administrators, faculty, students, and others involved in the program; the results are used to modify and improve the program as well as to provide the basis for planning.

8.5 Both the processes and the results of program evaluation are incorporated in institutional accreditation review.

Appendix B
ACRL Guidelines for
Extended Campus Library Services

Prepared by
The Task Force to Review the Guidelines
for Extended Campus Library Services
Mary Joyce Pickett, Chair

ASSOCIATION OF
COLLEGE & RESEARCH
LIBRARIES

Approved by the ALA Standards Committee at the 1990 Annual Conference

This revision of the "Guidelines for Extended Campus Library Services" was prepared by a task force appointed prior to the ALA Midwinter Meeting in 1988. The members were Lynn LaBrake, University of Central Florida; Barton Lessin, Wayne State University; Colleen Power, California State University, Chico; Julie Todaro, Austin Community College, Rio Grande Campus; and Mary Joyce Pickett, Illinois Institute of Technology (chair). In establishing the need for revision, the task force examined the professional literature, testimony from hearings on the existing guidelines held at the July 1988 ALA Annual Conference and at the October 1988 Off-Campus Library Services Conference, input from previous users and the Extended Campus Library Service Discussion Group, and information received from regional and professional accrediting agencies. The proposed draft revision was published in the May 1989 *C&RL News*, and hearings were held at the June 1989 ALA Annual Conference. This draft was revised in response to hearing testimony

Introduction

Library resources and services in institutions of higher education must meet the needs of main campuses, off-campus or extended campus programs, courses taken for credit or noncredit, continuing education programs, courses attended in person or by means of electronic transmission, or other means of distance education. The 1981 Guidelines for Extended Campus Library Services, designed to assist in the organization and provision of these resources and services, were scheduled for ACRL review. The task force determined that a revision was necessary based on the following factors: nontraditional study becoming a more commonplace element in higher education; an increase in diversity of educational opportunities; an increase in the number of unique environments where educational opportunities are offered; an increased recognition of the need for library resources and services at locations other than main campuses; an increased concern and demand for equitable services for all students in higher education, no matter where the classroom may be; a greater demand for library resources and services by faculty and staff at extended campus sites; and an increase in technological innovations in the transmittal of information and delivery of courses.

These revised guidelines are designed to outline direction, support a process, stress overall coordination, and support the educational objectives of the extended campus program. The audience for the "Guidelines" includes library staff planning for and managing these extended campus services, other library staff working with extended campus library staff, faculty, administrators at all levels within the educational institution, and sponsors of academic programs as well as accrediting and licensure agencies.

Definitions

"Extended campus community" covers all those individuals and agencies that are directly involved with academic programs offered away from the traditional academic campus including students, faculty, researchers administrators, and sponsors.

"Extended campus library services" refers to those services offered in support of academic courses and programs offered away from the main campus of the institution responsible for the academic program. These courses may be taught in traditional or nontraditional ways. This definition also includes services to individuals who are involved off campus regardless of where credit is given. The definition does not include nontraditional students pursuing on-campus academic programs.

"Parent institution" refers to the institutional entity responsible for the offering of academic courses and programs off campus.

"Library" denotes the academic library directly associated with the parent institution offering the off-campus program unless otherwise noted.

Philosophy

This document assumes the following statements:
The parent institution is responsible for providing support that addresses the information needs of its extended campus programs. This support should provide library service to the extended campus community equitable with that provided to the on-campus community.

The library has primary responsibility for identifying, developing, coordinating, and providing library resources and services that address the information needs of the extended campus community.

Effective and appropriate services for extended campus communities may differ from those services offered on campus. The requirements of academic programs should guide the library's responses to defined needs.

Where resources and services of unaffiliated local libraries are to be used to support information needs of the extended campus community, the library, or, where appropriate, the parent institution is responsible for the development of written agreements with those local libraries.

The extended campus library program shall have goals and objectives that support the provision of resources and services consistent with the broader institutional mission.

Management

It is the responsibility of library management to identify, plan, and oversee library services and resources in support of extended campus programs. The library administration should

1. assess the needs of its extended campus community for library resources, services, and facilities;
2. prepare a written profile of the extended community's information needs;
3. develop a written statement of immediate and long-range goals and objectives which address the needs and outline the methods by which progress can be measured;
4. involve academic community representatives, including the extended campus faculty and students, in the formation of the objectives and the regular evaluation of their achievement;
5. assess the existing library support, and its availability and appropriateness;
6. participate with administrators and teaching faculty in the curriculum development process and in course planning to ensure appropriate library resources and services are available;
7. promote library support services to the extended campus community.

Additional areas of management responsibility are covered in the sections on Finances, Personnel, Facilities, Resources, and Services.

Finances

The parent institution should provide continuing financial support for addressing the library needs of the extended campus community. This financing should be

1. related to the formally defined needs and demands of the extended campus program;
2. allocated on a schedule matching the parent institution's budgeting cycle;
3. identified within the parent institution's budget and expenditure reporting statements;
4. accommodated to arrangements involving external agencies, including affiliated, but independently supported, libraries.

Personnel

Personnel involved in the management and coordination of extended campus library services may include campus and library administration, the librarian managing the services, additional professional staff in the institution, and support staff from a variety of departments.

The library should provide professional and support personnel sufficient in number and of the quality necessary to attain the goals and objectives of the extended campus program including:

1. a librarian to plan, implement, coordinate, and evaluate library resources and services addressing the information needs of the extended campus community;
2. persons with the capacity and skills to identify informational needs and respond to them flexibly and creatively;
3. classification, status, and salary scales for extended campus library staff that are equivalent to those provided for other library employees.

Facilities

The library should provide facilities, equipment, and communication links sufficient in size, number, and scope to attain the objectives of the extended campus programs. Arrangements may vary and should be appropriate to programs offered.

Examples of suitable arrangements include but are not limited to the following:

1. access to facilities through agreements with a nonaffiliated library;
2. designated space for consultations, ready reference collections, reserve collections, electronic transmission of information, computerized data base searching and interlibrary loan services;
3. a branch or satellite library.

Resources

Access to library materials in sufficient number, scope, and formats should be provided to

1. support the students' needs in fulfilling course assignments (e.g., required and supplemental reading and research papers) and enrich the academic programs;
2. support teaching and research needs;
3. accommodate other informational needs of the extended campus community as appropriate.

Programs granting associate degrees should provide access to collections that meet the "Association of College and Research Libraries (ACRL) Standards for Community, Junior and Technical College Learning Resources Programs." Programs granting baccalaureate or master's degrees should provide access to collections that meet the standards defined by the "ACRL Standards for College Libraries." Programs offering doctorate degrees should provide access to collections that meet the standards defined by the "ACRL Standards for University Libraries."

Services

The library services offered the extended campus community should be designed to meet effectively a wide range of informational and bibliographic needs. Examples that may help meet these needs include the following:

1. reference assistance;
2. computer-based bibliographic and informational services;
3. consultation services;
4. a program of library user instruction designed specifically to meet the needs of the extended campus community;
5. assistance with nonprint media and equipment;
6. reciprocal borrowing, contractual borrowing, and interlibrary loan services;
7. prompt document delivery such as a courier system or electronic transmission;
8. access to reserve materials;
9. promotion of library services to the extended campus community.

Appendix C
Awarding Credit for Extrainstitutional[1] Learning

The following statement by the ACE Commission on Educational Credit and Credentials has been approved by the ACE Board of Directors and endorsed by the Council on Postsecondary Accreditation.

The American Council on Education recommends that postsecondary education institutions develop policies and procedures for measuring and awarding credit for learning attained outside their sponsorship.

American society abounds in resources for learning at the postsecondary level. Public, private, and proprietary education institutions exercise the central, but not exclusive, responsibility for instruction and learning. Association, business, government, industry, the military, and unions sponsor formal instruction. In addition, independent study and reading, work experiences, the mass media, and social interaction contribute to learning and competency.

Full and effective use of all educational resources is a worthy education and social goal. Achieving this goal will depend to a large extent on providing equitable recognition for extrainstitutional learning:

- Educational credentials have a significant bearing on the economic, professional, and social status of the individual. This social equity requires that equivalent learning, regardless of where and how it is achieved, be incorporated into the system of rewards for learning and competency.

- Recognition encourages learning and contributes to pedagogical effectiveness. Teaching students what they already know is both stultifying to them and wasteful of educational and personal resources.

Postsecondary education institutions legally authorized and accredited to award degrees and other educational credentials have a special responsibility to assess extrainstitutional learning as part of their credentialing function.

In the development of institutional policies and procedures, the American Council on Education recommends the following guidelines and resources.

Guidelines

1. Reliable and valid evaluation of student achievement is the sine qua non in awarding credit. Experience—whether acquired at work, in social settings, in the library, at home, or in the formal classroom—is in itself an inadequate basis for awarding credit. Increased attention in choosing evaluation procedures and techniques and more thorough evaluation are necessary when learning has been attained without participation in a program of study prescribed by an educational institution and offered by its faculty.

2. In determining whether it is appropriate to accept a student's extrainstitutional learning to the institution's mission, curricula, and standards for student achievement. Learning should be articulated, documented, and measured in these terms.

3. Institutions should evaluate extrainstitutional learning only in subject-matter fields in which they have or can arrange for faculty expertise or where they can rely on nationally validated examinations or other procedures for establishing credit equivalencies. Institutions should award credit in these areas only if the quality of learning meets their standards for student achievement. Normally, institutions should

---

[1] Extrainstitutional learning is defined as learning that is attained outside the sponsorship of legally authorized and accredited postsecondary educational institutions. The term applies to learning acquired from work and life experiences, independent reading and study, the mass media, and participation in formal courses sponsored by associations, business, government, industry, the military, and unions.

evaluate learning and award credit only in subject fields in which they offer courses or curricula. However, if the acquisitions of college-level learning outcomes has been demonstrated in an area not taught by the institution but related to the student's program of study, an exception may and ought to be made.

4. Institutions awarding credit for extrainstitutional learning should develop clearly stated policies regarding administrative responsibility, student eligibility, means of assessment, recording of results on transcripts, storage of documentation, student fees, and maximum number of credits allowable. Information on these and related institutional policies and procedures should be disseminated to students and faculty for maximum awareness and utilization.

5. Institutional policy should include provision that the institution's policies and procedures for awarding credit for extrainstitutional learning should be subject to periodic reevaluation.

Appendix D
Supplemental References

CAEL Publications

The Council for Adult and Experiential Learning (CAEL) is an independent, nonprofit international association of colleges and universities, corporations, unions, government agencies, organizations, and individuals. Its mission is to expand lifelong learning opportunities for adults and to advance experiential learning and its assessment.

The books listed below may be ordered, prepaid by check, VISA, or Master Card from CAEL Publications, 223 West Jackson Boulevard, Suite 510, Chicago, IL 60606. Telephone: (312) 922-5909. Please include $5.00 shipping and handling for the first book and $1.25 for each book thereafter.

Assessing Learning: Standards, Principles and Procedures, by Urban Whitaker, 1989, Softcover, 122 pages, $15.95.

> In this definitive guide to evaluating learning, Mr. Whitaker outlines the principles of good practice and standards of excellence in the assessment of learning, no matter where that learning has taken place.
> The book includes chapters on the following: definitions, propositions, and assumptions about traditional and experiential learning; teacher-, self-, and undirected learning and the assessment process and rules for assessing learning; standards for assessing learning; principles and procedures for assessing prior experiential learning; administrative measures to safeguard quality assurance; misconceptions; and malpractice.

Earn College Credit for What You Know (Second Edition), by Lois Lamdin, 1991, 200 pages, $19.95.

> At colleges and universities across the United States, you can earn credit for college-level learning and skills you already possess, if you can demonstrate to experts in the field that you possess the knowledge and skills you claim to have. One of the most effective ways to do this is to assemble a portfolio for assessment. This revised edition of *Earn College Credit for What You Know* includes an overview of prior learning assessment practices and a step-by-step guide on how to assemble your own portfolio to document your learning. This second edition of the 1985 best seller has added a new section on career and academic decision making, as well as a consumer's guide to postsecondary education and a section on surviving and thriving in college. The section on portfolio-assisted assessment has been significantly expanded, and there is new information on testing programs and assessment in technical areas. A state-by-state listing of those colleges and universities that currently have comprehensive assessment programs, based on a recent CAEL survey, is included in a new appendix.

Prior Learning Assessment: Results of a Nationwide Institutional Survey, by Mary Fugate and Ruth Chapman, 1992, Softcover, 152 pages, $19.95.

> The result of a 1991 CAEL survey to document the use and acceptance of various prior learning assessment (PLA) methodologies in postsecondary institutions throughout the United States, this important new book provides comprehensive information for a wide variety of audiences:
> - individual adults
> - members of higher education associations and commissions
> - education services officers
> - human resources or training organization personnel within corporations
> - faculty and staff at academic institutions
> - decision-makers in accrediting bodies
> - all others interested in the current state of prior learning assessment.
>
> For this survey, questionnaires were mailed to two key administrative officers at 3,694 academic institutions throughout the United States. For the purpose of the survey, the term "prior learning assessment" was defined broadly to include all modes of assessing learning gained outside the classroom. The detailed questionnaire addressed:
> - standardized examinations, including Advanced Placement (AP), College Level Examination Program (CLEP), American College Testing Proficiency Examination Program (ACT/PEP) and the Defense Activity for Nontraditional Education Support (DANTES) examinations

- course challenge or departmental examinations
- American Council on Education credit recommendations on both military education and training (ACE/Military) and on corporate education and training programs (ACE/PONSI)
- individualized prior learning assessment programs, including portfolio-assisted assessments, oral interviews, and competence demonstration
- transferability of assessment credits.

Your Hidden Credentials: The Value of Personal Learning outside of College, by Peter Smith, 1986, 180 pages, $7.95.

A self-help book for adults, *Your Hidden Credentials*, focuses on identifying and appreciating personal learning. It describes the role that personal learning has as the foundation for increased work satisfaction and further education. The book includes profiles of adult learners who have identified their personal learning and expanded their earning power on the basis of this knowledge. It also provides examples of how to transform difficult turning points in life into smooth transitions to greater opportunities; how to find an adult-friendly college that meets your educational needs; and how to determine your unknown skills and knowledge.

ACE Publications

For more information on the following two ACE publications, please contact American Council on Education/Oryx Press, Series on Higher Education, 4041 N. Central Ave., Phoenix, AZ 85012-3397.

The National Guide to Educational Credit for Training Programs, 1993, Softcover, 1120 pages, $49.95.

Published annually, this is the standard guide to credit recommendations for formal learning acquired off campus. An essential tool for counselors, advisers, and other training and education officials, it describes in detail some 2,000 courses offered by more than 180 business, professional, labor, government, and voluntary organizations from AT&T to the YWCA. Here is authoritative, up-to-date information on the content, materials, methods, goals, sites, dates offered, and credits recommended for each course. The guide reports the evaluations of the Program on Noncollegiate Sponsored Instruction of ACE's Center for Adult Learning and Educational Credentials.

The 1992 Guide to the Evaluation of Educational Experiences in the Armed Services, Softcover; 4 volumes, $19.95 each.

Published biennially in four convenient volumes, the guide describes courses offered by each service branch and the Department of Defense. Organized by ACE identification numbers, the entries list title and service number, dates, location, credit recommendation, and other basic data for each course. Also includes a keyword and course number index (softcover).

For more information on the following publication, please contact Joan Schwartz, American Council on Education, Center for Adult Learning and Educational Credentials, One Dupont Circle, Washington, DC 20036-1193.

Guide to Educational Credit by Examination (Third Edition), Joan Schwartz, Editor.

This revised edition will help officials at postsecondary institutions to award appropriate credit for learning acquired outside of their sponsorship, thus facilitating the decision making on awarding credit for prior learning through the use of examinations. Through the Center for Adult Learning and Educational Credentials, the ACE recommends credit for more than 350 tests including the College Board's CLEP, the DANTES Subject Standardized Tests, the State University of New York's Regents College Examination, and ACT/PEP, as well as several certification programs. This edition provides information on ACE's test and program review process; test content; faculty evaluators' judgments about test quality; minimum scores required for credit; and ACE's recommendations for the type and amount of credit to be awarded for each test.

Appendix E
Elements of a Model Policy for Awarding Credit for Extrainstitutional Learning

American Council on Education
The Center for Adult Learning and Educational Credentials
Washington, DC

April 1989

Extrainstitutional learning is defined as learning that is attained outside the sponsorship of legally authorized and accredited postsecondary education institutions. The term applies to learning acquired from work and life experiences, independent reading and study, the mass media, and participation in formal courses sponsored by associations, business, government, industry, the military and unions.

I. Example Statement of General Policy

Degree credit shall be awarded for postsecondary-level extrainstitutional learning. Such credit awards shall be made under protocols designed to ensure that reliable and valid measures of learning outcomes are or have been applied.

Rationale

Adult students are demanding that their learning acquired in extrainstitutional settings be assessed and that appropriate degree-related credit be awarded. This is a reasonable request and also one in keeping with the national interest. Full and effective use of all educational resources is a worthy educational and social goal. Achieving this goal will depend to a large extent on providing equitable recognition for extrainstitutional learning.

American society abounds in resources for learning at the postsecondary level. Postsecondary education institutions legally authorized and accredited to award degrees and other educational credentials accordingly have a special responsibility to assess extrainstitutional learning as part of their credentialing function.

Educational credentials have a significant bearing on the economic, professional, and social status of the individual. It follows that social equity requires that equivalent learning regardless of where and how it is achieved be incorporated into the system of rewards for learning and competency. Recognition encourages learning and contributes to teaching effectiveness. Teaching students what they already know is both stultifying to them and wasteful of educational and personal resources.

Through reliable and valid assessment of extrainstitutional learning, more persons can be enabled to enter college and work successfully toward degrees and other academic goals. Many of these individuals are those who have been educationally disadvantaged in the past.

II. Example Policy for Administrative Responsibility

Responsibility for administering policies and procedures for awarding credit for extrainstitutional learning rests with the academic vice president (or other designated senior academic official).

Rationale

Awarding credit is an academic matter. Therefore, administrative responsibility for the policies and procedures pertaining to awarding credit for extrainstitutional learning should be assigned to the institution's senior academic official. Policy implementation and application may be delegated to other institutional officials such as deans, department chairpersons, and registrars. However, oversight of their policy implementation and application is performed by a senior academic official.

Example of Application of the Policy

The academic vice president delegates to the institutional registrar the responsibility for transcripting credit awarded on the basis of recommendations in the ACE Guides (the policy was approved through the institution's usual governance procedures) and provides the registrar with guidelines for performing this responsibility. Included in the guidelines are a series of steps to follow in determining how to apply the ACE credit recommended for a course whose title is not the same as the title of any course offered by the institution.

The ACE guide recommends three semester hours in automotive maintenance, but the institution's courses are more specific and carry titles such as Tune-Up 1, Auto Brakes, and Automatic Transmission 1. In accordance with the guidelines, the registrar compares course descriptions in the institution's catalog with the course description in the guide, finds that the learning outcomes acquired through Tune-Up 1 match very closely the learning outcomes acquired through the military's automotive maintenance course, and transcripts three semester hours in Tune-Up 1.

III. Example Policy on Learning That Will Be Evaluated and Who Will Conduct the Evaluations

Extrainstitutional learning related to subject areas, courses, and programs of study will be evaluated for registered students. Established institutional evaluation procedures will be followed, using one or more of the authorized publications and methods for effecting assessment. Students of any age may apply for credit for extrainstitutional learning at any time during a period of enrollment.

Rationale

The learning that is evaluated must be in subject areas in which faculty expertise is available or in which expertise can be arranged. This expertise is essential for conducting evaluations and making credit-award decisions. If subject-matter experts do not conduct the evaluations and make the decisions, the credibility of the activity is suspect.

Although the great majority of students requesting credit for extrainstitutional learning will be of relatively mature years, it is possible that young adult students may have acquired learning in extrainstitutional settings. Providing a student can document the attainment of appropriate learning outcomes, he or she should receive credit regardless of age. Although most applications for award of extrainstitutional learning credit will be received at the time of enrollment from new students, it is possible that students already enrolled may realize that they, too, have extrainstitutional learning experiences that might qualify for credit awards. It is also possible that enrolled students, especially those who are employed, will continue to learn in noncollegiate settings and will want their learning assessed. Student initiatives with respect to extrainstitutional learning assessment shall not be limited or restricted to the initial term of enrollment.

Example of Application of the Policy

A 19-year-old student has been enrolled at Local College for two years and is about to enter her junior year. At the time of enrollment it did not occur to her that the foreign language requirement might be satisfied with a language other than one of those taught at the institution. This student's parents were refugees from Hungary who entered the United States in 1958. The Hungarian language is spoken in the home, and the student speaks the language fluently. The student is able to document to the satisfaction of the institution's language faculty, through evaluation done by a person in the community fluent in Hungarian, that she is, indeed, proficient in Hungarian. She received six credits in Hungarian that satisfy the foreign language requirement for the bachelor's degree.

IV. Publications and Methods Recommended for Use in Awarding Credit for Extrainstitutional Learning

Nine publications and methods are permitted for use in awarding credit for extrainstitutional learning. These publications and methods are (1) ACE *Guide to the Educational Experiences in the Armed Forces, Credit* for *Training Programs*; (2) ACE *National Guide to Educational Credit for Training Programs;* (3) ACE *Guide to Credit by Examination;* (4) New York Regents *Guide to Educational Programs in Noncollegiate Organizations;* (5) College Entrance Examination Board Advance Placement Program (CEEB/AP); (6) department challenge examinations and/or faculty end-of-course examinations; (7) degree-relevant extrainstitutional learning credit awarded and transcripted by other accredited institutions, as well as that credit transcripted by ACE on the Army/ACE Registry Transcript System (AARTS) and the Registry of Credit Recommendations (ROCR); (8) subject-matter experts at the faculty's request; and (9) individual portfolios using Council for Adult and Experiential Learning (CAEL) or other standardized guidelines. In addition, advice on using other publications and methods for awarding credit for extrainstitutional learning may be sought from the American Council on Education.

Rationale

For nearly 40 years, the *Guide to the Evaluation of Educational Experiences in the Armed Services* has been the standard reference work for recognizing learning acquired in the military. More recently the *National Guide to Educational Credit for Training Programs* and *The Guide to Credit by Examination* have attained similar stature. ACE has worked cooperatively with the Department of Defense, the armed services, business, industry, labor unions, other organizations providing education and training, and test publishers, as well as with accredited colleges and universities in developing the credit recommendations presented in the guide series. All recommendations carried are the result of careful and periodic review by evaluation teams that consist of university and college faculty members who are subject-matter experts. All evaluation teams work under policies and procedures approved by the ACE Commission on Educational Credit and Credentials and under protocols and supervision provided by the staff of the ACE Center for Adult Learning and Educational Credentials.

The policies and procedures used to develop the exhibits in the New York Regents *Guide to Educational Programs in Noncollegiate Organizations* are similar to those used by the American Council on Education. The CEEB/AP program permits high school students to demonstrate the attainment of college-level learning outcomes; the important factor is that learning outcomes are attained, not where the learning took place (in a high school) or who taught the course (usually a high school teacher). The practice of administering departmental or

individual faculty member challenge examinations or end-of-course examinations is long standing and permits the faculty members to make direct judgments about the equivalence of learning for specific course.

Credit transcripted on the basis of extrainstitutional learning should be treated the same as that transcripted for courses; in both instances, the faculty of the sending institution has attested to the student's attainment of required learning outcomes. Credit transcripted on ACE's Army/ACE Registry Transcript System (AARTS) and Registry of Credit Recommendations (ROCR) for the Army component of the Military Evaluations Program and participants in the Program on Noncollegiate Sponsored Instruction (PONSI) should also be treated as that transcripted for courses. In these instances, teams of faculty members from accredited colleges and universities have evaluated the learning and judged its equivalence to learning acquired on campuses.

Sometimes the expertise to evaluate extrainstitutional learning is not available on the faculty; in these instances, the faculty can designate an expert to conduct the evaluation. Criteria for selection of outside experts should be established.

The portfolio assessment guidelines promulgated by CAEL are widely accepted by faculty assessors and are considered exemplary. The portfolio provides a reliable method for evaluating learning outcomes acquired individually, as opposed to a set of learning outcomes acquired by large numbers of persons, such as through a course offered by the U.S. Army for soldiers.

Example of Application of the Policy

A student (soldier), upon entering Local College, provides an AARTS transcript that confirms completion of a course entitled Advanced Geodetic Surveyor at the Engineer School, Fort Belvoir, Virginia, in October 1981, while holding the rank of sergeant in the U.S. Army. Information on the transcript and in the ACE *Guide to the Evaluation of Educational Experiences in the Armed Services* indicates that the soldier completed this course when it was taught at Fort Belvoir between January 1977 and November 1983. Its objectives were to train warrant officers and senior noncommissioned officers in advanced geodetic survey techniques. The course was delivered by means of lectures and practical exercises in advanced geodetic surveying techniques including map compiling, vertical and horizontal control surveys, gravity, astronomic observations, and mathematics. The guide recommends that a college or university award six semester hours in geodesy at the upper division baccalaureate level; this recommendation also appears on the AARTS transcript. After review of this recommendation, Local College awards this student six semester hours of credit in geodesy toward completion of a planned major in mathematics.

V. Example Policy on Maximum Number of Credits That May Be Awarded for Extrainstitutional Learning

The maximum number of credits that may be awarded for extrainstitutional learning is three-fourths the number required for a degree.

Rationale

Most postsecondary education institutions have a requirement that stipulates that a minimum of one-fourth of the credits required for a degree must be earned in residence. The balance of the required credits, then, could be awarded on the basis of extrainstitutional learning. However, the credits awarded for extrainstitutional learning and those earned in residence would have to satisfy all degree requirements before a degree could be awarded. In the absence of a residency requirement, all degree requirements conceivably could be met through extrainstitutional learning.

Example of Application of the Policy

John Smith is a newly registered student at Local College. He is a financial vice president of a major U.S. corporation, CPA, and licensed realtor; he is fluent in three foreign languages—German, French, and Spanish; he has published seven articles in domestic and foreign journals and has contributed chapters in two books on international economics; he is knowledgeable about foreign countries and cultures as a result of having lived abroad for 11 years, and he is proficient in computer programming (COBOL and FORTRAN).

On the basis of Mr. Smith's demonstrated knowledge, skills, and competencies, the faculty awarded him 106 credits. The college requires 124 credits for a degree and has a 24-credit residency requirement. Therefore, Mr. Smith must earn 24 credits in residence. What courses does he take to earn 24 credits? His academic advisers decided, and Mr. Smith concurred, that he lacked knowledge about the environment, a special focus and thrust of the college's general education requirement. He took courses to satisfy this requirement and was awarded a degree.

VI. Example Policy on Recording Credits Awarded for Extrainstitutional Learning on Transcripts

The credit awarded for extrainstitutional learning shall be transcripted in the same manner as credits awarded for course completions.

Rationale

The faculty members have either evaluated the learning or approved the other means by which credit can be awarded. They have verified that learning has occurred and is equivalent to the learning acquired in their courses and programs. Therefore, special notation or differentiation of courses and credits awarded on the basis of extrainstitutional learning is unnecessary.

Example of the Application of the Policy

Examples of the way in which Mr. Smith's credit was transcripted are as follows:

Acct. 261	Financial Info. Systems	3 semester hours
Acct. 360	Fin. Reporting Theory and Practice	3 semester hours
Computer Science 251	Principles of Programming-FORTRAN	4 semester hours
Computer Science 252	Principles of Programming-COBOL	4 semester hours
German 101	Elementary German	4 semester hours
German 201	Intermediate German	4 semester hours
German 309	Advanced Conversation	3 semester hours

VII. Example Policy on Retention of the Documentation of Extrainstitutional Learning

Documents used to verify the award of credit for extrainstitutional learning shall be retained for one calendar year.

Rationale

The length of time documentation for the credits awarded for extrainstitutional learning shall be retained should be consistent with the length of time documentation for credits awarded for classroom learning is retained. Consistency facilitates equitable handling of student documents and represents sound recordkeeping practices.

Example of Application of the Policy

Local College keeps students' final exams on file for one calendar year, after which they are shredded. Mr. Smith's documentation—copies of articles and chapters he authored, copies of his computer programs, notes and summaries of interviews faculty members had with him, etc.—were kept on file for one calendar year and were then shredded.

VIII. Student Fees for Assessing Extrainstitutional Learning

A fee for the assessment of extrainstitutional learning shall be charged.

Rationale

Assessing extrainstitutional learning, transcripting the credits awarded, etc., are valuable services to students. These services require faculty and staff time. Students should, therefore, pay a fee for these services just as they pay fees for other institutional services.

Example of Application of the Policy

The fee for assessing extrainstitutional learning and for transcripting the results at Local College is based on the average hourly salaries for various faculty ranks (assistant professor, professor, etc.) and administrative positions plus the costs for benefits and administrative services, which are computed as percentages of salaries. The average hourly salaries are multiplied by the amount of time spent in performing the evaluation and administrative functions, rounded up to the half-hour. The fee for assessing Mr. Smith's extrainstitutional learning and for transcripting the results was $880.00.

IX. Example Policy on Oversight of the Program/Activity

An oversight committee, broadly representative of the institution's divisions/departments, shall be appointed (by the program administrator or through the institution's usual means of appointing committees). The major function of this committee is to review the credit-award decisions to ensure consistency across the institution.

Rationale

To protect the integrity and credibility of the activity, consistency is absolutely necessary. If either the faculty or the students perceive that credit awards are made capriciously, their confidence in the activity will be lost. When this occurs, the activity will no longer be feasible.

Example Application of the Policy

The oversight committee detected that, when a faculty evaluation team for portfolio assessment was comprised of three specific faculty members, the credit awards seemed overly generous. The oversight committee recommended to the administrator that these three faculty members should not comprise a team. The administrator discussed the credit-award information with the three faculty members, and they agreed with the oversight committee's recommendation, which was then implemented.

X. Example Policy on Program Evaluation

The Program for assessing extrainstitutional learning shall be evaluated on an annual basis by the academic vice president or his/her designee(s).

Rationale

It is sound administrative practice to evaluate programs on a regular basis to determine whether program objectives are being met. It is especially important to evaluate new programs so that problems are detected early on and changes can be made, if necessary. Evaluation should probably be done jointly by program staff and the staff of the Office of Institutional Research.

Example of Application of the Policy

At Local College, responsibility for program evaluation is assigned to the Office of Institutional Research, but the Office involves the program staff. Program evaluation includes, but is not limited to, an indepth look at the academic performance of students who have received credit for extrainstitutional learning. Recent data showed that their overall performance, in terms of GPA, was higher than that of the student body as a whole; the average number of credits carried each semester was equivalent to the average number carried by the student body as a whole; they were enrolled in all academic departments of the college, etc. Credit awards were examined by age categories and by assessment instrument used. This information was useful to the college faculty and administrators in deciding to continue the program.

Appendix F
Self-Regulation Initiatives: Guidelines for Colleges and Universities—Joint Statement on Transfer and Award of Academic Credit

Joint Statement on Transfer and Award of Academic Credit

This statement is directed to institutions of postsecondary education and others concerned with the transfer of academic credit among institutions and award of academic credit for extrainstitutional learning. Basic to this statement is the principle that each institution is responsible for determining its own policies and practices with regard to the transfer and award of credit. Institutions are encouraged to review their policies and practices periodically to ensure that they accomplish the institution's objectives and that they function in a manner that is fair and equitable to students. Any statements, this one or others referred to, should be used as guides, not as substitutes, for institutional policies and practices.

Transfer of credit is a concept that now involves transfer between dissimilar institutions and curricula and recognition of extrainstitutional learning, as well as transfer between institutions and curricula of similar characteristics. As their personal circumstances and educational objectives change, students seek to have their learning, wherever and however attained, recognized by institutions where they enroll for further study. It is important for reasons of social equity and educational effectiveness, as well as the wide use of resources, for all institutions to develop reasonable and definitive policies and procedures for acceptance of transfer credit. Such policies and procedures should provide maximum consideration for the individual student who has changed institutions or objectives. It is the receiving institution's responsibility to provide reasonable and definitive policies and procedures for determining a student's knowl-edge in required subject areas. All institutions have a responsibility to furnish transcripts and other documents necessary for a receiving institution to judge the quality and quantity of the work. Institutions also have a responsibility to advise the students that the work reflected on the transcript may or may not be acceptable for a receiving institution.

Institutions have a responsibility to make this distinction, and its implications, clear to students before they decide to enroll. This should be a matter of full disclosure, with the best interests of the student in mind. Institutions also should make every reasonable effort to reduce the gap between credits accepted and credits applied toward an educational credential.

Unaccredited Institutions

Institutions of postsecondary education that are not accredited by COPA-recognized accrediting bodies may lack that status for reasons unrelated to questions of quality. Such institutions, however, cannot provide a reliable, third-party assurance that they meet or exceed minimum standards. That being the case, students transferring from such institutions may encounter special problems in gaining acceptance and transferring credits to accredited institutions. Institutions admitting students from unaccredited institutions should take special steps to validate credits previously earned.

Foreign Institutions

In most cases, foreign institutions are chartered and authorized by their national governments, usually through a ministry of education. Although this provides for a standardization within a country, it does not produce useful information about comparability from one country to another. No other nation has a system comparable to voluntary accreditation. At the operational level, three organizations—the National Council on the Evaluation of Foreign Student Credentials (CES), the National Association for Foreign Student Affairs (NAFSA), and the National Liaison Committee on Foreign Student Admissions (NLC)—often can assist institutions by distributing general or specific guidelines on admission and placement recommendations are to be evaluated in terms of the programs and policies of the individual receiving institutions.

Validation of Extrainstitutional and Experiential Learning for Transfer Purposes

Transfer-of-credit policies should encompass educational accomplishment attained in extrainstitutional settings as well as at accredited postsecondary institutions. In deciding on the award of credit for extrainstitutional learning, institutions will find the services of the American Council on Education's Center for Adult Learning and Educational Credentials helpful. One of the center's functions is to operate and foster programs that determine credit equivalencies for various modes of extrainstitutional learning. The center maintains evaluation programs for formally structured courses offered by the military and civilian noncollegiate sponsors such as businesses, corporations, government agencies, and labor unions. Evaluation services are also available for examination programs, for occupations with validated job proficiency evaluation systems, and for correspondence courses offered by schools accredited by the National Home Study Council. The results are published in a guide series.

Another resource is the General Educational Development (GED) Testing Service, which provides a means for assessing high school equivalency.

For learning that has not been validated through the ACE formal credit recommendations process or through credit-by-examination programs, institutions are urged to explore the Council for Adult and Experiential Learning (CAEL) procedures and processes. Pertinent CAEL publications designed for this purpose are available from CAEL National Headquarters, 223 West Jackson Boulevard, Suite 501, Chicago, IL 60606.

This statement originally was developed by three national associations whose member institutions and organizations are directly involved in the transfer and award of academic credit—the American Association of Collegiate Registrars and Admission Officers, the American Council on Education, and the Council on Postsecondary Accreditation. In 1990, a fourth national association, the American Association of Community and Junior Colleges, joined the original three by officially approving the statement. The need for such a statement came from an awareness of the growing complexity of transfer policies and practices, which have been brought about, in part, by the changing contours of postsecondary education. With increasing frequency, students are pursuing their education in a variety of institutional and extrainstitutional settings. Social equity and the intelligent use of resources require that validated learning be recognized wherever it takes place. This statement is intended to serve as a guide to institutions in the development or review of policies dealing with transfer and award of credit. It is under periodic review by the four associations, and reactions would, of course, be welcome. Comments may be directed to Henry A. Spille, Vice President and Director of the Center for Adult Learning and Educational Credentials.

Robert H. Atwell, President ACE

Appendix G
National Universities Degree Consortium

The National Universities Degree Consortium (NUDC) was established to develop and distribute integrated, external degree completion programs to potential nontraditional students that are delivered in a flexible, off-campus format accessible by adult and part-time students nationwide. The consortium consists of nine land grant and comprehensive universities. It is a nonprofit corporation with a board of directors who established the consortium to respond to widespread requests from potential nontraditional students.

By joining resources, NUDC enables delivery of rigorous nonresidential education for degree completion throughout the nation. The coursework is pooled for delivery by way of cablecast television, interactive multimedia, interactive computer networks, teleconference, live instruction, telecourses, and correspondence study.

The nine land grant universities—Colorado State University, Kansas State University, University of New Orleans, University of Oklahoma, University of South Carolina, Oklahoma State University, Utah State University, University of Maryland University College, and Washington State University—offer accredited bachelor's degree programs with the assistance of the cablecast facilities of ME/U: The Education Network. The NUDC courses are received at local cable companies or by satellite. If the student cannot receive the cablecast, arrangements are made for the student to receive video tapes of the classes.

A bachelor's degree in management is offered by University of Maryland University College which stresses the integration of contemporary management theory and practice. Three additional degree programs are being developed and will be offered in 1993. The social science degree with an emphasis in criminal justice will be offered by Washington State University. The Bachelor of Science in Interdisciplinary Social Science and the Bachelor of Science in Agriculture, Animal Science, and Industry are under development from Kansas State University. By calling the ME/U Education Center at (800) 777-MIND, you can enroll in courses supporting these degrees.

For students who wish to learn at home or at work, access to registration and course materials is easy. Most courses can be completed within a semester, and all NUDC approved courses lead to a degree.

The student education center at ME/U provides centralized services for students seeking degree information by calling (800) 777-MIND. Students can enroll, pay tuition, and receive the course syllabus and textbooks. Instructions for cablecast schedule or tape delivery are provided. Voice mail is offered to students and their professors for access to each other. Initial academic advising is provided.

Alphabetical Index of Institutions

Index to Fields of Study

Letters in parentheses show the level of degree offered at each college for the field of study listed. *A* indicates an *associate's degree*; *B* indicates a *bachelor's degree*; *D* indicates a *doctorate degree*; *J* indicates a *Juris Doctor degree;* and *M* indicates a *master's degree.*

Accounting
    Albright College (B), 144
    Alvernia College (A) (B), 145
    Barry University (B), 30
    Bemidji State University (B), 226
    Birmingham-Southern College (B), 1
    Central Washington University (B), 178
    City University (A) (B), 263
    Dominican College (B), 116
    Gardner-Webb College (B), 125
    Georgian Court College (B), 112
    ICS Center for Degree Studies (A), 246
    Iowa Wesleyan College (B), 51
    Marymount College (B), 118
    Marywood College (B), 247
    Minneapolis Community College (A), 96
    Northwood Institute (A) (B), 224
    Regents College (B), 235
    Simpson College (B), 55
    University of Wisconsin-River Falls (B), 191
    Upper Iowa University (B), 217
    Villanova University (B), 153
Administrative Science
    Gannon University (B), 147
    Guildford College (B), 126
Advertising
    Marquette University (B), 187
    Northwood Institute (A), 224
    Syracuse University (M), 237
Aeronautics
    Embry-Riddle Aeronautical University (A) (B), 206
Aerospace Engineering
    Auburn University (M), 192
    University of Colorado (M), 21
Agriculture
    Kansas State University (B), 218
    University of Wisconsin-River Fall (B), 271
American Studies
    Saint Joseph College (B), 25
Anthropology
    Johnson State College (B), 259
Architecture
    Boston Architectural Center (B), 75
Art
    Georgian Court College (B), 112
    Johnson State College (B), 259
    Nebraska Wesleyan University (A), 108
    Vermont College of Norwich University (M), 260

Art History
    Georgian Court College (B), 112
Art Therapy
    Vermont College of Norwich University (M), 260
Arts, unspecified majors
    Albertus Magnus College (B), 22
    Amber University (B) (M), 167
    Anne Arundel Community College (A), 68
    Aquinas College (A) (B), 88
    Atlantic Union College (B), 223
    Bethune-Cookman College (B), 31
    Board of Governors of State Colleges and
        Universities (B), 211
    Caldwell College (B), 111
    Capital University (B), 238
    Carroll College (B), 185
    Chabot College (A), 9
    Charter Oak College (A) (B), 205
    City Colleges of Chicago (A), 212
    City University of New York Baccalaureate
        Program (B), 114
    College of Our Lady of the Elms (B), 76
    College of St. Scholastica (B) (M), 93
    Columbia University (B), 115
    Concord College (B), 265
    Converse College (B), 159
    Creighton University (A) (B), 106
    Davis and Elkins College (B), 266
    DePaul University (B) (M), 44
    Dominican College (A), 116
    Edison State Community College (A), 133
    Empire State College/State University of
        New York (A) (B) (M), 234
    Fairfield University (B), 24
    Fairhaven College (B), 179
    Fairmont State College (B), 267
    Fordham University (B), 117
    Goddard College (B) (M), 258
    Guildford College (B), 126
    Harvard University Extension School (A), 79
    Hastings College (B), 107
    Hiram College (B), 134
    Judson College (B), 193
    Limestone College (A) (B), 161
    Longview Community College (A), 103
    Loras College (A) (B) (M), 53
    Marshall University (B), 183